# Advanced Analytics and
# Deep Learning Models

**Scrivener Publishing**
100 Cummings Center, Suite 541J
Beverly, MA 01915-6106

## Next-Generation Computing and Communication Engineering

**Series Editors: Dr. G. R. Kanagachidambaresan and Dr. Kolla Bhanu Prakash**

Developments in artificial intelligence are made more challenging because the involvement of multi-domain technology creates new problems for researchers. Therefore, in order to help meet the challenge, this book series concentrates on next generation computing and communication methodologies involving smart and ambient environment design. It is an effective publishing platform for monographs, handbooks, and edited volumes on Industry 4.0, agriculture, smart city development, new computing and communication paradigms. Although the series mainly focuses on design, it also addresses analytics and investigation of industry-related real-time problems.

*Publishers at Scrivener*
Martin Scrivener (martin@scrivenerpublishing.com)
Phillip Carmical (pcarmical@scrivenerpublishing.com)

# Advanced Analytics and Deep Learning Models

Edited by

## Archana Mire

*Computer Engineering Department, Terna Engineering College, Navi Mumbai, India*

## Shaveta Malik

*Computer Engineering Department, Terna Engineering College, Nerul, India*

and

## Amit Kumar Tyagi

*Vellore Institute of Technology (VIT), Chennai Campus, India*

WILEY

This edition first published 2022 by John Wiley & Sons, Inc., 111 River Street, Hoboken, NJ 07030, USA and Scrivener Publishing LLC, 100 Cummings Center, Suite 541J, Beverly, MA 01915, USA
© 2022 Scrivener Publishing LLC
For more information about Scrivener publications please visit www.scrivenerpublishing.com.

**Wiley Global Headquarters**
111 River Street, Hoboken, NJ 07030, USA

For details of our global editorial offices, customer services, and more information about Wiley products visit us at www.wiley.com.

**Limit of Liability/Disclaimer of Warranty**
While the publisher and authors have used their best efforts in preparing this work, they make no representations or warranties with respect to the accuracy or completeness of the contents of this work and specifically disclaim all warranties, including without limitation any implied warranties of merchantability or fitness for a particular purpose. No warranty may be created or extended by sales representatives, written sales materials, or promotional statements for this work. The fact that an organization, website, or product is referred to in this work as a citation and/or potential source of further information does not mean that the publisher and authors endorse the information or services the organization, website, or product may provide or recommendations it may make. This work is sold with the understanding that the publisher is not engaged in rendering professional services. The advice and strategies contained herein may not be suitable for your situation. You should consult with a specialist where appropriate. Neither the publisher nor authors shall be liable for any loss of profit or any other commercial damages, including but not limited to special, incidental, consequential, or other damages. Further, readers should be aware that websites listed in this work may have changed or disappeared between when this work was written and when it is read.

*Library of Congress Cataloging-in-Publication Data*

ISBN 978-1-119-79175-1

Cover image: Pixabay.Com
Cover design by Russell Richardson

Set in size of 11pt and Minion Pro by Manila Typesetting Company, Makati, Philippines

Printed in the USA

10 9 8 7 6 5 4 3 2 1

# Contents

## 15 Big Data in Healthcare: Applications and Challenges     351

*V. Shyamala Susan, K. Juliana Gnana Selvi*
*and Ir. Bambang Sugiyono Agus Purwono*

# Preface

Advanced analytics is a mixture of machine learning, artificial intelligence, graphs, text mining, data mining, semantic analysis. It is an approach to data analysis. Beyond the traditional business intelligence, it is a semi and autonomous analysis of data by using different techniques and tools. However, deep learning and data analysis both are the high centres of data science. Almost all the private and public organizations collect heavy amounts of data, i.e., domain specific data. Many small/large companies are exploring large amounts of data for existing and future technology. Deep learning is also exploring large amounts of unsupervised data.

In fact, it is a key benefit of big data. It is also effective for big data. Moreover, it is collecting an unlabelled and uncategorized raw data. There are some challenges also in big data related to the extraction complex patterns from the large amount of data, retrieving of fast information, tagging of data etc, deep learning can be used to deal these kinds of problems or challenges.

The purpose of this book is to help teachers to instruct the concepts of analytics in deep learning and how big data technologies are managing massive amounts of data with the help of Artificial Intelligence (AI), Machine Learning (ML), Deep Learning (DL) etc. In this book one will find the utility and challenges of big data. Those who are keen to learn the different models of deep learning, the connection between AI, ML and DL will definitely find this book as a great source of knowledge.

This book contains chapters on artificial intelligence, machine learning, deep learning and their uses in many useful sectors like stock market prediction, recommendation system for better service selection, e-healthcare, telemedicine, transportation. In last few interesting chapter like innovations or issue or future opportunities with fog computing/cloud computing or artificial intelligence are being discussed in this work for future readers/researchers.

Hence, this book will be convenient to the undergraduate and graduate students planning their careers in either industry or research. This will also

serve as a great source of learning to software engineers who are beginners
in the field of advanced analytics in deep learning.

**Dr. Archana Mire**
**Dr. Shaveta Malik**
**Dr. Amit Kumar Tyagi**
January 2022

# Part 1

# INTRODUCTION TO COMPUTER VISION

# Artificial Intelligence in Language Learning: Practices and Prospects

Khushboo Kuddus

*School of Humanities (English), KIIT Deemed to be University, Bhubaneswar, Odisha, India*

## Abstract

Fourth Industrial Revolution which features rapid expansion of technology and digital application is influencing almost all spheres of our lives. Artificial Intelligence (AI) has made an impact on the way we live and work, that is, from floor cleaning to instructing Alexa. AI has a great potential in the field of education. AI in education is an emerging field in educational technology. It has an enormous potential of providing digitalized and completely personalized learning to each learner. However, the idea of using AI in education is actually intimidating educators because there is a lot of misconception and misunderstanding regarding the use of AI in education. It is mainly because the educators are unaware of the pedagogical implication of it in education in general and language learning in particular. It is also because of the lack of critical reviews of the pedagogical implications and new approaches in adopting AI in education. Therefore, the present study attempts to explore how AI can be used to enhance language learning experiences. It discusses the tools that can be used to teach English effectively. It further aims to explain how AI can be used to foster learner's autonomy. It essentially envisions AI embedded learning in classrooms to enhance English language teaching learning experience and assist the teachers teach their lessons effectively. The findings bring into light some practical and innovative ways, AI can be integrated in ELT classroom to enhance the language teaching learning experience. It focuses on teaching pronunciation and increasing fluency by mimicking the sound pattern and using speech recognition and speech editing features. Moreover, it also highlights the personal approach to language learning by using Chatbot which provides text-to-speech and speech-to-text conversion, using technology to transcribe speech in order to

*Email*: khushboo3133@gmail.com

Archana Mire, Shaveta Malik and Amit Kumar Tyagi (eds.) Advanced Analytics and Deep Learning Models, (3–18) © 2022 Scrivener Publishing LLC

check the pronunciation, translate speech, and practicing conversation by using voice command like Google Assistant. Hence, the paper examines the potential application of AI in education and language learning in particular. Further, it explores the possibilities of implication of AI in classrooms adopting new learning approaches and pedagogical modifications.

*Keywords:* Artificial intelligence, intelligent computer-assisted language learning, natural language processing, networked learning, English language teaching, pedagogies, digital tools

## 1.1   Introduction

English language is one of the universal languages these days. It is not only the language of science, technology, higher education, aviation, travel, and tourism but also the language of the internet and information technology. There have been unprecedented changes in the field of English teaching and learning with the continuous advancement in Information Communication Technology (ICT) [1, 2]. The rapid advancement of technology has had a significant impact on the field of education, particularly language acquisition and teaching. The enormous development of technology has remarkably affected the field of education and especially language learning and teaching. The adoption of ICT with the present day technical trends in language teaching is extraordinary [3]. The teaching and learning has been made easier, active, personalized, authentic, and effective by integrating ICT in second language acquisition or foreign language learning. It has also resulted in a paradigm shift in the teaching and learning process, as well as changes in teachers' roles [4].

The importance of application of technology in second language learning was realized long back in 1930s which gave rise to the emergence of Computer-Assisted Language Learning (CALL) which was initially used only for the drilling exercises. Later, with the advancement of technology, CALL became more interactive using multimedia and Language Laboratory. Moreover, in the 21st century, the social dimensions of ICT expanded with the exponential growth of ICT which led to revitalization of CALL in the form of Web 2.0 tools, Mobile-Assisted Language Learning (MALL), and Network Learning (NL) and, later, the Intelligent CALL (ICALL) [5]. Having said that, it is the implication of Artificial Intelligence (AI) in Language Learning along with Computational Linguistics, Machine Learning, and Natural Language Processing (NLP).

This chapter discusses the potential application of AI in education and language learning in particular adopting new learning approaches and pedagogical modifications. Further, it explores the ways how AI can be used to enhance language learning experiences by fostering learner's autonomy and adaptability. It also discusses the AI tools that can be used to teach English effectively. It focuses on teaching pronunciation and increasing fluency by mimicking the sound pattern, using speech recognition and speech editing features and the personal approach to language learning by using Chatbot. Furthermore, the chapter concentrates on the inference of AI embedded learning for establishing a new trend in foreign language learning as well as the shift in teachers' roles. Hence, the aim of this chapter is to provide a few substantial examples of how AI may be used to improve the language learning experience, and why language teachers should embrace and incorporate AI into the teaching process rather than fear it.

## 1.2    Evolution of CALL

In the 1960s, the audio-lingual method was introduced for English language teaching (ELT), which essentially insisted on drill and practice which became quite easier with the incorporation of computer in teaching and learning language [6, 7]. By the 20th century, CALL had a great impact on language teaching and learning. CALL during 1960s and 1980s can be termed as Structural CALL, as during this period, the computers used in language learning were mainly for drills and practice. Following the Structural approach and Behaviorist theory of learning, the computers programs focused more on structured and rote learning than interactivity. During this period, accuracy in grammar and sentence structure were the primary aims for language learning. The second phase of CALL between 1980s and 1990s is known as Communicative CALL. Computers used during this period were majorly for constructing exercises to develop efficacious communication. During this period, the integration of computers in language learning was not only for accuracy but also for achieving fluency. It encouraged interaction not only with the computers but also with the fellow learners. From the 1990s to the early 21st century, integrative CALL was marked by increased access to digital resources and the Internet [8]. The advancement in technology and easy access to the internet encouraged the educators to invent flexible classroom language learning lessons that could be easily accessed even outside the classroom. In the early 21st century, the Integrative CALL continued to have an impact on language learning. Davies *et al.* argue that the field was infused with the era's "Web 2.0 fever" [9]. This included the emergence of a slew of new communities based on Web 2.0 tools like wikis, social networking sites, discussion boards, and virtual worlds. The best examples are Facebook groups, Instagram, and Twitter.

Technology has become an integral part of our lives. Its presence is ubiquitous right from the time we wake up till the time we sleep in various forms like alarms, smart phone, smart TV, smart AC, laptop, tablet, Whats App, You Tube, and many others. Technology has become so prevalent in every sector and at every level of education that it is impossible to imagine one's existence without it in any form. The majority of language learners around the world today use technology to access materials in their second and foreign languages, communicate with people all over the world, learn at their own pace, and take several language tests such as the TOEFL and IELTS [10–12]. Technology helps us get connected with anyone at any part of the world and so the language learners can easily get connected to larger connected networks of native language speakers where they can learn a language by getting directly exposed to the target language. Hence, it would not be wrong to say that the significant development of ICT has changed the way we understand learning and consequently has led to a shift from traditional approaches to teaching to networked teaching and learning.

In this context of language learning and teaching, it is worth noting that Warschauer and Kern coined the concept of Network-Based Language Teaching (NBLT), which focuses on communication [13]. According to Sharples et al., there is a fundamental correlation between learner-centered, personalized, interactive, collaborative, situated, lifelong, and ubiquitous New Learning and New Technology, which is well known for being mobile, user-friendly, and ubiquitous [14]. According to Jones, Networked Learning (NL) has emerged as a significant paradigm in which ICT is used to foster interaction and connections between teachers and learners, learners and other learners, and a learning community and its learning resources [15]. Further, with the Fourth Industrial Revolution which features rapid expansion of technology and digital application is influencing all spheres of our lives. AI has made an impact on the way we live and work, that is, from floor cleaning, using automatic induction heaters, driverless cars to instructing Alexa. According to Manns, the Fourth Industrial Revolution is being driven by the integration and amplification of emerging breakthroughs in AI, automation, and robotics, as well as the far-reaching connection between billions of people with mobile devices that provide unparalleled access to data and information [16]. Furthermore, AI now has major applications for language studies, thanks to advances in NLP, the advent of NL, and the technological ability to manage large amount of data.

## 1.3    Defining Artificial Intelligence

Artificial Intelligence (AI) is a branch of science that studies and develops devices aimed at stimulating human intelligence processes. The primary aim of AI is to improve the speed and efficacy of regular processes. As a result, the number of industries implementing AI is growing globally [17].

The term AI as defined by Russell and Norvig is Computational Intelligence, or Machine Intelligence, which encompasses a wide range of subfields in which "specific tasks, such as playing chess, proving mathematical theorems, writing poetry, and diagnosing diseases, can be performed" [18]. According to Housman, "AI is capable of two things: (1) automating repetitive tasks by predicting outcomes on data that has been labeled by human beings, and (2) enhancing human decision-making by feeding problems to algorithms developed by humans" [19]. To put it another way, AI registers assigned commands by performing the tasks repeatedly and then generates a decision pathway for humans by presenting alternatives. Moreover, Nabiyev describes AI as a computer-controlled device's ability to execute tasks in a human-like manner [20]. According to the author, human-like features include mental processes like reasoning, meaning formation, generalization, and learning from prior experiences. Nilsson goes on to describe AI as the full algorithmic edifice that mimics human intellect [21]. According to him, AI encompasses the development of the information-processing theory of intelligence.

## 1.4    Historical Overview of AI in Education and Language Learning

AI has evolved in terms of its philosophical approach over time. Intelligent Tutoring Systems (ITSs) were the first to incorporate AI into language learning in the 1980s aimed for personalized and autonomous learning. Early iterations of ITS were referred to as programs that sought to cater to the needs of learners by facilitating communication [22]. Another significant benefit of ITS was that it allowed for infinite repetitions and practice, something that could never be done with a human instructor. It was designed for the individual learner who wanted to improve their language skills by using tutoring systems. Despite of its advantages, several studies on integration of ITS in higher education found that it had moderate positive impact on the academic learning of college students [23]. However, after four decades, the more advanced and updated version of AI has revitalized the potential for personalized learning [24].

Although ITS made extensive use of drill and rote-learning mechanism built into the computer-based learning system, today's AI applications are much more advanced, with the same aim of catering to personalized learning. The fundamental difference between the previous model of ITS and the current model is that the former involved a student working in isolation using an ITS and the later engages students in a networked environment. This exposes the learner to the authentic and natural learning scenarios providing social context for language learning.

As mentioned earlier, the remarkable advancement in AI has brought a significant and inevitable shift from CALL to ICALL. With advancements in mobile technologies and their applications in language learning, CALL paved the way for MALL, and similarly, development in AI has led to the rise of a new academic field called ICALL. NLP technologies' language processing capabilities have numerous implications in the field of CALL, and the field of study that investigates and integrates such implementations is known as ICALL [25].

In the early 2000s, the Massive Open Online Courses (MOOCs) offered a highly required and cost effective alternative to the expensive higher education in the US and beyond. However, such courses could not facilitate learners' participation, peer learning, scaffolding, or large-scale connections with global learners. Because of these constraints, the MOOC movement has stalled when it comes to delivering education on a wide scale. In contrast, many well-known ongoing MOOC initiatives, such as Coursera, Khan Academy, Udemi, EdX, and Udacity, have used AI and NLP techniques to improve learners' engagement, active learning, and autonomy. This resurgence of AI, along with its strong NLP potential, has had a significant impact on second language education, as NLP-based tutoring systems can provide corrective input and adapt and customise instructional materials [5].

## 1.5 Implication of Artificial Intelligence in Education

There are myriad of implications of AI in language teaching and learning. There is multitude of ways that language learners and teachers can gain from integrating this technology. Some of the most relevant implications are the following.

### 1.5.1    Machine Translation

Cultural variation is one of the predominant barriers of communication which majorly occurs due to the difficulty in decoding the language, one is not familiar with. In such scenario, being bilingual or multilingual is a blessing which paves the way for enormous career opportunities and communication across the world. The language barrier is easily eradicated by innovative AI-based translation technologies like Google Translate. On a wide scale, such innovations have made significant progress in helping second language and foreign language learners. Google Translate initially supported only a few languages, but by 2016, it supported 103 languages at different levels, with over 500 million total users and over 100 billion words translated daily [26]. Since this translation service is so easily and widely accessible, second language learners are using it to enhance their learning beyond the four walls of the classroom. In contrast, Google's machine translation had been slammed for its accuracy because the translations are based on statistical machine translation rather than grammatical rules. Advanced and revised versions of Google Translate, on the other hand, exhibited higher accuracy [27].

### 1.5.2    Chatbots

Learners can communicate and learn from language chatbots in a natural way by integrating chatbots in mobile apps, which enhances the autonomy of the learning process. Duolingo is the most common language learning chatbot, with AI algorithms that can understand the context of use and respond contextually and uniquely to users. Chatbots have helped thousands of learners learn languages without being embarrassed or feel uncomfortable. There are other such language learning chatbots like Andy, Mondly, and Memrise.

Figures 1.1 and 1.2 show how the chatbots respond to users contextually and uniquely.

### 1.5.3    Automatic Speech Recognition Tools

The speech recognition tools identify spoken languages, analyze them, and convert them into text. This tool is of great help to the students with physical disabilities or the ones who are not comfortable with the keypad.

(Source: Ref [28])

**Figure 1.1** Chatbot responding to the user contextually.

(Source: Ref [29])

**Figure 1.2** Chatbot responding to the user contextually.

The Dragon transcription software was one of the first AI applications which transcribed text from voice. This application is significantly used for second language acquisition, especially for improving pronunciation. Furthermore, using Automatic Speech Recognition (ASR) and NLP techniques, software and online systems such as Carnegie Speech and Duolingo have provided foreign language education. These systems not only transcribe speech to text but also identify and correct language errors for users.

In addition, Google Assistant can be constructively integrated to enhance learners' proficiency and pronunciation. Students can ask simple questions to the Google assistant like "How's the weather today in…?", "How far is Delhi from Agra?", "When was Taj Mahal built?", and "What time is it in Malaysia now?". This is an excellent way to improve and assess students' communication skills while also ensuring that their pronunciation is intelligible. Some of the well-known speech-recognizing applications are mentioned in the timeline given in the following.

(Source: Ref [30])

### 1.5.4    Autocorrect/Automatic Text Evaluator

Applications like Autocorrect can be used to get feedback for text. The feedback provided is an actionable feedback about their writing related to claims and sources, topic development, coherence, and English conventions and word choice. It also provides synonyms for unfamiliar words that they may encounter while reading external sources. Such widely used applications based on AI are Writing Mentor and Grammarly which provide feedback about the text related to punctuation, sentence construction, and accuracy.

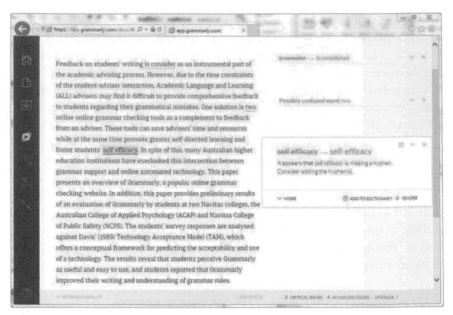

(Source: Ref [31])

### 1.5.5   Vocabulary Training Applications

There are applications with unique Machine Learning algorithm which facilitates completely personalized set of study materials by adapting the learning pattern and analyzing each learner's vocabulary strengths and weaknesses. Alphary is an AI-based application that helps students acquire and strengthen English vocabulary. These applications use the Oxford suite of Learner's Dictionaries and an integrated AI named FeeBu (Feedback ButterÖy) to mimic the behavior of a human English tutor who gives automated, intelligent feedback. It also automatically evaluates writing and analyzes grammatical mistakes [32].

### 1.5.6   Google Docs Speech Recognition

The widely known text processor Google Docs is a free and mobile friendly tool. The speech editing feature has been recently added to it. The voice recognition feature has evolved and it can help teachers in providing feedback of conversational activities. It can also be used to evaluate the intelligibility of the learners' speech by providing direct feedback in the form of text. The application can be creatively used for the maximum benefit of students.

### 1.5.7    Language MuseTM Activity Palette

The Language Muse TM Activity Palette is a fun way to improve learners' language skills. It is a web-based language-instruction program that uses NLP algorithms and lexical tools to generate language activities automatically and help English language learners' content comprehension and language skills enhancement. The online interface of the software for activity generation, assessment, and feedback is adaptable to MOOCs and several other online learning [33].

## 1.6    Artificial Intelligence Tools Enhance the Teaching and Learning Processes

### 1.6.1    Autonomous Learning

AI promotes personalized and autonomous learning. With the integration of AI, students always have easy access to learning. They can study at their own pace and space. They can study at any place and time they wish to. Students can clear their doubts at their own speed and time with AI-powered chatbots or AI virtual personal assistants like Google Assistant and Siri, without being humiliated in front of the entire class. AI personalizes studies to meet the needs of individual students, resulting in increased efficiency. AI has the potential to personalize digital language learning make for each learner, catering to their individual needs.

### 1.6.2    Produce Smart Content

The use of AI in education has paved the way for modern learning methods such as visualization, simulation, and web-based learning environments. Learners become more involved and engaged as a result of these new learning methods. Not only that, but AI also assists in the development and updating of lesson material, as well as customizing it for various learning goals and learners.

### 1.6.3    Task Automation

Evaluation is a time-consuming task that could be easily automated by the instructor using AI. It can automatically grade tests and even review essays, highlighting mistakes and recommending ways to prevent them in the future.

### 1.6.4   Access to Education for Students with Physical Disabilities

The innovative integration of AI in education broadens the ways of building multitude of constructive pedagogies to teaching and learning for students having learning disabilities. It also ensures access to education for physically challenged students like deaf or visually impaired. AI systems can be effectively trained to assist any group of special needs students.

## 1.7   Conclusion

If we look back in the timeline, we would realize that AI that we are living today was just a part of science fiction movies some years ago. Today, AI has become an inseparable part of our lives and it has made its space in almost all the spheres we can think of, right from business, banking, health, aviation to marketing, and now is slowly paving its way in the sphere of academics. AI in education is playing a significant role in augmenting teaching and learning. AI learning platforms facilitate autonomous learning, provides flexibility of space, pace, and time. Further, it facilitates personalized learning focusing on the learners' interest areas and considering the factors such as strengths, weaknesses, interests, and cultural background. AI-integrated online learning has augmented second language education across the globe manifolds.

Despite of AI having an enormous potential of enhancing the teaching and learning of foreign or second language, it still have certain challenges which need to be addressed. According to Lovett, despite advances in translation technology, there have been questions regarding Google Translate's grammatical accuracy and how it might be impacting the learner's process of building proficiency [34]. Furthermore, NLP is a complicated process, and accurately capturing all linguistic information is difficult. Further, the voice recognition also needs adjustments as sometimes it cannot understand heavy accents, articulation speech impediments, and soft voices. Therefore, further studies can be done to identify the solutions to the above stated problems. In addition, further research can also be done to identify the impact of AI on personalized learning, the grammar of the target language and on the proficiency of the language learnt. Moreover, a study on assessing the efficiency of AI on grading and evaluation can also be done.

AI is slowly paving its way into the sphere of academics through various technologies like Machine Learning and NLP, and it is surely going to foster the teaching and learning of second and foreign languages in the days to come.

# References

1. Warschauer, M., Of digital divides and social multipliers: Combining language and technology for human development, in: *Information and communication technologies in the teaching and learning of foreign languages: State of the art, needs and perspectives*, p. 46, 2004.

2. Khan, N.M. and Kuddus, K., Integrating ICT in English Language Teaching in Bangladesh: Teachers' Perception and Challenges. *Rupkatha J. Interdiscip. Stud. Humanit.*, 12, 5, 1, 2020.

3. Chatterjee, B. and Kuddus, K., Second Language Acquisition through Technology: A Need for Underdeveloped Regions like Jharkhand. *Res. Sch.- An International Referred e- J. Lit. Explor.*, 2, 2, 252, 2014.

4. Kuddus, K., Emerging Technologies and the Evolving Roles of Language Teachers: An Overview. *Lang. India*, 18, 81, 2018.

5. Kannan, J. and Munday, P., New trends in second language learning and teaching through the lens of ICT, networked learning, and artificial intelligence, in: *Vías de transformación en la enseñanza de lenguas con mediación tecnológica. Círculo de Lingüística Aplicada a la Comunicación*, vol. 76, Fernández Juncal, C. and Hernández Muñoz, N. (Eds.), p. 13, 2018, http://dx.doi.org/10.5209/CLAC.62495.

6. Davies, G., Walker, R., Rendall, H., Hewer, S., Introduction to new technologies and how they can contribute to language learning and teaching (CALL). Module 1.1, in: *Information and Communications Technology for Language Teachers (ICT4LT)*, G. Davies (Ed.), Thames Valley University, Slough, 2011, http://www.ict4lt.org/en/en_mod1-1.htm.

7. Levy, M., *CALL: context and conceptualisation*, Oxford: Oxford University Press, New York, 1997.

8. Warschauer, M., CALL for the 21st century. Paper presented at the *IATEFL and ESADE Conference*, Barcelona, Spain, 2 July, 2000, http://education.uci.edu/uploads/7/2/7/6/72769947/cyberspace.pdf.

9. Davies, G., Otto, S.E., Rüschoff, B., Historical perspectives on CALL, in: *Contemporary computer-assisted language learning*, p. 19, 2013.

10. Kuddus, K., Web 2.0 Technology in Teaching and Learning English as a Second Language. *Int. J. Engl. Lang. Lit.*, 1, 4, 292, 2013.

11. Dash, A. and Kuddus, K., Leveraging the Benefits of ICT Usage in Teaching of English Language and Literature, in: *Smart Intelligent Computing and Applications. Smart Innovation, Systems and Technologies*, vol. 160, S. Satapathy, V. Bhateja, J. Mohanty, S. Udgata (Eds.), pp. 225–232, Springer, Singapore, 2020.

12. Chatterjee, B. and Kuddus, K., Mass media Approach to Second Language Acquisition. *J. Engl. Stud.*, 10, 1, 10, 2015.

13. Warschauer, M. and Kern, R., *Network-based language teaching: Concepts and practice*, Cambridge University Press, New York, 2000.

14. Sharples, M., Taylor, J., Vavoula, G., A theory of learning for the mobile age, in: *Medienbildung in neuen Kulturräumen*, pp. 87–99, VS Verlag für Sozialwissenschaften, Switzerland, 2010.

15. Jones, C., *Networked learning: an educational paradigm for the age of digital networks*, Springer, Cham, Switzerland, 2015.

16. Manns, *UNESCO, Artificial Intelligence: Opportunities, threats and the future of learning*, Asia and Pacific Regional Bureau for Education, UNESCO Bangkok 2017.

17. Goksel, N. and Bozkurt, A., Artificial Intelligence in Education: Current Insights and Future Perspectives, in: *Handbook of Research on Learning in the Age of Transhumanism*, Sisman-Ugur, S. and Kurubacak, G. (Eds.), p. 224, 2019.

18. Russell, S.J., and Norvig, P., *Artificial intelligence, A modern approach*, 2nd ed, Pearson Education Inc., Upper Saddle River, New Jersey, 2003.

19. Housman, M., *Why 'augmented intelligence' is a better way to describe AI*, AINews, United Kingdom, 2018, https://www.artificialintelligence-news.com/2018/05/24/why-augmented-intelligence-is- a-betterway-to-describe-ai/.

20. Nabiyev, V.V., *Yapay zeka: İnsan bilgisayar etkileşimi*, Seçkin Yayıncılık, Ankara, 2012.

21. Nilsson, J., *Voice interfaces: Assessing the potential*, Nielsen Norman Group, USA, 2003, Retrieved from http://www.useit.com/alertbox/20030127.htm.

22. Self, J., The defining characteristics of intelligent tutoring systems research: ITSs care, precisely. *Int. J. Artif. Intell. Educ. (IJAIED)*, 10, 350, 1998.

23. Steenbergen-Hu, S. and Cooper, H., A meta-analysis of the effectiveness of intelligent tutoring systems on college students' academic learning. *J. Educ. Psychol.*, *106*, 2, 331, 2014.

24. Reiland, R., *Is Artificial Intelligence the Key to Personalized Education?*, Smithsonian Magazine, Smithsonian Magazine, USA, 2018. https://www.smithsonianmag.com/innovation/artificial-intelligencekey-personalized-education-180963172/, on March 15 2018.

25. Lu, X., *Natural Language Processing and Intelligent Computer-Assisted Language Learning (ICALL)*, The TESOL Encyclopedia of English Language Teaching, USA, 2018.

26. Turovsky, B., *Ten years of Google translate*, Google Translate Blog, Google, USA, 2016. https://blog.google/products/translate/ten-years-of-google-translate/

27. Turovsky, B., *Found in translation: More accurate, fluent sentences in Google Translate*, Blog. Google, USA, 15, 2016, https://www.blog.google/products/translate/found-translation-more-accurate-fluentsentences-google-translate/.

28. https://medium.com/@alejandra.riveraUX/adding-a-chat-feature-to-duolingo-a-ux-case-s tudy-73175b612120

29. https://images.app.goo.gl/3g7rVCnfyYBBVJZMA

30. https://www.google.co.in/url?sa=i&url=https%3A%2F%2Fwww.smartsheet.com%2Fvoice-assistants-artificial-intelligence&psig=AOvVaw35WN

WG91EdKuqWmYVQcvdI&ust=1617361257271000&source=images&cd=
vfe&ved=0CAIQjRxqFwoTCJC8hq7y3O8CFQAAAAAdAAAAABAD

31. https://www.researchgate.net/profile/Michelle-Cavaleri/publication/320618
419/figure/fig2/AS:697745916571656@1543366998696/Grammarly-feed
back-Free-version.jpg

32. https://www.intellias.com/ai-nlp-driven-language-learning-app/

33. Burstein, J., Madnani, N., Sabatini, J., McCaffrey, D., Biggers, K., Dreier, K.,
Generating Language Activities in Real-Time for English Learners using
Language Muse, in: *Proceedings of the Fourth ACM Conference on Learning
Scale (L@S'17)*, Association for Computing Machinery, NY, USA, pp. 213–
215, 2017, https://dl.acm.org/doi/10.1145/3051457.3053988.

34. Lovett, D., *Is Machine Translation a threat to language learning?*, The
Chronicle of Higher Education, Washington D.C., 2018.

# 2

# Real Estate Price Prediction Using Machine Learning Algorithms

**Palak Furia\* and Anand Khandare†**

*Department of Computer Engineering, Thakur College of Engineering and Technology, Mumbai, India*

## Abstract

For a long time since the very beginning, a continuous paradigm of selling and buying houses/land has continued to exist. The wealth of a man is often determined by the kind of house he/she buys, but this process had multiple people intermediate. However, with the increase in technology, this barter system has also changed a lot. With PropTech being the new upcoming thing to disrupt in the real estate market, using technology to complete the operations has made buying property very simple. It is seen as part of a digital transformation in the real estate industry, focuses on both the technological and psychological changes of the people involved, and could lead to new functions such as transparency, unprecedented data, statistical data, machine learning, blockchain, and sensors that are part of PropTech.

In India, there are number of websites, which collect the data for properties that are to sell, but there are cases where on different sites price vary for the same apartment, and as a result, there is a lot of obscurity [1, 2]. This project uses machine learning to predict house prices. One heuristic data commonly used in the analysis of housing price deficits is the Bangalore city suburban housing data. Recent analysis has found that prices in that database are highly dependent on size and location. To date, basic algorithms such as linear regression can eliminate errors using both internal and local features. The previous function of forecasting housing prices are basis of retrospective analysis and machine learning [6, 7]. A linear regression model and a decision tree model, using vague assumptions. In addition, a multi-dimensional object model with two training items is used to evaluate house prices where something that predicts the

---
*\*Corresponding author*: palakfuria18@gmail.com
*†Corresponding author*: anand.khandare@thakureducation.org

Archana Mire, Shaveta Malik and Amit Kumar Tyagi (eds.) *Advanced Analytics and Deep Learning Models*, (19–32) © 2022 Scrivener Publishing LLC "internal" cost of a house is used, and the non-objective component can count neighbors' preferences. The aim is to solve the problems of relapse where the target variable is the value and the independent variable region. We have used hot code coding in each of our institutions. The business application of this algorithm is that classified websites can directly use this algorithm to predict the values of new properties that are listed by taking variable input and predicting the correct and appropriate value.

*Keywords*: Machine learning, clustering algorithm, linear regression, LASSO regression, decision tree, support vector machine, random forest regressor

## 2.1    Introduction

We are in want of a right prediction at the real estate and the housing marketplace discipline. We see a mechanism that runs all through the residence shopping and promoting; buying a house may be a lifetime purpose for maximum of the people. There are lot of individuals making big errors when buying the houses; the majority are shopping for homes from the people they recognise with the aid of seeing the classified ads and everywhere in the grooves coming across the India. One of the not unusual hassles is shopping for the residences, which are too high priced and no longer really worth it [3]. From claiming valuation structures, additional techniques mirror those natures of asset and those conditions that are provided for [8, 9]. The assets would possibly properly, at the manner, alternate in open market underneath many situations and instances; people are unaware about the contemporary conditions and they start losing their cash [10]. The exchange in cost of residences would affect both the common people together with the financial system of country; to avoid such situations, there is a want of rate prediction. Many techniques are to use within the price prediction.

## 2.2    Literature Review

Statistical fashions have been a method to analyze and are expecting property expenses for a long term. In the work of Fik *et al.* (2003), a study to explain the housing costs version was carried out with the aid of studying the impact of vicinity capabilities at the property charges [11] (Piazzesi and Schneider; 2009). For those who foresee product costs in a different way, the association can be quite complicated. Price forecasts are number one within the import commercial enterprise quarter. But, forecasting from deliver call for can be complex due to the fact that there may be a consolidation energy alongside the way. A neural programming model wishes to predict inventory price. This gives an overlap between those shares and blessings.

Authors (Selim, 2009) [12] compared a few studies of artificial neural network deflection using 60% of residential price calculations, and a lot of comparisons have been made by estimating the performance of all their comparisons with different education sizes and choosing statistical lengths.

Authors (Wu and Brynjolfsson, 2009) [15] from MIT made an estimate of the way Google searches for global loan and income. The author is well aware about the near encounters between them in the fee of houses and the love for much priced houses. Data taken from net seek manner search queries the use of Google procedures and with the assistance of actual countrywide harmony-information gather each present of states.

The author provides a brief overview of how a random wooded algorithm is use for retrofitting and phase, power boost, and bag loading used as methods. It generates a lot of distinctions, and the difference between lifting and bagging as stated by Liaw *et al.* (2002) is the successive trees, calculating the weights of the objects and most will take predictions. Throughout the year 2001, Nghiep and Al (2001) proposed a randomized start-up that included fundraising and provided more randomly the entire random planning and postponement process, which is mentioned here in retrospect.

Eric Slone *et al.* (2014) improved the relationship among the various home factors and the number of residential queries analyzed using a simple linear regression and multiple linear regressions using a standard square method. Home square images have been used as descriptive variables in simple queues, and multi-line retouches include an increase in the measurement of the parcel of land, number of bedrooms, year of construction, and more descriptive.

## 2.3  Proposed Work

### 2.3.1  Methodology

There are classified websites where properties are inconsistent in terms of pricing of an apartment, and there are some cases where similar apartments are priced at different price point, and thus, there are a lot of intransparencies. Sometimes, the consumers feels that the pricing is not justified for a particular listed apartment, but there no way to confirm that either. We propose to use three machine learning algorithms: linear regression, LASSO regression, and decision tree algorithm. The tools required for the project are as follows: Python, Sklearn for model building, Jupyter notebook, visual studio code and Pycharm as IDE, Python flask for http server, HTML/CSS/Javascript for UI, Numpy and Pandas for data cleaning, and Matplotlib for data visualization.

## 2.3.2   Work Flow

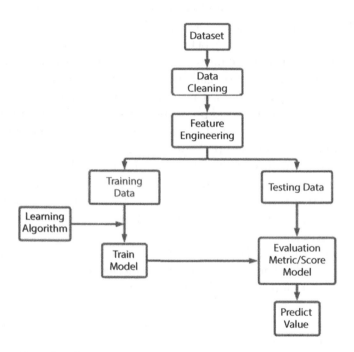

**Figure 2.1** Flow of work.

## 2.3.3   The Dataset

The selected dataset has element of the metropolis Bengaluru; it consists of nine columns with contents that is point out under in Table 2.1 and has 13,321 instances. Enforcement of real estate, infidelity in real estate builders inside the city, and actual property sales throughout India in 2017 have dropped by 7%. As an example, for a potential house owner, greater than 9,000 apartments and flats for sale vary between 42 and 52

**Table 2.1** Columns of dataset.

| Column name | Description |
|---|---|
| Area type | The kind of area the flat/plot is in. |
| Availability | If the land is currently available or not. |
| Location | Location of the land/plot. |
| Size | Number of bedrooms and hall kitchen in the flat. |
| Society | Name of the cooperating society. |
| Total square feet | Area of the plot in square feet. |
| Bath | Number of bathroom in the flat. |
| Balcony | Number of balcony in the flat. |
| Price | Price of the plot/flat. |

lakh, and it is observed that more than 7,100 apartments are within the budget 52 to 62 lakh, in step with a property file website Makaan.

## 2.3.4 Data Handling

### 2.3.4.1 Missing Values and Data Cleaning

First step is cleaning the data, for which we need to find the null values in the dataset. Figures 2.2 and 2.3 show the number of null values in every column. There are two methods of handling null value: first is that we can drop all the rows with null values, which will result in data loss; the other is that we could calculate the mean of all the values and replace all null values with the mean. Therefore, before cleaning the null value, we drop columns like society and balcony with multiple null values. Along with it, we also drop the columns like area type and availability, as our main goal is to predict the price.

In the size column, there are values with different attributes like 3 BHK and 3 BK, which means different; hence, to generalize, we will create a new column BHK. In this column, we would apply a function where we would tokenize each word; here, we keep the numbers and get rid of the other words. Therefore, we get a column BHK. In the total square feet column, there are entries where range is mention and not exact number; in this case, we replace it with the average of both the number.

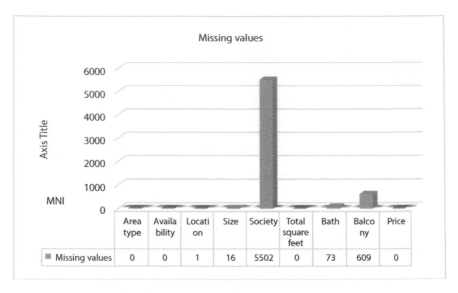

Missing values

| | Area type | Availa bility | Locati on | Size | Society | Total square feet | Bath | Balco ny | Price |
|---|---|---|---|---|---|---|---|---|---|
| ▣ Missing values | 0 | 0 | 1 | 16 | 5502 | 0 | 73 | 609 | 0 |

**Figure 2.2** Missing values.

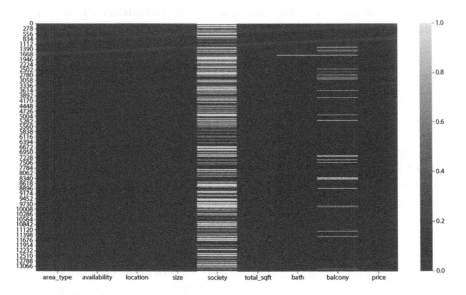

**Figure 2.3** Visualizing missing values using heatmap.

## 2.3.4.2    Feature Engineering

Feature engineering is the base that will help us further to remove outliers. Here, we combine two columns, apply the formula, and get price per

| | | |
|---|---|---|
| 2 | BHK | 5199 |
| 3 | BHK | 4310 |
| 4 | Bedroom | 826 |
| 4 | BHK | 591 |
| 3 | Bedroom | 547 |
| 1 | BHK | 538 |
| 2 | Bedroom | 329 |
| 5 | Bedroom | 297 |
| 6 | Bedroom | 191 |
| 1 | Bedroom | 105 |
| 8 | Bedroom | 84 |
| 7 | Bedroom | 83 |
| 5 | BHK | 59 |
| 9 | Bedroom | 46 |
| 6 | BHK | 30 |
| 7 | BHK | 17 |
| 1 | RK | 13 |
| 10 | Bedroom | 12 |

**Figure 2.4** Different BHK attribute.

square feet. Then, we find the number of unique location where we get 1,304 locations. Here, some of the locations are just mentioned once or twice; therefore, we set a threshold of 10, so all the locations that appear over five times are considered Figure 2.4.

### 2.3.4.3 Removing Outliers

Outliers are data points or errors, which represent extreme variations in our dataset. There are techniques to detect outlier; one of them is by visualization. We can graph box plot or scatter plot and, from the patterns, draw inference.

In BHK, there are some flat whose average area of one room is larger, which appears unusual, whereas in some instances, the number of bathroom is larger than number of rooms in the house, hence affecting the result.

The scatter chart was plotted to visualize price per square feet for 2 BHK and 3 BHK properties. Here, the blue points represent the 2 BHK and red

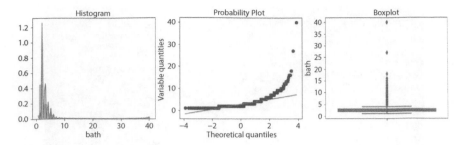

**Figure 2.5** Bath visualization.

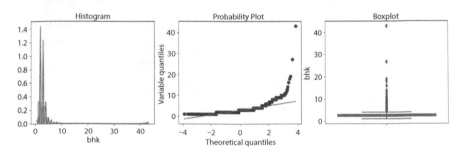

**Figure 2.6** BHK visualization.

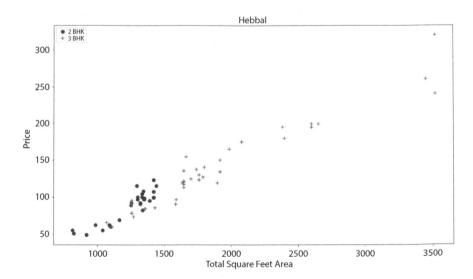

**Figure 2.7** Scatter plot for 2 and 3 BHK flat for total square feet.

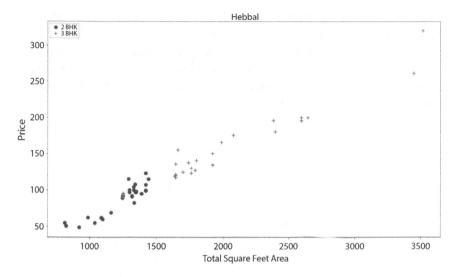

**Figure 2.8** Scatter plot for 2 And 3 BHK flat for total square feet after removing outliers.

points as 3 BHK plots. Based on Figures 2.5 through 2.8 the outliers was remove from the Hebbal region using the "remove bhk outliers function".

## 2.4    Algorithms

### 2.4.1    Linear Regression

Linear regression is an approach linear in nature to modeling the relationship connecting a scalar response and one or more explanatory variables. A prognostic modeling technique finds a relationship among independent variable and dependent variable. The independent variables can be categorical or continuous, while dependent variables are only continuous.

### 2.4.2    LASSO Regression

LASSO regression is another sort of linear regression; it makes use of shrinkage. Its data values are reduce in measurement in the route of a valuable point like mean. The system encourages easy and sparse models; the acronym "LASSO" is for the Least Absolute Shrinkage and choice Operator [4, 5]. L1 regularization is done with the aid of LASSO regression; it gives a sanction, which is equal to the absolute fee of the coefficients significance. This form of regularization outcomes in sparse fashions with much less coefficients; many coefficients can emerge as zero and are eliminated from the model. Huge penalties result in values close by to zero, which produces less difficult fashions. On the opposite, L2 regularization (e.g., ridge regression) does not bring about the exception of the coefficients or sparse models. This makes the LASSO higher to elucidate than the ridge.

### 2.4.3   Decision Tree

A selection tree is flowchart-like tree, in which a characteristic is represented by using inner node; the choice rule is represented with the aid of a branch and final results by way of each leaf node. The pinnacle node in a choice tree is called as the root node. It partitions the tree in a recursive way, namely, recursive partitioning. The time complexity is a characteristic of the range of statistics and the variety of attributes in the given records. Choice trees handle facts with high dimensionality and accuracy [13, 14].

### 2.4.4   Support Vector Machine

Support vector machine is a curated reading system and is used for classification and retrospective problems. The support vector machine is very popular, as it produces remarkable accuracy with low calculation power. It is widely used in segregation problems. It has three types: targeted, unsupervised, and reinforced learning. A support vector machine is a selected separator that is officially defined by separating the hyperplane. With the provision of training data, the release of advanced hyperplane algorithm that separates new models is labeled.

### 2.4.5   Random Forest Regressor

The Random Forest is a pliable and easy-to-use machine that produces good results most of the time with less time spent on hyperparameter setting. It has gained popularity because of its simplicity and the fact that it is use for split and reverse functions. Random forests are an amalgam of predictable trees in such a way that each tree is based on random vector values sampled independently and with the same distribution of all the trees in the forest. The general deforestation error changes as the limit of the number of trees in the forest grows.

### 2.4.6 XGBoost

XGBoost is a powerful way to build lower back-up fashions. The validity of this assertion can be characterized to the information of its (XGBoost) work with its students. Motive work includes job loss and time to get used to. It offers with the difference among actual values and expected values, e.g., how the model effects are from actual values. The typical loss features in XGBoost for deferral issues are reg: linear and, in binary categories, reg: logistics. Regularization parameters are as follows: alpha, beta, and gamma.

## 2.5   Evaluation Metrics

While working with regression fashions, it is very important to pick out an appropriate evaluation metric. It also addresses loss function for regression;

**Table 2.2**  Different evaluation metrics.

| Metric | Description | Formula |
|---|---|---|
| Mean squared error (MSE) | It is generally used in a regression function, to check how close the regression line to the dataset points is. | $MSE = \dfrac{1}{n}\sum\limits_{1=1}^{n}(yi - y_i^{\sim})^2$ |
| Root mean squared error (RMSE) | It is often referred as root mean squared deviation. Its purpose is to find error in the numerical predictive models. | $RMSE = \sqrt{\sum \dfrac{(Y_{Pred} - Y_{ref})^2}{N}}$ |
| Mean absolute error (MAE) | Similar to MSE, here, also, we take different between actual value and predicted value. | $MAE = \dfrac{1}{n}\sum\limits_{j=1}^{n}|y_j - y_j^{\sim}|$ |
| Coefficient of determination ($R^2$) | It is referred to as goodness of fit. The fraction of response/ outcome is explained by the model. | $R^2 = 1 - \dfrac{\sum_{i=1}^{n}(y_i - y_i^{\sim})^2}{\sum_{i=1}^{n}(y_i - y^{\sim})^2}$ |
| Pearson correlation coefficient | It measures the strength of association between two variables. | $r = \dfrac{\sum(X-\bar{x})(Y-\bar{y})}{\sqrt{\sum(X-\bar{x})^2}\sqrt{\sum(Y-\bar{y})^2}}$ |

few of them are mentioned in Table 2.2. If the distinction between the loss fee and the predicted value is less, then the loss/errors feature could be small and it characterized that the model is most suitable.

We can achieve RMSE just by taking square root of MSE. RMSE is very accessible with numerical prediction, to come across if any outliers are messing with the records prediction. Therefore, we select RMSE for version evaluation.

## 2.6    Result of Prediction

The dataset is divided into 80% of the training dataset and 20% of the testing dataset as seen in Table 2.3. The desired libraries were imported and GridSearchCV used to locate the satisfactory model. It compares the model on multiple regresses and different parameters and offers the best score among them. With the assistance of GridSearchCV, we have compared the algorithms, i.e., linear regression, LASSO regression, decision tree, support vector machine, random forest regressor, and XGBoost.

To aid this challenge, various device mastering algorithms are checked. It has been clear that XGBoost acts better with 85% accuracy and with an awful lot less blunders values. While this test is compared to the result, once those algorithms predicts properly. This task has been finished with the number one aim to determine the prediction for prices, which we have got efficiently completed using specific system analyzing algorithms like a linear regression, LASSO regression, decision tree, random forest, more than one regression, guide vector gadget, gradient boosted trees, neural networks, and bagging.

Consequently, it is clear that the XGBoost gives more accuracy in prediction in comparison to the others, and additionally, our research offers to locate the attributes contribution in prediction. In addition, python flask can be used as an http server and CSS/Html for creating UI for internet site. Therefore, one might agree with this that studies may be useful for the people and governments, and the future works are stated under every system, and new software program technology can assist in the future to expect the costs. Price prediction can be advanced by way of including many attributes like surroundings, marketplaces, and many different related variables to the houses.

**Table 2.3** Comparison of algorithm.

| | Model | Best score | RSME score | Error score | Accuracy percent |
|---|---|---|---|---|---|
| 0 | Linear regression | 0.790932 | 64.813703 | 0.209068 | 79% |
| 1 | LASSO regression | 0.803637 | 62.813241 | 0.196363 | 80% |
| 2 | Decision tree | 0.71606 | 70.813421 | 0.283936 | 72% |
| 3 | Support Vector Machine | 0.204336 | 126.440620 | 0.795664 | 20% |
| 4 | Random Forest Regressor | 0.884247 | 48.226644 | 0.115753 | 88% |
| 5 | XGBoost | 0.891979 | 46.588246 | 0.108021 | 89% |

# References

1. Bhagat, N., Mohokar, A., Mane, S., House price forecasting using data mining. *Int. J. Comput. Appl.*, 152, 2, 23–26, 2016.
2. Breiman, L., Bagging predictors. *Mach. Learn.*, 24, 2, 123–140, 1996.
3. Ganjisaffar, Y., Caruana, R., Lopes, C.V., Bagging gradient-boosted trees for high precision, low variance ranking models. *Proceedings of the 34th international ACM SIGIR conference on Research and development in Information Retrieval*, ACM, pp. 85–94, 2011.
4. Gu, J., Zhu, M., Jiang, L., Housing price forecasting based on genetic algorithm and support vector machine. *Expert Syst. Appl.*, 38, 4, 3383–3386, 2011.
5. Li, L. and Chu, K.-H., Prediction of real estate price variation based on economic parameters. *Applied System Innovation (ICASI), 2017 International Conference on*, IEEE, pp. 87–90, 2017.
6. Liaw, A., Wiener, M. *et al.*, Classification and regression by randomforest. *R. News*, 2, 3, 18–22, 2002.
7. Limsombunchai, V., House price prediction: Hedonic price model vs. artificial neural network. *New Zealand Agricultural and Resource Economics Society Conference*, pp. 25–26, 2004.

8. Mirmirani, S. and Cheng Li, H., A comparison of var and neural networks with genetic algorithm in forecasting price of oil. *Applications of Artificial Intelligence in Finance and Economics*, Emerald Group Publishing Limited, pp. 203–223, 2004.

9. Nghiep, N. and Al, C., Predicting housing value: A comparison of multiple regression analysis and artificial neural networks. *J. Real Estate Res.*, 22, 3, 313–336, 2001.

10. Patel, J., Shah, S., Thakkar, P., Kotecha, K., Predicting stock and stock price index movement using trend deterministic data preparation and machine learning techniques. *Expert Syst. Appl.*, 42, 1, 259–268, 2015.

11. Piazzesi, M. and Schneider, M., Momentum traders in the housing market: Survey evidence and a search model. *Am. Econ. Rev. Am. Econ. Assoc.*, 99, 2, 406–411, May 2009.

12. Selim, H., Determinants of house prices in turkey: Hedonic regression versus artificial neural network. *Expert Syst. Appl.*, 36, 2, 2843–2852, 2009.

13. Trafalis, T.B. and Ince, H., Support vector machine for regression and applications to financial forecasting, Neural Networks, 2000, *IJCNN 2000, Proceedings of the IEEEINNS-ENNS International Joint Conference on*, vol. 6, IEEE, pp. 348–353, 2000.

14. Willmott, C.J., On the validation of models. *Phys. Geogr.*, 2, 2, 184–194, 1981.

15. Wu, L. and Brynjolfsson, E., *The future of prediction: How google searches foreshadow housing prices and sales*, 2009.

# 3

# Multi-Criteria–Based Entertainment Recommender System Using Clustering Approach

Chandramouli Das, Abhaya Kumar Sahoo* and Chittaranjan Pradhan

*School of Computer Engineering, KIIT Deemed to be University, Odisha, India*

## Abstract

Multi-criteria recommender systems are such kind of models that are made to give a user-friendly environment to the user. These models are widely used in every sector of the world. Many leading companies are putting effort to make these multi-criteria recommender models effective by introducing new techniques and approaches. In the past, people used to done the recommendation manually. For example, if someone wants to buy something, then they used to ask other people who have bought that particular thing or people who has some knowledge on that thing. To take this process genuine, automatic, and more efficient, the concept of recommender system came. The first recommender system was based on single criteria. That is known as single-criteria recommender system. But in real-world scenario for recommendation, a model needs to look at more than one criterion. So, the multi-criteria recommender concept came in the picture. In this chapter, we will dig into various types of multi-criteria recommender systems. Here, we will see some innovative ideas, approaches, and methods, which are applied to a multi-criteria recommender system more efficient and effective. We will see how these new and innovative approaches give better result compared to the conventional recommender systems. Here, we have talked about so many different approaches of multi-criteria recommendation techniques done by various researchers around the globe. All these researches are done with the real-world datasets to solve the practical problems. We have also chosen five most likely research activities and explained in details how they have conducted their research and got a successful outcome. But before we dive into the hardcore details, we will see that how a recommender system was made. We talked about the various

*Corresponding author: abhayakumarsahoo2012@gmail.com

Archana Mire, Shaveta Malik and Amit Kumar Tyagi (eds.) Advanced Analytics and Deep Learning Models, (33–64) © 2022 Scrivener Publishing LLC

filtering techniques and the core working principles of a recommender system. At the end of the chapter, we have also discussed about the advantages and disadvantages of the recommender systems. Recommender system helps a business to grow higher and higher and also helps to analyze the risks. For these reasons, multi-criteria recommender systems are trending in the market and got high demand.

**Keywords:** Clustering, entertainment, mean absolute error, multi-criteria, recommender system

## 3.1    Introduction

In today's digital age, there is massive amount of information available over the internet; it provides the users with enormous amount of resources or services pertaining to any domain. As the information over the internet rises, the number of resources and options also tend to increase exponentially, causing information overload which eventually creates a lot of confusion among the clients, thus making the decision-making process strenuous [1].

Recommender systems are widely used in the decision-making process and deal with the information overload. Multi-criteria recommendation system is a type of recommender system that utilizes user's rating and preference on several criteria to make the optimal decision for the respective client. It can thus make a personalized recommendation based on the user's demands and choices. In this paper, we compare the performance of the recommendation system among three types of settings, first by using the ratings of all the criteria using the traditional approach, second by taking multiple-criteria preference as circumstance, and third by make use of chosen criteria ratings as circumstances. Thus, recommender system is a significant tool used in the decision-making process. It produces a recommendation list items to a client based on the client's previous likings [28–31].

The importance of recommender systems has been increasing day by day especially for the business applications, as the use of recommender system proved to be quite successful in the ecommerce sector like amazon. Many business applications started incorporating it in variety of other sectors including movie and music recommendation, books and e-books, tourism industry, hotels, restaurant's, news, etc. These systems assist the users in figuring out the most relevant information based on their needs instead of showing an indistinguishable amount of data that is irrelevant to the user. Hence, it is crucial for the recommender systems to have high predictive accuracy and allocate the desired items at the top of the recommendation list based on the specific user's requirements [16, 21].

The popularity of mobile devices among the users has increased the dependency on the mobile servers. People get lots of information including business information, product information, and recommendation information from the mobile devices. One of the important applications of mobile servers is movie recommendation. A movie recommendation system has been an effective tool in recommending movies to the users which, in turn, helps the viewers to cope with multiple movie options available and help them in finding the appropriate movies conveniently. However, recommendation is a complicated task as it involves various tastes of users, different genres of movies, etc. Hence, many techniques have been used to enhance the performance of the recommendation system [32].

We have a massive platform that can be used for giving individual thoughts and reviews. As there is so much data flowing over the internet, it is significant to derive new ways to collect and produce the information. Recommender system is an important component of many businesses, especially in the e-commerce domain. It usually exploits the preference history of the users to provide them with the suitable recommendations, whereas a traditional recommender system can provide only one rating value to an item [5, 24–26].

## 3.2    Work Related Multi-Criteria Recommender System

Multi-Criteria Recommender System (MCRS) is widely used in almost every sector. It has developed with time. Nowadays, we have many advance recommender systems. Recommender system models can be made by various methods like clustering technique, machine learning technique, deep learning techniques, neural networks, and big data sentiment analysis. There are many open source projects that are developing in the domain of MCRS. So, let us take a look on here.

Wasid and Ali came up with a MCRS based on the clustering approach. The primary objective of their method was to enhance recommendation performance by identifying more similar neighbors within the cluster of a specific user. To implement this method, they had done two major things. First, they extracted the users' preferences for the given items based on multi-criteria ratings. Second, on the basis of the preferences of the user, the cluster centers were defined [2].

Zheng proposed a utility-based multi-criteria recommender system that depends on the utility function. He built the utility function by applying the multiple-criteria ratings to measure the similarity between the vector of user evaluations and the vector of user expectations. To calculate the utility score, they had incorporated three similarity measures. In addition, three optimization learning-to-rank methods were used to learn the user expectations [3].

Tallapally et al. adopted a deep learning–based ANN architecture technique known as stacked autoencoders to ease the recommendations problems. The functionality of the traditional stacked autoencoders was enhanced to include the multiple-criteria ratings by adding an extra layer that acted like an input layer to the autoencoders. The multiple-criteria ratings input were connected to the intermediate layer. This intermediate layer comprised of the items or the criteria. This intermediate layer was further linked to N consecutive encoding layers [4].

Musto, Gemmis, Semeraro, and Lops used MCRS using aspect-based sentiment analysis. They utilized a structure for sentiment analysis and opinion mining. It automatically extracts sentiment scores and relevant aspects from users' reviews. They estimated the efficiency of the proposed method with other state-of-the-art baselines and compared the result [5].

García-Cumbreras et al. method utilizes the pessimistic and optimistic behaviors among users for recommender systems. The objective was to categorize the clients into distinct classes of two, namely, pessimist class and optimist class based on their cognition or behavior. The classes are defined on the report of the mean polarity of clients' rating and reviews. Then, the derived client's class is added as a latest attribute for the collaborative filtering (CF) algorithm [6].

Zhang et al. proposed an algorithm that considers virtual ratings or overall rating from the users' reviews by analyzing the sentiments of the user's opinions by using the emoticons that were also included in the reviews to mitigate the sparsity problem which still lies in the recommender systems [7].

Bauman et al. presented a recommendation system that suggested the items that comprised of the most significant aspects to improve the user's overall experience. These aspects were identified using the Sentiment Utility approach [8].

Akhtar et al. presented a technique for analyzing the hotel reviews and extracted some valuable information or knowledge from them to assist the service providers as well as the customers to help them identify the loop-holes and strengths in the service sector to improve their business performance [9].

Yang *et al.* presented a technique consisting of three main components namely aspect weight, opinion mining, and overall rating inference. The opinion mining component was responsible for extracting only the key aspects and opinions from the users' reviews based on which it computed a rating for each extracted aspect [10].

Dong *et al.* presented a method for CF that merges feature similarity and feature sentiments for recommending items, that having higher priority that are similar and better than the items in the users query [11].

Wang *et al.* proposed an approach on solving a problem when a user is particularly new to an environment. This problem is known as cold start problem. We will discuss about the cold start problem later in this paper. Most recommender systems collect the preferences of the users on some attributes of the items [12].

Musat *et al.* explained a method called topic profile CF (TPCF) that solved the problems occurring due to the data sparsity problems and non-person-alized ranking methods that led to difficulty in finding sufficient reliable data for making recommendations [13].

Jamroonsilp and Prompoon presented an approach for ranking the items based on user's reviews. They had considered five pre-defined aspects for the software items. The ranking of the software was computed by comparing the sentences analyzing the different clients' ratings for every software aspect. This was performed in three phases include gathering user reviews, analyz-ing the gathered reviews and doing the subsequent software ranking [14].

Zhang *et al.* proposed a method that utilized the aspect-level sentiment of the users' reviews with the support of helpfulness reviews [15].

Zheng, Shekhar, Jose, and Rai proposed a multi-criteria decision-making approach in the discipline of educational learning. At first, they integrated the context-awareness and the multi-criteria decision-making in the rec-ommender systems considering the educational data. Their experimental results were quite satisfactory, and it was realized that they were able to produce additional correct suggestions based on two different strategies of recommendations [17].

These are some of the works done by various scientists around the globe. There are thousands of projects which has been conducted or ongoing in the field of MCRS to make the system fully efficient. Nowadays, the leading companies are making using of the recommender systems. One of the best examples is the company Amazon that uses the recommender systems to give proper recommendation to their customers. Netflix is another company that uses multi-criteria recommender system to give a list of movies and web series suggestions to the user on the basis of the user's details and user's previous choices. So, day by day, new techniques are being applied in recommender systems to improve the accuracy.

## 3.3   Working Principle

The most basic question comes in mind that what is recommender system. A recommender system is a software or model that analyze a client's preference, and based on that, it generates a list of items for that client. A multi-criteria recommender system can be defined as recommender systems that collect information on multiple criteria. The basic working of recommender system is to predict accurate recommendation for a particular user. The recommender system or single-criteria recommender system explores only one criteria and give recommended result. This is the first ever recommender system concept. But for real-world problems, we cannot predict recommendation list by exploring only one criterion at a time. It will give false prediction. So, the MCRS concept comes in the field. These kinds of recommender system can explore multiple-criteria at a time and can give excellent accuracy (Figure 3.1).

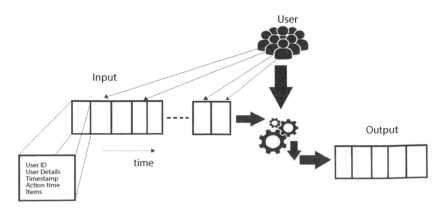

**Figure 3.1** Working principle of MCRS.

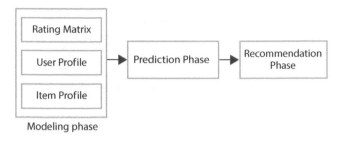

Modeling phase

**Figure 3.2** Phases of MCRS.

Recommender systems are widely used in e-commerce systems and movie industries and each and every sector. Suppose if we used amazon. com and buy a product, then before check out it shows similar kind of product as add on. This list of items is predicted by amazons very own recommender system. Similarly, if we use Netflix, then we can see that it always recommends new movies and web series to us. This prediction is based on generally two categories, on the basis of our previous choice and other one is on the basis of out Netflix account details. That is how recommender system generates a list which is most suitable to the user.

Every recommender system goes through three types of phases. Those phases are modeling phase, prediction phase, and recommendation phase.

Figure 3.2 explains the different phases of a recommender system. Now, we will see the each phases and their significance.

### 3.3.1   Modeling Phase

In modeling phase, its focus on preparing the data will be used in next two phase. As we can see in the diagram, it is also divided in three cases. First step is to build a ratio matrix. The rows of the matrix contain the name of the users, and columns contain the items and each cell contains rating, which by the user for a particular item. Now, it generates a user profile. This profile explains the preference of a user. It is mostly a vector and every user has their own private profile of preferences. In the third step, it generates a profile for the items which contains the features of the items.

### 3.3.2   Prediction Phase

It is the second phase of recommender system. The main objective is to estimate the rating or score of unrevealed or unspecified items for every client. This process is done by a utility function based on the extracted data which is provided by the modeling phase. Different filtering techniques are diagrammatically shown in Figure 3.3.

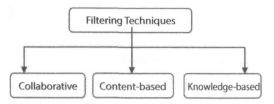

**Figure 3.3** Filtering techniques of MCRS.

### 3.3.3    Recommendation Phase

This the third phase of recommender system and also extension prediction phase. In this step, various methods are used to hold up clients' choice by predicting the most acceptable items. As per the user's interest, new items are recommended in this step.

These are the most three important phases of a MCRS. We use different kind of approaches in MCRS to predict good results. The most important and widely used approaches are content-based filtering, CF approach, and knowledge-based approach. We also have a hybrid approach. Now, we will take a deep look about all these approaches of MCRS.

### 3.3.4    Content-Based Approach

It generates the suitable recommendations for a client that depends on his previous behaviors. It analyzes the user's previous history like what liked, bought, or watched and accordingly it predicts. It generates a user profile for every user based on their previously selected items and recommends items to him based on similar features items which he liked before. It does not compare his preferences to the users to characterize each user. Content-based filtering approach is divided in three steps which are item representation, learning the user profile, and recommendations generator. In the item representation step, the information or the description of item is extracted to create item's characteristics. It produces the structured item's representation. In the next step, a user profile is generated. This user profile is based on the previous behavior such as liking or disliking, the rating or by writing some text comment given by the user for a particular item. This step is known as learning the user profile and the last step is recommendation generator. In this step, a list of recommended items is generated and compared it with the item's features of the client's profile. The item that is suitable or most likely is added to the prediction list [1].

This method has been executed in various domains like textual details such as websites, news, and articles and also used for recommending activities such as tourism, travel, TVs, and e-commerce industries. This method works very efficiently if the items size is moderate. This approach relies on content or characteristics of each item so it gives several advantages like it offers a high level personalization in recommendations; it can make its scale up when number of users increases, which means it is scalable. It can make recommendations with a particular interest of a user and it provided a very good security also. These are some advantages of content-based filtering approach [1].

### 3.3.5    Collaborative Filtering Approach

This technique is immense popular technique among all the multi-criteria recommender system. It interacts with multiple users and generates the recommendation list. If user1 has similarities in their preference with user2, then the item which is recommended to user2 will also be recommended to user 1. The hypothesis behind the following approach is that the clients agreeing other clients in the past will also agree in the future. For a new item, the relationship with user is determined by other users' review. We can represent as user terms matrix where each cell of the matrix represents the ratings given by clients for a particular item [1].

CF can be divided into two classes: model-based and memory-based. The memory-based approach is a kind of heuristic algorithm. It estimates the item's rating which depends on another client's ratings. It can also be classified into two methods: item-based and user-based. The other one, memory-based approach, recommends items based on the similar interests on other users. It analyzes the behavior of other clients like they purchased or liked or viewed before and then recommend the product to this client [1].

CF approaches have many advantages compare to all other filtering approaches like, sometimes, novel and unfamiliar items are recommended, it is very suitable and flexible in various domain, and it does not need to analyze the contents of a particular item [1].

These are some of the advantages of CF in MCRS.

### 3.3.6    Knowledge-Based Filtering Approach

This is comparatively a new approach than other two approaches. This method is used in those cases where both collaborative- and content-based approaches failed or cannot work properly. The situation happens when there is not enough ratings or reviews are at hand for a particular item for the recommendation process. It is generally happening for those that are hardly ever purchased like houses, cars, or financial services. The way this approach works that it extracts the client's perception for that domain for recommending the items that will satisfy his requirements the best. The core strength or advantage is that it does not need any previous rating of that problem. By using this approach, it can overcome the cold start problem. But it has a disadvantage also that it needs experienced engineering with all its attendant difficulties to understand the item domain satisfactorily [1].

There is another approach in the recommender system known as the hybrid approach. This approach is made to overcome the limitation of both collaborative and content-based filtering approach. It combines the strength of collaborative and content-based approach they are by combining multiple recommendation algorithm's implementations into a single recommendation system to improve the efficiency of the recommendation system which, in turn, would show better performance. The hybrid approach is generated by combining two or more algorithms. We must take care of two major points over here. First is keeping an account of the recommendation models that declare the required inputs and the determination of the hybrid recommender system. The second point is determining the strategy that will be used within the hybrid recommender. But there are also certain demerits prevailing in this hybrid approach like it not cost-effective, i.e., it is very expensive to implement because it is an amalgamation of other filtering methods. Moreover, it increases the complexity and, sometimes, needs outside data which is unavailable most of the time [1, 18].

## 3.4    Comparison Among Different Methods

Now, we will make a comparison between some methods used by researchers around the globe and will see about the result of their research.

### 3.4.1    MCRS Exploiting Aspect-Based Sentiment Analysis

In this research activity, Musto *et al.* proposed a CF technique based on MCRS, which utilizes the information to analyze users' interests conveyed by users' reviews.

In their experimental data analysis, they use many traditional models for evaluation. The outcomes showed the perception in back of this research [5].

Now, if we look in their experimental data analysis, then we can see that they have used three datasets. Those are Yelp, TripAdvisor, and Amazon.

**Table 3.1** Dataset statistics.

|                | Yelp    | TripAdvisor | Amazon    |
|----------------|---------|-------------|-----------|
| **Users**      | 45,981  | 536,952     | 826,773   |
| **Items**      | 11,573  | 3,945       | 50,210    |
| **Rating/Reviews** | 229,906 | 796,958 | 1,324,759 |
| **Sparsity**   | 99.95%  | 99.96%      | 99.99%    |

This framework is mainly for aspect extraction and sentiment analysis. For implementing this, we need different types of parameters. In the first step, we need to remove the words like "a", "and", "but", "how", "or", and "what". In the next step, we need to set the framework in between 10 and 50 for extracting the aspects and sub-aspects. To calculate the efficiency of sub-aspects, the main aspects were extricated, in some experimental session. As per the sentiment analysis algorithmic program, both "CoreNLP" and "AFINN-based" algorithms were used. They set KL-divergence score value as 0.1. They used both user-based and item-based CF system. Previously, they have used an advance version of Euclidean distance, which they introduced as multi-dimensional Euclidean distance for calculating the neighborhood. By their formula for all the dataset, neighborhood size was set to 10, 30, and 80, and they did it because the bigger neighborhoods will reduce in the efficiency of the proposed algorithm [5].

The effectiveness of their algorithmic program was planned by calculating the average of the Mean Average Error (MAE). Rival framework is used to calculate the matrices, to make sure the dependability in results [5].

### 3.4.1.1   Discussion and Result

In this demonstration, they analyzed discrete arrangements. Those are mainly based on aspect-based sentiment analysis. The results we can see in Tables 3.2 and 3.3. They stated the results picked up with AFINN sentiment analysis algorithm, due to space reasons. It did not come out with any major dissimilarity with the CoreNLP algorithm. As it is based on CF user-based approach, on Yelp dataset and Tripadvisor dataset, they took top 10 aspects from the datasets. Besides, the above results are better than the previous 50 aspects. Accordingly, they did not take a bigger space.

One more attractive result comes from the Yelp and TripAdvisor by use of sub-aspect which gave a significant improvement in performance.

**Table 3.2** Result comparison.

**Result of MCRS-Based CF Experiment 1**

| Configuration | | | Dataset | | |
| --- | --- | --- | --- | --- | --- |
| #neigh. | #asp. | Sub-asp | Yelp | TripAdvisor | Amazon |
| 10 | 10 | Y | 0.8362 | 0.7111 | 0.6464 |
| 10 | 10 | N | 0.841 | 0.7564 | 0.6335 |
| 10 | 50 | Y | 0.841 | 0.7269 | 0.6346 |
| 10 | 50 | N | 0.8364 | 0.8007 | 0.6276 |
| 30 | 10 | Y | 0.8461 | 0.7677 | 0.712 |
| 30 | 10 | N | 0.8473 | 0.7722 | 0.7122 |
| 30 | 50 | Y | 0.8474 | 0.7743 | 0.7101 |
| 30 | 50 | N | 0.8494 | 0.8003 | 0.714 |
| 80 | 10 | Y | 0.8579 | 0.7971 | 0.7584 |

**Result of Experiment 2**

| Configuration | Dataset | | |
| --- | --- | --- | --- |
| | Yelp | TripAdvisor | Amazon |
| Multi-U2U | **0.8362** | **0.7111** | **0.6276** |
| U2U-Euclidean | 0.886 | 0.8337 | 0.7254 |
| U2U-Pearson | 0.964 | 1.1222 | 0.9789 |
| Static-Multi-U2U | N.A. | 0.798 | N.A. |
| Multi-I2I | 0.864 | 0.8245 | 0.811 |
| I2I-Euclidean | 0.8745 | 0.8429 | 0.8117 |
| I2I-Pearson | 1.1794 | 0.8644 | 0.9679 |
| Static-Multi-I2I | N.A. | 0.8474 | N.A. |
| RatingSGD | 0.8409 | 0.745 | 0.8859 |

(Continued)

**Table 3.2** Result comparison. (*Continued*)

**Result of MCRS-Based CF Experiment 1**

| Configuration | | Dataset | | |
|---|---|---|---|---|
| #neigh. | Sub-asp | Yelp | TripAdvisor | Amazon |
| 80 | N | 0.8592 | 0.7953 | 0.7554 |
| 80 | Y | 0.859 | 0.7907 | 0.7544 |
| 80 | N | 0.8597 | 0.7995 | 0.7544 |

**Result of Experiment 2**

| Configuration | Dataset | | |
|---|---|---|---|
| | Yelp | TripAdvisor | Amazon |
| ParallelSGD | 0.8409 | 0.7449 | 0.8852 |
| ALSWR | 0.9545 | 0.9053 | 1.0354 |

**Result of MCRS Item–Based CF**

| Configuration | | Dataset | | |
|---|---|---|---|---|
| #asp. | Sub-asp | Yelp | TripAdvisor | Amazon |
| 10 | Y | 0.864 | 0.8245 | 0.811 |
| 10 | N | 0.8643 | 0.8252 | 0.8117 |
| 50 | Y | 0.8641 | 0.8254 | 0.8118 |
| 50 | N | 0.8648 | 0.826 | 0.8124 |

**Top 10 Main Aspects Extracted**

| | |
|---|---|
| Yelp | Place, food, service, restaurant, price menu, staff, drink, and lunch |
| TripAdvisor | Hotel, room, staff, location, service, breakfast, restaurant, bathroom, price, view |
| Amazon | game, graphic, story, character, player price, gameplay, controller level, and music |

Here, the maximum efficiency came by using the top 50 aspects. For a better understanding of this, we need to do further investigations [5, 20].

It is noted that, to get better efficiency, we need to configure all the datasets in top 10 neighbors.

In the next step, they compared the algorithm with matrix factorization (MF) algorithms for getting better baselines. Besides, it is specified that TripAdvisor dataset has an unchangeable set of six features. For every analysis like "Cleanliness", "location", "value", "service", "sleep quality", and "overall". They have differentiated their way with a MCRS algorithm that depends on those aspects. In Table 3.5, we can see that their method gets the better of against all the baselines. These results surely established that their perception, since they proved that their approach could overpower both strategies exploiting single ratings and MCRS algorithms.

When multiple-criteria user-to-user CF is used as recommender algorithm, then the best overall results are obtained [5].

### 3.4.2   User Preference Learning in Multi-Criteria Recommendation Using Stacked Autoencoders by Tallapally *et al.*

Here, they come up with a stacked autoencoders which is a DNN approach to use the multiple-criteria ratings. They implemented a model which is configured to analyze the connection in the middle of every client's criteria and general rating efficiency. Test outcomes are based on practical datasets like Yahoo! Movies dataset and TripAdvisor dataset. It illustrates that this approach can perform both single-criteria systems and multi-criteria approaches on different performance matrix [4].

Now, if we look on their proposed performance evaluation and result analysis, then it will be cleared that how much efficiency this model can achieve.

#### 3.4.2.1   *Dataset and Evaluation Matrix*

In this paper, they have used two datasets based on real world from tourism and movie domains that are used to evaluate the performance. They hold on to the sample data of the users who reviewed at least five hotels and hotels that were reviewed by at least five users to obtain working data subset from TA.

They used subset that carry more than 19,000 rating instances by more than 3,100 users with around 3,500 hotels which has a high sparsity of 99.8272%. In addition, YM data are generated as shown in Tables 3.3 to 3.5. For analyzing the performance of this method, they used Mean

**Table 3.3** Dataset.

**Result = YM 10-10**

**Result = YM 20-20**

| Technique | MAE | GIMAE | GPIMAE | F1 | Technique | MAE | GIMAE | GPIMAE | F1 |
|---|---|---|---|---|---|---|---|---|---|
| MF [10] | 0.8478 | 0.7461 | 0.6765 | 0.5998 | MF [10] | 0.7397 | 0.6077 | 0.57 | 0.6698 |
| 2016_Hybrid AE [23] | 0.7811 | 0.6595 | 0.8269 | 0.7042 | 2016_Hybrid AE [23] | 0.7205 | 0.6008 | 0.783 | 0.7578 |
| 2011_Liwei Liu [13] | 0.6574 | 0.5204 | 0.6574 | 0.664 | 2011_Liwei Liu [13] | 0.6576 | 0.5054 | 0.6576 | 0.6828 |
| 2017_Learning [22] | 0.6576 | 0.5054 | 0.6576 | 0.6629 | 2017_Learning [22] | 0.8254 | 0.5958 | 0.8131 | 0.7544 |
| 2017_CCC [27] | 0.6374 | 0.624 | 0.7857 | 0.5361 | 2017_CCC [27] | 0.6798 | 0.6095 | 0.7159 | 0.5585 |
| 2017_CCA [27] | 0.6618 | 0.6015 | 0.799 | 0.5343 | 2017_CCA [27] | 0.6691 | 0.6042 | 0.6971 | 0.5641 |
| 2017_CIC [27] | 0.6719 | 0.6542 | 0.7743 | 0.5327 | 2017_CIC [27] | 0.7029 | 0.6218 | 0.7064 | 0.5677 |
| Extended_SAE_3 | 0.5783 | 0.487 | **0.6501** | 0.7113 | Extended_SAE_3 | 0.5906 | 0.4959 | 0.6523 | 0.7973 |
| Extended_SAE_5 | **0.564** | **0.4842** | 0.6503 | **0.7939** | Extended_SAE_5 | **0.5798** | **0.4834** | **0.6306** | **0.807** |

(*Continued*)

**Table 3.3** Dataset. (*Continued*)

Result = TA 5-5

Result = YM 5-5

| Technique | MAE | GIMAE | GPIMAE | F1 | Technique | MAE | GIMAE | GPIMAE | F1 |
|---|---|---|---|---|---|---|---|---|---|
| MF [10] | 1.2077 | 1.3055 | 0.8079 | 0.4491 | MF [10] | 1.2961 | 1.2755 | 0.6204 | 0.4882 |
| 2016_Hybrid AE [23] | 0.6531 | 0.6022 | 0.8406 | 0.6789 | 2016_Hybrid AE [23] | 0.7691 | 0.6314 | 0.8244 | 0.6798 |
| 2011_Liwei Liu [13] | 0.772 | 0.5262 | 0.6282 | 0.6102 | 2011_Liwei Liu [13] | 0.7233 | 0.575 | 0.7232 | 0.6706 |
| 2017_Learning [22] | 0.6204 | 0.5907 | 0.6103 | 0.6907 | 2017_Learning [22] | 0.6514 | 0.5019 | 0.5824 | 0.7107 |
| 2017_CCC [27] | 0.6737 | 0.5878 | 0.5901 | 0.4497 | 2017_CCC [27] | 0.6888 | 0.6242 | 0.7577 | 0.538 |
| 2017_CCA [27] | 0.6914 | 0.6124 | 0.6095 | 0.4826 | 2017_CCA [27] | 0.6891 | 0.5417 | 0.5972 | 0.564 |
| 2017_CIC [27] | 0.7129 | 0.6536 | 0.6814 | 0.4636 | 2017_CIC [27] | 0.7012 | 0.642 | 0.7439 | 0.537 |
| Extended_SAE_3 | 0.5674 | 0.521 | 0.5379 | **0.7458** | Extended_SAE_3 | 0.608 | 0.4636 | 0.5673 | **0.7109** |
| Extended_SAE_5 | **0.5593** | **0.5075** | 0.549 | 0.7384 | Extended_SAE_5 | **0.5854** | **0.4633** | **0.5592** | 0.6073 |

Absolute Error (MAE) which is known for its simplicity, accuracy, and popularity [4].

### 3.4.2.2   Training Setting

Here, they trained their stacked autoencoder with the three-hidden layers and five-hidden layers, and also, they applied sigmoid and hyperbolic tangents. In sigmoid transfer function, the data are transformed in between 0 and 1. In hyperbolic tangents, the data are transformed in between −1 and 1. They used mini batch GD Optimizer and Adam Optimizer for regularization. Dropout regularization is added to each hidden layer with probability p = 0.5. Research was done for dissimilar parameters. Finest parameter values are shown in the research work. In this proposed approach, 90% of data are utilized for training purposes along with the rest samples for testing purposes [4].

### 3.4.2.3   Result

To compare this approach with single- as well as multi-criteria rating systems, they implemented the approach with some different research result proposed by different researchers. Those are MF, 2016 Hybrid AE [23] and multi-criteria recommendation techniques: 2011 Liwei Liu [13], 2017 Learning [22], three approaches from [27] (2017 CCC, 2017 CCA, and 2017 CIC). Certain procedures are used on all the functioning datasets. The results are shown in Tables 3.1 to 3.3. Conventional matrix factorization got the most ever loss in terms of MAE, GIMAE, and GPIMAE with values 1.2077, 1.3055, and 0.8079, respectively, as shown in Table 3.1. In terms of mean absolute error and F1, 2017 Pref Learning carry out superior to existing single and multi-criteria rating techniques. However, this method performs well in all the existing methods. It can be seen that MF got the maximum loss and least F1. Their preferred extended stacked autoencoder approach went beyond all the methods sufficiently in various evaluation metrics, as shown in Table 3.2. Similar trends are also found on the other datasets, YM 10-10 and YM 20-20 in Tables 3.3 and 3.4, respectively [4].

### 3.4.3   Situation-Aware Multi-Criteria Recommender System: Using Criteria Preferences as Contexts by Zheng

Inside this research activity, they tried to implement the new methods which manage criteria likings as contextual situations. To be specific, they trust that one portion of multi-criteria preferences may be observed as contexts and the other part managed in the conventional way in MCRS. They differentiate the suggestion efficiency between three settings. First one is applying every criteria rating in the conventional way. Second setting that they used is managing every criteria preference as contexts and the last one issuing preferred criteria ratings as contexts. Their demonstrations are depending on two practical rating datasets. It reveals that managing criteria priorities as contexts can upgrade the efficiency of module recommendations if those are being selected very carefully. They have used a hybrid model which selects criteria preference as contexts and solve remaining part in traditional way. They have illustrated this proposed model and got very efficient result and the model becomes the winner of their experiment [19].

Now, we will see its experimental evaluation and result to ensure its efficiency.

### 3.4.3.1   Evaluation Setting

They have very limited datasets which have multiple-criteria ratings for experiment. For this research, they use two popular real-world datasets: TripAdvisor dataset and Yahoo! Movies dataset. Successively, they used 80% of rated moves or hotels for training purposes and rest 20% for the testing purpose. They evaluated and compared the algorithms which are declared placed to calculate the prediction of rating. They predicted in general ratings mentioned by users on every item for test set, along with calculate efficiency by the very popular mean absolute error method [19].

### 3.4.3.2   Experimental Result

The outputs are revealed in Figure 3.4. If we take a sincere look, then we will find that the data tags on above of every bar present the rate of development by HCM in correspondence with other methods. In association with algorithms, biased MF represented the outcomes that are generated by the biased MF algorithm. The present results formed on the aggregation-based approach that takes benefits of multiple-criteria ratings. The aggregation is the hybrid model that merges user-specific aggregation models with item-specific aggregation models. In this paper, the proposed models are FCM, PCM, and HCM. In PCM, they choose the most authoritative criteria as contexts using information gain. They tried many selections and combinations here and represented the best selections in this research work [19].

First, biased MF does not require more details like multi-criteria ratings or contexts. So, for this reason, it is the worst model here. As FCM

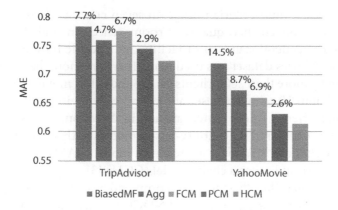

**Figure 3.4** Result comparison.

carries outpour efficiency than the Agg method in the TripAdvisor dataset, so applying contexts as criteria preference will not be inadequate choice every time. Choosing the most influential criteria, PCM performs better Agg in those two datasets. Eventually, they observed, HCM is the finest predictive model with the shortest mean absolute error. It has enough to provide remarkable improvements compared with other models and depends on the statistical paired t-test. To be more specific, it is fit to acquire 4.7% and 8.7% improvements in balancing with the aggregation model, 6.7% and 6.9% improvements compared with the FCM, in the TripAdvisor and Yahoo! Movies datasets, respectively. They have proved that HCM performs better than PCM in this experiment [19].

### 3.4.4 Utility-Based Multi-Criteria Recommender Systems by Zheng

In this research activity, they introduced a utility-based multi-criteria recommendation algorithm. In this algorithm, they studied customer expectations by dissimilar learning to rank approaches. Their experimental outputs are depending on practical datasets. It demonstrates the usefulness of these approaches [3].

#### 3.4.4.1 Experimental Dataset

In this research activity, they used two practical datasets where ratings are scaled between 1 and 5. The TripAdvisor data had used. In this dataset, it has more than 22,000 ratings provided by more than 1,500 clients with around 14,000 plus hotels. Every client rated at least 10 ratings. These ratings relate to multi-criteria ratings on seven criteria. Those criteria are cost-effective, convenience, quality of rooms, check-in, and cleanliness of the hotel and general standard of facility and specific business facilities. The Yahoo! Movies dataset was used here. There are more than 62,000 ratings given by more than 2000 clients on around 3,100 movies. Every client rates minimum 10 ratings. These ratings are related with multiple-criteria ratings on furrieries. Those critters are acting, direction, stories, and visual effects. They compared their utility-based models with some approaches. The approaches are MF, linear aggregation model (LAM), hybrid context model (HCM), and criteria chain model (CCM) [3].

They evaluated the efficiency of recommender form on the top 10 recommendations by using accuracy and NDCG to calculate the efficiency. To calculate the utility scores, they used three measures. By applying Pearson correlation, they get little improved results rather than applying cosine similarity. They found that Euclidean distance was the bad choice. They represented the best outcome by using Pearson correlation [3].

### 3.4.4.2 Experimental Result

As we can see in Figure 3.5, it represents the results the experiment. FMM becomes the best performing baseline method for the TripAdvisor data, but LAM and CCM beat MF by 1%. Here, HCM performs even lower than the MF approach. Through applying the utility-based method, the UBM by applying the listwise ranking can perform well the FMM method. If they use the pointwise and pairwise ranking optimizations, then the other UBM models will fail to beat FMM. From Yahoo! Movies dataset, all methods can perform the MF method that does not consider multi-criteria ratings. To be to detail, the UBM using listwise ranking can upgrade NDGC and precision by 6.3% and 5.4% in the TripAdvisor data, and 4.1% and 8% in FMM in comparison with Yahoo! Movies data [3].

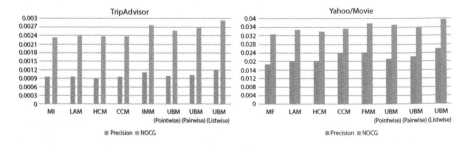

**Figure 3.5** Experimental result.

### 3.4.5    Multi-Criteria Clustering Approach by Wasid and Ali

In this research activity, they suggested a clustering method to use multiple-criteria rating into conventional recommendation system successfully. To generate more on the mark recommendations, they evaluate the intra-cluster client matches by applying Mahalanobis distance approach. Then, they collated their method with the conventional CF [2].

Now, we will take a look on their experimental evaluation and result for its efficiency.

### 3.4.5.1    Experimental Evaluation

To implement this proposed approach, they have used Yahoo! Movies dataset. This dataset consists of 62,156 rating provides by 6,078 users on 976 movies. To make it simple, they have extracted those clients that have rated to minimum 20 movies. This condition satisfies 484 users and 945 movies, and they have total 19,050 ratings. Then, every client's rating is splitted arbitrarily into training and testing set. They took 70% of data for training purpose and remaining 30% of data for testing purpose. Then, they calculate the distance between clients successfully. They selected top 30 most equivalent users for the neighborhood set formation. To evaluate this proposed approach, they used the most popular Mean Absolute Error (MAE) performance matrix. MAE is very popular because of its simplicity and accuracy as we have seen before. It matches the goal of the experiment. The mean absolute error estimates the derivation of actual and predicted client ratings [2].

### 3.4.5.2    Result and Analysis

The dataset which they have used contain both single-criteria and multiple-criteria user provided ratings. Table 3.4 represents the difference between their way with the conventional approach for both non-clustering and clustering environment. Here, they have compared their experimental result with Pearson collaborative recommender (PCRS) approach. Table 3.4 conveys the result between PCRS with their proposed Mahalanobis distance recommendation scheme (MDRS). It is very transparent that their method MDRS performed much superior than traditional PCRS. These results are based on mean absolute error method. This proposed MDRS approach works better for both on clustering and clustering environments which is shown in Figure 3.6 [2].

They also have shown the graphical implementation of this table which is in both non-clustering and clustering environments. The Mahalanobis

**Table 3.4** Comparison among clustering and non-clustering approach.

| Approach | MAE (non-clustering) | MAE (clustering) |
|----------|----------------------|------------------|
| PCRS | 2.4577 | 2.2734 |
| MDRS | 2.3094 | 2.1751 |

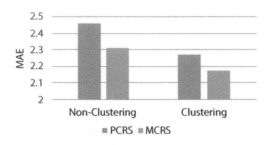

**Figure 3.6** Result.

distance–based method gives better result than the Pearson collaborative recommender approach. If the mean absolute error values are lower, then it means it is a better result. By that result, we can also see that the non-clustering–based technique always have less performance than clustering approaches. So, the clustering approach is better [2].

They have consolidated the multiple-criteria ratings into the conventional CF-based recommender system using K-means algorithm. Their method treats the third dimensional as multi-criteria, the clustering parameters as the clustering parameter of the clients, to handle the dimensionality. Their approach depends on thinking like each user has unique opinion and criteria. Therefore, to compare each user, the most important concern of this work is to find out clients' segments with alike client. Mahalanobis distance method is used here to create most exact neighbors for every client within the cluster. In the result, we can clearly see that this technique is more effective and accurate than the traditional approach [2].

## 3.5   Advantages of Multi-Criteria Recommender System

Multi-criteria recommender system is used to make user experience easier or make things easy for each and every user. If we take a look on business perspective, then this system is used to grow a business.

**Table 3.5** Comparison among existing methods in MCRS.

| Author name | Research work | Work done | Method name | Challenges |
|---|---|---|---|---|
| Yong Zheng | Utility-Based Multi-Criteria Recommender System (2019) | Implemented a new recommender system approach which dominates many the traditional approaches. | Utility-based approach. | Issue of overexpectation, which may contribute finer-grained recommendation models |
| Dharahas Tallapally, Rama Syamala Sreepada, Bidyut kr. Patra, Korra Sathya Babu | User Preference Learning in Multi-Criteria Recommendation Using Stacked Auto Encoders | Implemented a recommender system using extended version of autoencoder named as stacked autoencoder. | Stacked Autoencoder, An unsupervised deep neural network approach. | This approach is still now in improvement state, and this approach cannot work in user review system. |
| Mohammed Wasid, Rashid Ali | An Improved recommender System based on Multi-criteria Clustering Approach (2018) | Implemented Multi-criteria recommender system using Clustering approach which gives getting better result than traditional recommender Systems. | K-means Clustering, Mahalanobis Distance. | This particular algorithm assumes that each client has individual opinion which is dissimilar to each other for every criterion. |

*(Continued)*

**Table 3.5** Comparison among existing methods in MCRS. (*Continued*)

| Author name | Research work | Work done | Method name | Challenges |
|---|---|---|---|---|
| Yong Zheng | Situation-Aware Multi-Criteria Recommender System: Using Criteria Preferences as Contexts (2017) | Implemented a recommender system using criteria preference as context approach that gives a better result. | Aggregation approach, Full Contextual Model, Partial Contextual Model, Hybrid Contextual model. | Does not work well for all the cases. Its need improvement. |
| CataldoMusto, Marco de Gemmis, Giovanni Semeraro, Pasquale Lops | A Multi-criteria Recommender System Exploiting Aspect-based Sentiment Analysis of Users' Reviews (2017) | Implemented a recommender system using users review. | Taking out Aspects and Sentiment from Reviews, then feed it in multi-criteria recommender algorithm based on collaborative filtering technique. | This research work is still in improvement state. It can be improved further. |

In business point of view, if a customer comes in any platform, then the main work of the owner and the staff is to satisfy the customer needs. They will make sure that the customer must have a good experience and got their desired thing. This is the main work of a recommender system. For this particular reason, many companies are adopting this multi-criteria recommender system [33].

Here are some benefits in businesses perspective that can be achieved by using MCRS:

### 3.5.1   Revenue

MCRS has a big role in generating the revenue. Years of research, execution, and experiments, many researchers from all over the world made various types of recommender systems. Many different types of algorithms are executed and explored to get good accuracy. When a customer came to buy a particular thing then the MCRS shows him some similar things and accessories so that the customer will buy that too. This is one of the job of MCRS and also one of the effective ways to generate better revenue.

### 3.5.2   Customer Satisfaction

By a survey, it is seen that, many times, customers tend to look at their product recommendation from their last browsing for a better opportunity for good products. Suppose a customer browses as it and leave and after sometime he come again, then it would be a great help if their previous browsing sessions are available. It is also good for the recommender system because it will generate an item list based on the user's previous data and recommend those items to the customer. So, this is how MCRS plays an important role in customer satisfaction.

### 3.5.3   Personalization

If we take a look into our daily life, then we will understand that we also take recommendations to buy a product. These recommendations are mostly given by our family members and friends. We followed their recommendations because we trust them. This is the sole element which is implementing the MCRS to build among system and the user. The more suitable product system will predict for the user, the more the user will trust the MCRS and will buy the recommended product. That is how by personalization a customer will come to that platform again and again.

### 3.5.4   Discovery

Every recommender system can be used as a tool. The leading companies discover new ways to apply the recommender system as a tool. For example, iTunes uses "Genius Recommendations" which is a very efficient multi-criteria recommender tool, and Amazon uses "Frequently Bought together" which can also be customized by the user also. These are some innovative ways of using the multi-criteria recommender systems.

### 3.5.5   Provide Reports

This is an integral part of personalization system. It is also used to make trust with the clients. It helps to make solid decisions about the site or the direction of a campaign. In order to create a drive-in, sales client generates offers on slow moving product based on their report.

In the present time, online sales are generally more satisfying. So, every company wants to do something extra. An e-commerce company can use different types of filtering technique like collaborative, content-based, hybrid filtering as we have studied before to make an effective recommendation engine. For example, Amazon has super successful multi-criteria recommender engine which recommends several things as add on very efficiently and that attract a client or a customer to buy more and more things from the same platform. It follows the sole of every recommender system that the only way to truly engage with customer is to communicate with each as an individual.

## 3.6   Challenges of Multi-Criteria Recommender System

There are some common challenges which every MCRS faces. Some of them are as follows.

### 3.6.1   Cold Start Problem

This problem faces recommender system when a client came for the first time in that platform or when a new item is added on that platform. When someone comes for the first time in any platform, recommender system does not have any information about that client. Because the client have not rated any product or have not surfed anything. If a new item is added in platform, then it also does not have any rating of its quality, durability, etc. This is known as cold start problem. A huge number of research works has done to overcome this this problem [34].

### 3.6.2   Sparsity Problem

This is also a very important problem that all recommender systems are facing nowadays. It happens when user has large history list. The list contains everything like list of items he bought or list of movies he watched or listed of music he listened and even his previous surfing list. Sparsity happens when the user does not give rating after buying items or after watching movies. Rating is the most fundamental element for a MCRS. Because of lack of rating, a recommender system does not able to understand that whether the client liked that particular thing or not [34].

### 3.6.3   Scalability

Scalability is related to the multi-criteria recommender systems own performance. Generally, recommender system does not consume many resources. It is designed such a way that it gives best accuracy by using minimum resource. Recommender system needs to recommend a list of items to the user. But with time, the number of users increases, the number of items also increases, and the recommendation list is also increasing [34].

### 3.6.4   Over Specialization Problem

When a MCRS is able to know about the choices of a particular client, then it creates a boundary and shows according to their choice without discovering new items and other options with time. This situation is known as over specialization problem [34].

### 3.6.5   Diversity

If a user spends a long time in a platform, then the recommender system has a lot of information about him. If he orders almost same kind of things, then the recommender system generates the recommendation list that is based on the same category only [34].

### 3.6.6   Serendipity

Every recommender system should have an objective that to surprise people by recommending new product and make interest in the user [34].

### 3.6.7    Privacy

For recommender system privacy is very important. As the recommender system knows some information about the user, it should not be going to the outside world. The users need to understand which data is required to approve more ideally items to them and how it used [34].

### 3.6.8    Shilling Attacks

It happens when a user became malicious or unethical. Many times, it is observed that user starts giving false rating in some items. If it happens, then either the rating of that good item will drop down and that item will no longer recommended or a bad quality item will get more good ratings and will be recommended more by MCRS. This is known as shilling attack [34].

### 3.6.9    Gray Sheep

Gray sheep takes place normally in CF systems. Here, the belief of a client does not identify with any group and consequently. It is no able to acquire the advantage of recommendations [34].

## 3.7    Conclusion

In this chapter of MCRS, we understood the definition of a recommender system, its growing importance, and applications in various sectors. Further, we discussed about the different phases of a recommender system. Moreover, we deeply analyzed the three different filtering techniques associated with the recommender system that includes collaborative, content-based, and knowledge-based filtering techniques. In addition, we also discussed about the hybrid filtering techniques. To have a better understanding on the concept of the recommender system, we considered five research activities conducted by various researchers across the globe. Lastly, we also discussed about the various advantages and the challenges prevailing in the recommender system.

Nowadays, recommender systems are widely used in various aspects, with the passage of time, the recommender systems are being modified and are showing better performance. New techniques are implemented in the recommender system to derive a better prediction [1].

# References

1. Al-Ghuribi, S.M. and Noah, S.A.M., Multi-criteria review-based recommender system–the state of the art. *IEEE Access,* 7, 169446–169468, 2019.
2. Wasid, M. and Ali, R., An improved recommender system based on multi-criteria clustering approach. *Proc. Comput. Sci.,* 131, 99–101, Jan. 2018.
3. Zheng, Y., Utility-based multi-criteria recommender systems, in: *Proc. 34th ACM/SIGAPP Symp. Appl. Comput.,* pp. 2529–2531, 2019.
4. Tallapally, D., Sreepada, R.S., Patra, B.K., Babu, K.S., User preference learning in multi-criteria recommendations using stacked auto encoders. Presented at the *Proc. 12th ACM Conf. Recommender Syst.,* Vancouver, BC, Canada, 2018.
5. Musto, C., de Gemmis, M., Semeraro, G., Lops, P., A multi-criteria recommender system exploiting aspect-based sentiment analysis of users' reviews. Presented at the *Proc. 11th ACM Conf. Recommender Syst.,* Como, Italy, 2017.
6. García-Cumbreras, M. Á., Montejo-Râez, A., Díaz-Galiano, M.C., Pessimists and optimists: Improving collaborative filtering through sentiment analysis. *Expert Syst. Appl.,* 40, 17, 6758–6765, 2013.
7. Zhang, W., Ding, G., Chen, L., Li, C., & Zhang, C. (2013). Generating virtual ratings from chinese reviews to augment online recommendations. ACM Transactions on intelligent systems and technology (TIST), 4(1), 1–17.
8. Bauman, K., Liu, B., Tuzhilin, A., Aspect based recommendations: Recommending items with the most valuable aspects based on user reviews, in: *Proc. 23rd ACM SIGKDD Int. Conf. Knowl. Discovery Data Mining,* pp. 717–725, 2017.
9. Akhtar, N., Zubair, N., Kumar, A., Ahmad, T., Aspect based sentiment oriented summarization of hotel reviews. *Proc. Comput. Sci.,* 115, 563–571, Jan. 2017.
10. Yang, C., Yu, X., Liu, Y., Nie, Y., Wang, Y., Collaborative filtering with weighted opinion aspects. *Neurocomputing,* 210, 185–196, Oct. 2016.
11. Dong, R., O'Mahony, M.P., Schaal, M., McCarthy, K., Smyth, B., Sentimental product recommendation, in: *Proc. 7th ACM Conf. Recommender Syst,* pp. 411–414, 2013.
12. Wang, F., Pan, W., Chen, L., Recommendation for new users with partial preferences by integrating product reviews with static specications, in: *Proc. Int. Conf. Modeling, Adaptation, Pers.,* pp. 281–288, 2013.
13. Musat, C.C., Liang, Y., Faltings, B., Recommendation using textual opinions, in: *Proc. Int. Joint Conf. Artif. Intell.,* pp. 2684–2690, 2013.
14. Jamroonsilp, S. and Prompoon, N., Analyzing software reviews for software quality-based ranking, in: *Proc.10th Int. Conf. Elect. Eng./Electron., Comput., Telecommun. Inf. Technol. (ECTI-CON),* May 2013, pp. 1–6.

15. Zhang, Y., Liu, R., Li, A., A novel approach to recommender system based on aspect-level sentiment analysis, in: *Proc. 4th Nat. Conf. Electr., Electron. Comput. Eng. (NCEECE)*, pp. 1453–1458, 2015.
16. Kermani, N.R. and Alizadeh, S.H., A hybrid multi-criteria recommender system using ontology and neuro-fuzzy techniques. *Electron. Commer. Res. Appl.*, 21, 50–64, 2017.
17. Wang, Y., Wang, M., Xu, W., A sentiment-enhanced hybrid recommender system for movie recommendation: a big data analytics framework. *Wireless Communications and Mobile Computing*, 2018, 2018.
18. Zheng, Y., Utility-based multi-criteria recommender systems. In: *Proceedings of the 34th ACM/SIGAPP Symposium on Applied Computing*, pp. 2529–2531, 2019, April.
19. Zheng, Y., Situation-aware multi-criteria recommender system: using criteria preferences as contexts. In: *Proceedings of the Symposium on Applied Computing*, pp. 689–692, 2017, April.
20. Tallapally, D., Sreepada, R. S., Patra, B. K., Babu, K. S., User preference learning in multi-criteria recommendations using stacked auto encoders. In: *Proceedings of the 12th ACM Conference on Recommender Systems*, pp. 475–479, 2018, September.
21. Hassan, M. and Hamada, M., Improving prediction accuracy of multi-criteria recommender systems using adaptive genetic algorithms. In: *2017 Intelligent Systems Conference (IntelliSys)*, pp. 326-330, IEEE, 2017, September.
22. Hassan, M. and Hamada, M., A neural networks approach for improving the accuracy of multi-criteria recommender systems. *Appl. Sci.*, 7, 9, 868, 2017.
23. Hassan, M. and Hamada, M., Performance comparison of featured neural network trained with backpropagation and delta rule techniques for movie rating prediction in multi-criteria recommender systems. *Informatica*, 40, 4, 2016.
24. Zheng, Y., Criteria chains: a novel multi-criteria recommendation approach. In: *Proceedings of the 22nd International Conference on Intelligent User Interfaces*, pp. 29–33, 2017, March.
25. Ryngksai, I. and Chameikho, L., Recommender Systems: Types of Filtering Techniques. *Int. J. Eng. Res. Technol.*, Gujarat, 3, 2278-0181, 251–254, 2014.
26. Lakshmi, S.S. and Lakshmi, T.A., Recommendation Systems: Issues and challenges. *(IJCSIT) Int. J. Comput. Sci. Inf. Technol.*, 5, 4, 5771–5772, 2014.
27. Sharma, L. and Gera, A., A Survey of Recommendation System: Research Challenges. *Int. J. Eng. Trends Technol. (IJETT)*, 4, 5, 1989–1992, 2013.
28. Khusro, S., Ali, Z., Ullah, I., Recommender systems: issues, challenges, and research opportunities. In: *Information Science and Applications (ICISA) 2016*, pp. 1179–1189, Springer, Singapore, 2016.
29. Maan, T., Gupta, S., Mishra, A., A Survey On Recommendation System. *International Conference on recent innovations in management, Engineering, Science and technology (RIMEST2018)*, pp. 543–549, 2018.

30. Mahmoud, H., Hegazy, A., Khafagy, M.H., An approach for big data security based on Hadoop distributed file system. *2018 International Conference on Innovative Trends in Computer Engineering (ITCE)*, Aswan, pp. 109–114, 2018.

31. Mohamed, M.H., Khafagy, M.H., Ibrahim, M.H., Recommender systems challenges and solutions survey. In: *2019 International Conference on Innovative Trends in Computer Engineering (ITCE)*, pp. 149-155, IEEE, 2019, February.

32. Sahoo, A.K., Pradhan, C., Bhattacharyya, S., Privacy towards GIS Based Intelligent Tourism Recommender System in Big Data Analytics, in: *Hybrid Computational Intelligence: Research and Applications*, p. 81, 2019.

33. Mallik, S. and Sahoo, A.K., A Comparison Study of Different Privacy Preserving Techniques in Collaborative Filtering Based Recommender System, in: *Computational Intelligence in Data Mining*, pp. 193–203, Springer, Singapore, 2020.

34. Sahoo, A.K. and Pradhan, C., Accuracy-Assured Privacy-Preserving Recommender System Using Hybrid-Based Deep Learning Method, in: *Recommender System with Machine Learning and Artificial Intelligence: Practical Tools and Applications in Medical, Agricultural and Other Industries*, pp. 101–120, 2020.

# 4

# Adoption of Machine/Deep Learning in Cloud With a Case Study on Discernment of Cervical Cancer

Jyothi A. P. [1,2*], S. Usha[2,3] and Archana H. R.[3]

*¹Dept. of CSE, RVITM, Bengaluru, Karnataka, India*
*²Dept. of CSE, RND, RRCE, Bengaluru Karnataka, India*
*³Dept. of ECE, BMSCE, Bengaluru, Karnataka, India*

## Abstract

Machine learning (ML) utilizes calculations to parse information and settle on educated choices dependent on what it has realized. Deep learning (DL) is a subfield of ML. While both fall under the general classification of artificial intelligence, profound realizing is the thing that controls the most human-like manmade consciousness.

The association between ML/DL and cloud computing is the interest for resources. Where cloud computing becomes possibly the most important factor is the quick capacity to turn up new servers with a pre-characterized picture and change assets on the fly. You may need 100 servers up chipping away at your calculation, yet you do not need those hundred servers up consistently, which would be a misuse of cash. With cloud computing, you can turn up any number of servers you need, work on the algorithm, and, at that point, destroy the machines again when complete.

This book chapter discusses on adoption of ML/DL in cloud. It covers introduction, background study, description of ML/DL, connection between ML/DL and cloud, ML/DL algorithms, a project implementation on discernment of cervical cancer by using ML/DL in cloud with its design methodology and results, applications like cognitive cloud, chatbots, and smart personal assistants, IoT cloud, business intelligence, AI-as-a-Service, etc., along with advantages and conclusion related to adoption of ML/DL in cloud.

---

*\*Corresponding author:* jyothiarcotprashant@gmail.com

---

Archana Mire, Shaveta Malik and Amit Kumar Tyagi (eds.) *Advanced Analytics and Deep Learning Models*, (65–110) © 2022 Scrivener Publishing LLC

Definite and blunder-free location can spare lives. Prior identification of cervical disease was finished by a tiny smear test dependent on the figuring of boundaries of the phone core of the example, for example, its shape and size as smear is broke down to magnifying lens is an incredibly testing task. Thus, Digital Image Processing procedure is required to distinguish anomalies in human cell. Subsequently, a thorough AI procedure has been proposed in this book section. The proposed method gives the highlights and state of cytoplasm, nucleus in the cervix cell. KNN and SVM are used with the highlights and state of the divided cell and contrasted and obscure cervix cell test with this procedure. The precision pace of 86% for SVM and 70% for KNN is accomplished.

While ML/DL makes cloud computing much more enhanced, efficient, and scalable, the cloud platform expands the horizon for ML/DL applications. Thus, both are intricately interrelated, and when combined into a symbiotic relationship, the business connotations can be tremendous.

*Keywords*: Machine learning, deep learning, KNN, SVM, cloud, AI, cervical cancer

## 4.1    Introduction

Artificial Intelligence (AI) utilizes calculation to parse data, gains from that information, and settles on educated choices dependent on what it has realized. Machine Learning (ML)/Deep Learning (DL) are a subdomain AI. Both come under the broad category of artificial brainpower, thoughtful realizing is the obsession that reins the most human being-like artificial consciousness.

Both of these subsets of AI are some manner or another linked with data, which makes it plausible to articulate to an explicit type of understanding. On the other hand, you should know that profound knowledge require substantially more data than a conventional AI computation. The purpose in the wake of this is that profound knowledge organizations can recognize a variety of mechanism in neural organization layers presently when in excess of 1,000,000 information focuses communicate. AI calculations, then again, are equipped for learning by pre-modified models.

Distributed computing is the on-request ease of access of personal computer framework resources, predominantly data stockpile and power. It portrays server farms available to several patrons over the Internet.

The association between ML/DL and cloud processing is the interest for assets. ML/DL is a cycle that requires a ton of preparing power. Numerous

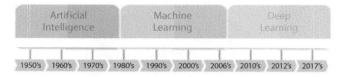

**Figure 4.1** Advancement of artificial intelligence.

individuals keen on this will consolidate many workers without a moment's delay to chip away at a calculation, and request power that is not effectively available on committed facilitating stages, and so on. The advancement of artificial intelligence and the evolution with deep learning and machine learning is signified in Figure 4.1.

Where distributed computing becomes possibly the most important factor is the fast capacity to turn up new workers with a pre-characterized picture, and change assets on the fly. You may need 100 workers up chipping away at your calculation; however, you do not need those hundred workers up consistently in any case, which would be a misuse of cash.

With distributed computing, you can turn up quite a few workers you need, chip away at the calculation, and, at that point, obliterate the machines again when complete.

As more cloud administration suppliers and organizations understand the capability of ML/DL in the cloud, it will prod the interest for cloud ML/DL stages. Although ML/DL makes distributed computing substantially more upgraded, effective, and versatile, the cloud stage grows the skyline for ML/DL applications. Hence, both are complicatedly interconnected. When consolidated, the business undertones might be gigantic. The interrelativity of AI, ML and DL is represented in Figure 4.2.

Preparing ML models in the cloud bodes well. Why? Among numerous reasons, it permits you to prepare on a lot of information with ample figure and maybe train numerous models in equal. Additionally it is not difficult to do! On Google Cloud Platform, you can utilize Cloud ML Engine to prepare AI models in Tensor Flow and other Python ML libraries (for example, scikit-learn) without dealing with any foundation. To do this, you should place your code into a Python bundle (for example, add setup.py and __init__.py records). Likewise, it is a best practice to put together your code into a model.py and task.py.

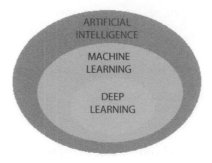

**Figure 4.2** AI, ML, and DL.

Man-made reasoning as a scholastic order was established in 1950s. As a matter of fact, the "man-made intelligence" phrase was instituted by John McCarthy, an American PC researcher. As indicated by John McCarthy, AI is "The discipline and designing and construction of canny machinery, particularly clever PC programs".

Despite the fact that it was not as of not earlier period, it evicted to be essential for way of life on account of advance in massive data accessibility and reasonable elevated processing power. AI performs at its greatest possible level by fusion of lot of record gathering with rapid, iterative prepare, and shrewd computations. This permits the AI programming to gain naturally, since examples or highlights given that huge informational indexes. It is regular nowadays we witness AI news and models on the standard news broadcast. Seemingly, the ubiquity achievement with public mindfulness was AlphaGo man-made consciousness program that finished humankinds, 2,500 years of incomparability in May 2017 at the old tabletop game GO utilizing an AI calculation called "support learning". At that point, these sorts of AI news become part of our day by day processes with self-driving vehicles, Alexa/Siri, continuous face recognition at air terminals, person genome ventures, Amazon/Netflix, AI specialists, hand compose response, Email advertising calculation, and the rundown can continue forever, whereas profound neural organization, the most outstanding type of AI, that is, at maximum tip of the Gartner's support series to say a sign of swelled requirements, personal working vehicles include just completed large number of miles with generally good security accounts.

AI innovations will keep upsetting in 2019 and will turn out to be considerably more broadly accessible because of moderate distributed computing and huge information blast. We do not remember some other tech space right now that draws in so many brilliant individuals and tremendous assets from both the open source/creator network and the biggest ventures simultaneously.

## 4.2    Background Study

The key idea [1] is to subjectively drop units (close by their relationship) from the neural association during planning. This keeps units from co-changing unreasonably. This in a general sense decreases overfitting and gives critical redesigns over other regularization techniques.

A leftover knowledge structure [2] to support the arrangement of major neural relations that are liberally more considerable than those used as of now. We explicitly reformulate the layers as learning extra limits with respect to the layer commitments, as opposed to learning unreferenced limits. We give broad definite verification demonstrating to facilitate these leftover associations that are easier to improve and can get accuracy from fundamentally comprehensive implication.

Getting ready Deep Neural Networks [3] is jumbled in a manner that the spread of every layer of information vary all through planning, as the restrictions of the precedent layer vary. We insinuate this speculate as inside covariate shift and tackle the problem by normalizing input layers. It is applied to a forefront picture request method. This achieves comparative exactitude with numerous places less planning steps and beats the principal method by a gigantic cutting edge.

Convolutional Neural Networks (CNNs) [4] encompass set up when an astounding class of models for representation confirmation issue. Enabled by these results, we give an expansive careful estimate of CNNs for huge degree video gathering by means of an additional dataset of one million YouTube accounts having a mark with 487 classes.

Another dataset [5] with the goal of pushing the top tier in article affirmation by setting the subject of thing affirmation concerning the more broad request of scene understanding. Our dataset contains photos of 91 things types that would be successfully undeniable by a 4 year old. Finally, we give design execution assessment to skipping box and division distinguishing proof outcomes using a Deformable Parts Model.

Another scene-driven data base [6] carried places with in excess of 7 million stamped pictures of scenes. We propose new methods to consider the thickness and assortment of picture datasets and show that places is as thick as other scene datasets and has more prominent assortment.

Another framework for surveying generative models through a hostile cycle [7], in which we as a whole the while train two models: a generative model G that gets the data scattering and a discriminative model D that evaluates the probability that a model came from the arrangement data rather than G.

In most current trackers, to adapt to regular picture changes, a classifier is ordinarily prepared with deciphered and scaled example patches. A scientific model for datasets of thousands of deciphered patches was proposed [8]. By indicating that the subsequent information lattice is circulant, we can diagonalize it with the discrete Fourier change, diminishing both stockpiling and calculation by a few significant degrees.

To give an ideal audit on multi-name learning, authors contemplate [9] the issue where every model is spoken to by a solitary example while related with a bunch of marks at the same time.

Tentatively evaluate the consensus versus explicitness of neurons [10] in each layer of a significant convolutional neural association and report two or three astounding results. Flexibility is conflictingly affected by two specific issues: (1) the specialization of higher layer neurons to their extraordinary task to the burden of execution on the goal task, which was typical and (2) improvement challenges related to separating networks between co-changed neurons, which was not envisioned.

We evaluate 179 classifiers rising up out of 17 families [11] (discriminate assessment, Bayesian, neural associations, maintain rule-based classifiers, vector machines, decision trees, stacking, boosting, firing, and various get-togethers, summarized straight models, nearest neighbor, deficient least squares and head portion backslide, determined and multinomial backslide, different flexible backslide splines, and unique techniques). We utilize 121 informational indexes from UCI information base to consider the classifier conduct, not subject to the informational index assortment. The champs are the arbitrary backwoods (RF) variants executed in R and got to through caret and the SVM with Gaussian bit actualized in C utilizing LibSVM.

Information Vault, a Web-scale probabilistic information base that joins extractions from Web content (got through investigation of text, plain information, page structure, and human explanations) with earlier information got from existing information stores for developing information bases [12]. We utilize managed AI techniques for combining particular data sources. The Knowledge Vault is significantly greater than any recently distributed organized information store and highlights a probabilistic derivation framework that figures aligned probabilities of truth accuracy.

Figuring for unpleasant nearest neighbor organizing [13] and evaluate and contrast them and past computations. To scale to colossal enlightening records that would somehow not fit in the memory of a lone machine, we propose a scattered nearest neighbor organizing framework that can be used with any of the figuring portrayed in the paper.

Present status of the theoretical investigation and sensible advances on Extreme learning machine (ELM) [14]. Beside portrayal and backslide, ELM has starting late been connected for gathering, feature decision, illustrative learning, and various other learning tasks. In light of its remarkable viability, ease, and incredible hypothesis execution, ELM has been applied in a combination of spaces, for instance, biomedical planning, PC vision, structure conspicuous evidence, and control and progressed mechanics.

Work targets giving an extensive prologue to the idea float transformation that alludes to an online regulated learning [15] situation when the connection between the info information and the objective variable changes over the long haul.

To improve the invariance of CNN initiations [16] without debasing their discriminative force, this paper presents a basic however powerful plan called multi-scale order less pooling (MOP-CNN).

We plan to distinguish all occurrences of a class in a picture and, for each example, mark the pixels that have a place with it. We call this errand Simultaneous Detection and Segmentation (SDS) [17].

A lot of highlight determination techniques are accessible in writing [18] because of the accessibility of information with many factors prompting information with extremely high measurement.

This paper tends to the issue of face alignment for a solitary picture. We show how a group of relapse trees can be utilized to gauge the face's milestone positions straightforwardly from a scanty subset of pixel powers, accomplishing super-real-time execution with top notch expectations [19].

An ebb and flow focal point of extraordinary examination in example arrangement [20] is the blend of a few classifier frameworks, which can be constructed following either the equivalent or various models and additionally datasets building.

The investigation of different methods and conversation being completed, the paper by Rajashekar *et al.* [21] depicts a screening system made for a pragmatic screening structure that could be extensively sent. The structure digitizes Pap smear slides and does cell level and smear level assessment on digitized smear and, in conclusion, portrays the smear as either interesting or dubious. Obviously, conventional smears were screened out with no human intercession while questionable smears were sent for ace cytologist survey.

A negligible exertion mono layer slide availability method has also been perceived which produces mono layer slides of significant worth commensurate to that of financial systems at much lesser cost.

Aabha Phatak *et al.* [22] portray that cervical malignant growth can well spring of affecting women planetary and its rate is increasing. Early end can wind up being very instrumental in lessening the cervical disease mortality. Assurance using clinical picture assessment is expanding speedy acknowledgment in this way, a robotized demonstrative system using picture planning procedures has been proposed in the paper, in which may wind up being a manual for the radiologists and expect a critical occupation in early revelation of malignancy. It presents division and plan techniques using which the envisioned mechanized decision genuinely steady organization limits.

Zhi Lu *et al.* [23] presented and assessed the framework submitted to the chief covering cervical cytology picture segmentation challenge, in biomedical prescription. This was figured out to stimulate the new development and seat stamping of methods fit for separating solitary cells from covering cell knocks in cervical cytology pictures, which is an essential for the improvement of the chance work of PC upheld assurance systems for cervical harm.

Mustafa N *et al.* [24] purposeful computerized imaging strategies accessible to give reserve of irregularity structure additionally work demonstrating locals of premium (ROI) and cluster alongside scatter investigation.

## 4.3   Overview of Machine Learning/Deep Learning

Simulated intelligence incorporates PCs discovering how they can perform tasks without being unequivocally modified to do in that capacity. It incorporates PCs picking up from data gave with the objective that they do certain endeavors. For direct tasks alloted to PCs, it is possible to program estimations prompting the machine how to execute all methods expected to deal with the recent concern; on the PC's part, no learning is required. For additional created tasks, it might be going after for a human to truly make the necessary computations. Before long, it can wind up being all the more remarkable to help the machine with developing its own computation, rather than having human engineers show each necessary development.

The control of AI utilizes different ways to deal with instruct PCs to achieve errands where no completely good calculation is accessible. In situations where huge quantities of potential answers exist, one methodology is to mark a portion of the right answers as legitimate. This would then be able to be utilized as preparing information for the PC to improve

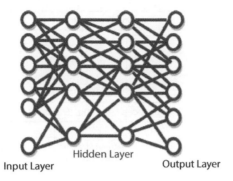

**Figure 4.3** Working network of deep learning.

the algorithm(s) it uses to decide right answers. For instance, to prepare a framework for the errand of computerized character acknowledgment, the MNIST dataset of manually written digits has regularly been utilized.

Profound learning calculations use regulated and unaided learning calculations to prepare the yields through the conveyed inputs. The underneath circles are spoken to as neurons that is interconnected. The neurons are grouped into three diverse progressive systems of layers as shown in Figure 4.3. The main neuron level for example input layer gets the information and passes it to the primary concealed layer. The concealed layers play out the calculations on the got information. The greatest test under neural organizations creation is to choose the quantity of neurons and various shrouded layers. At long last, the yield layer delivers the necessary yield.

This is the essential progression of working. Presently, comes where the technique for calculation is clarified. Each association between the neurons comprises of loads, it means the centrality of the information esteems. To normalize the yields, an enactment work is utilized. For preparing the organization, two significant measures are thought of. The first is to make a huge informational collection and the second is enormous computational force. The "somewhere down" in profound learning implies the quantity of shrouded layers the model is utilizing to prepare the informational index.

Workings of DL can be summarized in four last focuses:

1. ANN requests a blend from paired true/false inquiries.
2. Extracting numeric qualities from squares of information.
3. Sorting the information according to the got answers.
4. A last point is stamping/marking the information.

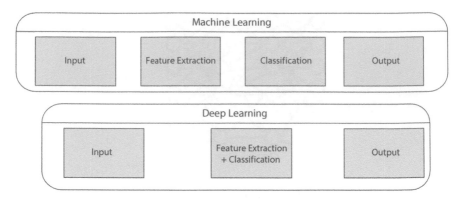

**Figure 4.4** Difference between ML and DL.

## 4.4   Connection Between Machine Learning/Deep Learning and Cloud Computing

The connection is the demand for resources. ML is a process that requires a lot of processing power. Many people interested in this will combine hundreds of servers at once to work on an algorithm and demand power that is not straightforwardly available on committed hosting platform.

Where cloud computing comes into play, it is the rapid ability to spin up new servers with a pre-defined image and change resources on the fly. You may want 100 servers up working on your algorithm, but you do not want those hundred servers up at all times otherwise, which would be a waste of money.

With cloud computing, you can spin up any number of servers you want, work on the algorithm, and then destroy the machines again when complete. An underlying difference between ML and DL is shown in Figure 4.4. A comparitive study of DL and ML is given in Table 4.1

## 4.5   Machine Learning/Deep Learning Algorithm

Three diverse knowledge methods in ML algorithms are shown in Figure 4.5.

### 4.5.1   Supervised Learning

Input is called preparation set and has a label as well as outcome, for instance, a supply price at a time. A model is entity from beginning to end

Table 4.1  Comparison of DL and ML.

| Attributes | Deep Learning | Machine Learning |
|---|---|---|
| Definition | It is a subset of AI with the steady spotlight on accomplishing more noteworthy adaptability through considering the entire world as a settled progressive system of concepts. | It is a sub-part of artificial knowledge. It permits the machines to prepare with different datasets and anticipate dependent on their encounters. |
| Working mechanism | Neural networks help in deciphering the highlights of information and their connections in which significant data is handled through different phases of preparing the data. | It uses mechanized calculations to foresee the choices for the future and demonstrating of capacities dependent on the information took care of to it. |
| Management | All the calculations are self-coordinated after the usage for result getting and information analysis. | All the investigation is overseen by investigators to assess distinctive variable under the different datasets. |
| Functional examples | Practical models are remote helpers, shopping and amusement, facial acknowledgment, interpretations, drugs, and vision for driverless vehicles. | Practical models are discourse acknowledgment, clinical conclusion, measurable exchange, arrangement, expectation, and extraction. |
| Information points | Data focuses are utilized for examination typically numbered in millions. | Data focuses are utilized for investigation as a rule numbered in thousands. |
| Preparing time | Considering bigger boundaries, profound learning sets aside a long effort for training. | Machine learning calculations ordinarily sets aside less effort for examination, going from a couple of moments to hours. |

(*Continued*)

**Table 4.1** Comparison of DL and ML. (*Continued*)

| Attributes | Deep Learning | Machine Learning |
|---|---|---|
| **Considered algorithms** | It utilizes neural networks. | It uses calculations like straight relapse, arbitrary timberland, and KNN. |
| **Output** | The yield is typically assorted like a score, a component, grouping, or basically a text. | The yield for this calculation is normally a numeric worth like an arrangement. |

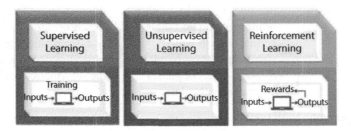

**Figure 4.5** Types of ML.

of a training cycle in which it is needed to craft prospect and is adjusted while those forecasts are not correct. The groundwork cycle proceeds until the representation achieves an ideal degree of accuracy on the research information. Model issues are classification and regression. A representation of Supervised Learning Algorithm is as shown in Figure 4.6.

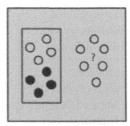

Supervised Learning
Algorithms

**Figure 4.6** Supervised learning algorithm.

## 4.5.2 Unsupervised Learning

Information is not marked and does not include an identified outcome. A representation is unit by final structure at hand in the data. This may be to remove common guidelines. It could be during a statistical cycle to efficiently diminish surplus, or it very well may be to coordinate information by likeness. Model problems are alliance, size decrease and membership rule learning. Model computations are the Apriori estimate and K-Means. A representation of Supervised Learning Algorithm is as shown in Figure 4.7.

## 4.5.3 Reinforcement or Semi-Supervised Learning

Records are a combination of named as well as unnamed models. At hand is an ideal plan concern; however, the model should gain proficiency with the structures to sort out the information just as make expectations. A representation of Supervised Learning Algorithm is as shown in Figure 4.8.

Model issues are order and relapse. Model computations are extension of flexible strategies that formulate suspicions concerning how to make obvious the unnamed info. The method is based on observation and initial preparation and gaffe to bring about objectives or inflate return. The specialist settles on an alternative by noticing its current circumstance.

In the event that the insight is negative, the result changes its masses to have the choice to mend on an every other requisite preference at any time. Various learning techniques can be mapped as shown in Figure 4.9.

### 4.5.3.1 Outline of ML Algorithms

While crunching information to display business choices, you are most normally utilizing directed and unaided learning strategies. An interesting issue right now is semi-administered learning techniques in zones, for example, picture order where there are huge datasets with not so many marked models.

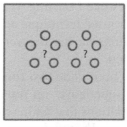

Unsupervised Learning
Algorithms

**Figure 4.7** Unsupervised learning algorithm.

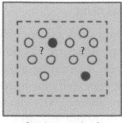

Semi-supervised
Learning Algorithms

**Figure 4.8** Reinforcement algorithm.

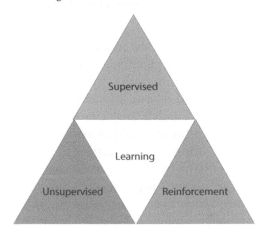

**Figure 4.9** Supervised, unsupervised, and reinforcement learning.

## Algorithms Grouped by Resemblance

Calculations are frequently gathered by comparability regarding their capacity; for instance, tree-based strategies and neural organization motivated techniques. It is the most valuable approach to assemble calculations and it is the methodology we will use here. This is a helpful assembly strategy, yet it is not great. There are still computations that possibly will just find a way into numerous classes like Learning Vector Quantization together with a neural organization roused technique and an occasion-based strategy. It has additional divisions having the very name that depicts hitch along with set of computation.

These computations had been done two times or by picking the social affair that sincerely is the "superlative" on top form. This segments a list of the well-known AI calculations that gathered the manner in which we believe is the most instinctive. The rundown is not thorough in both the gatherings or the computations, yet it is delegate and valuable to understand a thought of the set of the ground.

It would be ideal if you note the following: There is a solid predisposition toward calculations utilized for grouping and relapse, the two most predominant directed AI issues you will experience.

### a. Regression Algorithms
Regression is worried about displaying the connection among factors that is iteratively sophisticated utilizing a proportion of blunder in the expectations prepared by the model which is represented in Figure 4.10.

Relapse techniques are a set of measurements and co-selected into factual AI. This might be befuddling on the grounds that we can employ regression to incorporate indirect method for class of computation. Truly, relapse is a cycle.

The well-known relapse calculations are as follows:

- Ordinary Least Squares Regression (OLSR)
- Linear Regression
- Logistic Regression
- Multivariate Adaptive Regression Splines (MARS)
- Locally Estimated Scatterplot Smoothing (LOESS)

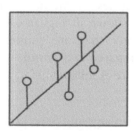

Regression Algorithms

**Figure 4.10**  Regression algorithms.

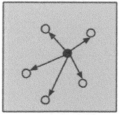

Instance-based
Algorithms

**Figure 4.11**  Instance-based algorithms.

## b. Instance-Based Algorithms

This erudition method is a choice issue specifying occasions or instances of preparing information which are considered significant or needed.

These techniques regularly build up an information base for model facts and contrast new-fangled statistics with the information base that utilizes comparability evaluation to locate the most excellent counterpart and to make an estimate. Example-based strategies are additionally called champ that brings home all the glory methods and memory-based education. Representation of Instance based algorithms is shown in Figure 4.11. Zero-in lays on the portrayal of the put-away cases with comparability estimates utilized among occasions.

Few well-known algorithms in this are as follows:

- k-Nearest Neighbor (kNN)
- Learning Vector Quantization (LVQ)
- Self-Organizing Map (SOM)
- Locally Weighted Learning (LWL)
- Support Vector Machines (SVM)

## c. Regularization Algorithms

An expansion technique which take care of method dependent on their unpredictability, preferring less difficult models that are, moreover, improved at adding up as shown in Figure 4.12. We took regularization computations independently that are famous, ground-breaking, and straightforward changes prepared to dissimilar strategy.

The famous algorithms are as follows:

- Ridge Regression
- Least Absolute Shrinkage and Selection Operator (LASSO)
- Elastic Net
- Least-Angle Regression (LARS)

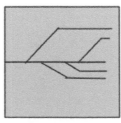

Regularization
Algorithms

**Figure 4.12** Regularization algorithms.

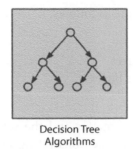

Decision Tree
Algorithms

**Figure 4.13** Decision algorithms.

### d. Decision Tree Algorithms

These techniques develop a method of choices through dependent on authentic estimation of traits in the records. Options diverge in tree structure until a forecast option is ready for a specified proof. Choice trees are frequently quick, precise, and a major top choice for AI.

The most well-known choice tree calculations are as follows:

- Classification and Regression Tree (CART)
- Iterative Dichotomiser 3 (ID3)
- C4.5 and C5.0 (various adaptations of an incredible methodology)
- Chi-Squared Automatic Interaction Detection (CHAID)
- Decision Stump
- M5
- Conditional Decision Trees

### e. Bayesian Algorithms

This method is concerned with Bayes Theorem for classification and regression.

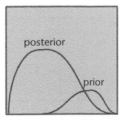

Bayesian Algorithms

**Figure 4.14** Bayesian algorithms.

Few famous algorithms are as follows:

- Naive Bayes
- Gaussian Naive Bayes
- Multinomial Naive Bayes

## f. Clustering Algorithms

Clustering depicts the set of matter and the set of plans. These are constantly synchronized through demonstrating approach. These strategies are apprehensive about incorporating normal structure data to paramount.

Mainstream grouping calculations are as follows:

- k-Medians
- Expectation-Maximization (EM)
- Hierarchical Clustering

## g. Association Rule Learning Algorithms

These techniques separate guidelines that better clarify noticed connections among factors in information.

Standards like this have significance in scientifically valuable association in enormous database abused by an association.

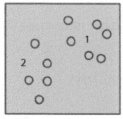

Clustering Algorithms

**Figure 4.15** Clustering algorithms.

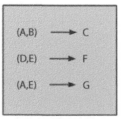

Association Rule
Learning Algorithms

**Figure 4.16** Association rule learning algorithms.

The algorithms are follows:

- Apriori algorithm
- Eclat algorithm

## h. Artificial Neural Network Algorithms

ANN is methods motivated by the arrangement and additional ability of innate neural organizations.

It is a tremendous subdomain with inclusion of many computations and methodologies.

We have isolated out DL from neural organizations due to the gigantic development and prevalence in the domain.

- Perceptron
- Multilayer Perceptrons (MLPs)
- Back-Propagation
- Stochastic Gradient Descent
- Hopfield Network
- Radial Basis Function Network (RBFN)

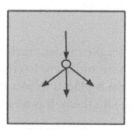

Artificial Neural Network
Algorithms

**Figure 4.17**   Artificial neural network algorithms.

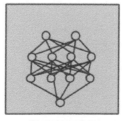

Deep Learning
Algorithms

**Figure 4.18**   Deep learning algorithms.

### i. Deep Learning Algorithms
They are a cutting edge update to ANN that misuse bountiful modest calculation.

We are worried about construction of a lot higher and other mind-boggling neural organizations, and many techniques are worried about huge datasets of marked simple information, for example, picture, text, sound, and video.

### j. Dimensionality Reduction Algorithms
Like bunching strategies, size decreases look and abuses the natural structure in the information, however, for this situation, in a solo way or request to sum up or portray information utilizing less data.

This can be helpful to envision dimensional information or to improve information which would then be able to be utilized in a managed learning technique. A significant number of these strategies can be adjusted for use in grouping and relapse.

- Principal Component Analysis (PCA)
- Principal Component Regression (PCR)
- Partial Least Squares Regression (PLSR)
- Multidimensional Scaling (MDS)

### k. Ensemble Algorithms
These techniques are more fragile model, freely prepared having expectations that are consolidated here and there to create the common forecast.

A large amount of exertion is placed to sort powerless students to consolidate and the manners to join them. It is an incredible category of strategies and is famous.

- Stacked Generalization (Stacking)
- Gradient Boosting Machines (GBM)

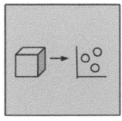

Dimensional Reduction
Algorithms

**Figure 4.19** Dimensional reduction algorithms.

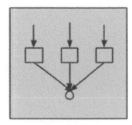

Ensemble Algorithms

**Figure 4.20**  Ensemble algorithms.

- Gradient Boosted Regression Trees (GBRT)
- Random Forest

The generally accepted DL algorithms are as follows:

a. Convolutional Neural Network (CNN)
b. Recurrent Neural Networks (RNNs)
c. Generative Adversarial Networks (GAN)

## A. Convolutional Neural Networks

This is one of most mainstream applied DL cases. They are extraordinary for image/video handling applications. They are deep counterfeit neural organizations that are utilized fundamentally to group, grouping them by proximity. These are computations that can differentiate faces, people, road signs, tumours, blossoms, and numerous different parts of visual information. Self-driving vehicles or robots will expand use its abilities. The mainstream applied commercial cases are likely optical character acknowledgment (OCR) to digitize text to computerize information section as shown by an example in Figure 4.21.

CNN calculation views the picture distinctively versus the human being cerebrum. Each picture is a three-dimensional variety of numbers, known as pixels where you have width, stature, and profundity. Width and tallness relies upon the picture goal. The third measurement (profundity) is Red-Green-Blue (RGB) values for the shading code (except if you are utilizing a dark and white picture as information). The perception of an image by the system on applying DL is as shown in Figure 4.22.

Profound learning CNNs get these pictures to go all the way through a progression of convolution layers with channels (Figure 4.23).

At first, these channels do not have the foggiest idea where to search for picture highlights like edges or bends and the recently referenced loads are arbitrary numbers (like a child with new brain). We normally have an

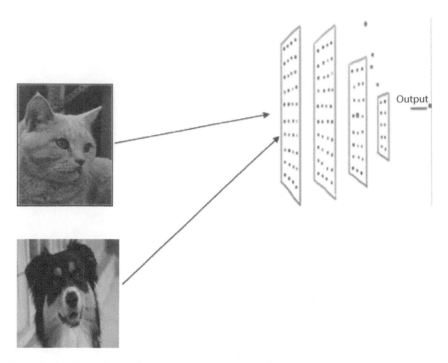

**Figure 4.21**  Convolutional Neural Networks. Source: https://search.creativecommons.org/photos/e6d6b916-ea50-4ade-9c23-283fa6e3dd6b.

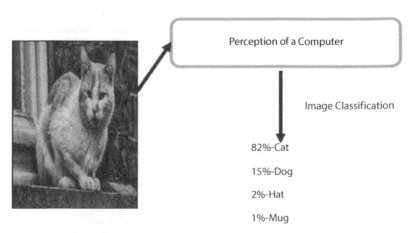

**Figure 4.22**  How our DL algorithm sees an image. Source: https://search.creativecommons.org/photos/812ca736-2128-4652-aa36-2095cc23d359.

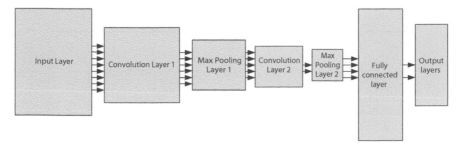

**Figure 4.23** Convolution layers.

enormous preparing informational index with a huge number of pictures with pre-recognized marks. The model first makes a forward pass, computes the underlying loads, makes a forecast of the result name (for example this is a canine), and contrasts it and reality that is the current preparing set marks. Since this is a preparation set, we definitely realize the result names, hence relying upon the achievement of the forecast, and a misfortune work is determined and the organization makes a back pass while refreshing its loads. The manner in which the PC can change its loads to diminish the misfortune is through a technique gotten back to engendering. Presently, the model plays out a retrogressive pass through the organization, which is figuring out which loads contributed most to the misfortune and discovering approaches to calibrate these loads so the misfortune diminishes through continuous passes.

At first, the determined misfortune is required to be extremely high and it is relied upon to diminish to a base after many (yet fixed) seasons of forward/in reverse passes. Toward the end, ideally, the organization should be prepared all around, so the loads of the layers are tuned accurately.

At that point, run test to have the option to see whether CNNs model works. We ought to have an alternate arrangement of pictures in addition to its separate marks and go through the testing set of pictures by the CNNs. We contrast the yields with the test set to check whether and how well our organization functions! Normally, the more information you have, the better your model could be tuned through preparing and test. That is why huge information empowers profound learning. For an adequate model, fit to be utilized for genuine situations, we keep modifying the method.

It is much perplexing yet excessively significant and rearranged rationale for the vast majority of Artificial Neural Networks.

One more genuine illustration of PC vision is in real life in China. Alibaba dispatched City Brain System in its origination in China where an AI community streamlines the traffic lights.

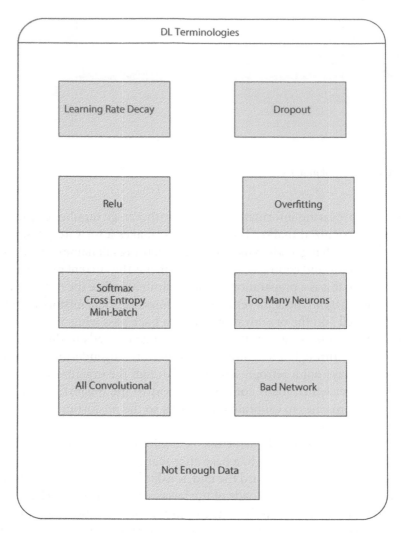

**Figure 4.24** DL terminology examples.

CNN like calculations as of now rule our everyday life: Facebook—programmed labeling, Google—photograph exploration, and Pinterest—house channel personalization.

### B. Recursive (Recurrent) Neural Networks (RNN)

Utilized reciprocally this organization is only a speculation of an intermittent organization by a similar abbreviation. A RNN essentially utilizes past information sources inside the estimations. Let us assume you are examining penmanship. Another approach to consider RNNs is that they have

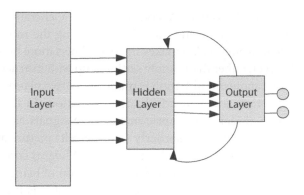

**Figure 4.25** Neural network.

```
DUKE VINCENTIO:
Well, your wit is in the care of side and that.

Second Lord:
They would be ruled after this chamber, and
my fair nues begun out of the fact, to be conveyed,
Whose noble souls I'll have the heart of the wars.

Clown:
Come, sir, I will make did behold your worship.
```

**Figure 4.26** AI or real Shakespeare?

a "memory" which catches data about what has been determined up until this point. RNN can recall the previous sources of info, to give a major edge over other counterfeit neural organizations with regards to consecutive and setting touchy assignments, for example, discourse acknowledgment.

They are viewed as perhaps remarkable model for Natural Language Processing. They are likewise utilized for verbal communication interpretations, forming music, composing books, compose AI tweets, Tesla AI, and have kept in touch with mainstream profound learning RNN articles to additionally allude to.

### C. Generative Adversarial Networks (GAN)
They were made by Ian Goodfellow, who is as of now staff research expert at Google Brain, and his associates from the University of Montreal in 2014.

Yann LeCun, the head of Facebook AI communicated: "Generative Adversarial Networks is the most hypnotizing thought concerning the most recent ten years in Machine Learning". GAN makes the neural nets more human by permitting it to CREATE rather than simply setting it up with instructive records.

A generative antagonistic affiliation is made out of two neural affiliations: a generative affiliation and a discriminative affiliation. In the beginning stage, a Generator model takes capricious change signals as information and produces a self-confident disorderly (counterfeit) picture as the yield. Sensibly with the assistance of the Discriminator, it begins conveying photographs of a specific class that give off an impression of being genuine.

The Discriminator which is the rebuke of Generator is managed both the made pictures comparably as a specific class of pictures at the same time, permitting it to tell the generator how the genuine picture takes after.

Generator and Discriminator are setting one as opposed to the accompanying (as such the "ineffectively organized") and battle during the preparation where their fiascos push against one another to improve practices (through back propagation). The objective of the generator is to pass without being gotten while the objective of the discriminator is to see the fakes.

Coming about to appearing at a specific point, the Discriminator will be not prepared to tell if the make picture is an authentic or a bogus picture,

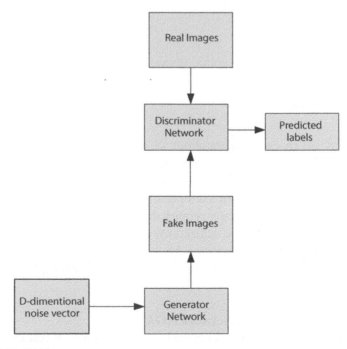

**Figure 4.27** GAN.

and that is the place where photographs can be seen of a specific being made by out Generator that never genuinely exist! Specialists now and again depict this as the generative affiliation trying to "trick" the discriminative affiliation, which should be set up to see unequivocal plans of models continually.

These may be well utilized for expanding goal of a picture, reproducing mainstream pictures or compositions or creating a picture from text, delivering photograph practical portrayals of item models, and producing reasonable discourse sound of genuine individuals just as delivering style/ stock shots.

GANs are exceptionally well known in online media. Be careful with profound phony recordings! In the event that input with sufficient faces informational index, it can make totally innovative phony faces that are excessively sensible yet additionally do not exist! The following is NVIDIA's AI delivering counterfeit human photographs utilizing this.

Profound Learning for NLP: It picked up tremendous prominence as of late gratitude to AI. It has the capacity of PCs to examine, comprehend,

**Figure 4.28** GAN examples. Source: https://github.com/junyanz/CycleGAN.

**Figure 4.29** GAN example. Source: https://github.com/junyanz/CycleGAN.

*Edmond de Belamy*

**Figure 4.30** GAN used to create painting. Source: Wikipedia. GANs were used to create the 2018 painting *Edmond de Belamy*.

and create individual language, with discourse. For instance, you can do assumption investigation given any content. It can make AI suggestions in the wake of parsing through film/book surveys or web. It is capable of running chatbots/advanced partners for front end errands utilizing text or sound associations. Alexa/Siri/Cortana/Google Assistant are the celebrated computerized personas utilizing NLP motors.

Phases of NLP are a language alliance, empowering individuals to speak. Google Assistant can settle on a couple of decisions. Other realized utilized cases are venture hunt or assessment taking out (opinion investigation). As of now, an enormous decision of this motors that are promptly accessible in the direction of implant into regular uses like call focuses, talk bots, interpreters, auto-indicators, spam channels, as well as the fresh immense area of computerized colleagues.

Text and/or Speech Engine
Natural Language Processing (NLP)
Machine and Deep Learning

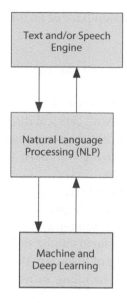

**Figure 4.31** AI in chatbots.

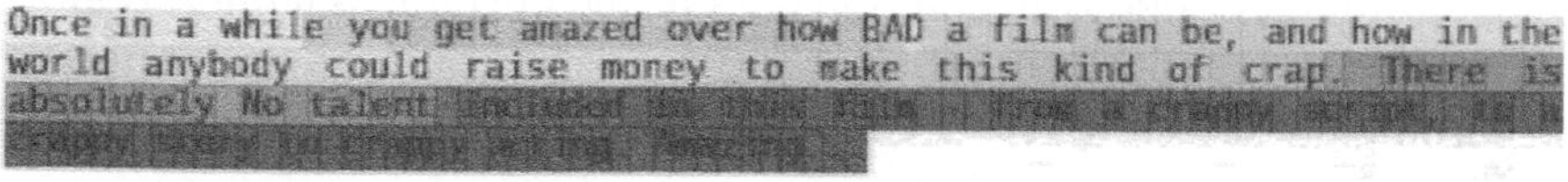

Once in a while you get amazed over how BAD a film can be, and how in the world anybody could raise money to make this kind of crap. There is absolutely No talent

**Figure 4.32** Behavior of the sentiment neuron. Colors show the type of sentiment.

## 4.6 A Project Implementation on Discernment of Cervical Cancer by Using Machine/Deep Learning in Cloud

Cervical malignancy is the first reason for death among ladies across the globe because of disease. Careful and mistake-free recognition can spare lives. Prior location of cervical cancer was finished by a minute smear test dependent on the count of boundaries of the cell core of the example, for example, its shape and size as smear is examined to magnifying lens is a very testing task. Subsequently, Digital Image Processing procedure is required to distinguish variations from the norm in human cell. Thusly, an extensive AI method has been proposed in this paper. The proposed procedure gives the highlights and state of cytoplasm and core in the cervix cell. KNN and SVM are prepared with the highlights and state of the divided cell and contrasted and obscure cervix cell test with this strategy. The precision pace of 86% for SVM and 70% for KNN is accomplished.

### 4.6.1    Proposed Work

Presently, cervical malignant growth is the deadliest disease across the globe. The principle situation with cervical disease is that it cannot be seen in beginning phases as it does not show any disorder until definitive stages. Consequently, the true organizing will assist with giving fastidious treatment to the person in question.

The specific apparatuses for this reason incorporate Pap test, Computed tomography check (CT/CAT), Biopsy, Magnetic reverberation imaging (MRI), Positron discharge tomography examine (PET), Cystoscopy, Laparoscopy X-beam, and so forth can be utilized with picture preparing methods to get the organizing of disorder. The point of this task is to plan and build up a novel picture handling moved toward dependent on ML framework to help in cervical cancer discovery at beginning phase. Our methodology is cloud-based, so the calculation is not kept to a particular area.

Utilization of cloud is an additional preferred position as it offers opportunity to get to results from any spot and specialists can begin treatment at beginning phase as it were.

The destinations are as follows:

- To the salvage activity time and the quantity of salvage administrators.
- To get an exact area and phase of a tumor.
- To diminish the demise rate.
- To get the visual substance of the tumor to know the condition as right on time as conceivable utilizing picture handling.

### 4.6.1.1    MRI Dataset

Cervical malignant growth is the disease emerging from the cervix which is the diminished piece of the uterus. This work utilizes MRI as the diagnosing device in DICOM (Digital Imaging and Communications in Medicine) design is taken as the contribution to this work. Converting the picture into dim scale further more evacuates the messiness and it gets better picture quality to acquire greater possibility in identifying the pro tolerance. The dataset consist of 24 inmates with narrowly progressive cervical cancer.

### 4.6.1.2    Pre Processing

The important step in our prospective technique includes the following.

#### 4.6.1.2.1    Image Enhancement

Upgrade progress the splendor of discolored pictures by means of the gamma adjustment and likelihood circulation of predominance pixels. The improvement strategies are grouped into two direct upgrade techniques aberrant improvement method. In undeviating upgrade methods, the picture differentiation can be straight forwardly characterized by a particular complexity term. In backhanded upgrade, techniques endeavor to improve picture differentiate by redistributing the likelihood thickness.

The adaptive gamma correction (AGC) is devised as the image contrast can be enhanced intelligently retrieved by Gamma correction, which is a nonlinear operation. Gamma correction is used to amend brightness or darkness of image pixels. Image lightness can be revised according to the gamma value. Scope of Gamma is 0.0 to 10.0; if the rate is less than 1.0,

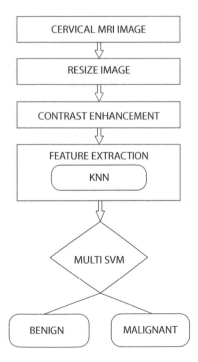

**Figure 4.33** Flowchart of the methodology.

then the image gets dark. If the rate is greater than 1.0, then the image gets light. If gamma value is equal to one, then there are no changes in an image.

#### 4.6.1.2.2    Image Segmentation

This is a crucial part. The breaking of an image into relevant format is called image segmentation. Desire of division is to change the depiction of a picture pixel into uncomplicated aspect. The approach is classified on two properties, i.e., discontinuity and similarity. Occupying this property, it has Edged-based and Region-based division. The division that depends on brokenness property of pixels is considered as boundary- or edge-based strategy. The Region-based division is partitioning of an image into analogous areas of connected pixels. The Region-based method involves thresholding, region growing, region splitting, and merging. The fundamental thought is to choose an ideal dim level edge an incentive for differentiating object of enthusiasm for a picture from the help the dim level dissemination. Otsu method is used frequently. This requires computing gray-level images of global thresholding which depends only on gray-level pixels of the image.

#### 4.6.1.3    Feature Extraction

Getting a measure of assets expected to depict colossal arrangement of information are called appearance extraction. The look embraced for measurable KNN highlights.

The highlights are as follows:

    i.    Contrast
    ii.   Correlation
    iii.  Energy
    iv.  Homogeneity
    v.   Mean
    vi.  Standard deviation (std)
    vii. Entropy (I)
    viii. Root Mean Square (RMS).
    ix.  Variance (var).
    x.   Smoothness
    xi.  Kurtosis
    xii. Skewness
    xiii. Inverse Difference Medium

**Multi-Support Vector Machine**
SVM just order information into two classes. This capacity eliminates the limitations via "looking" for the right class for each column in the test informational index. Preparing test in help vector machine is divisible by a hyperplane. This hyperplane is processed by the choice function; point limit arranging should be possible into gatherings. There are two sorts of classifier are utilized to arrange the better outcome. The back spread and feed forward classifiers are not distinguishing a few vermin in a picture, yet SVM gives better outcome. SVM is a non-direct classifier and is a moving AI calculation.

Ex: Training set = [1 10;2 20;3 30;4 40;5 50;6 66;3 30;41 42];
Test set = [3 34;1 14;22 25;62 63];
Group Train = [1;1;2;2;3;3;2;2];
Results = multisvm (Training set, Group Train, Test set);
Disp("multi class problem");
Disp(results).

### 4.6.2 Design Methodology and Implementation

Stage 1: Input the MR picture.
Stage 2: Enhance the MR picture utilizing Adaptive gamma remedy technique.
Stage 3: The improved picture is then portioned utilizing Otsu's division strategy.
Stage 4: Features are currently removed utilizing KNN highlight extraction.
Stage 5: Classification of the picture is finished utilizing SVM classifier.
Stage 6: Staging of each picture is the resultant yield.

**Input Specification**
The input/dataset of the proposed system is magnetic resonance image (MRI) in DICOM format; this DICOM images are converted into "Joint Photographic Expert Group" (JPEG) format as shown in the following figures.

**Output specification**
After computing, the output is classified as two stages as follows:

    i.   Benign
    ii.  Malignant.

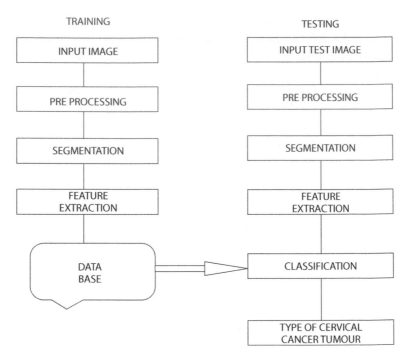

**Figure 4.34** Flowchart includes training and testing.

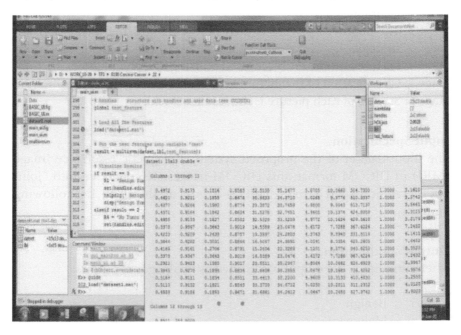

**Figure 4.35** Values of the trained dataset matrices.

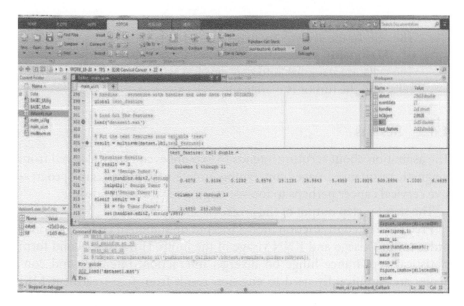

**Figure 4.36** Values of the tested datasets matrices.

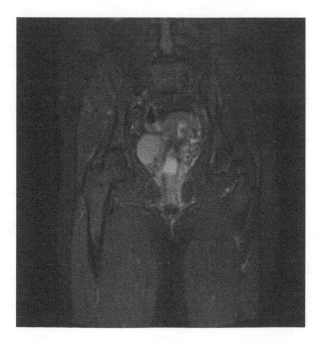

**Figure 4.37** Sample cervical cancer magnetic resonance image (MRI).

**i.    Benign**
The cells in the growth are usual, it is benign.
**ii.    Malignant.**
The cells are irregular and can develop widely; they are cancerous cells, and the tumor is malignant.

### 4.6.3    Results

The aspiration about scrutiny intends to explore even if trait derived from magnetic resonance images concerning inmate with provincially progressive cervical cancer perhaps to foresee staging regarding syndrome.

The step-by-step output of the project is shown below:

Precise SVM contradiction model was put up stationed on both second-order texture visage and KNN visage of the lump. However, second form statistical appearance hinge on diverge, interaction, intensity, and congruity are significantly used to envision result from free treatment MRI

**Figure 4.38**  Loading the MRI image from datasets.

**Figure 4.39**  Contrast enhancement.

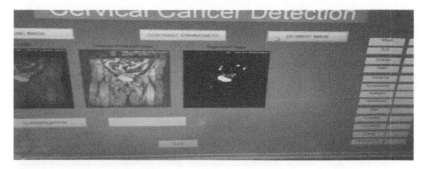

**Figure 4.40** Image segmentation.

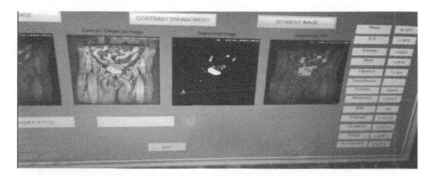

**Figure 4.41** Segmented region of interest (ROI).

of cervical cancer cyst. Thus, texture features surpass features along with numerical characteristics for cancer stage conclusion, which depends on cyst size. Thus, the exact staging will advise regime to the sufferer as resolution to the prospect work also surpasses to anticipate the treatment according to the staging will serve the radiologist for an improved medication advice.

## 4.7    Applications

At the point when combined with the intensity of distributed computing, AI could be considerably more advantageous. This blend is named "the keen cloud". The current use of cloud includes registering, stockpiling, and systems administration. In any case, with the component of AI mixed in the cloud, the capacities of the cloud will increment unfathomably. The insightful cloud gets equipped for gaining from the tremendous measure of information put away in the cloud, to develop expectations and break

**Figure 4.42** After classification, cervical cancer (ROI) tumor is found.

**Figure 4.43** After classification, cervical cancer region of interest (ROI) tumor is not found.

down circumstances. This will fill in as a keen stage to perform errands much productively.

Distributed computing gives two essential requirements to run an AI model well along with low pricing and preparing capability to critical situation with massive measures to care about information. To begin with, it gives versatile and eases registering, and it is an extraordinary method to store and handle enormous volumes of information. Accordingly, the mixture of cloud with AI benefits both these orders. The effect of AI on cloud is most prominent in the accompanying angles.

### 4.7.1   Cognitive Cloud

The cloud stores gigantic measures of information which turns into the wellspring of learning for ML calculations. Billions of individuals throughout the world use its stages to store information; it is a superb open door for ML calculations to use that information and gain from it. In different words, ML calculations can move the cloud worldview from distributed computing to intellectual registering.

Psychological figuring relates to innovation stages that are planned on the standards of AI and sign handling. It fuses AI, regular language preparing, discourse/object acknowledgment, human-PC connection, and story age.

When implanted with ML capacities, the cloud becomes "Psychological Cloud" which does intellectual figuring applications available for the regular mass. IBM Cognitive and Microsoft's Azure Cognitive Services are incredible instances of this—these stages permit to create keen applications with no issue.

### 4.7.2    Chatbots and Smart Personal Assistants

Chatbots and individual colleagues have come up with both the individual and business scene. Savvy remote helpers like Alexa can play out a variety of undertakings for you and even collaborate with you like another person. Anyway created they may be, chatbots and menial helpers are still at their early stage. They are as yet advancing, as yet learning. Henceforth, it is normal for them to have limitations. When coordinated with cloud, chatbots and savvy individual aides may have a huge group of information available to them to gain from. Therefore, their learning capacities will get an extensive lift. With time, chatbots and individual partners will advance to totally get rid of any type of human being intercession or backing.

### 4.7.3    IoT Cloud

IoT Cloud is a cloud stage explicitly intended to store and deal with the information created by the Internet of Things (IoT). Sales force's IoT Cloud is controlled by Thunder—a "hugely adaptable continuous occasion preparing motor".

IoT Cloud can allow goliath measures of information created by associated gadgets, sites, and clients and trigger activities for ongoing reactions. It tends to be utilized for different genuine situations.

### 4.7.4    Business Intelligence

On account of ML/DL distributed computing, business insight (BI) administrations are additionally getting progressively shrewd. Cloud ML has two-overlap payback for BI. The cloud stage can store tremendous volumes of client along with friends' information, and ML calculations can measure also break down that information to discover inventive arrangements.

With client information close by, ML calculations can help organizations pick up a more inside and out and better comprehension of their intended interest group-buying conduct, inclinations, needs, problem areas, and so forth Likewise, organizations can make item improvement and advertising methodologies to help deals and increment ROI.

ML has a huge concern in client experience and fulfilment. Organizations comprehend to clients and improved; they make items that can address their trouble spots and needs. This prompts elevated consumer loyalty. Additionally, ML calculations can make instinctive suggestion motors and chatbots for better client experience.

This is only an aspect to blend ML/DL calculations, and also distributed computing is getting better with the BI frameworks.

### 4.7.5   AI-as-a-Service

Cloud administration suppliers offer AI abilities by means of open-source AI-as-a-Service (AIaaS) stages. This is a profoundly practical method of sending AI functionalities to organizations.

It offers clients a large group of AI devices and functionalities needed for AI/ML model structure, astute mechanization, intellectual registering, and significantly more. Obviously, it is very quick and productive. It provides extraordinary assistance to comprehend ML and cloud in a better way.

## 4.8   Advantages of Adoption of Cloud in Machine Learning/Deep Learning

The cloud compensation per-utilize method is useful for busty AI or ML/DL outstanding burdens. It makes it simple for endeavors to try different things with ML/DL abilities and upgrade as undertakings to get into creation and request increments. The cloud makes canny capacities available without need of progressed abilities in computerized reasoning or information science. AWS and Google Cloud Platform, etc., offer many ML/DL choices that do not need profound information on AI, AI hypothesis, or a group of information scientists. ML is not any more a popular expression—it is a living truth within recent memory that has brought forth various extraordinary callings in the Data Science area.

From being an innovation that was once too far for little and medium-sized endeavors, ML is currently a standard innovation, because of the public cloud. Today, the top distributed computing stages like Amazon (AWS), Google (ML Engine), and Microsoft (Azure) have democratized

AI and ML and made it both available and reasonable. Both of all shapes and sizes cloud stages are reevaluating AI and ML to make advance administrations that can set these problematic innovations inside the hierarchical structures. Of the multitude of administrations offered by the cloud, ML stages are one of the quickest developing administrations. This is fundamentally a result of the adaptability with which they can be turned out. In spite of other cloud-based administrations, cloud ML stages can be conveyed through a large group of various conveyance models, including psychological registering, GPU-based processing, robotized AI, and ML model administration. As an expanding number of ventures across all mechanical areas are utilizing ML, it is boosting the work prospects in this space. As indicated by Indeed's 2019 report of "The Best Jobs in the US", Machine Learning Engineer is the highest level employment with an amazing 344% development and a normal base compensation of $146,085 every year! Also, with cloud developing as a significant objective for ML-based tasks and administrations, vocations in the cloud are soaring too. Indeed, even in India, it is one of the most generously compensated occupations for freshers. It is assessed that by 2021, the absolute income for distributed computing administrations will surpass $300 billion.

AI in the cloud is the new pattern in the business since when joined, the potential and abilities of both ML and the cloud duplicate. Since ML in the cloud does not request a particular arrangement of cutting edge aptitudes (an essential information on ML ideas and the cloud stage will do), it presents a superb open door for profession building. Additionally, the cloud makes ML models/benefits considerably more versatile, offering enough degree for meeting dynamic business prerequisites. Utilizing AI on the cloud, undertakings would first be able to test and convey more modest tasks on the cloud and afterward scale up as need and request increments. The compensation per-utilize model further makes it simple to get to more complex abilities without the need to acquire new progressed equipment.

## 4.9    Conclusion

A significant pattern as of now, being seen in the profound learning market, is the expanding fuse of profound learning arrangements in the clinical business. These arrangements help medical care explores pick up better experiences into the clinical properties and advantages of different medications and mixes. Moreover, this innovation helps the guardians better dissect the clinical history of patients with the goal that the best treatment plans can be recommended to them. Additionally, these arrangements can likewise be consolidated alongside different clinical imaging strategies, for example, CT sweeps, ECG, and MRI checks for the successful determination of numerous basic illnesses and problems, which, thusly, helps in the better treatment of these infections.

The picture acknowledgment class recorded the most noteworthy development under the application division of the profound learning market during the most recent couple of years. This is attributed to the huge necessity of profound learning arrangements in picture acknowledgment applications, because of their capacity to help clients in the location and ID of articles and examination of computerized pictures. By building a task.py, we can handle hyperparameters as order line contentions, which permits us to decouple our model rationale from hyperparameters. A key advantage is this permits us to handily shoot various positions in equal utilizing various boundaries to decide an ideal hyperparameter set (we can even utilize the worked in hyperparameter tuning administration!). At last, the docopt bundle consequently creates a parser for our task.py record, in view of the utilization string that the client composes.

# References

1. Hinton, G.E., Krizhevsky, A., Srivastava, N., Sutskever, I., Salakhutdinov, R., Dropout: A simple way to prevent neural networks from overfitting. *J. Mach. Learn. Res.*, 15, 1929–1958, 2014.
2. He, K., Ren, S., Sun, J., Zhang, X., Deep residual learning for image recognition, 2016, CoRR, abs/1512.03385.
3. Ioffe, S. and Szegedy, C., Batch Normalization: Accelerating deep network training by reducing internal covariate shift. *ICML*, 2015.
4. Fei-Fei, L., Karpathy, A., Leung, T., Shetty, S., Sukthankar, R., Toderici, G., Large-scale video classification with convolutional neural networks. *IEEE Conference on Computer Vision and Pattern Recognition*, 2014.
5. Belongie, S.J., Dollár, P., Hays, J., Lin, T., Maire, M., Perona, P., Ramanan, D., Zitnick, C.L., Microsoft COCO: Common Objects in Context. *ECCV*, 2014.
6. Lapedriza, À., Oliva, A., Torralba, A., Xiao, J., Zhou, B., Learning deep features for scene recognition using places database. *NIPS*, 2014.
7. Bengio, Y., Courville, A.C., Goodfellow, I.J., Mirza, M., Ozair, S., Pouget-Abadie, J., Warde-Farley, D., Xu, B., Generative adversarial nets. *NIPS*, 2014.
8. Batista, J., Caseiro, R., Henriques, J.F., Martins, P., High-speed tracking with kernelized correlation filters, 2015, CoRR, abs/1404.7584.
9. Zhang, M. and Zhou, Z., A review on multi-label learning algorithms. *IEEE TKDE*, 2014.

10. Bengio, Y., Clune, J., Lipson, H., Yosinski, J., How transferable are features in deep neural networks, 2014, CoRR, abs/1411.1792.
11. Amorim, D.G., Barro, S., Cernadas, E., Delgado, M.F., Do we need hundreds of classifiers to solve real world classification problems. *J. Mach. Learn. Res.*, 2014.
12. Dong, X., Gabrilovich, E., Heitz, G., Horn, W., Lao, N., Murphy, K., Zhang, W., Knowledge vault: A web-scale approach to probabilistic knowledge fusion, in: *Proceedings of the 20th ACM SIGKDD international conference on Knowledge discovery and data mining ACM*, 2014, August.
13. Lowe, D.G. and Muja, M., Scalable nearest neighbor algorithms for high dimensional data. *IEEE Trans. Pattern Anal. Mach. Intell.*, 2014.
14. Huang, G., Huang, G., Song, S., You, K., Trends in extreme learning machines: A review. *Neural Networks*, 2015.
15. Bifet, A., Bouchachia, A., Gama, J., Pechenizkiy, M., Zliobaite, I., A survey on concept drift adaptation. *ACM Comput. Surv.*, 2014.
16. Gong, Y., Guo, R., Lazebnik, S., Wang, L., Multi-scale orderless pooling of deep convolutional activation features. *ECCV*, 2014.
17. Arbeláez, P.A., Girshick, R.B., Hariharan, B., Malik, J., Simultaneous detection and segmentation. *ECCV*, 2014.
18. Chandrashekar, G. and Sahin, F., A survey on feature selection methods. *Int. J. Comput. Electr. Eng.*,
19. Kazemi, V. and Sullivan, J., One millisecond face alignment with an ensemble of regression trees. *Proc. IEEE Conf. Comput. Vis. Pattern Recognit.*, 2014.
20. Corchado, E., Graña, M., Wozniak, M., A survey of multiple classifier systems as hybrid systems. *Inform. Fusion*, 16, 3–17, 2014.
21. Deepak, R.U., Kumar, R.R., Byju, N.B., Natarajan, P., Pour-nami, C., Sibiu, S., Bengtsson, E., Sujathan, K.R., Computer assisted Pap Smear Analyser for Cervical cancer screening using Quantitative Microscopy. *J. Cytol. Histol.*, 2015.
22. Phatak, A. and Barbadekar, A.B., Classification of MR images of cervical cancer using SVM and ANN. *Int. J. Sci. Res. (IJSR)*, 2015.
23. Mustafa, N., Mat Isa, N.A., Mashor, M.Y., Othman, N.H., New features of cervical cells for cervical cancer diagnostic system using neural network. *Int. J. Simul. Syst. Sci. Technol. (IJSSST)*, 2008.
24. Lu, Z., Carneiro, G., Bradley, A.P., Ushizima, D., Nosrati, M.S., Bianchi, A.G.C., Evaluation of three Algorithms for the segmentation of overlapping Cervical Cells. *IEEE J. Biomed. Health Inform.*, 21, 2, March 2017.
25. Baldi, P. and Brunak, S., *Bioinformatics: A Machine Learning Approach*, MIT Press, Cambridge, MA, 2002.
26. Jyothi, A.P. and Usha, S., Interstellar-based topology control scheme for optimal clustering performance in Wireless Sensor Network. *Int. J. Commun. Syst.*, 33, 8, 1–16, May 2020.
27. Miller, T., Explanation in artificial intelligence: Insights from the social sciences. 267, 1–38, February 2019.

28. Zhang, J., Zheng, Y., Qi, D., Li, R., Yi, X., Li, T., Predicting citywide crowd flows using deep spatio-temporal residual networks. 259, 147–166, June 2018.

29. Albrecht, S.V. and Stone, P., Autonomous agents modelling other agents: A comprehensive survey and open problems - Open access. 258, 66–95, May 2018.

30. Eppe, M., Maclean, E., Confalonieri, R., Kutz, O., Schorlemmer, M., Plaza, E., Kühnberger, K.U., A computational framework for conceptual blending - Open access. 256, 105–129, March 2018.

31. Anshelevich, E., Bhardwaj, O., Elkind, E., Postl, J., Skowron., P., Approximating optimal social choice under metric preferences. 264, 27–51, November 2018.

32. Beck, H., Dao-Tran, M., Eiter, T., LARS: A logic-based framework for analytic reasoning over streams. 261, 16–70, August 2018.

33. Leottau, D.L., Ruiz-del-Solar, J., Babuška, R., Decentralized reinforcement learning of robot behaviors. 256, 130–159, March 2018.

34. Bozzato, L., Eiter, T., Serafini, L., Enhancing context knowledge repositories with justifiable exceptions. 257, 72–126, April 2018.

35. Ganian, R. and Ordyniak, S., The complexity landscape of decompositional parameters for ILP. 257, 61–71, April 2018.

36. Lowalekar, M., Varakantham, P., Jaillet, P., Online spatio-temporal matching in stochastic and dynamic domains. 261, 71–112, August 2018.

37. Benedikt, M., Grau, B.C., Kostylev, E.V., Logical foundations of information disclosure in ontology-based data integration. 262, 52–95, September 2018.

38. Li, F., Qian, Y., Wang, J., Dang, C., Jing, L., Clustering ensemble based on sample's stability. 273, 37–55, August 2019.

39. MacAlpine, P. and Stone, P., Overlapping layered learning. 254, 21–43, January 2018.

40. Law, M., Russo, A., Broda, K., The complexity and generality of learning answer set programs - Open access. 259, 110–146, June 2018.

41. Martínez-Plumed, F., Prudêncio, R.B.C., Martínez-Usó, A., Hernández-Orallo, J., Item response theory in AI: Analysing machine learning classifiers at the instance level. 271, 18–42, June 2019.

42. Jyothi, A.P. and Sakthivel, U., CFCLP- "A Novel clustering framework based on combinatorial approach and linear programming in WSN". *2nd International Conference on Computing and Communications Technologies (ICCCT)*, pp. 49–54, 2017, Chennai.

43. Zhou, J.T., Pan, S.J., Tsang, I.W., A deep learning framework for Hybrid Heterogeneous Transfer Learning. 275, 310–328, October 2019.

44. Baldi, P., Sadowski, P., Lu, Z., Learning in the machine: Random backpropagation and the deep learning channel. 260, 1–35, July 2018.

45. Gaggl, S.A., Linsbichler, T., Maratea, M., Woltran, S., Design and results of the Second International Competition on Computational Models of Argumentation. 279, February 2020.

46. Gottifredi, S., Tamargo, L.H., García, A.J., Simari, G.R., Arguing about informant credibility in open multi-agent systems. 259, 91–109, June 2018.

47. Rigas, E.S., Ramchurn, S.D., Bassiliades, N., Algorithms for electric vehicle scheduling in large-scale mobility-on-demand schemes. 262, 248–278, September 2018.
48. Fazzinga, B., Flesca, S., Furfaro, F., Complexity of fundamental problems in probabilistic abstract argumentation: Beyond independence. 268, 1–29, March 2019.
49. de Campos, C.P., Scanagatta, M., Corani, G., Zaffalon, M., Entropy-based pruning for learning Bayesian networks using BIC. 260, 42–50, July 2018.
50. Nikolaou, C., Kostylev, E.V., Konstantinidis, G., Kaminski, M., Grau, B.C., Horrocks, I., Foundations of ontology-based data access under bag semantics - Open access. 274, 91–132, September 2019.
51. Bonatti, P.A., Rational closure for all description logics. 274, 197–223, September 2019.

# 5

# Machine Learning and Internet of Things–Based Models for Healthcare Monitoring

**Shruti Kute[1]\*, Amit Kumar Tyagi[1,2]†,**
**Aswathy S.U.[3]‡ and Shaveta Malik[4]**

*[1]School of Computer Science and Engineering, Vellore Institute of Technology,*
*Chennai, Tamil Nadu, India*
*[2]Centre for Advanced Data Science, Vellore Institute of Technology, Chennai,*
*Tamil Nadu, India*
*[3]Department of Computer Science and Engineering, Jyothi Engineering College,*
*Cheruthuruthy, Thrissur, Kerala, India*
*[4]Terna Engineering College, University of Mumbai, Mumbai, India*

## Abstract

We all know what life matters to us and also, if anything happens to human life in form of any mental or physical issues, the immediate priority is given to healthcare field. So, with the help of vast and advanced technology, it particularly made this field much easier and produces accurate and efficient results. With that note, ML and IoT are the combos that made a great change in medical field, bringing so many efficient systems that made every single life of doctors and nurses process easier. This paper brings out some ML-IoT models that have been used by researchers during recent years, and also, it will be useful for other research specialists out there to be inspired and to try new aspect that could potentially help other healthcare workers out there. We also discussed the challenges of integrating ML-IoT that could be taken care and solved in future.

*Keywords:* Internet of Things, machine learning, neural networks, E-healthcare

*\*Corresponding author*: shrutikute99@gmail.com
*†Corresponding author*: amitkrtyagi025@gmail.com
*‡Corresponding author*: aswathy.su@gamail.com
Amit Kumar Tyagi: ORCID: 0000-0003-2657-8700

Archana Mire, Shaveta Malik and Amit Kumar Tyagi (eds.) Advanced Analytics and Deep Learning
Models, (111–126) © 2022 Scrivener Publishing LLC

## 5.1   Introduction

The fundamental portion of the life is medical services. Medical services are the upkeep and improvement of well-being by means of anticipation and finding of diseases. Any cracks or irregularities that are available profound underneath the skin can be determined with the assistance of the analytic hardware like CT, MRI, PET, SPECT, and so forth. Some of conditions that may be unusual such as coronary episode and epilepsy are recognized even before they happen. As the expansion of ordinary people continues, an unaccountable change of mood of disease increases among masses which potentially create strain to recent medical frameworks. So, the main aim will be to reduce the stress atmosphere of medical area frameworks while keeping up its nature which brings out the basic idea level of this process. So, the answer to control the weights over the medical area frameworks will be Internet of Things (IoT). Caring patients without full monitoring is a big failure and also leads to some other cause. Thereby, further exploration to cope up with both explicit and implicit medical cases that a continuous monitoring advancement is needed. A few related works have recently studied explicit zones and innovations that are identified with IoT medical care. A broad study is introduced in, with center put around monetarily accessible arrangements, potential applications, and remaining issues. Every subject is considered independently, as opposed to as a component of an all-encompassing framework. Integration of data mining and stockpiling can be done in framework while evaluating them. In order to reduce the expenses for treatment, RFID is used in American clinics. Various wearable frameworks have been proposed to give dependable remote transmission of information. As IoT has numerous advantages in the field of healthcare, the only concern is the security in which numerous data are been passed while implementation and also while a user uses this end product. So, securing them is a great challenge.

There are much better advancements say Artificial Intelligence (AI), which could potentially build such accurate and efficient models for medical fields. Machine Learning (ML) is a subset of AI in which there is only feeding of certain algorithm in which machine itself learns and perform its own trained model (some includes web look, spam sifting, promotion position, and stock exchanging). ML increases equivalent significance and acknowledgment as that of big data and cloud computing by investigating those huge pieces and streamlining the errand of information researchers in an automatic process. Expansive scale educational assortments are accumulated and inspected in different territories, from planning sciences to relational associations, business, bio atomic exploration, and security. Calculations done by AI model will be stacked in memory; however, there is an equal need for much advancement to acquire that generous data which literally brings some experiences in real-life world. ML will be good algorithm for these kinds of fields that could potentially intake huge and complex data.

Motivation: The motto of this paper is to define some recent advancements that happened in the healthcare service with the help of ML and IoT integration. It will be also helpful to many researchers out there who can read and be inspired with and make new other proposal that could potentially help to develop new models.

Organization of work: The introduction part is in Section 5.1, and rest of the sections is as follows: Section 5.2 depicts literature survey of some of the models followed by Section 5.3 with interpretable ML in healthcare followed by opportunities of ML in healthcare in Section 5.4. Section 5.5 deals with integration of ML-IoT and models related to that. Section 5.6 discusses about applications of machine learning in Medical and Pharma sector. Section 5.7 depicts challenges while integrating them, and finally, Section 5.8 is the conclusion.

## 5.2    Literature Survey

Here, we discuss some of recent advancements in healthcare that have been taken care by ML and IoT integration. Samir Jadhav [1] proposed a disease prediction using ML in IoT environment. Here, they integrate IoT and Body Sensor Network (BSN) in which they include sensors like pulse rate sensor, temperature sensor, and blood pressure sensor for collecting continuous data. During the training phase, they collect the data from online repository and are given under pre-processing. After errors are cleaned; then, they are saved in database. In testing phase, with the help of six wearable sensors, an atmosphere of IoT is created in order to collect data and they are given to Fuzzy Random Forest (FRF) classifier for prediction, and while evaluating this model, they gain an accuracy of 93.5%. Ganesan and Sivakumar [2] proposed a heart disease prediction and diagnosis using ML and IoT. They used UCI dataset for training and testing of this model. They also used wearable IoT gadgets for collecting data that are linked with human body. In final stage, they use classifiers such as J 48, Logistic Regression (LR), multilayer perceptron (MLP), and SVM, in which, when they evaluate with certain parameters like accuracy, precision, recall, F-score, and kappa value, they found that J 48 outperforms better with 91.4%. Deva Priya Isravel *et al.* [3] proposed an improved ML-IoT model for heart disease predictions. IoT atmosphere is created using LM35 temperature sensor, public sensor, AD8232 ECG sensor, and Arduino Uno, and continuous data are collected, and for training and testing phases, they use VA medical center, long beach, Cleveland Clinic foundation UCI dataset. They are given to classifiers like Naïve Bayes, KNN, and decision tree, in which decision tree outperform better than other methods.

A wearable architecture based on the IoT was proposed in [4] to test the ECG signals. This device provides a portable platform that uses a nonintrusive wearable sensor to capture ECG signals from the patient and send them to the IoT cloud through Bluetooth or ZigBee powered smart phone technologies. In order to find the disease, data collected in the cloud can be accessed by a professional for further processing using data analytics. The data analytics procedure for data cleaning, storage, review, and generation in real-time of notification warnings to the specialist concerned can be carried out by accessing the remote server. ML methods are used to promote the early diagnosis of heart disease. The research was conducted in from the health data collection to study the irregular functions of the heart. Using ML classification algorithms such as SVM, Adaboost, artificial neural network (ANN), and Naïve Bayes, the amplitude and interval periods of the cardiac waves were analyzed to identify the signals was seen in [5]. Identifying correct classifiers can assist the doctor in making diagnostic and prompt patient quality decisions. There are numerous ways of diseases of arrhythmia that are linked to heart rhythm disorders. Statistical and dynamic features are important for the extraction of ECG signals to ensure proper diagnosis. Heart rate variability is therefore computed in this paper [6] to produce warnings when the patient is affected by arrhythmia disease. In [7], the outlier-based warning system was used in a data-driven approach to classify patient anomaly data to minimize measurement errors. The system proved to be productive when qualified datasets were evaluated in a real-time system. Novel pre-processing for the classification of ECG data is suggested in the following section.

## 5.3   Interpretable Machine Learning in Healthcare

While the utilization of ML and counterfeit intelligence in medication has its foundations in the most recent days of the field, it is just lately that there has been a push toward the acknowledgment of the need to have medical care arrangements controlled by ML. This has driven specialists to propose that it is just a short time before ML will be pervasive in medical care.

Notwithstanding the acknowledgment of the estimation of ML in medical care, obstacles to additional appropriation remain. Particularly in basic use cases that incorporate clinical dynamic, there is some indecisive in the organization of such models in light of the fact that the expense of model misclassification is possibly high. Medical care swarms with conceivable "high stakes" uses of ML calculations: anticipating understanding danger of sepsis (a possibly hazardous reaction to contamination), foreseeing a patient's probability of readmission to the clinic, and foreseeing the requirement for end-of-life care. Interpretable ML along these lines permits the end client to grill, comprehend, troubleshoot, and even improve the ML framework. There is a lot of chance and interest for interpretable ML models in such circumstances. Interpretable ML models permit end clients to assess the model, preferably before a move is made by the end client, for example, the clinician. By clarifying the thinking behind forecasts, interpretable ML frameworks give clients motivations to acknowledge or dismiss expectations and proposals.

Reviews of ML frameworks in spaces like medical services and the criminal equity framework uncover that the choices and suggestions of ML frameworks might be one-sided. Accordingly, interpretability is expected to guarantee that such frameworks are liberated from inclination and reasonable in scoring distinctive ethnic and social gatherings. In conclusion, ML frameworks are previously settling on choices and suggestions for a huge number of individuals around the globe (for example, Netflix, Alibaba, and Amazon). These prescient calculations are having troublesome effects on society and bringing about unexpected results like deskilling of doctors. While the use of ML techniques to medical care issues is unavoidable given that intricacy of dissecting huge measures of information, the need to normalize the desire for interpretable ML in this space is basic. Verifiably, there has been a compromise between interpretable ML models and execution (exactness, review, F-Score, AUC, and so on) of the forecast models. That is, more interpretable models like regression models and decision trees regularly perform less well on numerous forecast undertakings contrasted with less interpretable models like slope boosting, Deep Learning (DL) models, and others. Specialists and researchers have needed to adjust the longing for the most exceptionally performing model to that which is enough interpretable. Over the most recent couple of years, analysts have proposed new models which display superior just as interpretability, e.g., GA2M, rule-based models like SLIM, falling principal records, and model refining. Be that as it may, the utility of these models in medical services has not been convincingly shown because of the uncommonness of their application.

The absence of interpretability in ML models can conceivably have unfavorable or even hazardous results. Consider a situation where the experiences from a discovery models are utilized for operationalization without the acknowledgment that the prescient model is not prescriptive in nature. For instance, consider Caruana *et al.* [8] chip away at building classifiers for naming pneumonia patients as high or generally safe for in-clinic mortality. A neural organization, basically, a black box as far as interpretability, ends up being the best classifier for this issue. Examination of this issue with relapse models uncovered that one of the top indicators showed restraint history of asthma, a constant pneumonic infection. The model was foreseeing that given asthma, a patient had a lower danger of in-clinic demise when conceded for pneumonia. Truth be told, the inverse is valid—patients with asthma are at higher danger for genuine complexities and sequelae, including demise, from an irresistible aspiratory infection like pneumonia. The asthma patients were, truth to be told, given more convenient consideration of a higher keenness than their partners without asthma, accordingly causing an endurance advantage. Likewise, spillage from information can mislead models or misleadingly swell execution during testing, anyway clarifications can be utilized to amend models when such issues surface. While there is a call to apply interpretable ML models to an enormous number of areas, medical services are especially testing because of medicolegal and moral necessities, laws, and guidelines, just as the genuine alert that must be utilized while wandering into this space. There are moral, lawful, and administrative difficulties that are remarkable to medical care given that medical services choices can immediately affect the prosperity or even the life of an individual. Guidelines like the European Union's General Data Protection Regulation (GDPR) require associations which utilize understanding information for expectations and proposals to give on request clarifications. The powerlessness to give such clarifications on request may bring about enormous punishments for the associations in question. Hence, there are financial just as administrative and well-being motivating forces related with interpretable ML models.

## 5.4   Opportunities in Machine Learning for Healthcare

ML has a huge part in technology advancements, and it has a wider part in every fields. Due to its accurate and efficient nature of model and the capability to analyze the complex data in a much simplistic way, it brings various applications that have been put forwarded by so many specialists out there. When comes to medical aspect, ML gives much hand-hand systems that could potentially make the service much accurate and efficient. So, here are some of medical related applications of ML:

a. **Identifying Diseases and Diagnosis:** One of the main difficult stages while implementing ML over this medical field is to identifying the disease and analyzing them. In case of identifying tumor stage, various hereditary related diseases also can be identified. A genome-based sequencing of tumor is developed by IBM Watson Genomics which makes fast and accurate results. ML is being used in Berg, the biopharma goliath an oncology section to create remedial medicines for curing the tumor. P1vital's PReDicT (Predicting Response to Depression Treatment) is also used for analyzing and providing treatment in several clinical conditions.

b. **Medication Discovery and Manufacturing:** ML is also being used in the medication part in which it needs R&D advances, such as sequencing and accurate medication that could potentially help in treating diseases that are multifactor. As of now, the AI strategies include solo realizing which can distinguish designs in information without giving any expectations. As an example, we take Hanover which is created by Microsoft that uses ML for treatment of malignant growth and also for other purposes and also for medication that is customisable for AML (Acute Myeloid Leukemia).

c. **Clinical Imaging Diagnosis:** DL is a subset of ML also being advanced in this area much wider in which these two combined to give computer vision (CV). With the help of these advancements, Microsoft created a device that could take inner shot of body that could use as further analysis.

d. **Customized Medicine:** Customized medicines can, in addition to the fact that more are successful by matching individual well-being with prescient investigation, likewise be ready for additional exploration and better infection appraisal. Right now, doctors are restricted to browsing a particular arrangement of determinations or gauge the danger to the patient dependent on his suggestive history and accessible hereditary data. As the nature of ML is progressing in which the Oncology department of IBM Watson is in the frontline in order develop such medicine based on the medical history that could potentially help various treatment. Coming years will be ML-IoT–based advancements that bring various devices that could intake vast data.

e. **ML-Based Behavioral Modification:** Conduct alteration is a significant piece of preventive medication, and since the time the expansion of ML in medical services, incalculable new businesses are springing up in the fields of malignant growth avoidance and distinguishing proof, understanding therapy. An organization called Somatrix which does a B2B2C-based analysis in which they also use ML in order perceive signals that are being used in daily lives.

f. **Brilliant Health Records:** Keeping up modern well-being records is a thorough cycle, and keeping in mind that innovation has had its influence in facilitating the information passage measure, truly even now, a dominant part of the cycles set aside a great deal of effort to finish. The main aim of ML is to build a model which we can invest less time and cash and, on that basis, classification of records is another process where ML comes in play where we use OCR tool for recognising text (for instance, Google Cloud Vision API ad MATLAB integration for ML-based penmanship). Nowadays, MIT has been in frontline for developing such model that helps in classification records, recommendation, and so on.

g. **Clinical Trial and Research:** ML is not that much affected in the case of trials and research as it requires a ton of time and research. When we apply ML on this area that could help in distinguishing these trials and predict the outcomes, this could potentially be helpful for scientists.

h. **Publicly Supported Data Collection:** Publicly supporting is extremely popular in the clinical field these days, permitting analysts and professionals to get to a huge measure of data transferred by individuals dependent on their own assent. When it comes to medication, publicly available dataset is much greater in terms of implication. A research kit developed by Apple uses facial recognition, as ML technology collects data and potentially helps to cure Aspergers and Parkinson disease. IBM also collaborated with Medtronic lately which collects data and makes accessible insulin with help of publicly available data.

i. **Better Radiotherapy:** This is one of the searched sessions where ML has been constantly applicable. With the help of ML, it is much simple and easier to analyze the clinical images and classify with accurate results with help of several models. By using ML models, we can classify it as ordinary or irregular, sore or non-injury, and so forth. An algorithm is developed by Google's DeepMind Health that could potentially help UCLH specialists that recognize contrast malignant images.

j. **Flare-Up Prediction:** AI and ML are being such great technology that could use for prediction of future and today; researchers approach a lot of information gathered from satellites, ongoing web-based media refreshes, site data, and so forth. ANN helps to gather this data and foresee everything from jungle fever episodes to serious persistent irresistible infections. Foreseeing these flare-ups is particularly useful in underdeveloped nations as they need critical clinical framework and instructive frameworks (e.g., ProMED-mail).

## 5.5 Why Combining IoT and ML?

As we know, IoT and ML need each in which IoT handles very large continuous data and can be enhanced by ML algorithms [9]. Since IoT connects many devices, it does have many imperfections like speed and accuracy of data while transmission. But when ML combines with IoT, it not only mimics like a human brain but also learns the pattern of its own. So, with the amount of data that is being generated by these IoT will be given to these machine models that could use this in learning stage that potentially improves the intelligent of physical devices.

### 5.5.1 ML-IoT Models for Healthcare Monitoring

ML has revolutionized in so many fields due to its accurate and efficient results and inside that DL also came as part of ML where it took ML into another level. Some of models related to DL and IoT in respective to healthcare are put forwarded. Wei-Long Zheng *et al.* [10] proposed emotion classifier based on EEG with the help of deep networks. They proposed deep neural network that could potentially classify into positive and negative. The emotional stage switching is analyzed by Hidden Markov Model (HMM) and Deep Belief Network (DBN). Here, features are extracted and are given to this model for further classification. This model is compared with other like KNN, SVM, and Graph Regularized

Extreme Learning Machine (GELM), in which the proposed model shows improved results than other like 87%. Musaed Alhussein and Ghulam Muhammad [11] proposed a voice pathology detection with the help of DL. They use a framework by using a mobile in which neural networks are performed. The dataset they used is Saarbrucken voice disorder in which it contains voices required for classifier to analyze. Here, they use CNN in specific VGG-16 network and so as other CaffNet models for further analysis. Initially, signals from smart mobile sensors capture data from patients, and then, they are transmitted to a machine and then to cloud where DL is performed. Once it is detected by the server cloud, cloud manager will send the decision to doctor where he analyzes these voice signals and then provides a feedback back to cloud. Then, this will return those to patient where he/she given a god medical care. As they evaluated this model with database, they used they get an accuracy of 98.7%, and in future, they add like dividing those voice signals into several band-limited and parallelly applying other CNN models. Also, a fusion of voice and EEG signals to can be added as input for further deep fusion strategy.

Jose Granados *et al.* [12] proposed a multichannel monitoring and classification of ECG signals with neural networks. Here, they try to classify the 12-lead config ECG in which they set a device of five multichannels that is connected with cloud via gateway of smartphone. By using GATT as protocol on this gateway, they can enable the notification, and with the help of WebSocket, they collect the data and these are passed to CNN in which they classify into different types of arrhythmias. They also added that in future they can implement energy efficient model and also FPGA-based neural networks. Trang Pham *et al.* [13] proposed a DeepCare which is a neural network which reads medical records, stores, deduces the current disease, and also predicts the outcomes of future. They use Long Short-Term Memory (LSTM) in order to avoid those irregularity events. Once all this is set up, at every step, they need to find the hidden state which will be using as future trajectory part. The three steps they do is disease progression followed by recommending interventions and then, finally, future risk prognosis. For this model performance, they collected data from regional Australian hospital. The priority they take in dataset contains a) admissions that have incomplete data of patients and b) patients who have less than two admissions. The limitation of this was that they build this for coded data and numerical data can be included, for that they need to extract feature vector per series.

Further, Dong Nie *et al.* [14] proposed a model that could produce CT from MRI images. For this, they use Generative Adversarial Network (GAN) with the help of fully connected network (FCN). To solve the discontinuity problem occurring in 2D CNN, they take 3D FCN for evaluating CT from MRI images. Then, they use the image gradient difference-based loss function for reducing blurriness of CT image obtained as output. Finally, they use auto-context model for refining the output. The dataset is of Alzheimer's Disease Neuroimaging Initiative (ADNI) and contains 16 subjects of both MRI and CT, and also, they use pelvic dataset contains 22 subjects of MRI and CT images. Edward Chol *et al.* [15] proposed a GAN for generating multilabel records of patients. By using GAN, they can generate high-dimensional variables that are discrete say binary, count features, etc. For this, the Palo Alto Medical Foundation (PAMF) dataset contains 258,000 patient records of 10-year-old. They also propose a minibatch averaging in order to avoid the collapse that can happen in mode, so as to increase the efficiency using batch normalization.

## 5.6 Applications of Machine Learning in Medical and Pharma

The main applications of ML technique in healthcare are as follows:

**Identifying Diseases and Diagnosis:** ML application play a vital role in identifying the deadly disease such as cancer and genetic disorder which are very difficult to identify by manual operation. This ML application provides a feasible way for the identification and diagnosis of disease and also provides a routine clinical condition for the affected person.

**Drug Discovery and Manufacturing:** An early stage drug development method is one of the principal clinical applications of ML. This also comprises of R&D innovations such as next-generation pattern and precise medicine that can help define potential mechanisms for multifactorial disease therapy. Currently, ML includes supervised learning techniques that can recognize patterns in data without prediction.

**Medical Imaging Diagnosis:** The breakthrough technology called CV is the responsibility of ML and DL. Microsoft's Inner Eye initiative operates as a diagnostic image tool to analyze images. As ML becomes easier and explanatory, more data sources from different medical imaging sources are to be expected to form part of this diagnostic process powered by AI.

**Machine Learning-Based Behavioral Modification:** Behavioral modification is an important component of preventive medicine, with several start-ups being produced in cancer prevention and identification, patient management, etc., after the proliferation of computers in health-care. Somatix is a B2B2C-based data analytics company that has launched an ML-based framework to identify movements we make in our every-day lives to help us understand and make appropriate adjustments to our unconscious actions.

**Better Radiotherapy:** Radiology is one of the most common applications in the field of ML in healthcare. The analyses of the medical image have sev-eral discrete variables which can occur at any time. Many tumors, cancer focuses, etc., cannot be modeled simply by means of complex equations. As ML-based algorithms learn from several different samples, diagnosing and finding variables is easier. The classification of artifacts like lesions into categories such as normal or abnormal lesions or lesion, etc., is one of the most common applications of ML in analyzing medical images.

## 5.7   Challenges and Future Research Direction

Even though ML and DL have that huge potential for integrating with so much other technology, we should also look for some challenges that could be evaluated and incorporated as well [16]:

a. Massive scale of IoT data: As IoT is generating huge and continuous real time data that could be a challenge to ML/DL in terms of time consumption and the complexities in the structure. As the data instances increases, so as the accu-racy of that model will be increase and also the resources need to develop this model also gets increased. So, for that, these models can be run in a distributed framework in a parallel processing way, but further research is also need to develop this issue.

b. Data pre-processing: In the case of IoT, it is hard to find and pre-process such massive data that contains errors.

c. High velocity: Even though IoT produce such vast data at a certain rate in which processing such fast data and ana-lyzing them is challenging and the solution is to reduce is that by providing online learning. Also, further research is needed for integrating online learning with ML/DL models.

d. Heterogeneity: However, these ML/DL models analyze many different data and the challenge arrives while man-aging them in order to avoid conflicts between the formats.

e. Requirement of large IoT data sets: As these ML models are performed under large dataset in which IoT may or may not provide that large data that is potentially needed for a ML model to perform.

f. Models for IoT devices: Making a model that is as much constrained with IoT in which both could perform well is another task need to be taken care.

Further, the readers are suggested to refer work [17–24] to know more about raised issues in healthcare services and solutions provided by AI-based techniques for the healthcare application.

Also, many future research opportunities have been discussed in [17–24] for future researchers, i.e., to find a problem for their research.

## 5.8    Conclusion

This proposed work mainly focus on patient heath monitoring by integrated the concept of IoT and ML, which will help us to determine and diagnose the deadly disease in an efficient way. This paper mainly focused on the advances of ML and IoT in healthcare section and also discussed some of the advance works that have been put forwarded by researchers in past years. Authors also attempt to address the challenges that could be solved in future integration of ML and IoT when implementing over healthcare. This paper also helps other researchers out there to analyze and to be inspired to create further models that could potentially help healthcare workers in many diagnostic areas.

## References

1. Yadav, S. and Jadhav, S., Machine learning algorithms for disease prediction using IoT environment. *Int. J. Eng. Adv. Technol. (IJEAT)*, 8, 6, 4303–4307, August 2019.

2. Ganesan, M. and Sivakumar, N., IoT based heart disease prediction and diagnosis model for healthcare using machine learning models. *2019 IEEE Int. Conf. Syst. Comput. Autom. Netw. (ICSCAN)*, 1–5, 2019. DOI: 10.1109/ICSCAN.2019.8878850.

3. Isravel, D.P., Darcini S, V.P., Silas, S., Improved heart disease diagnostic IoT model using machine learning techniques. *Int. J. Sci. Technol. Res.*, 9, 02, 4442–4446, February 2020.

4. Yang, Z., Zhou, Q., Lei, L., Zheng, K., An IoT-cloud based wearable ECG monitoring system for smart healthcare, *J. Med. Syst.*, 286, 2016.

5. Celin, S. and Vasanth, K., ECG signal classification using various machine learning techniques. *J. Med. Syst.*, 42, 2018, 10.1007/s10916-018-1083-6.

6. Kalaivani, R.L.D.V., Machine learning and IoT-based cardiac arrhythmia diagnosis using statistical and dynamic features of ECG. *J. Supercomput.*, 9/2020, 47–55, 2019, https://www.springerprofessional.de/en/the-journal-of-supercomputing-9-2020/18221258

7. Hauskrecht, M., Batal, I., Valko, M., Visweswaran, S., Cooper, G.F., Clermont, G., Outlier detection for patient monitoring and alerting. *J. Biomed. Inform.*, 46, 1, 47–55, February 2013, https://www.sciencedirect.com/science/journal/15320464.

8. Caruana, R., Lou, Y., Gehrke, J., Intelligible models for HealthCare: Predicting pneumonia risk and hospital 30-day readmission. *Proc. 21th ACM SIGKDD Int. Conf. Knowl. Discov. Data Mining*, 46, 1, February 2013.

9. Vilmate Blog, open source: https://vilmate.com/blog/why-use-ai-enabled-iot-in-healthcare/, Pattern Recognit Lett., pp. 346–353, 2020, https://www.ncbi.nlm.nih.gov/pmc/articles/PMC7217772/.

10. Zheng, W.-L., Zhu, J.-Y., Peng, Y., Bao-Liang, L., EEG-based emotion classification using deep belief networks. *IEEE Int. Conf. Multimed. Exp.*, 346–353, 2014.

11. Alahussein, M. and Muhammad, G., Voice pathology detection using deep learning on mobile healthcare framework. *Appl. Sci.*, 10, 3723, 1–13, 2020.

12. Granados, J., Westerlund, T., Zheng, L., Zou, Z., IoT platform for real-time multichannel ECG monitoring and classification with neural networks, in: *11th International Conference on Research and Practical Issues of Enterprise Information Systems (CONFENIS)*, pp. 181–191, Shanghai, China, Oct. 2017.

13. Pham, T., Tran, T., Phung, D., Venkatesh, S., Predicting healthcare trajectories from medical records: A deep learning approach. *J. Biomed. Inform.*, 69, 218–229, 2017, https://www.sciencedirect.com/science/journal/15320464.

14. Nie, D., Trullo, R., Lian, J., Ruan, C.P.S., Wang, Q., Shen, D., Medical image synthesis with context-aware generative adversarial networks, 417–425, 2018.

15. Choi, E., Biswal, S., Malin, B., Duke, J., Stewart, W.F., Sun, J., Generating multi-label discrete patient recordsusing generative adversarial networks, in: *Proceedings of Machine Learning for Healthcare 2017*, vol. 68, JMLR W&C Track, 2017.

16. Saleem, T.J. and Chishti, M.A., Deep learning for Internet of Things data analytics. *Digit. Commun. Netw.*, 2019.

17. Nair, M.M. and Tyagi, A.K., Privacy: History, Statistics, Policy, Laws, Preservation and Threat Analysis. *J. Inf. Assur. Sec.*, 16, 1, 24–34, 11p. 2021.

18. Tyagi, A.K., Nair, M.M., Niladhuri, S., Abraham, A., Security, privacy research issues in various computing platforms: A survey and the road ahead. *J. Inf. Assur. Sec.*, 15, 1, 1–16, 16p, 2020.

19. Tyagi, A.K. and Nair, M.M., Deep learning for clinical and health informatics, in the book, in: *Computational Analysis and Deep Learning for Medical Care: Principles, Methods, and Applications*, 28 July 2021, https://doi.org/10.1002/9781119785750.ch5.

20. Kumari S., Vani V., Malik S., Tyagi A.K., Reddy S., Analysis of text mining tools in disease prediction. In: *Hybrid Intelligent Systems. HIS 2020. Advances in Intelligent Systems and Computing*, A., Abraham, T., Hanne, O., Castillo, N., Gandhi, T., Nogueira Rios, T.P., Hong (eds.), vol. 1375, Springer, Cham., 2021, https://doi.org/10.1007/978-3-030-73050-5_55

21. Gudeti, B., Mishra, S., Malik, S., Fernandez, T.F., Tyagi, A.K., Kumari, S., A novel approach to predict chronic kidney disease using machine learning algorithms, in: *2020 4th International Conference on Electronics, Communication and Aerospace Technology (ICECA)*, pp. 1630–1635, Coimbatore, 2020, doi: 10.1109/ICECA49313.2020.9297392.

22. Tyagi, A.K., Gupta, M., Aswathy S.U., Ved, C., Healthcare solutions for smart era: An useful explanation from user's perspective, in: *Recent Trends in Blockchain for Information Systems Security and Privacy*, CRC Press, 2021.

23. Tyagi, A.K. and Chahal, P., Artificial intelligence and machine learning algorithms, in: *Challenges and Applications for Implementing Machine Learning in Computer Vision*, IGI Global, 2020. DOI: 10.4018/978-1-7998-0182-5.ch008.

24. Tyagi, A.K., and Rekha, G., Challenges of applying deep learning in real-world applications, in: *Challenges and Applications for Implementing Machine Learning in Computer Vision*, p. 92–118. IGI Global 2020, DOI: 10.4018/978-1-7998-0182-5.ch004.

# 6

# Machine Learning–Based Disease Diagnosis and Prediction for E-Healthcare System

**Shruti Suhas Kute[1], Shreyas Madhav A. V.[1*],**
**Shabnam Kumari[2] and Aswathy S. U.[3]**

*[1]School of Computer Science and Engineering, Vellore Institute of Technology,*
*Chennai, Tamil Nadu, India*
*[2]SRM Institute of Science and Technology, Chennai, Tamil Nadu, India*
*[3]Department of Computer Science and Engineering, Jyothi Engineering College,*
*Cheruthuruthy, Thrissur, Kerala, India*

## Abstract

The rapid development of IoT and AI technologies over the past decade has resulted in the rise of several medical applications for digitizing the healthcare sector. One important domain within healthcare is that has yielded maximal benefits due to the integration of emerging technologies in medical diagnostics. The diagnosis of a disease requires an in-depth analysis of a patient's symptoms, genetic history, environmental conditions, and so on. In a traditional healthcare system, doctors arrive at informed conclusions by studying the data presented to them by the patients and their health records. The advent of IoT and deep learning has caused a metamorphosis of conventional medical diagnostics into automated decision-making systems powered by machine learning. The requirements of doctor's intervention at every step are minimized and consultations are made after initial automated screening tests. Several machine learning frameworks have been established in the past for the diagnosis of a wide collection of diseases including different forms of cancer, Alzheimer's disease, skin condition, etc. The integration of machine learning–based inferences with IoT-based healthcare systems has been established and is projected to become mainstream during the upcoming years. This paper focuses on the existing role of IoT and machine learning applications in detecting and identifying the presence of medical conditions in patients.

---

*\*Corresponding author:* shreyas.madhav@gmail.com

Archana Mire, Shaveta Malik and Amit Kumar Tyagi (eds.) Advanced Analytics and Deep Learning
Models, (127–148) © 2022 Scrivener Publishing LLC

This chapter places a special focus on conditions affecting the heart and the brain, two of the most vital organs in the human body.

**Keywords:** Healthcare, Internet of Things, human intelligence, machine intelligence

## 6.1  Introduction

IoT's role in healthcare has changed people's lives, particularly more seasoned patients, by empowering steady and remote monitoring of medical problems. The major benefits are yielded by individuals living alone and in need of medical care. On the occurrence of any unsettling development or changes in the standard behavior of a patient, the IoT component of the healthcare system can facilitate instant communication to relatives and concerned well-being suppliers. IoT frameworks have come to fruition in the healthcare industry to ease the diagnostic and monitoring processes involved in patient care. Fall identification frameworks for elderly homes are a prominent example of IoT inpatient monitoring [1]. The frameworks do not exclusively operate on alarms but also dispatches communication models, similar to voice help and camera recognition to lower and panic by providing constant status updates [2]. Such implementations will empower more seasoned grown-ups to act with the framework unafraid of an expectation to absorb information. The extended IoT-based fall discovery framework enables family and guardians to be immediately advised of the occasion and distantly screen the person. Incorporated at stretches a reasonable home air, the extended IoT-based fall discovery framework will improve the norm of life among more established grown-ups. IoT networks provide instant intercommunication and increase the efficiency of daily processes in healthcare. IoT implementations help provide a better patient experience with reduced error rates, with the ability to monitor and attend to patients from the comfort of their homes. The end node devices of the network that are in direct interaction with the patient play a crucial role of collecting data on the patient's condition and the overall environment. Any anomalous changes in the patient's vitals or condition are constantly monitored with regular updation to the concerned healthcare professionals.

While IoT applications are gaining traction in the field of healthcare, the integration of deep learning models will help escalate the beneficial attributes of IoT to the next level. The proactive nature of the technology and data collection capacities makes it one of the most suitable technologies for integration with machine learning applications. Deep learning is a subspace of artificial intelligence (AI) and is widely regarded for its efficiency in tackling computer vision problems. Its functioning depends on learning various degrees of reflection and portrayal of the data provided to it. Computational models are available in the profound discovery that comprises different handling layers to learn the features of information with various degrees of reflection. Image analysis of X-rays, MRIs, and CT scans can help detect aberrations in the organ's nature. While deep learning of images can help arrive at visual determinants of a disease, the analysis of large amounts of sample data can help develop patterns that are cannot be efficiently extracted by a human. Monitoring gene expression levels also plays a huge role in assessing hereditary diseases [3] and is immensely dependent upon machine learning. The combinational advantages of reliable data collection and communication of IoT networks with the learning capability of machine learning accelerate the diagnosis of patients in real-time. This chapter discusses the application of machine learning models in IoT healthcare systems for diagnosing heart and brain-related health problems. The topics of this chapter cover the machine learning techniques employed in biomedical imaging, brain tumor classification based on machine learning and IoT, early detection systems for dementia machine learning applications for a real-time monitoring of Arrhythmia patients using IoT, and IoT machine learning integration for diagnosis and prediction of medical conditions.

## 6.2 Literature Survey

IoT is spreading expeditiously in these recent years and its positive attributes in everyday life and applications are snowballing. It is essentially a network that interfaces web-associated genuine gadgets, vehicles, structures, and implants with actual science, programming, sensors, actuators, and organization property to gather and trade data. It is been used in a lot of areas, such as transportation and conveyance space, climate expectations [5], and for individual and social applications. It is very predictable since the IoT can constitute almost 50 billion articles by 2020. The ascent in the number of web-associated gadgets and IoT that were initially aligned toward developing smart homes has enabled us to have houses with great technological improvements to make accommodation safe and comfortable. These web associated gadgets form the outer layer of a network of gadgets called the Internet of Things (IoT). Telemedicine is furthermore another IoT application that has been making progress over the previous few years [6]. With the development of smart systems administration and processing, IoT applications have a splendid and boundless future in enhancing the management of other technologies. Be it engineers, specialists, business people or researchers, it is time they considered M2M correspondence as an adaptable innovation that utilizes normal gear in more up to date implementations [7]. Developing the pace of the maturing populace and making medical services reasonable and accessible in distant territories are two key difficulties that the medical care industry must stay aware of. The vital resources of the Indian restorative administration structure are a direct result of its overall arranged helpful staff. Different undertakings have been made to upgrade the nature and nature of human administrations given by these offices. Khambete examines the undertakings that have been made to upgrade the well-being structure. Likewise, it features the weaknesses of therapeutic staff, well-being issues, and the reasonable moves which ought to be made in thought to improve the idea of human administrations in India.

Medical diagnosis is of prime interest for the application of AI solutions that are compatible with an IoT framework. Priyan Malarvizhi Kumar *et al.* introduced three-level engineering of IoT with AI calculation for coronary illness early identification. They have proposed three-level structures to store and cycle through enormous amounts of information which are delivered via wearable devices. Level 1 spotlights an assortment of information from different sensors, level 2 uses Apache HBase for putting away a huge volume of information into cloud computing, while level 3 uses Apache Mahout for creating calculated relapse-based expectation models. At last, it does a ROC examination to get a nodal investigation of coronary illness. In 2016, Mingyu Park *et al.* implemented a novel seat framework that records and pictures the user's activities through a cell phone application to enable the clients to address their uneven stance. They had utilized weight sensors and tilt detecting even though they had utilized I-Beacon and Bluetooth innovation for correspondence reasons which send information with low force utilization. It is an Arduino usage that mostly recognizes different client stances. This usage supplements the client to sit effectively with the acknowledgment of their own present status by giving instinctive and envisioned information progressively to cell phone applications. The left and the right side show a genuine versus ideal stance with the weight appearing around and around with red/yellow/green and orange tones. This is a genuine case of IoT innovation.

Cloud and IoT-based m-medical care applications have been delivered and realized for noticing the certified seriousness level and diagnosing them according to the earnestness. The wearable and implanted IoT devices are utilized as IoT contraptions. These devices are used to accumulate the remedial data from far off regions. The quick assessment can be accumulated as helpful data that are assembled through IoT contraptions, associated with the human body. Related restorative data is delivered by using the UCI Repository dataset and the helpful sensors for envisioning everyone who has been impacted with diabetes very. The came about data will be spared securely by applying five particular periods of an as of late proposed stockpiling technique, for instance, data stockpiling, data recuperation, data accumulation, data partitioning, and data blending. Cloud computing is a stage that awards on-interest for coordinated admittance to planning executives. This state works outside of anybody's capacity to see and is utilized to get information from the shrewd things, take a gander at and decipher this information and give electronic perceptions to the client. This is additionally generally a dazzling part for frameworks since this will make a market with a ton of occasions to make a driving force for clients of IoT applications. The assessment of this information in the cloud will routinely be performed by colossal information assessment and AI assessments. AI enables these calculations to develop themselves by getting from their information input. A WSN is a course of action of self-choice sensors that send their information through the structure to a focal zone. An IoT structure can utilize a WSN for the assortment of information for a lot of clients. Until now, not many out of each odd IoT framework will utilize one since there are different particular possible outcomes. The total information is just the fundamental advance of an IoT framework; further, this information must be isolated and changed into critical data or gave to different articles. The sensors used for the WSN achieve the probability to make any action splendid and the giant headway in these sensors is apparently the guideline improvement that started the IoT progression.

Deep learning techniques to interpret MRI scans require the medical images to be preprocessed and reconstructed to achieve a proper diagnosis [4]. The visual features and pixel information can help establish dominant patterns in the patient's scans to identify underlying diseases. Cloud-based health diagnosis systems that generate user diagnosis results by operating on the server-side are prominent in several medical and healthcare centers to provide preliminary general screening of a patient. Pre-trained classification and prediction models play a huge role in efficiently identifying the disease labels. Wearable technology and computational learning have ensured the omnipresent nature of healthcare systems in tackling diseases primarily affecting senior citizens like Parkinson's disease [8]. One observed trend in the analysis of existing technology is the special importance placed upon heart and brain conditions due to their criticality and threat to life. The sedentary lifestyles of the population have resulted in a massive surge in the total number of heart disease patients over the past decade. IoT healthcare systems and associated modeling techniques elevate the efficiency of cardiovascular conditions and abnormalities [9]. Hybrid machine learning techniques have also facilitated this mitigation [10]. Several frameworks have been developed for the process of monitoring heart patients using multi-domain technologies like fog computing, deep learning, and IoT [11]. Similar deep learning and IoT developments have also been established for brain tumor segmentation and localization [12]. In this chapter, we emphasize the prominent brain and heart diseases and state-of-the-art technology that has been developed with the hopes of combating them.

## 6.3 Machine Learning Applications in Biomedical Imaging

AI appears to have the option to "see" patterns that are past human observation. This disclosure has prompted significant and expanded revenue in the field of AI—explicitly, how it very well may be applied to clinical pictures. AI is a strategy for perceiving features and understanding their significance in clinical pictures. Pixel-based analysis of the AI calculation framework at that point recognizes the best mix of these picture highlights for grouping the picture or processing some measurement for the given picture locale. There are a few strategies that can be utilized, each with various qualities and shortcomings. There are open-source variants of a large portion of these AI techniques that make them simple to attempt to apply to pictures. A few measurements for estimating the presence of a calculation exist; nonetheless, one must know about the conceivably related traps that can bring about misdirecting measurements. All the more as of late, deep learning has begun to be utilized; this strategy has the advantage that it does not need a picture include distinguishing proof and figuring as an initial step; rather, highlights are recognized as a feature of the learning cycle. AI has been utilized in clinical imaging and will have a more noteworthy impact later on. Those working in clinical imaging must know about how AI functions.

Computer-supported discovery and conclusion performed by utilizing AI calculations can assist doctors with interpreting clinical imaging discoveries and lessen translation times. These calculations have been utilized for a few testing undertakings, for example, aspiratory embolism division with Computed Tomography (CT) angiography, polyp recognition with virtual colonoscopy or CT in the setting of colon malignant growth, bosom malignancy discovery, and conclusion with mammography, cerebrum tumor division with medical reverberation (MR) imaging, and identification of the psychological condition of the mind with practical MR imaging to analyze neurologic sickness (e.g., Alzheimer illness). Respiratory disease detection from chest scans and x-rays have also helped control communicable diseases like COVID-19, pneumonia, and so on. Low dose protocols of frequent tests and screening for combined PET/CT scans can be disadvantageous in the fact that the ability to visually comprehend them requires precision. That precision is enhanced by applying image enhancement techniques to provide an image similar to a standard PET/CT scan [13]. These altered images can be fitted easily into a deep learning model to get accurate results. Apart from diseases exhibiting internal symptoms, conditions that present externally like skin lesions and ulcers [14] have also been efficiently classified using machine learning techniques. Image segmentation processing is to identify the regions of injury from images of the wound. Sudden changes in a person's skin color or texture is a cause of concern and may be the symptom of a major underlying disease. Machine learning algorithms were applied based upon RGB analysis and extraction of GLCM features to characterize the inherent visual presentation of skin disease [15]. The study tested out several ML models for a wide array of diseases including psoriasis, eczema, and fungal infections. Skin cancer research has also been accelerated by the advent of AI computations and machine intelligence. Ensemble machine learning techniques have shown significant progress in the early detection of malign melanoma [16] and made use of texture, color, and skeleton of the affected area to grade the disease. In most cases of medical imaging, it is essential to establish a proper region of interest to focus on the most important features of the disease present in the image. Segmented images eliminate unnecessary background information. CNN architecture models are the most used in deriving medical inferences and diagnosing diseases. One particular field of interest where CNNs are employed is for the processing of carotid artery ultrasounds [17]. Several similar systems have been proposed for accelerating the process of patient diagnosis. The application of deep learning solutions to the biomedical image is highly accurate and removes the need for doctoral intervention during the preliminary stages of a diagnosis.

## 6.4   Brain Tumor Classification Using Machine Learning and IoT

Brain tumors drastically reduce the life expectancy of a person and, in most cases, are terminal. This is considered as one of the major problems that affect one of the most vital organs of our body. Radiologists have been employing several imaging techniques including X-ray, Magnetic Resonance Imaging (MRIs), Ultrasound, and Computed Tomography (CT) to monitor any abnormal visual growths. Convolutional Neural Network (CNN), a kind of deep learning system is normally utilized for picture arrangement undertakings including object location, confinement, and characterization. It learns the highlights naturally, eliminates manual element extraction, and consequently wipes out the human intercession. CNN typically requires a dataset for preparing that is named and in this way, it is a regulated learning technique motivated by creature visual cortex. The convolutional layer comprises channels for applying on input picture and afterward after the produced information is passed to the Pooling layer. Highlight maps are created at every convolution layer. It is obtained through registering convolutions between neighborhood fixes and weight vectors ordinarily called channels. Highlight maps are a gathering of nearby weighted entities. To improve the effectiveness of preparing, channels are applied over and over. This cycle assists with lessening the number of boundaries during learning measures. To deal with more unpredictable highlights, this cycle is presented and utilized. Finally, completely associated layers are functioning as an ordinary neural organization. The last learning stage maps the highlights to the anticipated yields. Generally, most extremely profound convolutional neural organizations are set up with set convolution layers, thick layers, sub-testing layer, and delicate max layer. The overall philosophy of applying the deep learning models and structures to identify, find, and foresee the tumor.

Automation of MRI-based detection of brain tumors has been achieved with the flow of the process including image filtering, noise removal, thresholding, and feature extraction from the regions of interest [18]. Grayscale MRIs are processed to isolate discrepancies in the brain structure and identify abnormal growths in scans with low color scale variations. These models always satisfy the accuracy requirement specified for human doctors while completing the process efficiently in much lesser time. The variability of brain tumors in structure and size showcases the need for robust systems that maintain accuracy in their diagnosis. Recent developments in novel feature representation strategies for tissue segmentation in multimodal images, for exploration and extraction of the local and overall information. Feature learning kernels were modality-specific random forests [19]. Sparse representation–based contour modeling techniques were employed in the later stages to visualize the analyzed information on the MRI scans. Morphological processing of medical images is extremely useful in making the feature extraction process easier, especially in the case of brain MRIs. It enables the disregarding of impulse noises that have affected the image during the time of capture [20]. The usage of region-based convolutional neural networks for localization and isolation of the tumor growing region helps enhance the robustness of the brain tumor detection system [21].

In recent times, several frameworks have been progressing toward wide stream implementations for classifying brain tumor images. Optimization of tumor parameters and the registration of brain tumor images (ORBIT) is a famous application of the aforementioned domain [22]. The integration of IoT technology with machine learning has been particularly helpful in the case of brain tumor recognition. The prediction of brain tumors by utilizing IoT to extract physical symptoms related to brain tumors [23]. Fractal-based IoT frameworks integrated with cloud services have also propelled the detection process of brain tumors.

## 6.5    Early Detection of Dementia Disease Using Machine Learning and IoT-Based Applications

Dementia, a sickness of the mind, assaults intellectual exercises such as memory, sanity, and thought. The risk of dementia increases with age and may also be caused due to severe injuries, with around 65% of the cases inferable from Alzheimer's illness. Note that a dementia increment is its terminal nature without an early diagnosis. The process cycle of conclusion includes three stages. The first step is achieved by getting a consultation from a doctor. The second stage introduces the body and mind to a variety of neuropsychological tests. The diagnosis is finalized by getting an MRI scan of the patient. Several modern methodologies are geared toward the early determination of dementia by methods for neuropsychological testing pair with segment data. Usually utilized testing measures abide by the Mini-Mental State Examination (MMSE), the Consortium to Establish a Registry for Alzheimer's Disease (CERAD), the Blessed Orientation-Memory-Concentration Test (BOMC), the Montreal Cognitive Assessment (MoCA), a short source meeting to distinguish dementia (AD8), and the General Practitioner Assessment of Cognition (GPCOG), with each introducing certain focal points and constraints. CERAD and MMSE are most often incorporated since they are indifferent to the subject's sex, instruction, culture, or religion.

Machine learning strategies have been brought into determining the outcomes of the aforementioned tests as they are computationally uniform, resulting in minimal errors and inequalities. This provides a chance to eliminate human error in a process that is extremely delicate and determinant of the patient's future. Experiments to decide the capacity of AI calculations to take over the neuropsychological and extract significant segmentation have been looked into extensively in the hope of digitizing the early detection of dementia. Chen and Herskovits investigated the implementations of SVM and Bayesian Classifiers for evaluating the members affected by early dementia. Joshi *et al.* employ AI and neural organization strategies for ordering dementia states to improve the precision over present dementia screening instruments and MMSE. The discoveries clearly demonstrated the accuracy and precision of the combined tests by employing AI. Trambaiolli and Lorena recently utilized information from electroencephalography tests to group patients with ordinary comprehension and Alzheimer's or MCI by learning the EEG example of Alzheimer's patients utilizing the SVM calculation. Accordingly, EEG Epochs indicated 79.9% exactness and the SVM result was about 87%. Williams and Weakley explored the Clinical Dementia Rating score and implemented a strategy for screening dementia utilizing Decision Tree, Naive Bayes, SVM, and Artificial Neural Networks (ANN), and. The consequences of the assessment of the seriousness of dementia indicated that Naive Bayes was the most exact and SVM had the least precision. Cho and Chen proposed a leveled twofold layer structure for the early conclusion of dementia. This is a model that predicts early analysis of dementia utilizing a Bayesian organization in the top-layer after analytic expectation with FCM and PNN calculation in the base-layer when a psychological test, for example, MMSE and CERAD is performed. In this model, the exactness of FCM and PNN was 74% and 69%, separately, however, MCI and dementia were not very much ordered when contrasting ordinary, MCI, and dementia. Shankle and Mani performed CDR expectations utilizing AI techniques and electronic clinical records. For Naive Bayes, the precision was the most noteworthy, while for different calculations, it was lower than Bayesian, yet it was about 70% exact.

The conclusion of dementia comprises an enormous piece of evaluating the diverse intellectual capacities for common deficiencies in thinking processes. This results in doctors deciphering tests that bring about clashing results: Rather than the previously mentioned considerations, a two-layered various leveled approach for assessing and making differentiations between ordinary, MCI, and early dementia can propel the accuracy of the diagnosis. This methodology is obtained from the dementia focus on symptomatic techniques which include a three-way blend of intellectual testing, neuropsychological screening, and early detection of the disease. In this exploration, we plan to utilize neuropsychological and segment data to foresee ordinary, MCI, and dementia inside our proposed model by applying seven habitually utilized AI models including Naive Bayes, Logistic Regression, Random Forest, Bayes Network, Begging, SVM, and MLP. Immediate intuitional diagnosis is provided which can help attain informed conclusions by the physicians.

## 6.6 IoT and Machine Learning-Based Diseases Prediction and Diagnosis System for EHRs

Other methodologies in healthcare utilize AI to associate patient's EHR information, including gene and drug history analysis, to measure infection hazard, as indicated by an investigation distributed in cell patterns. While EHRs contain significant data about patients' medical issues and the consideration they get, these records are not generally exact. EHRs may not be immediate markers of patients' actual well-being states at various focuses as expected, yet rather reflect clinical cycles, patients' cooperation with the framework, and the accounting cycle.

Specialists from Massachusetts General Hospital built up a system that utilizes AI to gather data on patients' findings and drugs over the long run, as opposed to from free well-being records. "Over the previous decade, billions of dollars have been spent to initiate significant utilization of EHR frameworks. For a large number of reasons, notwithstanding, EHR information is as yet perplexing and have adequate quality issues, which make it hard to use this information to address squeezing medical problems, particularly during pandemics, for example, COVID-19, when quick reactions are required," said lead creator Hossein Estiri. "In this paper, we propose a calculation for abusing the worldly data in the EHRs that is contorted by layers of authoritative and medical care framework measures." Investigations uncovered that this consecutive methodology can precisely anticipate the probability that a patient may really have a hidden infection.

"The worldly connections encoded in the new methodology catch a portion of the complexities of the clinical cycle that are lost in the traditional methodology," the scientists noted. For instance, coronary supply route

**Table 6.1** Literature review of existing technological works on Alzheimer's disease.

| Applications | Methodology | $N_s$ | Performance |
|---|---|---|---|
| Diagnosis of Alzheimer's disease | NBC, RF, RLO, RS, and SVM | 27 | Accuracy = 97.14% |
| Diagnosis of Alzheimer's disease | SVM | 53 | Accuracy = 96.23% |
| Diagnosis of dementias | LR and SVM | 29 | Accuracy = 93% |
| Detection of Alzheimer's disease related regions | SVM | 126 | Accuracy = 92.36% |
| Predicting mild cognitive impairment patients for conversion to Alzheimer's disease | LDS | 164 | AUC = 0.7661 |
| Predicting mild cognitive impairment patients for conversion to Alzheimer's disease | GA and SVM | 458 | Sensitivity = 76.92%; Specificity = 73.23%; Accuracy = 75% |
| Identification of dissociable multivariate morphological patterns | LC | 801 | AUC = 0.93 |
| Identification for Alzheimer's disease and mild cognitive impairment | EM and SVM | 338 | Alzheimer's disease: sensitivity = 84.86%, specificity = 91.69%, accuracy = 88.73%; Mild cognitive impairment: sensitivity = 79.07%, specificity = 82.7%, accuracy = 80.91% |

*(Continued)*

**Table 6.1** Literature review of existing technological works on Alzheimer's disease. (*Continued*)

| Applications | Methodology | N$_s$ | Performance |
|---|---|---|---|
| Identification for Alzheimer's disease and mild cognitive impairment | DCNN | 900 | Alzheimer's disease: sensitivity = 98.89%, specificity = 97.78%, accuracy = 98.33%; Mild cognitive impairment: sensitivity = 92.23%, specificity = 91.11%, accuracy = 92.12% |
| Identification for Alzheimer's disease and mild cognitive impairment | DCNN | 142 | Alzheimer's disease: sensitivity = 85%, specificity = 82%, accuracy = 85%; Mild cognitive impairment: sensitivity = 84%, specificity = 81%, accuracy = 85% |
| Identification of genes related to Alzheimer's disease | DT and QAR | 33 | 90 genes are related to Alzheimer's disease |
| Identification of genes related to Alzheimer's disease | ELM, RF, and SVM | 31 | Sensitivity = 78.77%; Specificity = 83.1%; Accuracy = 74.67% |

infection followed by chest torment in the clinical record was discovered to be more helpful in anticipating the advancement of cardiovascular breakdown than both of the components all alone or in an alternate request.

In the Table 6.1, literature review of existing technological works on Alzheimer's disease can be found. The new methodology could give suppliers new bits of knowledge into regular infections, and feature designs that may be more subtle to parental figures. "Our investigation does not depend on single demonstrative codes yet rather depends on groupings of codes with the desire that a succession of important attributes over the long run is bound to speak to reality more than a solitary component," Estiri said. "Also, the AI figures out a large number of patients and can discover groupings that a doctor would probably never recognize all alone as pertinent, yet really are related to the infection." The strategy could likewise help distinguish infection markers that are interpretable by clinicians. This could prompt new computational models for recognizing and approving new sickness markers and for propelling clinical revelations. The proposed perspective about clinical records could likewise help recognize patients in a network who are in danger of building up an assortment of different illnesses and suggest their assessment by medical services rehearses. The consequences of the investigation exhibit the utility and estimation of fleeting information in the EHR, and how this data can be utilized to advise care rehearsals.

RS, random subspace; DCNN, deep convolutional neural network; DT, decision tree; ELM, extreme learning machine; GA, genetic algorithm; SVM, support vector machine; LC, lasso classification; LDS, low density separation; NBC, Naive Bayes classifier; QAR, quantitative association rules; RF, random forest; RLO, random linear oracle; EM, expectation-maximization; LR, logistic regression.

## 6.7    Machine Learning Applications for a Real-Time Monitoring of Arrhythmia Patients Using IoT

Constant checking of dangerous cardiovascular sickness like arrhythmia utilizing wearable sensors and IoT gadgets clears approaches to versatile well-being (m-well-being) frameworks. Cell phones with ML applications, wearable sensors, and IoT gadgets are the significant advances of the existing arrhythmia observing frameworks. In-house nonstop cardiovascular checking is extant with the utilization of AI procedures to foresee the side effects of arrhythmia by ordering the information acquired from the UCI vault. The physiological sign electrocardiogram (ECG) is considered to portray the irregular conduct of the cardiovascular framework [24]. Our primary curiosity is techniques to anticipate the side effects of arrhythmia with the examination and order of information acquired from the patients utilizing sensors or cell phones to the information arranged at the archive. Precision and proficiency of the proposed arrangement have been established by dissecting the huge arrangement of information with the field gathered ECG signals. Well-being observing and its connected advancements is an appealing exploration region. The ECG has consistently been a well-known estimation plan to evaluate and analyze cardiovascular illnesses (CVDs). The quantity of ECG checking frameworks in the writing is extending dramatically. Henceforth, it is extremely hard for scientists and medical care specialists to pick, look at, and assess frameworks that serve their necessities and satisfy the checking prerequisites. This highlights the requirement for a checked reference managing the plan, grouping, and investigation of ECG observing frameworks, serving the two analysts and experts in the field. Exhaustive, master confirmed scientific categorization of ECG observing frameworks and abroad, a precise survey of the writing has been established in the past [25]. This gives proof-based help to basically understanding ECG observing frameworks' segments, settings, highlights, and difficulties. Henceforth, a conventional design model for ECG checking frameworks, a broad examination of ECG observing frameworks' worth chain is led, and a careful survey of the important writing, characterized against the specialists' scientific categorization, have been introduced, featuring difficulties and latest technologies.

Deep learning techniques have been established to consider the arrhythmia as a non-linear Delay Differential Equation (DDE) time series analysis where lightweight CNN networks can be used to grade and monitor the patients. This is associated with IoT sensors that detect the irregular beating of the heart [26]. Other similar solutions include Lightweight Arrhythmia Classification with Deep Learning (DL-LAC) method that is based upon a single-lead ECG trace and does not require noise-filtering and manual feature extraction steps. Virtualized deployment of these models to the IoT microcontrollers raises the hope for combating medical problems with the full force of emerging technologies [27]. ECG arrhythmia data has also been inputted to multiple machine learning models to ensure the compatibility of a computational model with the given medical data. Support Vector Machine–based classification proved most efficient in terms of accuracy and precision [28]. The classification has proven much faster and has an accuracy over the acceptable rate of proper diagnosis by an authorized physician [29].

## 6.8   IoT and Machine Learning–Based System for Medical Data Mining

Medical services determination is a developing exploration region. Different calculations and strategies for an early finding and arrangement of illnesses have been proposed by numerous analysts. The K implies calculation requires a quicker preparation time depends on the size of the clinical information. To speed up, Hussain *et al.* proposed an equal cycle approach dependent on the Xilinx Virtex4 XC4VLX25 FPGA to quicken the five K implies grouping of the clinical informational collection. In 2013, Chauhan *et al.* planned a coronary illness-related forecast model by utilizing different data mining procedures. In view of this model and the utilization of the J48 characterization calculation, a higher precision was accomplished. In 2015, Gelogo *et al.* featured the utilization of a universal clinical framework, which depends on IoT engineering, for the expectation of neurotic conditions. In 2015, Delen *et al.* anticipated the bosom malignancy endurance rate utilizing data mining techniques. To anticipate the endurance rate, the creators utilized two mainstream data mining calculations including neural organizations and DT with a measurable strategy (calculated relapse). Rajkumar *et al.* planned a classifier for thyroid infections. Their proposed multilayer perceptron (MLP) calculation orders and determines the obsessive stage with improved precision. In 2017, Verma *et al.* presented another structural model for understudy medical care arrangements. They executed the k crease cross-approval approach in their model to analyze the examples and registered the outcomes dependent on boundaries, for example, exactness, explicitness, and affectability. Jain *et al.* proposed a keen methodology for the recognizable proof of the H1N1 pig seasonal infection utilizing AI calculations. This methodology can be utilized by the public authority and different offices to arrange and anticipate infections. In 2018, Singh *et al.* planned a viable coronary illness expectation framework to figure the danger level utilizing an MLP neural organization. Verma and Sood proposed a strategy dependent on IoT and cloud computing for the confirmation of the obsessive status and forecast of infections. The creators zeroed in on understudy medical services and sterilization. Verma and Sood distributed a methodical audit of data mining calculations dependent on emotional wellness strategies, which quickly sums up the use of information digging calculations for the expectation of the danger components of different sicknesses. Bioinformatics research on data mining assumes an imperative function in medical services and clinical findings. Verma *et al.* quickly summed up different AI calculations just as equal figuring for the expectation of obsessive conditions. In our proposed framework, the utilization of a fluffy classifier and its FPGA execution builds the precision which lessens the calculation time that is needed for the forecast of cardiovascular illnesses.

Lastly, researchers are encourged to refer to articles [30–37] to learn more about emerging technologies and their uses in e-healthcare (including open issues and challenges).

## 6.9 Conclusion and Future Works

This chapter discusses the existing machine learning applications in the field of medical diagnosis and the integrative possibilities of the established models with IoT networks. Biomedical imaging is a crucial step in the testing processes carried out to understand the biological and physiological characteristics of a patient. The brain and the heart are two of the most vital organs of our body and deserve the proper recognition for contributing toward the development of robust imaging techniques in the field of medicine. Early brain tumor detection saves millions of lives every year and the introduction of machine learning servicing has only increased the efficiency of the process. IoT and cloud services can propel the ML frameworks to function in remote and household conditions. This can assist diagnose and monitor patients from the comfort of their homes. Dementia is another slow-growing illness that becomes highly critical to people in their old age. Exploration of electronic health records can help monitor the history of illnesses and the medical treatment received by the patient. The computational nature of AI can crawl through huge stacks of medical data to attain a clear understanding of a patient's medical status.

Heart conditions are also long term and can cause great stress and hardships for the patient. In this chapter, we take a closer look at arrhythmia and the related technological applications that have enabled us to ease the condition. ECG observing frameworks have been concentrated altogether in the writing. The multi-dimensional parts of these frameworks make it hard for specialists, clinical professionals, and others to choose, among these frameworks, those that satisfy their checking needs, coordinate the setting of their utilization, and backing the necessary infection observing prerequisites. The current advancements in ECG observing frameworks utilized deep learning, AI, big data, and IoT to give a productive, cost-proficient, completely associated, and incredible checking framework. Empowering innovations give immense occasions to the headway of ECG observing frameworks. IoT gets far off, unconstrained networks and administrations that influence information and encourage opportune, important, and basic choices for a superior way of life. Moreover, fog handling and cloud preparing add to an expanded occasion to improve productivity and satisfy various sought after adaptable application administrations. Moreover, blockchain innovation empowers security over a dispersed climate for different exchanges all through the various layers of the ECG observing framework design.

As a future work, investigating the field of mechanical technology and medical services robotization can possibly change the up and coming age of ECG observing frameworks and to disentangle automated helped medical procedure methods, older consideration, and far off and in-emergency patient checking. Mechanical helped a medical procedure ought to be performed with higher accuracy, control, and improved vision, preparing for the progressive medical services of tomorrow. Further future examination headings incorporate investigating the utilization of the quickly developing IoT and brilliant associated gadgets for preventive medical services and supporting the recognition of patients' unordinary clinical issues or a change in personal conduct standards. Likewise, customized checking frameworks ought to be raised to the following level as far as being profoundly redone as per patients' necessities and intelligence to permit extraordinary designs and transformations to clients' prerequisites for superior personal satisfaction. At long last, another conceivable exploration course is to add more insight to the patients' environmental factors, for instance, inserting more sensors in the rug to precisely identify patients' developments to set up standards of conduct and distinguish any irregularities, as recommended. IoT systems are starting to dominate healthcare, and this chapter takes this mainstream change into consideration to discuss the adaptations of ML application to interoperable systems.

# References

1. Kong, X., Meng, Z., Meng, L., Tomiyama, H., A Privacy Protected Fall Detection IoT System for Elderly Persons Using Depth Camera. *2018 International Conference on Advanced Mechatronic Systems (ICAMechS)*, Zhengzhou, pp. 31–35, 2018.

2. Saadeh, W., Butt, S.A., Altaf, M.A.B., A Patient-Specific Single Sensor IoT-Based Wearable Fall Prediction and Detection System. *IEEE Trans. Neural Syst. Rehabil. Eng.*, 27, 5, 995–1003, May 2019.

3. Pirooznia, M., Yang, J.Y., Yang, M.Q. *et al.*, A comparative study of different machine learning methods on microarray gene expression data. *BMC Genomics*, 9, S13, 2008, https://doi.org/10.1186/1471-2164-9-S1-S13.

4. Lundervold, A.S. and Lundervold, A., An overview of deep learning in medical imaging focusing on MRI. *Z. Med. Phys.*, 29, 2, 102–127, https://doi.org/10.1016/j.zemedi.2018.11.002, 2019.

5. Salam, A., Internet of Things for Environmental Sustainability and Climate Change, in: *Internet of Things for Sustainable Community Development. Internet of Things (Technology, Communications and Computing)*, Springer, Cham, https://doi.org/10.1007/978-3-030-35291-2_2, 2020.

6. Albahri, A.S., Alwan, J.K., Taha, Z.K., Ismail, S.F., Hamid, R.A., Zaidan, A.A., Albahri, O.S., Zaidan, B.B., Alamoodi, A.H., Alsalem, M.A., IoT-based telemedicine for disease prevention and health promotion: State-of-the-Art. *J. Netw. Comput. Appl.*, 173, 102873, https://doi.org/10.1016/j.jnca.2020.102873, 2021.

7. Tyagi, A.K., Gupta, M., Aswathy S.U., Ved, C., Healthcare solutions for smart era: An useful explanation from user's perspective, in: *Recent Trends in Blockchain for Information Systems Security and Privacy*, CRC Press, 2021.

8. Romero, L.E., Chatterjee, P., Armentano, R.L., An IoT approach for integration of computational intelligence and wearable sensors for Parkinson's disease diagnosis and monitoring. *Health Technol.*, 6, 167–172, 2016, https://doi.org/10.1007/s12553-016-0148-0.

9. Khan, M.A., An IoT Framework for Heart Disease Prediction Based on MDCNN Classifier. *IEEE Access*, 8, 34717–34727, 2020.

10. Ganesan, M. and Sivakumar, N., IoT based heart disease prediction and diagnosis model for healthcare using machine learning models. *2019 IEEE International Conference on System, Computation, Automation and Networking (ICSCAN)*, Pondicherry, India, pp. 1–5, 2019.

11. Tuli, S., Basumatary, N., Gill, S.S., Kahani, M., Arya, R.C., Wander, G.S., Buyya, R., HealthFog: An ensemble deep learning based Smart Healthcare System for Automatic Diagnosis of Heart Diseases in integrated IoT and fog computing environments. *Future Gener. Comput. Syst.*, 104, 187–200, 2020, https://doi.org/10.1016/j.future.2019.10.043.

12. Madhupriya, G., Guru, N.M., Praveen, S., Nivetha, B., Brain Tumor Segmentation with Deep Learning Technique. *2019 3rd International Conference on Trends in Electronics and Informatics (ICOEI)*, Tirunelveli, India, pp. 758–763, 2019.

13. Nai, Y. *et al.*, Improving Lung Lesion Detection in Low Dose Positron Emission Tomography Images Using Machine Learning. *2018 IEEE Nuclear Science Symposium and Medical Imaging Conference Proceedings (NSS/MIC)*, Sydney, Australia, pp. 1–3, 2018.

14. Seixas, J.L., Barbon, S., Mantovani, R.G., Pattern Recognition of Lower Member Skin Ulcers in Medical Images with Machine Learning Algorithms. *2015 IEEE 28th International Symposium on Computer-Based Medical Systems*, Sao Carlos, pp. 50–53, 2015.

15. Hegde, P.R., Shenoy, M.M., Shekar, B.H., Comparison of Machine Learning Algorithms for Skin Disease Classification Using Color and Texture Features. *2018 International Conference on Advances in Computing, Communications and Informatics (ICACCI)*, Bangalore, pp. 1825–1828, 2018.

16. Sabri, M.A., Filali, Y., El Khoukhi, H., Aarab, A., Skin Cancer Diagnosis Using an Improved Ensemble Machine Learning model. *2020 International Conference on Intelligent Systems and Computer Vision (ISCV)*, Fez, Morocco, pp. 1–5, 2020.

17. Sudha, S., Jayanthi, K.B., Rajasekaran, C., Sunder, T., Segmentation of RoI in Medical Images Using CNN- A Comparative Study. *TENCON 2019 - 2019 IEEE Region 10 Conference (TENCON)*, Kochi, India, pp. 767–771, 2019.

18. Shahriar Sazzad, T.M., Tanzibul Ahmmed, K.M., Hoque, M.U., Rahman, M., Development of Automated Brain Tumor Identification Using MRI Images. *2019 International Conference on Electrical, Computer and Communication Engineering (ECCE)*, Cox'sBazar, Bangladesh, pp. 1–4, 2019.

19. Ma, C., Luo, G., Wang, K., Concatenated and Connected Random Forests With Multiscale Patch Driven Active Contour Model for Automated Brain Tumor Segmentation of MR Images. *IEEE Trans. Med. Imaging*, 37, 8, 1943–1954, Aug. 2018.

20. Sharma, Y. and Meghrajani, Y.K., Brain tumor extraction from MRI image using mathematical morphological reconstruction. *2014 2nd International Conference on Emerging Technology Trends in Electronics, Communication and Networking*, Surat, pp. 1–4, 2014.

21. Sharma, Y. and Meghrajani, Y.K., Brain tumor extraction from MRI image using mathematical morphological reconstruction. *2014 2nd International Conference on Emerging Technology Trends in Electronics, Communication and Networking*, Surat, pp. 1–4, 2014.

22. Zacharaki, E.I., Shen, D., Lee, S., Davatzikos, C., ORBIT: A Multiresolution Framework for Deformable Registration of Brain Tumor Images. *IEEE Trans. Med. Imaging*, 27, 8, 1003–1017, Aug. 2008.

23. Rahman, M.L., Shehab, S.H., Chowdhury, Z.H., Datta, A.K., Predicting the Possibility of Being Malignant Tumor based on Physical Symptoms using IoT. *2020 IEEE Region 10 Symposium (TENSYMP)*, Dhaka, Bangladesh, pp. 26–30, 2020.

24. Devadharshini, M.S., Heena Firdaus, A.S., Sree Ranjani, R., Devarajan, N., Real Time Arrhythmia Monitoring with Machine Learning Classification and IoT. *2019 International Conference on Data Science and Engineering (ICDSE)*, Patna, India, pp. 1–4, 2019.

25. Baig, M.M., Gholamhosseini, H., Connolly, M.J., A comprehensive survey of wearable and wireless ECG monitoring systems for older adults. *Med. Biol. Eng. Comput.*, 51, 5, 485–95, 2013 May.

26. Sakib, S., Fouda, M.M., Fadlullah, Z.M., Nasser, N., Migrating Intelligence from Cloud to Ultra-Edge Smart IoT Sensor Based on Deep Learning: An Arrhythmia Monitoring Use-Case. *2020 International Wireless Communications and Mobile Computing (IWCMC)*, Limassol, Cyprus, pp. 595–600, 2020.

27. Sakib, S., Fouda, M. M., Fadlullah, Z. M., Nasser, N., Alasmary, W., A proof-of-concept of ultra-edge smart IoT sensor: A continuous and lightweight arrhythmia monitoring approach. *IEEE Access*, 9, 26093–26106, 2021.

28. Shimpi, P., Shah, S., Shroff, M., Godbole, A., A machine learning approach for the classification of cardiac arrhythmia. *2017 International Conference on Computing Methodologies and Communication (ICCMC)*, Erode, pp. 603–607, 2017.

29. Bulbul, H.I., Usta, N., Yildiz, M., Classification of ECG Arrhythmia with Machine Learning Techniques. *2017 16th IEEE International Conference on Machine Learning and Applications (ICMLA)*, Cancun, pp. 546–549, 2017.

30. Nair, M. M., Tyagi, A. K., Sreenath, N., The future with industry 4.0 at the core of society 5.0: Open issues, future opportunities and challenges. *2021 Int. Conf. Comput. Commun. Inform. (ICCCI)*, 1–7, 2021.

31. Varsha, R., Nair, S.M., Tyagi, A.K., Aswathy, S.U., RadhaKrishnan, R., The future with advanced analytics: A sequential analysis of the disruptive technology's scope. In: *Hybrid Intelligent Systems. HIS 2020. Advances in Intelligent Systems and Computing*, A. Abraham, T. Hanne, O. Castillo, N. Gandhi, T. Nogueira Rios, T.P. Hong (eds.), vol. 1375. Springer, Cham., 2021, https://doi.org/10.1007/978-3-030-73050-5_56

32. Tyagi, A.K., Nair, M.M., Niladhuri, S., Abraham, A., Security, privacy research issues in various computing platforms: A survey and the road ahead. *J. Inform. Assur. Sec.*, 15, 1, 1–16, 16p, 2020.

33. Madhav, A.V.S. and Tyagi, A.K., The world with future technologies (Post-COVID-19): Open issues, challenges, and the road ahead. In: *Intelligent Interactive Multimedia Systems for e-Healthcare Applications*, A.K. Tyagi, A. Abraham, A. Kaklauskas (eds.), Springer, Singapore, 2022, https://doi.org/10.1007/978-981-16-6542-4_22.

34. Mishra, S. and Tyagi, A.K., The role of machine learning techniques in Internet of Things based cloud applications. AI-IoT book, Springer, 2021.

35. Pramod, A., Naicker, H.S., Tyagi, A.K., Machine learning and deep learning: Open issues and future research directions for next ten years, in: *Computational Analysis and Understanding of Deep Learning for Medical Care: Principles, Methods, and Applications*, 2020, Wiley Scrivener, 2020.

36. Nair, M.M. and Tyagi, A.K., Privacy: History, statistics, policy, laws, preservation and threat analysis. *J. Inform. Assur. Sec.*, 16, 1, 24–34, 11p, 2021.

37. Tyagi, A.K., Fernandez, T.F., Mishra, S., Kumari, S., Intelligent automation systems at the core of industry 4.0. In: *Intelligent Systems Design and Applications. ISDA 2020. Advances in Intelligent Systems and Computing*, A. Abraham, V. Piuri, N. Gandhi, P. Siarry, A. Kaklauskas, A. Madureira (eds.), I, vol. 1351, Springer, Cham., 2021, https://doi.org/10.1007/978-3-030-71187-0_1.

# Part 2
# INTRODUCTION TO DEEP LEARNING AND ITS MODELS

# 7

# Deep Learning Methods for Data Science

**K. Indira[1], Kusumika Krori Dutta[1]\*, S. Poornima[2]
and Sunny Arokia Swamy Bellary[3]**

*[1]M.S. Ramaiah Institute of Technology, Bengaluru, India
[2]Anna University, Chennai, India
[3]Charlotte, NC, United States*

## Abstract

Deep learning network (DLN) is defined as the neural network characterized by complex connected layers to handle a large volume of data, automatic extraction of features, and representation learning for identification and regression problems. This concise chapter on deep learning (DL) methods for data science takes readers through a series of program-writing tasks that introduce them to the use of different DL techniques in various areas of artificial intelligence (AI). It covers zen and tao of the various types of DL methods such as convolutional neural network, recurrent neural network (RNN), denoising autoencoder (DAE), recursive neural network, deep reinforcement learning, deep belief networks (DBNs), and long short-term memory (LSTM), i.e., starting from architecture, learning rules, mathematical model to programing aspects explained in this chapter. The developed and emerging structures of DLN has been applied in applications according to the depth of computational graph, learning, and performance. The knowledge of merits and demerits of each method can train reader toward selection of best suited technique for a given problem statement. For example, the evolution of RNN-based DL architecture innovated many applications in time series, biological, speech-to-text conversion, which has sequence dependent data. RNN handles both real values (time series) and symbolic values of variable length inputs. This chapter covers varieties of application with example to give reader an overall learning. The formulation of this chapter highlights the improvement in applications (such as language, text, signal, and image processing) by modifications in network configuration. This AI technique summarizes the necessity, development,

*\*Corresponding author:* kusumika@msrit.edu

Archana Mire, Shaveta Malik and Amit Kumar Tyagi (eds.) Advanced Analytics and Deep Learning Models, (151–180) © 2022 Scrivener Publishing LLC

strength, and weakness of DLN models used in data science which will integrate all the basic cores of engineering in near future.

*Keywords*: Deep learning, RNN, CNN, DBN, LSTM, deep reinforment learning, recursive NN

## 7.1    Introduction

Artificial neural networks or ANNs are the computational systems modeled after the biological neural networks of physical brains and designed to mimic them. They consist of an input layer, multiple hidden layers in between, and an output layer. Each layer has numerous processing units called neurons.

A neuron, the basic unit of a neural network, takes multiple inputs and returns a single output. In a feedforward neural network, the neuron outputs in one layer are fed as input to the succeeding layer neurons. The input layer, the first layer of the chain, receives input signals from the user, and the output layer is the last layer in the chain which returns its outputs to the user. A neural network may have multiple inputs and multiple outputs.

Deep learning (DL) also known as deep neural networks [1–3] is based on ANN concept where more number of layers or more numbers of neurons in each layer or both, i.e., deeper layers, and more numbers of neurons are used. More number of layers provides more iteration and increases efficiency of the net but at the same time it increases complications in handling. Whereas, more number of neurons provides ability to extract more features from the given datasets.

In this chapter, some of the DL methods are discussed in details.

## 7.2    Convolutional Neural Network

Convolution generates a signal by combining two signals mathematically. For grayscale images (2D data), the convolution operation between a filter (kernel) $W^{k_1 \times k_2}$ and an image $X^{N_1 \times N_2}$ is given by Equation (7.1). This equation allows the kernel to be centered on pixel of interest.

$$Y(i,j) = \sum_{a=-\frac{k1}{2}}^{\frac{k1}{2}} \sum_{b=-\frac{k2}{2}}^{\frac{k2}{2}} X(i-a, j-b) W\left(\frac{k1}{2}+a, \frac{k2}{2}+b\right) \qquad (7.1)$$

Thus, if the image is 2D, a 2D filter is used to slide over the input image, and if the image is color (RGB), a 3D case, a 3D filter is used which is refereed as a volume, and to perform convolution, 3D filter will slide over the volume over the 3D input and the effect is that 2D convolution operation is performed on a 3D input as the filter is moved right or left and not along the depth. Thus, multiple filters can be used to get multiple feature maps. If the input is of dimension Width $(W_1)$ × Height $(H_1)$ × Depth $(D_1)$, the spatial filter is of size (F × F), with the depth of the filter is the same as depth of input. To apply the kernel at the corners, pad inputs appropriately (P) and use strides S which defines the interval at which the filter is applied. The dimensions of the output with Width (W2) × Height (H2) is given in Equations (7.2) and (7.3), respectively.

$$W_2 = \frac{W_1 - F + 2P}{S} \tag{7.2}$$

$$H_2 = \frac{W_2 - F + 2P}{S} \tag{7.3}$$

The depth of the output layer depends on the quantity of filters used. If K such filters are used, then the output dimension will be $W_2 \times H_2 \times K$. In case of traditional machine learning, hand-crafted features such as SIFT, HOG, and LBP are extracted, whereas in CNN [4–7], there are multiple layers of meaningful filters/kernels for extracting the features. These kernels are treated as parameters and weights are learned through backpropagation.

Some of the issues faced by fully connected neural network (FNN) such as networks cannot learn the same features (e.g., edges) at different places in the input images and the network is computationally expensive for large images are solved in a CNN. In CNN, the issues are solved by having local receptive field and weight sharing. In local receptive field, hidden layers are connected to local patches of the layer below to capture the local relationship in pixels, reducing the number of parameters in the model. Weight sharing reduces the number of parameters of the model and enables translation invariance of neural network to images. There is another layer called pooling layer which aggregates information including minor variations and reduces the size of the previous layer output and thus eases performance of further layers.

Other variants of convolution are dilated convolution and transpose convolution. In dilated convolution, the dilated rate controls the spacing between values in the kernels. Transpose convolution also known as deconvolution is used for learnable up sampling.

Backpropagation is a widely used algorithm to train CNN. In this algorithm, gradients are computed through recursive application of chain rule. Optimizers are used to change the weights and learning rate of the network to reduce the losses. Gradient descent is the first-order optimization algorithm, and the loss is transferred between layers through backpropagation, and the weights are modified so that the loss is minimized. Variants of gradient descent such as stochastic gradient descent (SGD) and mini-batch gradient descent (MBGD) can be employed for training the model. Other types of optimizers such as Adagrad, Adadelta, and Adam optimizers are used to update the weights with minimum loss.

## 7.2.1   Architecture

The CNN model consists of four layers, namely, two convolution layers, one max pooling layer, and one fully connected (FC) layer wherein every layer neuron is connected with every neuron in the neighbor layer. In convolution layers, there are sixteen $3 \times 3$ filters to perform feature extraction, the max pooling layer to reduce the dimensions of feature maps, the number of learning parameters, and computations to be executed by the model. The FC layer performs the classification task. The two convolution layers are followed by ReLu activation. It helps to alleviate vanishing gradient problem and introduces an amount of non-linearity in the model. The last FC layer is succeeded by softmax activation function. This ensures that the output of all the neurons in the final layer is in the range [0, 1]. The output indicates the probability that the input belongs to that particular class. Dropout randomly ignores a certain fraction of the total neurons. It helps to prevent overfitting and hence helps the model to generalize better.

## 7.2.2   Implementation of CNN

Optical character recognition (OCR) is preferred for implementation and testing Kannada text [7]. The printed text document is scanned and the scanned image is pre-processed to extract lines, words, and characters in an image. In the training phase, the individual characters are trained, and in the testing phase after pre-processing, the individual characters are recognized and converted into a machine edible format (e-book, pdf, etc.).

Kannada text has 49 phonemic letters (Varnamaale) which is grouped as 13 vowels, 34 consonants, and two special characters (Anuswara and Visarga). The script has its own numerals, vowel modifiers, and consonant modifiers. The combination of vowel and consonant is called Syllable (Akshara). Vowels are independent of consonants, whereas the consonants are dependent on the vowels. The consonants are divided into Vargeeya and Avargeya Vyanjanas. The number of possible combination of Kannada characters is 623,893. But, while recognizing a character in a word, first, the base character is recognized, and then, the vowel modifiers and Vatt Aksharas are recognized and appended to base character. The complexity is reduced from 623,893 to just having 340 classes for the main aksharas and 32 for the vattaksharas. Data samples of Kananda main aksharas and Vatt Aksharas are shown in Figures 7.1A and B respectively.

Convolutional neural networks are used for training Main Aksharas and Vatt Aksharas. The block diagram for training of CNN is illustrated in Figure 7.2.

For the Main Aksharas dataset, all the images are separately resized to dimensions 15×20, 25×20, 30×20 and 40×20 respectively, thus creating four different datasets which contain the same images but differ in their dimensions. These datasets are separately used to train four different CNN models, namely CNN1, CNN2, CNN3 and CNN4. For the Vatt Aksharas dataset, all the images are separately resized to dimensions 15×15, 20×15, 30×15 respectively. These datasets are again separately used to train three different CNN models, namely CNN5, CNN6 and CNN7.

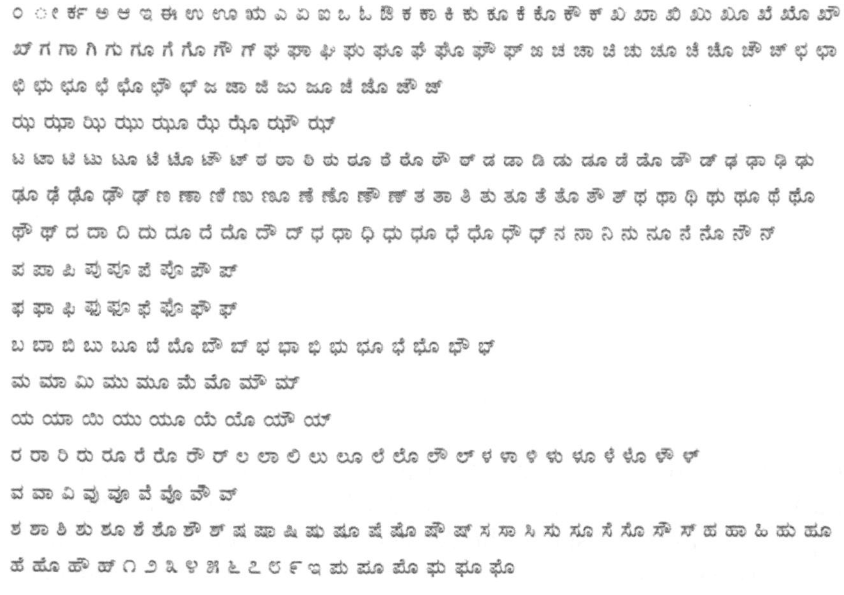

**Figure 7.1 (A)** Kannada Main Aksharas.

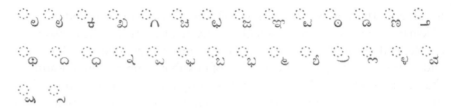

**Figure 7.1 (B)** Kannada Vatt Aksharas.

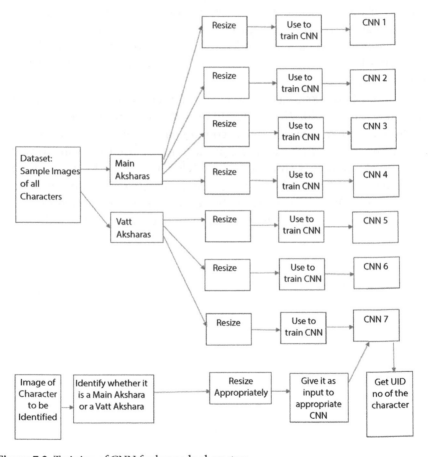

**Figure 7.2** Training of CNN for kannada characters.

The character to be predicted is determined whether it is a Main Akshara or a Vatt Akshara. In case it is a Main Akshara, it is resized to height 20 keeping the width constant. The Aspect Ratio is multiplied by a factor of 20. It is assigned to the appropriate CNN by implementing the below mentioned decision rules:

- If the width is less than or equal to 20, is assigned to CNN1
- If the width is greater than 20 but less than or equal to 25, it is assigned to CNN2
- If the width is greater than 25 but less than or equal to 35, it is assigned to CNN3
- If the width is greater than 35, it is assigned to CNN4

In case it is a Vatt Akshara, it is resized to height 15 keeping the width constant. The Aspect Ratio is multiplied by a factor of 15. It is assigned to the appropriate CNN by implementing the below mentioned decision rules:

- If the width is less than or equal to 20, is assigned to CNN5
- If the width is greater than 20 but less than or equal to 25, it is assigned to CNN6
- If the width is greater than 25, it is assigned to CNN7

The idea behind using separate CNNs to predict a Main Akshara and a Vatt Akshara is due to the fact that in Kannada script, several Main Aksharas and the corresponding Vatt Aksharas look similar and if only one CNN is used for prediction, there is a fair chance that it may mispredict. The idea behind using more than one CNN for predicting either a Main Akshara or a Vatt Akshara is due to the fact that a CNN cannot take in inputs with variable dimensions. Using a single CNN for all characters, ignoring the Aspect Ratios will again result in the model mispredicting. Hence, the Aspect Ratios of the characters are considered, and then the characters are resized and fed to the appropriate CNN.

## 7.2.3   Simulation Results

The dataset for implementation consists of Kannada Main aksharas and vattaksharas as shown in Figures 7.1A and B. There are 340 classes for the main aksharas and 32 classes for the vattaksharas. The average number of samples collected for each class is 50. Input scanned image is segmented into lines, words, and characters and the segmented character is collected to form a database of Main aksharas and vattaksharas. These training samples are fed to the appropriate CNN model. The model is trained using a batch size of 32, for 15 epochs. The weights are updated using RMS prop optimizer with cross entropy loss function. The trained model is saved and then used for testing. In the testing phase, the sample image shown in Figure 7.3A is given to the system to extract lines, words, and characters and the individual character is recognized by the trained

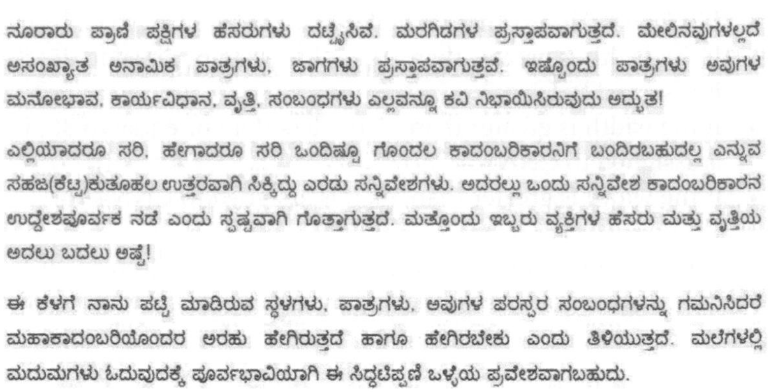

ನೂರಾರು ಪ್ರಾಣಿ ಪಕ್ಷಿಗಳ ಹೆಸರುಗಳು ದಟ್ಟಿಸಿವೆ. ಮರಗಿಡಗಳ ಪ್ರಸ್ತಾಪವಾಗುತ್ತದೆ. ಮೇಲಿನವುಗಳಲ್ಲದೆ ಅಸಂಖ್ಯಾತ ಅನಾಮಿಕ ಪಾತ್ರಗಳು, ಜಾಗಗಳು ಪ್ರಸ್ತಾಪವಾಗುತ್ತವೆ. ಇಷ್ಟೊಂದು ಪಾತ್ರಗಳು ಅವುಗಳ ಮನೋಭಾವ, ಕಾರ್ಯವಿಧಾನ, ವೃತ್ತಿ, ಸಂಬಂಧಗಳು ಎಲ್ಲವನ್ನೂ ಕವಿ ನಿಭಾಯಿಸಿರುವುದು ಅದ್ಭುತ!

ಎಲ್ಲಿಯಾದರೂ ಸರಿ, ಹೇಗಾದರೂ ಸರಿ ಒಂದಿಷ್ಟೂ ಗೊಂದಲ ಕಾದಂಬರಿಕಾರನಿಗೆ ಬಂದಿರಬಹುದಲ್ಲ ಎನ್ನುವ ಸಹಜ(ಕೆಟ್ಟ)ಕುತೂಹಲ ಉತ್ತರವಾಗಿ ಸಿಕ್ಕಿದ್ದು ಎರಡು ಸನ್ನಿವೇಶಗಳು. ಅದರಲ್ಲಿ ಒಂದು ಸನ್ನಿವೇಶ ಕಾದಂಬರಿಕಾರನ ಉದ್ದೇಶಪೂರ್ವಕ ನಡೆ ಎಂದು ಸ್ಪಷ್ಟವಾಗಿ ಗೊತ್ತಾಗುತ್ತದೆ. ಮತ್ತೊಂದು ಇಬ್ಬರು ವ್ಯಕ್ತಿಗಳ ಹೆಸರು ಮತ್ತು ವೃತ್ತಿಯ ಅದಲು ಬದಲು ಅಷ್ಟೆ!

ಈ ಕೆಳಗೆ ನಾನು ಪಟ್ಟಿ ಮಾಡಿರುವ ಸ್ಥಳಗಳು, ಪಾತ್ರಗಳು, ಅವುಗಳ ಪರಸ್ಪರ ಸಂಬಂಧಗಳನ್ನು ಗಮನಿಸಿದರೆ ಮಹಾಕಾದಂಬರಿಯೊಂದರ ಅರಹು ಹೇಗಿರುತ್ತದೆ ಹಾಗೂ ಹೇಗಿರಬೇಕು ಎಂದು ತಿಳಿಯುತ್ತದೆ. ಮಳೆಗಳಲ್ಲಿ ಮದುಮಗಳು ಓದುವುದಕ್ಕೆ ಪೂರ್ವಭಾವಿಯಾಗಿ ಈ ಸಿದ್ಧಟಿಪ್ಪಣಿ ಒಳ್ಳೆಯ ಪ್ರವೇಶವಾಗಬಹುದು.

**Figure 7.3 (A)**  Sample image.

ನೂರಾರು ಪ್ರಾಣಿ ಪಕ್ಷಿಗಳ ಹೆಸರುಗಳು ದಟ್ಟಿಸಿವೆ ಮರಗಿಡಗಳ ಪ್ರಸ್ತಾಪವಾಗುತ್ತದೆ ಮೇಲಿನವುಗಳಲ್ಲದೆ ಅಸಂಖ್ಯಾತ ಅನಾಮಿಕ ಪಾತ್ರಗಳು ಜಾಗಗಳು ಪ್ರಸ್ತಾಪವಾಗುತ್ತವೆ ಇಷ್ಟೊಂದು ಪಾತ್ರಗಳು ಅವುಗಳ ಮನೋಭಾವ ಕಾರ್ಯವಿಧಾನ ವೃತ್ತಿ ಸಂಬಂಧಗಳು ಎಲ್ಲವನ್ನೂ ಕವಿ ನಿಬಾಯಿಸಿರುವುದು ಅದ್ಭುತ! ಎಲ್ಲಿಯಾದರೂ ಸರಿ ಹೇಗಾದರೂ ಸರಿ ಒಂದಿಷ್ಟೂ ಗೊಂದಲ ಕಾದಂಬರಿಕಾರನಿಗೆ ಬಂದಿರಬಹುದಲ್ಲ ಎನ್ನುವ ಸಹಜ(ಕೆಟ್ಟ)ಕುತೂಹಲ ಉತ್ತರವಾಗಿ ಸಿಕ್ಕಿದ್ದು ಎರಡು ಸನ್ನಿವೇಶಗಳು ಅದರಲ್ಲೂ ಒಂದು ಸನ್ನಿವೇಶ ಕಾದಂಬರಿಕಾರನ ಉದ್ದೇಶಪೂರ್ವಕ ನಡೆ ಎಂದು ಸ್ಪಷ್ಟವಾಗಿ ಗೊತ್ತಾಗುತ್ತದೆ ಮತ್ತೊಂದು ಇಬ್ಬರು ವ್ಯಕ್ತಿಗಳ ಹೆಸರು ಮತ್ತು ವೃತ್ತಿಯ ಅದಲು ಬದಲು ಅಷ್ಟೇ ಈ ಕೆಳಗೆ ನಾನು ಪಟ್ಟಿ ಮಾಡಿರುವ ಸ್ಥಳಗಳು ಪಾತ್ರಗಳು ಅವುಗಳ ಪರಸ್ವರ ಸಂಬಂಧಗಳನ್ನು ಗಮನಿಸಿದರೆ ಮಹಾಕಾದಂಬರಿಯೊಂದರ ಅರಹು ಹೇಗಿರುತ್ತದೆ ಹಾಗೂ ಹೇಗಿರಬೇಕು ಎಂದು ತಿಳಿಯುತ್ತದೆ ಮಳೆಗಳಲ್ಲಿ ಮದುಮಗಳು ಓದುವುದಕ್ಕೆ ಪೂರ್ವಭಾವಿಯಾಗಿ ಈ ಸಿದ್ದಟಿಪ್ಪಣಿ ಒಳ್ಳೆಯ ಪ್ರವೇಶವಾಗಬಹುದು

**Figure 7.3 (B)**  Output edible text.

model and then converted to edible output text as shown in Figure 7.3B. The errors obtained from the system are highlighted. The designed model is tested with different paragraphs and prediction accuracy is noted and is tabulated in Table 7.1. The overall accuracy of the model is 81.76%.

### 7.2.4   Merits and Demerits

The system is able to produce edible text for any font size but if character images consist of two Aksharas in a single image, which should ideally have been further segmented into separate Aksharas results in misprediction by the CNN and hence results in erroneous output. Further, in the

**Table 7.1** Model prediction accuracy.

| Input paragraph no. | No. of input words | Correct output | Incorrect output | Accuracy (in %) |
|---|---|---|---|---|
| 1 | 82 | 73 | 09 | 89.02 |
| 2 | 40 | 34 | 06 | 85 |
| 3 | 42 | 34 | 08 | 80.95 |
| 4 | 52 | 41 | 11 | 78.84 |
| 5 | 24 | 18 | 06 | 75 |
| Overall | | | | 81.76 |

rare case where two Vatt Aksharas are present, the character segmentation again results in an image with both of them, rather than separate images.

### 7.2.5  Applications

Linguistic Translational Applications centred around Kannada can be developed which translates content from Kannada to any other language and vice versa. These applications will be of great use to people living in Karnataka who do not know the native language.

## 7.3  Recurrent Neural Network

A grand astuteness of ANNs is utilized to compute the cognition models of human nervous systems. The development of ANN in sundry applications such as image apperception and relegation, self-driving conveyances, and data analytics and prognostication, animation games proved that the performance of ANN models is equal to or better than that of the human. The fundamental architectures of ANN accept dependent multidimensional data and perplex its structure according to the application requisite. The evolution of recurrent neural networks (RNN)–predicated DL architecture innovated many applications in time series, biological, and verbalization to text conversion, which has sequence dependent data. RNN handles both genuine values (time series) and symbolic values of variable length inputs. Semantic interpretation of text utilizing time layered RNN structure found incipient research areas such as sentiment analysis, machine translation, and information analytics [8–15, 27–30].

RNN holds recollection in the form of obnubilated layers. In RNN, the information is transferred among individual layers of the network and the sequence positions. While the conventional ANN gets perplexed with variable length inputs for single layer, RNN accepts single input for multiple layers corresponds to each position of sequence. The input in each layer has kindred modeling parameters which reiterates the architecture throughout the network, and hence, "Recurrent Neural Network" defines as a self-loop in the obnubilated layer neuron enables recurrence of the antecedent output. The obnubilated neuron of RNN holds the summary of precedent inputs of same sequence, which differentiates it from other aliment-forward networks.

## 7.3.1   Architecture

RNN is a model where the first layer output is given as input to the next neuron layer as shown in Figure 7.4. In conventional neural networks, all the neuronal inputs and outputs are independent of each other. In circumstances where the presage the next word of a sentence is preferred, there is a desideratum to recollect the antecedent words. Thus, RNN is chosen to satisfy this requirement using an obnubilated Layer. The main and most consequential feature of this model is obnubilated state, which recollects some information about a sequence.

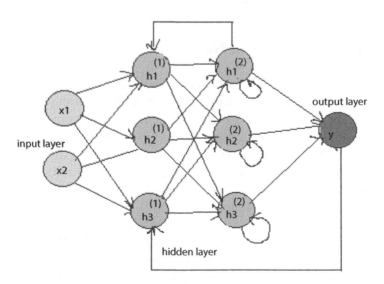

**Figure 7.4** Recurrent neural network architecture.

## 7.3.2    Types of Recurrent Neural Networks

Based on the working principle, RNNs are of three types: a) Simple RNN, b) Gated Recurrent Units (GRUs), and c) Long Short-Term Memory (LSTM) Networks.

### 7.3.2.1    Simple Recurrent Neural Networks

A Simple RNN has three layers: input, hidden, and output. Based on the architecture, simple RNN is of two types: i) Elman Networks and ii) Jordan Networks. In case of Elman Networks, sets of context units are fed from hidden layer is connected, which can store value of previous hidden layer units and sequence prediction. Whereas, the output layer of Jordan Network feed the sets of context unit as shown in Figure 7.5.

Let us consider

$x_t$: input vector

$h_t$: hidden layer vector

$o_t$: output vector

$y_t$: target vector

$b_x$: bias vector (input layer)

$b_h$: bias vector (hidden layer)

$b_o$: bias vector (output layer)

$W_x$, $W_h$: weight parameter matrix

$e(\cdot)$, $f(\cdot)$: a nonlinear Activation function (e.g., tanh and sigmoidal)

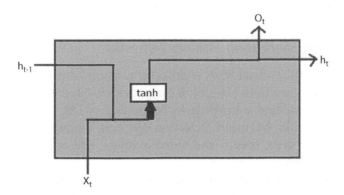

**Figure 7.5** Simple RNN.

For total time steps of T:

*Feedforward Phase (h$_t$, y$_t$, L$_t$, L):* For the given sequence input, the RNN computes the hidden state output and model output as follows:

$$g_t = W_x x_t + W_h h_{t-1} + b_h \tag{7.4}$$

$$ht = e(W_x x_t + W_h h_{t-1} + b_h) \tag{7.5}$$

$$z_t = W_h h_t + b_o \tag{7.6}$$

$$o_t = f(h_t) \tag{7.7}$$

In case of evanescent gradient, the contribution of faraway time steps were disoriented, and hence, the cognition is implemented with only more proximate time step information. RNN with this circumscription is not opportune for long-term–dependent sequences with this structure. If the normalized gradient of loss function elevates exponentially, then the product will not be a scalar in exploding gradient condition. The cognition of RNN with this circumscription becomes unstable and the network may get crashed. More the number of layers (k) in obnubilated state, the normalized scalar values become spectral matrix form which makes the cognition involute and arduous. Then, the norm of all the matrix is computed utilizing chain rule to learn gradient issues. Thus, the RNN model is simple and potent, and the training of RNN has evanescent and exploding inhibitions with many deep layers.

The gradient limitations have been handled using delayed neural networks, optimization methods, penalties, regularization technique, clipping of gradients, graded leakage units, LSTMs, and GRUs.

### 7.3.2.2   Long Short-Term Memory Networks

LSTMs follow an artificial RNN architecture, which has both feedforward and feedback connections [16–26]. It can process entire sequence of data at a time, so, this method got popularity in the field of DL. It has wide range of applications like Intrusion Detection Systems, connected, unsegment handwriting analysis, speech and video analysis, and anomaly detection in network traffic.

It has one cell and three gates, i.e., input, output, and forget gate (as shown in Figure 7.6), where the role of the cell is to remember values at random time intervals and gates control the flow of information between the cells or if anything can be dropped out.

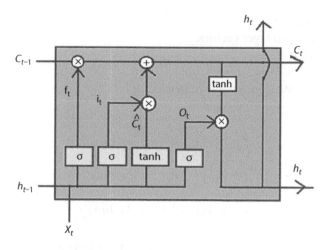

**Figure 7.6** Long short-term memory networks.

*Advantages of LSTMs:*

- It can perform processing of dataset, classification from the dataset.
- Based on times series data, it can make predictions.
- It has ability to bridge unknown lapses between events in the flow.
- It can address the issues of vanishing gradient of traditional RNNs.
- It is not sensitive to gap length unlike Hidden Markov Models and other sequence learning techniques.
- LSTMs are strongly capable to achieve classical results in all the machine translation applications.

*Disadvantages of LSTMs:*

- For fine precision counting time steps to achieve, additional counting methods may be required.
- Number of gate requirement is more as each memory cell block requires an input and one output gate.
- It shows constant error as shown in conventional feedforward architecture while presented entire string at a time as input.
- Just like other feedforward networks, LSTMs also have "regency" problem.

Let us consider:
$hC_t$, $hh_t$: hidden layer vectors.
$x_t$: input vector.
$bias_f$,$bias_i$,$bias_c$,$bias_o$: bias vector.
$Wt_f$, $Wt_i$, $Wt_c$, $Wt_o$: parameter matrices.
$\sigma$, tanh: activation functions.

$$f_t = \sigma(Wt_f.[\,h_{t-1},\,x_t\,] + bias_f) \tag{7.8}$$

$$i_t = \sigma(Wt_i.[\,h_{t-1},\,x_t\,] + bias_i) \tag{7.9}$$

$$o_t = \sigma(Wt_o.[\,h_{t-1},\,x_t\,] + bias_o) \tag{7.10}$$

$$h\check{C}_t = tanh(Wt_c.[\,hh_{t-1},\,x_t\,] + bias_c) \tag{7.11}$$

$$hC_t = f_t \odot hC_{t-1} + i_t \odot \check{C} \tag{7.12}$$

$$hh_t = o_t \odot tanh(hC_t) \tag{7.13}$$

### 7.3.2.3   Gated Recurrent Units (GRUs)

In RNN, GRUs are gated mechanisms. It has fewer parameters compared to LSTMs with similar architecture with forget gate. GRUs are of two types i) fully gated unit and ii) minimal gated unit. It is introduced mainly to prevent vanishing gradient, issue of standard RNN using update and reset gate.

The fully gated unit (as shown in Figure 7.7) has several variations, based on bias combinations and gating done using previous hidden state.

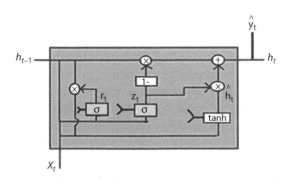

**Figure 7.7** Fully gated version.

The most simplified form of GRU is known as minimal gated unit. Main three types are shown as Type1, Type 2, and Type 3 in Figures 7.8, 7.9, and 7.10, respectively.

Let us consider:

$hh_t$: hidden layer vectors.

$x_t$: input vector.

$z_t$: update gate vector

$r_t$: reset gate vector

$bias_z$, $bias_r$, $bias_h$: bias vector

$Wt_z$, $Wt_r$, $Wt_h$: parameter matrices.

$\sigma$, tanh: activation functions.

If $\sigma(x) \in [0, 1]$, then alternative activation functions are also possible.

The operator $\odot$ denotes the Hadamard product

$$z_t = \sigma(Wt_{z.}[\,hh_{t-1}, x_t\,] + bias_z) \qquad (7.14)$$

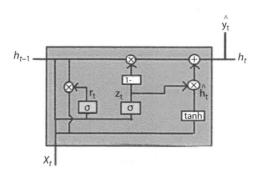

**Figure 7.8**  Type 1 GRU.

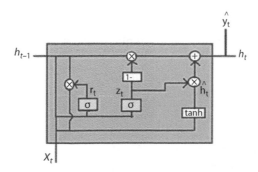

**Figure 7.9**  Type 2 GRU.

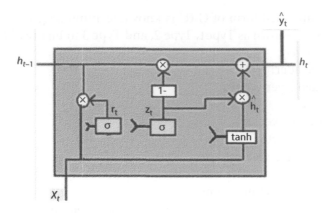

**Figure 7.10** Type 3 GRU.

$$r_t = \sigma(Wt_{r.}[\, hh_{t-1}, x_t\,] + bias_r) \qquad (7.15)$$

$$hh_t = (1 - z_t) \odot hh_{t-1} + z_t \odot tanh(Wt_h \, .[\, r_t \odot hh_{t-1}, x_t] + bias_h) \qquad (7.16)$$

*Type 1:* Each gate only depend on bias and previous hidden state

$$z_t = \sigma(Wt_z \, hh_{t-1} + bias_z) \qquad (7.17)$$

$$r_t = \sigma(Wt_r \, hh_{t-1} + bias_r) \qquad (7.18)$$

*Type 2:* Each gate only depend on previous hidden state without bias

$$z_t = \sigma(Wt_z \, hh_{t-1}) \qquad (7.19)$$

$$r_t = \sigma(Wt_r \, hh_{t-1}) \qquad (7.20)$$

*Type 3:* Each gate only depend on bias and not previous hidden state

$$z_t = \sigma(bias_z) \qquad (7.21)$$

$$r_t = \sigma(bias_r) \qquad (7.22)$$

*Minimal Gated Unit:*
In case of minimal gated unit, the update vector ($z_t$) and reset vector ($r_t$) is merged into a forget gate ($f_t$).

$$f_t = \sigma(W_f [\, hh_{t-1}, x_t\,] + bias_f)  \tag{7.23}$$

$$hh_t = f_t \odot hh_{t-1} + (1 - f_t) \odot tanh(Wt_h \cdot [\, f_t \odot hh_{t-1}, x_t] + bias_h)  \tag{7.24}$$

where
$x_t$: input vector
$hh_t$: output vector
$f_t$: forget vector
$Wt_f$, $Wt_h$, and $bias_f$, $bias_h$: parameter matrices and bias vectors

### 7.3.3    Merits and Demerits

#### 7.3.3.1    Merits

a.  A RNN recollects all information at time intervals as LSTMs can recollect anterior inputs in time series presages.
b.  RNN can be combined with convolutional layers to stretch the pixel neighborhood for effective performance.

#### 7.3.3.2    Demerits

a.  It has vanishing and exploding gradients.
b.  It is difficult to training a RNN.
c.  It is unable to execute lengthy sequences with tanh and ReLu activation functions.

### 7.3.4    Applications

RNNs are utilized in many applications ranging from seizure detection to cryptography and from verbalization apperception to stock market prognostication. Very importantly, its appreciable applications are unsegmented, connected, often temporal in nature and appropriate to physiological signals as they are recorded as one dimensional (1D) samples over time. Ergo, many research works have benefitted with the application of RNN features to physiological data such as

*   Physiological data additionally kenned as biomedical signals categorically bio-electrical signal categorizes and characterizes as follows:

- o Electroencephalogram (EEG): electrical signals engendered due to electrical activity in human encephalon.
- o Electrooculogram (EOG): signals engendered due to the vicissitude of potential of the cornea-retina region that subsists between the front side and back ends of human ocular perceiver.
- o Electrocardiogram (ECG): signals that are engendered from activity of human heart which are consequence of cardiac muscle depolarization and re-polarization during heartbeat.
- o Electromyogram (EMG): electrical signals engendered by skeletal muscles.

- Last 2 years, i.e., 2018 and 2019, it has been visually perceived a plethora of research development transpired on EEG and with utilizing EEG among the four other modalities or cumulation of two or more modalities. EEGs are majorly utilized because EEG predicated signal acquisition is more frugal and does not require any special equipment, the acquisition system is portable which makes it feasible for applications such as encephalon-computer interface, it has high temporal resolution with sampling rates between 250 and 2,000 Hz.
- Recent past, several experimental and theoretical work on statistical relegation techniques had been published. Many of the literatures prove that the DL models outperform compared to traditional models. In the following section, EEG modality utilizing RNN has been discussed. In the next section the prominent applications of EEG research such as Encephalon decoding and anomaly detection have been elaborated.

## 7.4   Denoising Autoencoder

Autoencoders are the neuron models used to cull and extract the data features. It has more nodes in the obnubilated layer than the inputs. It is jeopardizing to learn the soi-disant "Identity Function", withal called "Null Function", denoting that the output and input is equal, in order to model the Autoencoder network nugatory.

Denoising autoencoder (DAE) handles the quandary by corrupting the data intentionally by arbitrarily zeroing half of its own input values. Researches suggest to use 30% corrupted input as it depends on the magnitude of data and number of input nodes of the model. The loss function is calculated as the error magnitude between the pristine input and the obtained output which helps to learn the extraction or elimination features.

## 7.4.1    Architecture

In this type of architecture, the number of input and output remains the same, whereas hidden layer has variation in number of neuron as shown in Figure 7.11.

## 7.4.2    Merits and Demerits

One conspicuous drawback is your autoencoder may not work. It may always give you the average of the input set, or always reconstruct the input set precisely, or coalesce those two defects in surreptitious ways. Or it may work impeccably in the training set but fail miserably out of sample. One drawback compared to statistical analysis is you may miss paramount theoretical insights. This is not so much a drawback as the flip side of the advantage that the autoencoder picks up valuable relationships that would never occur to a human, either due to human preconceptions or because they are too intricate for humans to process. One drawback compared

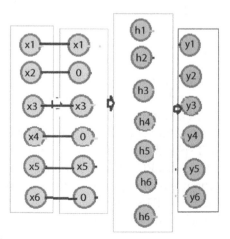

**Figure 7.11** Architecture of denoising autoencoder.

to statistical analysis is you may miss consequential theoretical insights. This is not so much a drawback as the flip side of the advantage that the autoencoder picks up valuable relationships that would never occur to a human, either due to human preconceptions or because they are too intricate for humans to process. The autoencoder might be more sensitive to input errors different from those in the training set or to transmutations in underlying relationships that a human would descry.

### 7.4.3   Applications

- Dimensionality reduction
- Recommendation system
- Image generation, compression, and denoising
- Feature extraction
- Sequence to sequence prediction

## 7.5   Recursive Neural Network (RCNN)

Natural language processing attracted more researchers to analyze speech or text used in multimedia, data mining, sensor, citation, and social networks (rcnn4). The graphical representation of RCNN enables researchers to handle highly complex data [31]. Recursive neural network help to identify many objects and the relation among them in a picture. While the graph properties are studied as graph classification, the vertex classification has been used to identify the label associated with the vertex of the graph. The vertex classification has been obtained using neighbor vertex and label information [32].

### 7.5.1   Architecture

A semisupervised recursive auto encoder (RAE) and supervised recursive neural tensor (RNT) network are the extended versions of RCNN [33]. The description of framework and function of RNT and RAE compared in Table 7.2 helps the reader to select the variant. NLP uses RAE to segment a sentence for further process. RNT splits the input as per its constitutents and label them.

Similar to recurrent model, RCNN also handles variable input length. It is used to segment sentence or image into various classes using backpropagation through structure (BPTS). The basic RCNN consists of a binary tree graph in which each node shares weight matrix [32]. The inputs of different length are fed at the bottom of tree and passes upwards toward the target in feedforward phase. The words are composed into a functions

**Table 7.2** Comparison between RCNN variants.

| | Recursive autoencoder | Recursive neural tensor |
|---|---|---|
| Framework | | |
| Components | Semisupervised learning<br>Multilayer<br>Reduced dimension in hidden layers<br>Softmax layer at the output layer | Supervised learning<br>Multiple encoding layers |
| Explanation | A single sentence composed of n word vectors are constructed as input nodes of a tree. The hidden nodes are reduced version of input nodes. The hidden output is fed to autoencoder at the top node of the tree which also has softmax layer to learn the label information. Fine tuning of word vectors helps to obtain information of label targets. | A single sentence breaks the large phrases and subphrases according to nouns and verbs. The large phrases N and V may have subphrase n or v. The tensor network is structured as tree in which machine learning–based constituent parsing has been used. The top-down configuration has a root with two leaf nodes. Each leaf node learns the semantic, sensitiveness, and context information by neural network. |
| Limitations | Requirement of known input vectors makes the batch training complex. The graph size increases with input length. | Parser dependent |

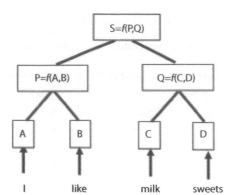

**Figure 7.12** Architecture of RCNN.

P and Q as shown in Figure 7.12 and then recursively constitutes to S function. Applying loss function to composite node S, the calculated loss is compared with predicted one. The errors are calculated using negative log likelihood criterion method and then weights are updated accordingly in back propagation phase. The labels of node are analyzed for emotions. The semantic analysis is further extended to NLP using LSTM units before the recursive phase of nodes [34].

### 7.5.2    Merits and Demerits

For a sequence of a length τ, the depth (quantified as the number of compositions of nonlinear operations) can be abbreviated from τ to O (log τ) and has to deal with long-term dependencies. The ability to structure a perfect tree for every requirement is always a crucial question.

### 7.5.3    Applications

The research papers used RCNN to split a sentence into a binary tree and fragments it using its semantic properties. Similarly, construction and reconstruction of images with many objects are analyzed using the types of RCNN. RCNN handles granular and hierarchical data by its tree construction. The applications of RCNN include the following:

- Paraphrasing detection
- NLP
- Speech-to-text transcription
- Image decomposition and reconstruction

- Forecasting short-term electrical load
- Identification and control of discrete nonlinear systems
- Sentiment analysis

## 7.6   Deep Reinforcement Learning

Reinforcement learning (RL) created enthusiasm to artificial intelligence (AI) researchers for its framework of learning ability from environment as human. It is a reward driven trial and error learning process from successful or failure experiences for future decisions. Atari Games, AlphaGo, Driverless car, and Teaching a robot are classical examples of practical RL of DLNs. The algorithm is built based on the balance between exploration and exploitation by extracting sensed inputs and generate them into state of actions. Stateless algorithms have also been developed for specific applications such as Naïve and E-greeding [31–33]. The algorithms has been briefed for a gambling problem in which getting high payoff by choosing correct slot machine is the task.

(i)   *Naïve Algorithm*:

   a.   Exploration: The number of trials will be fixed by the player for each slotter.
   b.   Exploitation: The slotter with highest payoff will be continued.

Finding highest payoff consumes more time with less output generated machines. The player will lose the game if the slotter is misidentified. Naïve algorithm will not be a good choice for realistic problems.

(ii)   ε - greeding Algorithm:

   a.   Exploration: From 'ε' fraction of trials, a slotter will be chosen randomly.
   b.   Exploitation: The best average payoff machine will be used for the $(1 - \varepsilon)$ trials.

Wrong choice of slotter is completely avoided using ε – greeding method. Small values of ε will lead to win at the cost of more exploitation time. Fixing the fraction using annealing method becomes the best strategy for succeeding the game.

## 7.6.1    Architecture

The RL systems are generally modeled as a simple neural network to evaluate and maximize rewards for each decision in an environment taken by the learner. The learner explores the accumulated data collected through his actions without prior knowledge and the system keep challenges learning process till he succeed. The continuous learning modifies the structure with respect to actions and rewards. If the neural network has more than one hidden layer, then it is referred as deep RL network. The learning process of DRL can be explained using Markov's decision model and Q learning model whose functions are described in Table 7.3.

## 7.6.2    Merits and Demerits

Although RL have many errors, it is preferred for its special features. An overperformed RL may have overload of states so that a portion of output may get discarded. DRL will not be able to solve simple quandaries. But in other way, the most celebrated benefits of utilizing DL can be as follows:

- No desideratum for feature engineering
- Best results with unstructured data
- No desideratum for labeling of data
- Efficient at distributing high-quality results
- The desideratum for lots of data
- Neural networks at the core of DL are ebony boxes

## 7.6.3    Applications

DRL networks have the following exciting applications by its dynamic learning in its framework during both exploration and exploitation phases.

- Driverless cars
- Robotic control and automation
- Stock market trading
- ad-placement optimization
- Business strategy planning
- Customized training systems for aircraft instructions

A deep belief network (DBN) is a propagative graphical model of neural network with multiple interconnected layers of obnubilated units. The layers of DBN detect the input features during the flow of information.

**Table 7.3** Comparison between Markov decision model and Q learning model.

| | Markov decision model | Q learning model |
|---|---|---|
| Framework | S0 → State Transition → S1; Policy, Action, Reward; Agent | S0 → State Transition → S1; Reward$_{S0}$, Action, Reward; Agent ← f(a, Y, Q$_0$) |
| Components | States, policy, action, reward, goal | States (S0, S1), action, reward, goal, learning rate (α), discount factor (γ), and optimal estimated reward (Q$_0$) at state (S1) |
| Explanation | It is a continuous process between states of an agent like performing an action, computing the result and ahead toward a goal based on deep learning network's output. Deterministic policy generates same action at every state whereas stochastic policy stimulates action based on probability calculations. | The value-based process guides the agent in decision-making of appropriate actions by calculating Q values. |
| Limitations | Direct solution is possible for lesser reward values. Iterative methods can be used for higher rewards. | Limited only to finite action and state spaces. Deep Q learning method is adapted when needed for function approximations. |

## 7.7 Deep Belief Networks (DBNS)

Initially, DBN learns to retrieve the input using probabilistic method and then relegates with supervised training. DBNs can be regarded as a composed simple and undirected unsupervised network [11]. A Restricted Boltzmann Machine (RBM) is an energy-predicated model propagated with an input layer and interconnected obnubilated layers. Its framework trains the network layers as an expeditious, such that contrastive divergence is applied to all the layers as well as its constituents.

The optical selectivity feature of DBNs which allows individual layer training at a time directed itself as one of the successful DL algorithms. A continuous DBN is an extended version of deep-notion network that accepts only decimals and not the binary.

### 7.7.1   Architecture

Untrained layers are stacked over a trained layer such that the input is transferred to the bottom layer which is being trained. The interconnected DBN layers function as a restricted Boltzmann machine network. The trained layer is reset with a training vector whose weights and bias values are allotted to the individual units. The training of stacked RBM is illustrated in Figure 7.13. The updating process is repeated until the stopping criterion is met.

### 7.7.2   Merits and Demerits

The advantages of DBN are efficient utilization of obnubilated layers (higher performance gain by integrating layers compared to multilayer perceptron) and robustness in relegation (size, position, color, view angle rotation). Hardware requisites for the net are the most sizably voluminous drawback for equipollent.

### 7.7.3   Applications

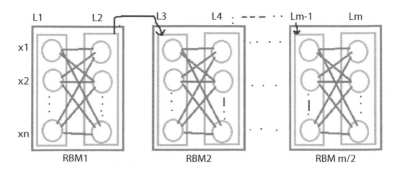

**Figure 7.13** Architecture of deep belief networks.

It has many attractive implementations and employments of DBNs in real-life applications with its own limitations.

- Apperceive, cluster and create image, video sequences
- Data capture

## 7.8   Conclusion

This chapter explains the basic working of the DLN structures along with literature applications. The formulation of this chapter highlights the improvement in applications (such as language, text, signal, image, or video processing) by modifications in network configuration. This AI technique summarizes the necessity, development, strength, and weakness of DLN models used in data science which will integrate all the basic cores of engineering in near future.

## References

1. Aggarwal, CC., *Neural Networks and Deep Learning- A Textbook*, Springer International Publishing AG, part of Springer Nature, Switzerland, 2018. https://doi.org/10.1007/978-3-319-94463-0
2. Patterson, J. and Gibson, A., *Deep Learning: A Practitioner's Approach*, 1st. ed, O'Reilly Media Inc., USA, 2017.
3. Yann, L., Bengio, Y., Hinton, G., Deep Learning, *Nature*, 521, 7553, 436–44, 2015. https://doi.org/10.1038/nature14539.
4. Bellary, S.A.S. and Conrad, J.M., Classification of Error Related Potentials using Convolutional Neural Networks, in: *2019, 9th International Conference on Cloud Computing, Data Science & Engineering (Confluence)*, IEEE, pp. 245–249, 2019, January.
5. Dutta, K.K. *et al.*, Classification of Kannada Hand Written Alphabets using Multi-Class Support Vector Machine with Convolutional Neural Networks. *International Conference on Innovative Computing and Cutting-edge Technologies, (ICICCT 2020)*, Thailand, 11-12 September 2020.
6. Dutta, K.K., Swamy, S.A., Banerjee, A., Chandan, R., Vaprani, D., Kannada character recognition using multi-class SVM method. *Proceedings of the Confluence 2021: 11th International Conference on Cloud Computing, Data Science and Engineering*, pp. 405–409, Jan. 2021.
7. Dutta, K.K., Sunny, S.A., Victor, A., Ayman Habib, M., Parashar, D., Kannada alphabets recognition using decision tree and random forest models.

*Proceedings of the 3rd International Conference on Intelligent Sustainable Systems, ICISS 2020*, pp. 534–541, 2020.

8. Dutta, K.K., Multi-Class Time Series Classification of EEG Signals with Recurrent Neural Networks, in: *2019 9th International Conference on Cloud Computing, Data Science & Engineering (Confluence)*, IEEE, Noida, India, pp. 337–341, 2019, https://doi.org/10.1109/CONFLUENCE.2019.8776889.

9. Abdelhameed, A.M., Daoud, H.G., Bayoumi, M., Deep convolutional bidirectional LSTM recurrent neural network for epileptic seizure detection, in: *2018 16th IEEE International New Circuits and Systems Conference (NEWCAS)*, IEEE, pp. 139–143, 2018, June.

10. Alhagry, S., Fahmy, A.A., El-Khoribi, R.A., Emotion recognition based on EEG using LSTM recurrent neural network. *Emotion*, 8, 10, 355–358, 2017.

11. Ghasemi, F., Pérez-Sánchez, H., Dehnavi, M.A., Fassihi, A., The Role of Different Sampling Methods in Improving Biological Activity Prediction Using Deep Belief Network. *J. Comput. Chem.*, 38, 10, 1–8, 2016.

12. Bresch, E., Großekathöfer, U., Garcia-Molina, G., Recurrent deep neural networks for real-time sleep stage classification from single channel EEG. *Front. Comput. Neurosci.*, 12, 85, 2018.

13. Dutta, K.K., Kavya, V., Swamy, S.A., Removal of Muscle Artifacts from EEG Based on Ensemble Empirical Mode Decomposition and Classification of Seizure Using Machine Learning Techniques, in: *2017 International Conference on Inventive Computing and Informatics (ICICI)*, IEEE, Coimbatore, pp. 861–866, 2017, https://doi.org/10.1109/ICICI.2017.8365259.

14. Şen, D. and Sert, M., Continuous valence prediction using recurrent neural networks with facial expressions and EEG signals. *2018 26th Signal Processing and Communications Applications Conference (SIU)*, Izmir, pp. 1–4, 2018.

15. Wang, F. *et al.*, Analysis for Early Seizure Detection System Based on Deep Learning Algorithm. *2018 IEEE International Conference on Bioinformatics and Biomedicine (BIBM)*, Madrid, Spain, pp. 2382–2389, 2018.

16. Gers, F.A., Schmidhuber, J.A., Cummins, F.A., Learning to Forget: Continual Prediction with LSTM. *Neural Comput.*, 12, 10, 2451–2471, 2000. https://doi.org/10.1162/089976600300015015.

17. Sutskever, I., *Training Recurrent Neural Networks*, PhD Thesis, University of Torondo, 2013.

18. Cai, J., Wei, C., Tang, X., Xue, C., Chang, Q., The Motor Imagination EEG Recognition Combined with Convolution Neural Network and Gated Recurrent Unit. *2018 37th Chinese Control Conference (CCC)*, Wuhan, pp. 9598–9602, 2018.

19. Patterson, J. and Gibson, A., *Deep Learning: A Practitioner's Approach*, 1st. ed, O'Reilly Media, Inc, California, 2017.

20. Attia, M., Hettiarachchi, I., Hossny, M., Nahavandi, S., A time domain classification of steady-state visual evoked potentials using deep recurrent-convolutional neural networks. *2018 IEEE 15th International Symposium on Biomedical Imaging (ISBI 2018)*, Washington, DC, pp. 766–769, 2018.

21. Li, M., Zhang, M., Luo, X., Yang, J., Combined long short-term memory based network employing wavelet coefficients for MI-EEG recognition. *2016 IEEE International Conference on Mechatronics and Automation*, Harbin, pp. 1971–1976, 2016.

22. Sun, M., Wang, F., Min, T., Zang, T., Wang, Y., Prediction for High Risk Clinical Symptoms of Epilepsy Based on Deep Learning Algorithm. *IEEE Access*, 6, 77596–77605, 2018.

23. Min, S., Lee, B., Yoon, S., Deep learning in bioinformatics. *Brief. Bioinform.* 18, 5, 851–869, 2017.

24. Rim, B., Sung, N.J., Min, S., Hong, M., Deep Learning in Physiological Signal Data: A Survey. *Sensors*, 20, 4, 969, 2020.

25. Ruffini, G., Ibanez, D., Castellano, M., Dubreuil-Vall, L., Soria-Frisch, A., Postuma, R., Gagnon, J.F., Montplaisir, J., Deep learning with EEG spectrograms in rapid eye movement behavior disorder. *Front. Neurol.*, 10, 806, 2019.

26. Lee, S., Hussein, R., McKeown, M.J., A Deep Convolutional-Recurrent Neural Network Architecture for Parkinson's Disease EEG Classification. *2019 IEEE Global Conference on Signal and Information Processing (GlobalSIP)*, Ottawa, ON, Canada, pp. 1–4, 2019.

27. Hochreiter, S. and Schmidhuber, J., Long short term memory. *Neural Comput.*, 9, 8, 1735–1782, 1997.

28. Tayeb, Z., Fedjaev, J., Ghaboosi, N., Richter, C., Everding, L., Qu, X., Wu, Y., Cheng, G., Conradt, J., Validating deep neural networks for online decoding of motor imagery movements from EEG signals. *Sensors*, 19, 1, 210, 2019.

29. Tsiouris, K.M., Pezoulas, V.C., Zervakis, M., Konitsiotis, S., Koutsouris, D.D., Fotiadis, D.I., A Long Short-Term Memory deep learning network for the prediction of epileptic seizures using EEG signals. *Comput. Biol. Med.*, 99, 24–37, 2018.

30. Hush, D., Abdallah, C., Horne, B., The recursive neural network and its applications in control theory. *Comput. Electr. Eng.*, 19, 4, 333–341, 1993. https://doi.org/10.1016/0045-7906(93)90054-U.

31. Lu, Q. and Getoor, L., Link-based classification. *Proceedings of the 20th International Conference on Machine Learning*, vol. 3, pp. 496–503, 2003.

32. Socher, R., Perelygin, A.Y., Wu, J., Chuang, J., Manning, C.D., Ng, A.Y., Potts, C., *Recursive Deep Models for Semantic Compositionality Over a Sentiment Treebank*, Emnlp, 2013.

33. Xu, Q., Wang, Q., Xu, C., Qu, L., Collective Vertex Classification Using Recursive Neural Network, *Comput. Sci.*, ArXiv, 2017.

34. Geron, L.S., *Recursive Neural Networks for Semantic Sentence Representation*, Thesis and Dissertation, City University of New York, Sep 2018.

**8**

# A Proposed LSTM-Based Neuromarketing Model for Consumer Emotional State Evaluation Using EEG

**Rupali Gill\* and Jaiteg Singh**

*Chitkara University Institute of Engineering and Technology, Chitkara University, Punjab, India*

### Abstract

Contemporary marketing methodologies like television commercials, newspaper advertisements, and billboards are used by marketers to sell products because they do not understand the psychology of the consumer toward a point of purchase. The advancement in the field of technology during the last decade has allowed various researchers to measure neurophysiological parameters to predict human buying behavior for better marketing. This research study aims to bridge the gap between traditional market research and neuromarketing research. EEG-based emotional state assessment in neuromarketing has been widely used. The major gap of neuromarketing is the lack of research work in machine learning methods for predicting and classifying customer preferences. Various approaches to machine learning for predicting and classifying user preferences have been thoroughly studied. An LSTM-based approach is adopted to detect consumer emotional states by using DEAP EEG signals. The findings showed that the proposed LSTM model can be used for EEG-based emotion recognition.

*Keywords*: Neuromarketing, brain-computer interface, deep learning, deep neural networks, EEG (electroencephalograph)

*\*Corresponding author*: rupali.gill@chitkara.edu.in

Archana Mire, Shaveta Malik and Amit Kumar Tyagi (eds.) Advanced Analytics and Deep Learning Models, (181–206) © 2022 Scrivener Publishing LLC

## 8.1   Introduction

Emotions play a key role player in humans' life, not only in interaction but also in crafting decisions. This has resulted in the phenomenal expansion of research domains like cognitive computing, human-computer interaction, sentiment analysis, user interface design, optimizing user experience, healthcare, and neuromarketing. These domains prominently compute and evaluate emotive responses to optimize results. User response can be recorded through numerous channels like subjective self-reports, facial expressions, speech analysis, physiological signals, and autonomic neurophysiological measurements. Techniques like functional Magnetic Resonance Imaging (fMRI), electroencephalography (EEG), eye gaze tracking, eye tracking using pupillometry, biometrics, and facial coding have been extensively used to understand the emotive state of respondents. This understanding is further used to trigger impulse decisions [1, 2]. Intrinsic connectivity within brain regions can help in predicting impulsivity of decision-making. Brain activity is considered to be a biomarker of the decision-making process [3, 4].

The process of decision-making involves the frontal lobe, insula, parietal lobe, and anterior cingulate cortex portions of the brain. Interactions within these regions of the brain are considered to be pivotal in the process of decision-making [4–9]. EEG and fMRI are best known for the unbiased natural feedback about any given stimulus and can be best used for decision assessment [4, 10–12]. These signals, being spontaneous and natural, cannot be faked; this makes them highly accurate in predicting decisions. EEG is easier to set up and because high temporal information recording can be used to develop a decision prediction system. In this chapter, an attempt has been made to develop an EEG and physiological information-driven intelligent framework to predict decisions. Measuring emotion states concerning any stimuli is highly demanding and may help in decision-making [13]. The same can be used to evaluate product designing strategies, packaging designing strategies, user interface design review, and marketing advertising assessments [14]. There is also a need to find advanced analytical methods for decision-making [15, 16]. The latest machine learning and deep learning approaches has led to the development of various predictions and planning analysis models. So, it can help us find an automatic method of extraction of features machine learning or deep learning to predict emotional state predictions [17].

The major research outlines of this work are as follows:

- To study and compare machine learning techniques with deep learning techniques to predict emotional states.
- To record the test dataset and find an appropriate feature extraction technique to be used for dimensionality reduction.
- To propose an long short-term memory (LSTM)–based framework from emotional state evaluation using EEG

The chapter starts with a comparative analysis of various techniques, which could be used to record, physiological and psychological responses of respondents. Subsequently, a summary of machine learning techniques explored by the research community to classify and predict emotions is provided. Later, an LSTM-based framework is proposed to instigate impulse decisions within respondents. The framework is trained over the benchmark dataset and tested with the proposed recorded dataset. Section 8.2 presents the background and motivation behind the current research. Section 8.3 elaborates an extensive review of machine learning and deep learning techniques. Section 8.4 provides a methodology and proposed system. Section 8.5 presents results and discussions, and Section 8.6 provides conclusion and future scope of the chapter.

## 8.2 Background and Motivation

Marketers spend a lot of money on promoting the usability or performance of goods. This is important during the pre-testing of various alternative advertising strategies before the launch and during the post-launch market analysis of the campaign. There are some traditional approaches to pre-test advertising. These approaches include self-reported approaches such as liking, recall or purchase intention, and neuromarketing [18–20]. Recently, companies such as Coca-Cola have begun to use neuromarketing strategies to test ads before the introduction of products to consumers [12]. This section describes different principles relevant to predicting emotion desires and the strategies used to record them. The scope, methods, intention, and classification techniques used so far in the prediction of emotions have been presented in the following sections.

### 8.2.1 Emotion Model

Emotion refers to a mental state that arises rationally rather than by attentive imposition and is often followed by physio-physiological changes that are important to the human cerebral system [22].

Emotion theories can be categorized into three major groups—physiological, neurological, and cognitive. On the basis these theories, two emotion models were defined namely discrete and dimensional. Discrete emotion models evaluate the distinct discrete emotions given by Ekman. They can be classified into six basic types—happy, sad, angry, disgust, fear, and surprise. Dimensional emotion models are the continuous emotions and are given by valence and arousal on the separate dimensions. Most dimensional models combine valence-arousal and excitement [18, 23, 24].

## 8.2.2    Neuromarketing and BCI

The term "neuromarketing" started to arise around 2002. A couple of businesses, for example, Sales Brain and Bright house, started offering consultations and studies, inspiring the use of knowledge and technologies into the industry of advertising of neuroscience [24]. Neuromarketing values the study of their consumer behavior [2, 25]. This approach was preferred by new executives such as Coca-Cola and Campbell's [20]. Neuromarketers used neuroscientific methods to manipulate consumer actions (i.e., needs, demands, and perceptions) while purchasing products [26]. This gave the inspiration of neuromarketers to evaluate the cerebral input activity of customers through ads and product methods [21].

Brain-computer interfaces (BCIs) are some of the latest innovations in the field of neuromarketing. The technology used helps in making an effective connection with the customers. BCIs do not need interference from nerves, muscles, to issue a command [27–29]. Different BCIs are used these days for emotion recognition tasks. The most common are EEG, fMRI, Positron Emission Tomography (PET), Magnetoencephalography (MEG), Steady State Topography (SST), and Transcranial Magnetic Stimulation (TMS). In addition other neuromarketing techniques like facial coding, galvanic skin reaction, skin conductance, and eye-tracking [30] are used for emotion recognition. Each technique has a specific functionality.

Neuromarketing includes advanced equipment and expertise that are beyond the scope of most of the businesses themselves. As executives decide to engage one of the many providers of neuromarketing services, they should consider the most critical features and differentiators of the available techniques [31].

Most emotive progressions occur in a very short duration of time—much faster than a blink of an eye. Also, actions that cause emotive progressions occur in a very short span varying from milliseconds to seconds, and EEGs with the greater temporal resolution are used to calculate brain action at a faster rate. The human brain generates enough activity, which is captured by the BCI as an EEG signal. EEG captures emotional processes in the time frame even in absence of behavioral changes. In short, EEG provides a low-cost, portable, and safe solution to record emotions for advertisement preference prediction [18, 20, 26].

### 8.2.3   EEG Signal

EEG technique is the most versatile and common when discussed in terms of brain research and its functioning. Its application deals with cognitive and emotive responses. The popularity is this device is due to its neutral measurements of emotive and cognitive responses [23, 32, 33]. EEG is commonly used in BCI communication networks to enable brain activity to be explicitly converted into commands to be used into emotive response recognition [34]. EEG is a record of the oscillation of electrical potentials of the brain as a result of ion current flow between brain neurons [1]. These neural actions consist of two unique types: (1) rhythms and (2) transient behavior. Rhythms are neural oscillations, rhythms based on the biological activity of the adrenals. The electrical activity is indicated in the human scalp by assessing the variants. EEG electrical activity is characterized by the division of frequencies into groups called alpha, delta, theta, and gamma. Human brain waves are composed of five major frequency bands called delta, theta, alpha, beta, and gamma [13, 35]. These activities are logged using electrodes mounted over the cortex right on the scalp. Other EEG signals that have been obtained are the measurement of electrical activity at the scalp location of the electrode [36, 37].

The most common type of EEG device which is used is Emotive EPOC. In this device, electrodes are connected to the device. Emotiv EPOC consists of 14 EEG channels plus 2 reference channels providing optimum positioning for precise spatial resolution. The major challenges of using an EEG is a low signal-to-noise ratio (SNR) [15, 38, 39], a non-stationary signal [40, 41], difficulty in handling [42], and inter-subject variability [16]. The next section details related works done by researchers in the field of EEG for EEG-based feature extraction and classification.

## 8.3   Related Work

This section is classified into two categories: EEG-based study on machine learning and EEG-based studies on deep learning.

### 8.3.1   Machine Learning

Original studies [43] aimed at measuring human emotions using both peripheral and EEG physiological signals over short-term periods. The authors focused on a dimensional model of emotion detection using a recall-based acquisition procedure. A combination of the different features set at the decision level using the summary rule increased accuracy to 70%. Moreover, the refusal of non-confident samples eventually led to a classification accuracy of 80% for the three grades. The study in [44] is based on the music-recognized emotional response approach to brain activity. The authors performed a comparison based study to confirm the practicality of using hierarchical binary classifiers to improve the efficiency of classification compared to non-hierarchical methods using a dimensional emotional model. The results predict that SVM can be used as a solution to the problems of EEG-based multi-class emotional grouping.

Authors [45] developed an EEG emotion recognition that can work on finding emotion-specific EEG features and examining the effectiveness of classifiers when stimuli were listening to music. The research applied by SVM to the EEG signal provides a practical approach to emotional states in practical or clinical applications. The authors [46] proposed a scheme that combined Hybrid Adaptive Filtering (HAF) with Higher-Order Crossings (HOCs) analysis to initially process EEG signals to enhance underlying emotion information, by integrating dimensional model and genetic algorithm–based techniques, and then by applying a feature extraction analysis that resulted in a HOC-based vector feature. The adopted emotive induction technique was based on the Mirror Neuron Method to achieve an accurate representation of the emotive stimulus which have been used to evoke brain potentials. The authors [47] proposed an Emotion Recognition Method using estimated (ApEn) and wavelet entropy (WE) EEG signals. The algorithm could continuously classify valence levels on e-learning systems. MAHNOB-HCI was used by authors [48] to analyze the facial videos, audio-visual signals, eye-gaze points, and physiological signals of the peripheral/central nervous system. The experiment was conducted using two-dimensional model experiments based on consensus or disagreement. These results show the possible usages of the recognized modality and the importance of the SVM classifier for emotion recognition. Authors [49] presented a discrete emotional recognition model with the motive of retrieving effective tags for videos using EEG, the distance between eye gaze, and response from pupil using the MANHOB dataset. A single-participant cross-validation technique was used to experiment using the SVM classifier. The authors [50] used the differential entropy (DE) and its variants to record the EEG-based emotional states. The DE technique was compared with various frequency-domain techniques. These results indicated that the used method gave best results the identification of emotions than conventional frequency-domain techniques.

The research [51] aimed at assessing the application areas of a multimodal approach by using the dynamics of the EEG and sound properties of music content for the categorization of emotional valence and arousal. A study by authors [52] used a sample entropy (SampEn)–based emotional state recognition using a support vector machine (SVM)–weight classifier. One is to distinguish between positive or negative emotions with high arousal and the other between genitive emotions with different arousal states. The findings indicated that emotion-related channels were mostly located in the prefrontal region. The reasonable accuracy of the identification was demonstrated by rigorous validation procedures. Future research will focus on the impact of EEG data duration and frequency bands. The study [53] looked at the feasibility and suitability of the subject-dependent and subject-independent emotion classification using unimodal and multimodal physiological signals using the SVM classifier. EEG, ECG, and Skin Conductance (SC) were used to characterize emotion via a dimensional model. Emotions are created by images and classical music. The most accurate method of classifying valence and arousal is EEG and decision-level fusion, respectively.

The authors [54] proposed a model to classify the discrete emotional state of an individual while listening to the Quran. The brain signals were analyzed using a machine learning approach. The results indicate that two kinds of emotions -happy and unhappy arise while listening to Quran. The results of the data analysis were proposed approach based on subject-specific frequency bands for emotional state classification. The researchers [55] used both conventional and Iranian musical samples. The EEG signals were recorded while the participants were listening to musical selections. The features were based on the principle of efficient connectivity. The correlation of the extracted features was extracted through the dimensional model. Signals have been classified into different categories using connectivity-based features.

The researchers [56] proposed a feature-based Emotion Recognition Model using EEG. The dimensional model classified the valence and arousal dimensions using the SVM classifier. The results of the suggested solution surpassed other methods of identification. The authors [57] used a new technique for the identification of emotions that are investigated by the detection of single-trial ERPs linked to a particular level of emotions. The study [58] used the late positive potential (LPP) to pick the characteristics for the classification of emotions-negative, moderately negative, and neutral. The LPP-based EEG features were chosen under multiple frequency bands. Emotion classification was performed using the SVM and the K-nearest neighbors (KNN). Conclusions contained in the report provide experimental evidence that LPP components can be used for EEG-based emotion recognition. The authors [59] proposed an EEG-based BCI framework used for emotional recognition was proposed to detect two specific emotional states. The authors [53] assessed the efficiency of single-channel EEG dynamics using SVM and K-NN. The results show that K-NN achieves a better classification rate for SVM. Authors [60] introduced the classification of emotions triggered by viewing music videos. The authors have shown that there is a link between the user's self-assessment of arousal and valence and the frequency of their EEG behavior. The authors [61] proposed an approach to analyzing highly contaminated brain signals for the detection of emotions. The authors of the study [62] conducted the EEG-based emotion classification and visualized shifts in emotional states over time.

The authors [63] proposed an Emotive EEG function extraction technique: Kernel Self-Emotion Pattern (KEEP). Adaptive SVM is also proposed to resolve the issue of learning from excessive emotional EEG data sets. The combined use of KEEP and the adaptive SVM showed promising results for the valence and arousal classification model. The authors [64] proposed a novel approach to classifying different human emotions based on statistically weighted, self-regressive EEG signal modeling. The proposed algorithm is more efficient than current algorithms. The authors [65] examined the features of the bi-spectrum for quantifying emotions using the Valence-Arousal Emotion Model and arrived at the function vector via a backward sequential search.

The authors [66] focused on the study of the relationship between EEG signals and human emotions based on Emotion Recognition Studies using the Emotive EPoC Headset. The authors [67] proposed an efficient EEG-based emotional recognition algorithm based on spectral features and neural network classifiers. The temporal features were selected from the emotion-related EEG signals by the application of Gabor functions and the transformation of wavelets and the classification was performed using the probabilistic neural network (PNN). The research [68] examines the output of the proposed EEG-based Emotion Recognition Method, which used a self-organizing map to define boundaries between separable regions. A research was conducted to collect eight channels of EEG data from 26 healthy right-handed subjects in four emotional states when exposed to audio-visual emotional stimuli.

The authors [69] used the wireless EEG system in the body area network to explore the potential of EEG emotional valence monitoring for use in real-life circumstances. The analysis [70] gives a study of three EEG signals that feature extraction techniques-statistical characteristics, PSD-based features (Power Spectral Density), and HOC-based features (High Order Crossings). The research [35] focused on the differentiation between subjects' EEG responses to self-assessed music that is liked or not. The findings provided a way to build a generic brain-machine interface for recognition of music preferences. The authors [71] intend to establish a method for detecting and transmitting the changes in emotions displayed by the Central Nervous System (CNS) through the use of EEG signals. The authors analyzed and discussed implementation issues related to each phase of the system.

The authors [72] have introduced an Emotion Recognition System using a self-regressive (AR) model, a sequential forward feature selection (SFS), and a KNN classifier that uses EEG signals during emotional audio-visual inductions to investigate AR features based on the Levinson-Durbin recursive algorithm. The authors [73] used a dimensional model to classify emotions using a 10-channel EEG device. The comparative study was conducted using the help vector machine and the KNN classifiers, which produced promising results. The authors [74] looked at the first demonstration of the musical "BCI feeling". The EEG data included brain and non-brain behaviors. Popular Spatial Pattern classification gave 84% correct pseudo-online performance and five-of-five correct live performance classification.

The authors [75] presented a systematic analysis and a comparative assessment of the various approaches used to differentiate between positive and negative affective states based on their EEG-derived profiles. They contrasted the general and individualized models and classifiers by analyzing their efficacy in taking into account the variations inherent in neurophysiological data for user-dependent and user-independent data. The authors [76] experimented with the odor pleasantness perception using EEG and ECG signals. The results show that odor has no effect on gender, time evolution, and dataset material. The results show that the features of the ECG signals did not result in substantially non-random output in the experiment. The authors' research work [47] uses a dimensional model to understand physiological status.

The authors used non-linear methods for the extraction of features—the fractal dimension and the correlation dimension. The results show a high correlation between emotional states using a fractal dimension model. The authors [77] performed EEG-based study to find the relation between brain signals for emotion analysis. The results indicated that the change in EEG-based functional connectivity was significantly different between emotional states. Researchers [78] demonstrated a good performance assessment using implicit emotional tagging on naive subjects. An emotional tangibility metric was used to measure emotion recognition efficacy. The authors [79] proposed an algorithm to view EEG signals as the activation/deactivation of sources specific to the brain activity of interest.

The proposed algorithm, called Asymmetric Spatial Pattern (ASP), extracts pairs of space philters, with each philter corresponding to only one of the two sources. Experimental studies on actual data also show positive results for some asymmetric neurophysiological observations on brain emotion production. Research by [80] proposed a probabilistic classifier based on Bayes theory and supervised learning using a perceptron convergence algorithm. In the Bayes classifier, the weighted-log-posterior function is used for the vectors feature. The analysis was performed on DEAP datasets using EEG signals. The efficiency of the proposed approach is measured using the dimensional model. Work [81] proposed an approach to the mental state of patients using EEG signals.

For this reason, wavelet energy, changed energy, wavelet entropy, and statistical moments of brain electrical activity were used. As a part of the future work, it was suggested to fuse EEG signals with several other sensors (wearable sensors). The authors [82] fused the EEG and facial expressions features for implicit affective tagging using a dimensional model. They extracted a feature-level and decision-level fusion and demonstrated increased performance. The authors proposed [83] the Deep Brief Network (DBN) to recognize emotion in listening to music. The DBN gave better results when compared to SVM and decision tree in most cases of dimensional emotional model. It further recorded the time (FD) and time-frequency (DWT) domain classification features outperform PSD features for dynamic emotion recognition. The authors [84] used the EEG features to classify valence and arousal based on the decision tree algorithm. Significant correlations were found between the EEG features and the arousal and valence. The authors in the study [85] suggested the integration of brain and peripheral signals for the detection of emotions. Authors [86] used EEG signals to classify two emotions: happy and sad using common spatial patterns (CSPs) and linear-SVMs. The experimental results indicate that the gamma frequency range is suitable for EEG-based emotion recognition and classification. The authors [87] used brain signals for four different emotions using hybrid EEG signal features. The accuracy results of emotion classification and recognition were analyzed for three different age groups. The relationship between musical genres and human emotions is explored by the writers. The author [88] evaluated the EEG system Emotiv EPOC and compared it to NoldusFaceReader to distinguish emotions from the captured data. Authors [89] proposed a method for the identification of facial expression fusion based on EEG and facial-landmark detection. EEG signal processing and facial landmark are the main components of emotion recognition. SVM was used to capture facial landmarks and the results showed an improvement of 4.35% in facial emotion recognition and a 5.78% increase in facial emotion recognition using the fusion process. The research carried out so far studies the percentage-wise usage of EEG studies being carried out using various classification and regression algorithms.

Table 8.1 shows that, about 59% of cases, SVMs were used, using different characters. KNN was selected for about 13% of jobs; Linear Discriminant Analysis (LDA) was used by 6.34% of authors, while Quadratic Discriminant Analysis (QDA) was selected by 1.58%. Finally, Naive Bayes (NB) and Multi-Layer Perceptron Back Propagation (MLP-BP) were elected by 3.17% and 1.58%; each was selected by the authors to investigate the EEG signal using random forest, PNNs, short deep networks, and neural networks.

## 8.3.2 Deep Learning

Machine learning algorithms have many advantages, but they may not work well in producing integrated patterns that are not limited to various time-series databases. Also, the selection of key features in the main feature set is important and will require size reduction techniques. Besides, the removal and selection of features are computerized. For example, the computer costs of selecting a feature can increase significantly by increasing the size of the feature. In general, search algorithms may not be able to convert to the appropriate feature settings of the machine learning model. To address the difficulty of obtaining effective and dynamic features from time-series data, many researchers have focused on deeper learning methods.

Deep learning decreases the difficulty of extracting automated features during EEG raw data for machine learning models [90]. As an alternative, the hierarchical feature representation can be learned through machine learning models automatically. Therefore, the hierarchical representation removes the need for pre-processing. Many of the deep learning techniques, such as auto-encoders, fully convolutional neural networks (CNNs), and recurrent neural networks (RNNs), have a great and significant impact on computer vision, speech recognition, object recognition, natural language processing (NLP), and machine translation [91, 92]. Therefore, deep

**Table 8.1** Percentage-wise usage of machine learning algorithms.

| Algorithm name | % Age of EEG references | Count of references |
|---|---|---|
| Logistic regression | 1.58 | 1 |
| Naive Bayes | 3.17 | 2 |
| Support vector machine | 58.73 | 37 |
| Random forest | 1.58 | 1 |
| AdaBoost | 1.58 | 1 |
| Probabilistic Neural Network | 1.58 | 1 |
| K-Nearest Neighbor | 12.69 | 8 |
| LDA | 6.34 | 4 |
| Elman NN | 1.58 | 1 |
| QDA | 1.58 | 1 |
| BLDA | 1.58 | 1 |
| MLP-BP | 3.17 | 2 |
| RBF | 19.04 | 12 |
| DBF | 1.58 | 1 |
| Others | Nil | 0 |

learning models can grasp high-level data abstraction and it is used for building reconfigurable emotion recognition architectures in recent years.

Deep learning offers up to date precision in several activities, from object finding to speech detection. A small number of researchers [93] show that 40% of the deep learning studies are focused on CNN and 13% used RNN for research in EEG-based systems, and more than half of the studies used pre-processed data with machine learning techniques. The systematic analysis [94] indicates that the use of CNN, RNN, and back-propagation classification tasks, and findings show that these techniques outperform conventional neural network techniques.

The deep learning models require a broad study, varied set of data, and a large amount of data to identify the underlying structure. Also, machine learning provides a fast-paced model. The advantage of in-depth learning by machine learning is that it is very accurate.

Deep learning algorithms can be categorized as three types of forwarding neural networks [92], RNNs, and CNN [91, 92] as shown in Figure 8.1. In most state-of-the-art emotional recognition research, deep learning has been used for deep extraction/representation due to its effectiveness. Deep learning models have been used in the field of EEG-based emotional recognition [95]. The current research predicts that deep learning approaches have become predominant in physiological signal analysis for the identification of emotions. Research has been conducted using a DBN and has achieved a classification accuracy of 87.62% [96]. The authors in [97–99] adopted a deep CNN model to derive features for the identification of emotions and compared to linear SVM.

The deep learning models can be classified as shown in Figure 8.1. The next subsections details about these models.

### 8.3.2.1    Fast Feed Neural Networks

The FFNN is the simplest form of an artificial neural network. With this type of construction, the data flows to only one side, forward. That is, the flow of information begins in the installation layer, then in the "hidden" layer, and ends in the extraction layer. The network does not have a loop. The details depend on the output layers [100].

### 8.3.2.2    Recurrent Neural Networks

RNN is a multidisciplinary network that can store data on content nodes, allow it to read data sequences, and extract numbers or other sequences. In simple terms, in the artificial neural network, its communication

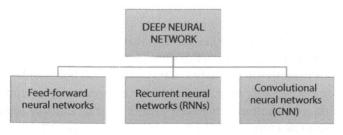

**Figure 8.1** Classification of deep neural network.

between neurons includes traps. RNNs are well-suited to process input sequences [91, 92]. For training EEG data, RNN is better to extricate the feature information as compared to other machine learning algorithms from EEG data. As informal, the transformation of raw EEG data is applied to the frequency spectrogram features for the input domain in RNN. The research has been carried out to classify seizures by applying RNN on raw EEG data and corresponding wavelet features [101]. LSTM techniques along with EEG data have been used to detect lapses [102]. Therefore, some of the authors proposed a three-stage technique for seizure finding in EEG signals; using Welch method power spectrum density, the dimensionality of description, time-series signals samples, and RNN [103]. Elman RNNs, a new architecture of RNN are used for the classification of EEG signals to understand brain mental states [104, 105]. A small number of researchers have used LSTM for EEG data [106, 107] either to predict or classify the brain emotional states. To extract EEG features from EEG data, some of the authors used wavelet transform for human brain state prediction [108]. Deep RNN has adopted quit layouts and weight loss activity with a common name. The structure based on the framework of the process of small speech processing has been used as a structural element of RNN to model the intra-expression potential for sensory recognition [109]. In conclusion, every effort has been made to replicate the neural networks of the EEG and its application areas for emotional awareness, diagnosis, and brain clarification. The neural network (NN) acquires the role of an assortment of applications due to the combined effect of feature extraction and segmentation availability on deep learning algorithms. The authors [110] used two layers of LSTM and four layers of neural networks for EEG-based signal classification. They used 1D gradient descent with a radial bias to enhance the accuracy of the proposed system.

### 8.3.2.3   Convolutional Neural Networks

CNN is a multi-layered network with a unique design that has been designed to extract more complicated data characteristics in each layer to get the result. CNN is well-suited for cognitive functions. CNN is widely-used when there is a random set of data (e.g., images) and its users need to extract information from it [92, 92]. CNNs have been widely used in recent image processing operations due to the removal of a feature from images by the convolution kernel. The details show by transferring all parts of the image to be extracted in bulk [111]. CNN works well with raw EEG data and volume range. CNN is used to train EEG data as it reduces audio performance; and thus, it reduces complexity training. Authors [112, 113] introduced a new method for extracting features and separating MI EEG for a single test. Research has been done to suggest a method of calculation to find memory performance that will be remembered or ignored by training EEG data while working on memory [114]. The combined approach of CNN and RNN has been used to train powerful features to automatically detect the presence of medical infections [115]. The authors tested CNN's new structure with four layers of conviction and three full layers of connectivity to add single-phase EEG separation to all subjects, aimed at enhancing the functioning of human segregation and autonomy [116–118].

## 8.4   Methodology of Proposed System

The response and effect of data from the EEG signal are based on a good choice of the output method and the partition algorithm. The current study highlights the possibility of the discovery of two emotional states—unpleasant and pleasant, using EEG statistics and categories. This section discusses the process, inclusion process, and other implementation details of the proposed EEG-based emotional acquisition process. The section provides a description of the proposed database and the DEAP database of the smiling model. We show the difference in RNN classification. Volunteers with no medical history reported in previous years were chosen to record the data.

For the research, the DEAP dataset is used, and the test dataset is recorded by the authors in a controlled environment using Emotiv Epoc.

Raw EEG data is collected from an EEG device designed by Emotiv Epoc: mapping of the 14+2 channels of EEG headset with DEAP data set. EEG headset used in the DEAP data set contains 32 channels. So, there was a need to map the channels.

DWT (Discrete Wavelet Transform) is applied in the form of raw EEG data. This algorithm separates the signal from certain bands and after using DWT and inverse DWT several times with the appropriate parameters, it is possible to extract alpha and beta waves from the signal at a small sample cost. A DWT is a method based on a limiting factor and a process of reducing size. The EEG signal was subdivided into multiple sub-bands using DWT and produced the best intermediate results to be incorporated into the classification engine. Next appropriate classification technique is applied for the extraction of emotions for decision-making.

### 8.4.1 DEAP Dataset

DEAP dataset was used as a test dataset. DEAP [119] is a publically available dataset for the analysis of human affective analysis in a multimodal way. The DEAP database has been used in so many times in various research studies for detection [120, 121]. An EEG and the physical gestures of the 32 participants were recorded as each watched 40-minute quotes for music videos. Participants rated each video according to levels of arousal, valence, likes/dislikes, dominance, and familiarity.

To set the true emotional states we referred to the rating scale mentioned in [119]. We used the DEAP self-report reports to identify selected areas using the nine-point Likert scale.

### 8.4.2 Analyzing the Dataset

For the current research, six emotions will be detected (happy, sad, angry, neutral, bored, and surprise) and emotions are mapped as valence arousal model with valence values as "positive, negative, and neutral" and arousal values as "high, medium, and low". The values are based on valence arousal model shown in Figure 8.2. The values are measured on a Likert scale. Classifying the dataset according to rules formed and by using mean of

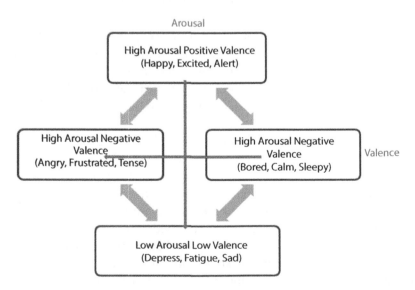

**Figure 8.2** Valence arousal model.

values, the states can be categorized into sub-states. For the classification of these emotions, RNN-LSTM will be used.

### 8.4.3    Long Short-Term Memory

Standard RNN preparation can be difficult due to gradient problems vanishing or exploding. This inhibits the network's ability to replicate gradients over long periods. This prevents a moderate dependency model between input data of human activities while studying movements with long rear windows. However, LSTM-based RNNs can simulate time series strings and their comprehensive dependencies by inserting common nodes with memory cells with internal and external duplication.

### 8.4.4    Experimental Setup

The data set was collected from 35 volunteers, comprising 30 males and 5 females of different age groups. Different responses were gathered from the participants while watching the video clips. EEG signals were acquired from 16(14+2) electrodes by using a 10-20 international standard placement system.

The data set was collected using the respondents who were made to sit in a controlled environment.

**Stimuli Video Clips:** Psychologists suggested that video duration is from one to ten minutes to elicit single emotion [122, 123]. For stimuli selection, 20 video clips were chosen to gather multiple responses from participants.

### 8.4.5    Data Set Collection

The experiment was conducted with 35 subjects, where each subject was shown 20 advertisements that caused some emotion. To detect EEG signals, the Emotiv Epoc headset of (14+2) channels was used for analysis. The EEG signal window video is divided into frames depending on the sampling frequency and duration of the video. There are 10 resultant emotions obtained so the number of emotions is multiplied by the number of frames. The number of features obtained is large in number. The advertisement clip of 1- to 2-minute duration is used as a stimulus to recognize the change in facial expression and EEG signals as in Figure 8.3.

All the equipment that was needed for the experiment such as a monitor, screen, computer, EEG machine, camera, was kept ready before

**Figure 8.3** EEG setup.

30 minutes of the session of data collecting. To ensure the participant is in a comfortable mood, a relaxation time of 10 minutes was given to relax the brain. Then, EEG headset was applied to each of the volunteers. The volunteers were selected with the prior permission of not applying oil on hair. The major things that trigger the emotion are color combination, brand, model presenting the advertisement, duration of the advertisement, and user interest in a product.

## 8.5    Results and Discussions

### 8.5.1    LSTM Model Training and Accuracy

The LSTM model here has six layers of LSTM, six layers of batch normalization, six dropout layers, and one dense layer, as well as many epochs. The accuracy of the model by using the LSTM model is predicted, as shown in Figure 8.4.

The accuracy graphs of DEAP as a training dataset and proposed dataset as validation set show a comparative result for 600 epochs. The results show that the model can be used for emotion prediction using the validation and test datasets, but there is a scope of improvement in the accuracy of the result.

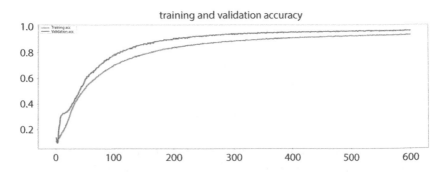

**Figure 8.4** Training and validation accuracy for DEAP dataset.

## 8.6    Conclusion

The chapter started with the introduction of emotion recognition and studying the gap between traditional market research, and neuromarketing research using EEG as the base technique. In the next section, the literature examined provided descriptions of the different machines. The review provided the following observations 1) The analysis shows that 58% of researchers used SVM as a classification technique to classify emotions 2) Machine learning techniques became more studied in 2016 and in-depth study models of EEG-based emotional recognition were released in 2020. The LSTM model was trained to check the emotional states for advertisements and was tested over the proposed dataset. The accuracy of the validation and test dataset was comparable, but there is a scope of improvement. For future work, we propose to improve the accuracy of the LSTM model with DWT as a dimensionality reduction technique for EEG-based emotion recognition.

## References

1. Abdulkader, S.N., Brain computer interfacing: Applications and challenges. *Egypt. Inform. J.*, *16*, 2, 213–230, 2015.
2. Agarwal, S. and Dutta, T., Neuromarketing and consumer neuroscience: current understanding and the way forward. *Decision*, *42*, 4, 457–462, 2015.
3. ALdayel, M.Y.-N., Deep Learning for EEG-Based Preference Classification in Neuromarketing. *Appl. Sci.*, *10*, 4, 1525–1548, 2020.
4. Alhagry, S.F.-K., Emotion recognition based on EEG using LSTM recurrent neural network. *Emotion*, *8*, 10, 355–358, 2017.
5. Ali, M.M., EEG-based emotion recognition approach for e-healthcare applications, in: *2016 eighth international conference on ubiquitous and future networks (ICUFN)*, IEEE, pp. 946–950, 2016.
6. Al-Nafjan, A., Hosny, M., Al-Ohali, Y., Al-Wabil, A., Review and classification of emotion recognition based on EEG brain-computer interface system research: a systematic review. *Appl. Sci.*, *7*, 12, 1239, 2017.
7. Alsolamy, M. and Fattouh, A., Emotion estimation from EEG signals during listening to Quran using PSD features. *7th International Conference on Computer Science and Information Technology (CSIT)*, IEEE, pp. 1–5, 2016.
8. Atkinson, J. and Campos, D., Improving BCI-based emotion recognition by combining EEG feature selection and kernel classifiers. *Exp. Syst. Appl.*, *47*, 35–41, 2016.
9. Bartra, O.M., The valuation system: a coordinate-based meta-analysis of BOLD fMRI experiments examining neural correlates of subjective value. *Neuroimage*, *76*, 412–427, 2013.

10. Bastos-Filho, T.F., Evaluation of feature extraction techniques in emotional state recognition, in: *2012 4th International conference on intelligent human computer interaction (IHCI)*, IEEE, pp. 1–6, 2012.

11. Baumgartner, T.S., Diminishing parochialism in intergroup conflict by disrupting the right temporo-parietal junction. *Soc Cogn. Affect. Neurosci.*, 9, 5, 653–660, 2014.

12. Bechara, A.D., Different contributions of the human amygdala and ventromedial prefrontal cortex to decision-making. *J. Neurosci.*, 19, 13, 5473–5481, 1999.

13. Benar, C.S.-C., Single-trial analysis of oddball event-related potentials in simultaneous EEG-fMRI. *Hum. Brain Mapp.*, 28, 602–613, 2007.

14. Berka, C. and Levendowski, D., EEG correlates of task engagement and mental workload in vigilance, learning, and memory tasks. *Aviat. Space Environ. Med.*, 78, B231–44, 2007.

15. Bhatti, A.M., Human emotion recognition and analysis in response to audio music using brain signals. *Comput. Hum. Behav.*, 65, 267–275, 2016.

16. Bigdely-Shamlo, N. and Mullen, T., The PREP pipeline: standardized preprocessing for large-scale EEG analysis. *Front. Neuroinform.*, 9–16, 2015.

17. Blankertz, B.L., Single-trial analysis and classification of ERP components—a tutorial. *NeuroImage*, 56, 2, 814–825, 2011.

18. Brown, L. and Bernard, G., Towards wireless emotional valence detection from EEG," in IEEE EMBS, in: *2011 Annual International Conference of the IEEE Engineering in Medicine and Biology Society*, vol. 2011, IEEE, pp. 2188–2191, 2011.

19. Buschman, T.J., Top-down versus bottom-up control of attention in the prefrontal and posterior parietal cortices. *Science, 315*, 5820, 1860–1862, 2007.

20. Cecotti, H. and Graser, A., Convolutional neural networks for P300 detection with application to brain-computer interfaces. *IEEE Trans. Pattern Anal. Mach. Intell.*, 33, 3, 433–445, 2010.

21. Chanel, G.K., Short-term emotion assessment in a recall paradigm. *Int. J. Hum. Comput. Stud.*, 67, 8, 607–627, 2009.

22. Chen, J.H., Electroencephalogram-based emotion assessment system using ontology and data mining techniques. *Appl. Soft Comput.*, 30, 663–674, 2015.

23. Clerc, M. and Bougrain, L., *Brain–Computer Interfaces 1: Foundations and Methods*, New York, Wiley, 2016.

24. Cole, S.V., Cycle-by-cycle analysis of neural oscillations. *J. Neurophysiol.*, 122, 2, 849–861, 2019.

25. Craik, A.H.-V., Deep learning for electroencephalogram (EEG) classification tasks: a review. *J. Neural Eng.*, 16, 3, 031001, 2019.

26. Critchley, H.D., Neural activity relating to generation and representation of galvanic skin conductance responses: a functional magnetic resonance imaging study. *J. Neurosci.*, 20, 8, 3033–304, 2000.

27. Davidson, P.R., EEG-based lapse detection with high temporal resolution. *IEEE Trans. Biomed. Eng.*, 54, 5, 832–839, 2007.

28. Duan, R.N., Differential entropy feature for EEG-based emotion classification, in: *2013 6th International IEEE/EMBS Conference on Neural Engineering (NER)*, IEEE, pp. 81–84, 2013.

29. Fayek, H.M., Evaluating deep learning architectures for Speech Emotion Recognition. *Neural Netw.*, *92*, 60–68, 2017.

30. Forney, E.M., Classification of EEG during imagined mental tasks by forecasting with Elman recurrent neural networks, in: *The 2011 International Joint Conference on Neural Networks*, IEEE, pp. 2749–2755, 2011.

31. Gao, Y.L., Deep learninig of EEG signals for emotion recognition, in: *2015 IEEE International Conference on Multimedia & Expo Workshops (ICMEW)*, IEEE, pp. 1–5, 2015.

32. Geisen, E. and Murphy, J., A Compendium of Web and Mobile Survey Pretesting Methods, in: *Advances in Questionnaire Design, Development, Evaluation and Testing*, pp. 287–314, 2020.

33. Gramfort A, S.D., Time-frequency mixed-norm estimates: sparse M/EEG imaging with non-stationary source activations. *NeuroImage*, *70*, 410–22, 2013.

34. Hadjidimitriou, S.K., Toward an EEG-based recognition of music liking using time-frequency analysis. *IEEE Trans. Biomed. Eng.*, *59*, 12, 3498–3510, 2012.

35. Hakim, A. and Levy, D.J., A gateway to consumers' minds: Achievements, caveats, and prospects of electroencephalography-based prediction in neuromarketing. *Wiley Interdiscip. Rev. Cogn. Sci.*, *10*, 2, e1485, 2019.

36. Hammou, K.A., The contributions of neuromarketing in marketing research. *J. Manage. Res.*, *5*, 4, 20, 2013.

37. Hatamikia, S.M., The emotion recognition system based on autoregressive model and sequential forward feature selection of electroencephalogram signals. *J. Med. Signals Sens.*, *4*, 3, 194, 2014.

38. Hosseini, S.A., Emotional stress recognition system using EEG and psychophysiological signals: Using new labelling process of EEG signals in emotional stress state, in: *2010 international conference on biomedical engine*, IEEE, pp. 1–6, 2010.

39. Huang, D.G., Asymmetric spatial pattern for EEG-based emotion detection, in: *The 2012 International Joint Conference on Neural Networks (IJCNN)*, IEEE, pp. 1–7, 2012.

40. Hwang, H.J., EEG-Based Brain-Computer Interfaces: A Thorough Literature Survey. *Int. J. Hum. Comput. Interact.*, *29*, 12, 814–826, 2013.

41. Jain, D.K., Extended deep neural network for facial emotion recognition. *Pattern Recognit. Lett.*, *120*, 69–74, 2019.

42. Jas, M. and Engemann, D.A., Autoreject: automated artifact rejection for MEG and EEG data. *NeuroImage*, *159*, 417–29, 2017.

43. Jatupaiboon, N.P.-N., Subject-dependent and subject-independent emotion classification using unimodal and multimodal physiological signals. *J. Med. Imaging Health Inform.*, *5*, 5, 1020–1027, 2015.

44. Jiang, J.Z., Single-trial ERP detecting for emotion recognition. *17th IEEE/ACIS International Conference on Software Engineering, Artificial Intelligence, Networking and Parallel/Distributed Computing (SNPD)*, IEEE, pp. 105–108, 2016.
45. Jiao, Z.G., Deep Convolutional Neural Networks for mental load classification based on EEG data. *Pattern Recognit.*, 76, 582–595, 2018.
46. Jie, X.C., Emotion recognition based on the sample entropy of EEG, in: *Biomedical materials and engineering*, vol. 24, pp. 1185–1192, 2014.
47. Jordão, I.L., Neuromarketing applied to consumer behaviour: an integrative literature review between 2010 and 2015. *Int. J. Business Forecasting Marketing Intell.*, 3, 3, 270–288, 2017.
48. Kaur, R.G., Cognitive emotion measures of brain, in: *2019 6th International Conference on Computing for Sustainable Global Development (INDIACom)*, IEEE, pp. 290–294, 2019.
49. Khalili, Z. and Moradi, H., Emotion recognition system using brain and peripheral signals: using correlation dimension to improve the results of EEG, in: *2009 International Joint Conference on Neural Networks*, IEEE, pp. 1571–1575, 2009.
50. Khosrowabadi, R.Q., EEG-based Emotion Recognition Using Self-Organizing Map for Boundary Detection, in: *2010 20th International Conference on Pattern Recognition*, pp. 4242–4245, 2010.
51. Koelstra, S.M., Deap: A database for emotion analysis; using physiological signals. *IEEE T. Affect. Comput.*, 3, 1, 18–31, 2011.
52. Koelstra, S.P., Fusion of facial expressions and EEG for implicit affective tagging. *Image Vis. Comput.*, 31, 2, 164–174, 2013.
53. Koelstra, S.Y., Single Trial Classification of EEG and Peripheral Physiological Signals for Recognition of Emotions Induced by Music Videos, in: *International Conference on Brain Informatics*, Springer, Berlin, Heidelberg, pp. 89–100, 2010.
54. Krain, A.L., Distinct neural mechanisms of risk and ambiguity: a meta-analysis of decision-making. *Neuroimage*, 32, 1, 477–484, 2006.
55. Kroupi, E.V., Subject-independent odor pleasantness classification using brain and peripheral signals. *IEEE T. Affect. Comput.*, 7, 4, 422–434, 2015.
56. Kumar, N.K., Bispectral analysis of EEG for emotion recognition. *Proc. Comput. Sci.*, 84, 31–35, 2016.
57. Lan, Z.L., Real-time EEG-based user's valence monitoring IEEE, in: *2015 10th International Conference on Information, Communications and Signal Processing (ICICS)*, IEEE, pp. 1–5, 2015.
58. Lee, Y.Y., Classifying different emotional states by means of EEG-based functional connectivity patterns. *PloS One*, 9, 4, 1–13, 2014.
59. Li Y, G.C., A self-training semi-supervised SVM algorithm and its application in an EEG-based brain computer interface speller system. *Pattern Recognit. Lett.*, 29, 9, 1285–1294, 2008.

60. Li, D.W., Facial expression recognition based on Electroencephalogram and facial landmark localization. *Technol. Healthcare*, *27*, 4, 373–387, 2019.
61. Li, G.L., Deep learning for EEG data analytics: A survey. *Concurr. Comput. Pract. Exp.*, e5199, 2019.
62. Li, M.L., Emotion classification based on gamma-band EEG, in: *2009 Annual International Conference of the IEEE Engineering in medicine and biology society*, IEEE, pp. 1223–1226, 2009.
63. Li, N.M., Resting-state functional connectivity predicts impulsivity in economic decision-making. *J. Neurosci.*, *33*, 11, 4886–4895, 2013.
64. Lin, M.H., Applying EEG in consumer neuroscience. *Eur. J. Marekting, 52*, 66–91, 2018.
65. Lin, Y.P., EEG-based emotion recognition in music listening: A comparison of schemes for multiclass support vector machine. *IEEE International Conference on Acoustics, Speech and Signal Processing*, IEEE, pp. 489–492, 2009.
66. Lin, Y.P., EEG-Based Emotion Recognition in Music Listening,". *IEEE Trans. Biomed. Eng.*, *57*, 7, 1798–1806, 2010.
67. Lin, Y.P., Exploring day-to-day variability in EEG-based emotion classification, in: *2014 IEEE International Conference on Systems, Man, and Cybernetics (SMC)*, IEEE, pp. 2226–2229, 2014.
68. Liu, Y.H., Single-trial EEG based emotion recognition using kernel Eigenemotion pattern and adaptive support vector machine, in: *2013 35th Annual International Conference of the IEEE Engineering in Medicine and Biology Society (EMBC)*, IEEE, pp. 4306–4309, 2013.
69. Lotte F, B.L., A review of classification algorithms for EEG-based braincomputer interfaces: a 10 year update. *J. Neural Eng.*, *15*, 031005, 2018.
70. Lou, S.F., An integrated decision-making method for product design scheme evaluation based on cloud model and EEG data. *Adv. Eng. Inform.*, *43*, 101028–1010236, 2020.
71. Makeig, S.L.-S., First demonstration of a musical emotion BCI, in: *International Conference on Affective Computing and Intelligent Interaction*, Springer, Berlin, Heidelberg, pp. 487–496, 2011.
72. Manor, R. and Geva, A.B., Convolutional neural network for multi-category rapid serial visual presentation BCI. *Front. Comput. Neurosci.*, *9*, 146, 2015.
73. Matlovič, T., Emotion Detection using EPOC EEG device, in: *Information and Informatics Technologies Student Research Conference (IIT. SRC)*, pp. 1–6, 2016.
74. Mehmood, R.M., A novel feature extraction method based on late positive potential for emotion recognition in human brain signal patterns. *Comput. Electr. Eng.*, *53*, 444–457, 2016.
75. Mikhail, M.E.-A., Using minimal number of electrodes for emotion detection using brain signals produced from a new elicitation technique. *Int. J. Auton. Adapt. Commun. Syst.*, *6*, 1, 80–97, 2013.

76. Minasyan, G.R., Patient-specific early seizure detection from scalp EEG. *J. Clin. Neurophysiol.: Off. Publ. Am. Electroencephalographic Soc.*, 27, 3, 163, 2010.

77. Mohammadi, Z.F., Wavelet-based emotion recognition system using EEG signal. *Neural Comput. Appl.*, 28, 8, 1985–1990, 2017.

78. Morin, C., Neuromarketing: The New Science of Consumer Behavior. *Society*, 48, 131–135, 2011.

79. Murugappan, M.M., Wireless EEG signals based neuromarketing system using Fast Fourier Transform (FFT), in: *2014 IEEE 10th International Colloquium on Signal Processing and its Applications*, IEEE, Kuala Lumpur, pp. 25–30, 2014.

80. Nagabushanam, P.G., EEG signal classification using LSTM and improved neural network algorithms. *Soft Comput.*, 1–23, 2019.

81. Nasehi, S.P., An optimal EEG-based emotion recognition algorithm using gabor features. *WSEAS Trans. Signal Process.*, 3, 8, 87–99, 2012.

82. Ni, Z.Y., Confused or not Confused? Disentangling Brain Activity from EEG Data Using Bidirectional LSTM Recurrent Neural Networks, in: *Proceedings of the 8th ACM International Conference on Bioinformatics, Computational Biology, and Health Informatics*, ACM, pp. 241–246, 2017.

83. Nosratabadi, S.M., State of the art survey of deep learning and machine learning models for smart cities and urban sustainability, in: *International Conference on Global Research and Education*, Cham, Springer, Cham, pp. 228–238, 2019.

84. Ohme, R.R., Analysis of neurophysiological reactions to advertising stimuli by means of EEG and galvanic skin response measures. *J. Neurosci. Psychol. Econ.*, 2, 21–31, 2009.

85. Pan, J.L., An EEG-based brain-computer interface for emotion recognition, in: *2016 international joint conference on neural networks (IJCNN)*, IEEE, pp. 2063–2067, 2016.

86. Patnaik, S.M., Deep RNN learning for EEG based functional brain state inference. *International Conference on Advances in Computing, Communication and Control (ICAC3)*, IEEE, pp. 1–6, 2017.

87. Petrantonakis, P.C., Emotion recognition from brain signals using hybrid adaptive filtering and higher order crossings analysis. *IEEE T. Affect. Comput.*, 1, 2, 81–97, 2010.

88. Petrosian, A.P., Recurrent neural network based prediction of epileptic seizures in intra-and extracranial EEG. *Neurocomputing*, 30, 1.4, 201–218, 2000.

89. Pham, T.D., Emotion recognition using the emotiv epoc device, in: *International Conference on Neural Information Processing*, Springer, Berlin, Heidelberg, pp. 394–399, 2012.

90. Ramadan, R.A., Basics of brain computer interface, in: *Brain-Computer Interfaces*, vol. 74, pp. 31–50, Springer Cham, Switzerland, 2015.

91. Ramadan, R.A., Brain computer interface: control signals review. *Neurocomputing*, 223, 26–44, 2017.

92. Romero, E.M., Margin maximization with feed-forward neural networks: a comparative study with SVM and AdaBoost. *Neurocomputing, 57,* 313–344, 2004.

93. Roy, Y.B., Deep learning-based electroencephalography analysis: a systematic review. *J. Neural Eng., 16,* 5, 051001, 2019.

94. Santhoshkumar, R. and Geetha, M.K., Deep Learning Approach for Emotion Recognition from Human Body Movements with Feedforward Deep Convolution Neural Networks. *Proc. Comput. Sci., 152,* 158–165, 2019.

95. Shahabi, H. and Moghimi, S., Toward automatic detection of brain responses to emotional music through analysis of EEG effective connectivity. *Comput. Hum. Behav., 58,* 231–239, 2016.

96. Shamwell, J.L., Single-trial EEG RSVP classification using convolutional neural networks, in: *Micro-and Nanotechnology Sensors, Systems, and Applications VIII,* vol. *9836,* p. 983622, 2016.

97. Shin, S.J., Brainwave-based Mood Classification Using Regularized Common Spatial Pattern Filter. *KSII T. Internet Inf., 10,* 2, 807–824, 2016.

98. Shu, L.X., A review of emotion recognition using physiological signals. *Sensors, 18,* 7, 2074, 2018.

99. Si, Y.L., Predicting individual decision-making responses based on single-trial EEG. *NeuroImage, 206,* 116333–116342, 2020.

100. Singh, J.G., Use of neurometrics to choose optimal advertisement method for omnichannel business. *Enterp. Inf. Syst., 14,* 2, 243–265, 2020.

101. Smith, M.E., Monitoring task loading with multivariate EEG measures during complex forms of human-computer interaction. *Hum. Factors, 43,* 3, 366–380, 2001.

102. Soleymani, M.A.-E., Continuous emotion detection using EEG signals and facial expressions, in: *2014 IEEE International Conference on Multimedia and Expo (ICME),* IEEE, pp. 1–6, 2014.

103. Soleymani, M.L., A Multimodal Database for Affect Recognition and Implicit Tagging. *IEEE T. Affect. Comput., 3,* 1, 42–55, 2012.

104. Soleymani, M.P., Multimodal Emotion Recognition in Response to Videos. *IEEE T. Affect. Comput., 3,* 2, 211–223, 2011.

105. Stikic, M.J., EEG-based classification of positive and negative affective states. *Brain-Comput. Interfaces, 1,* 2, 99–112, 2014.

106. Stober, S.S., *Deep feature learning for EEG recordings. arXiv preprint arXiv:1511.04306,* 2015.

107. Sun, X.Q., Remembered or forgotten?—An EEG-Based computational prediction approach. *PloS One, 11,* 12, 2016.

108. Suzuki, S.H., Learning to simulate others' decisions. *Neuron, 74,* 6, 1125–1137, 2012.

109. Tang, Z.L., Single-trial EEG classification of motor imagery using deep convolutional neural networks. *Optik, 130,* 11–18, 2017.

110. Thammasan, N.F., Application of deep belief networks in eeg-based dynamic music-emotion recognition, in: *2016 International Joint Conference on Neural Networks (IJCNN)*, IEEE, pp. 881–888, 2016.
111. Thodoroff, P.P., Learning robust features using deep learning for automatic seizure detection, in: *Machine Learning for Healthcare Conference*, pp. 178–190, 2016.
112. Tripathi, S.A., Using Deep and Convolutional Neural Networks for Accurate Emotion Classification on DEAP Dataset, in: *Twenty-Ninth IAAI Conference*, pp. 4746–4752, 2017.
113. Vijayan, A.E., EEG-based emotion recognition using statistical measures and auto-regressive modeling, in: *2015 IEEE International Conference on Computational Intelligence & Communication Technology*, IEEE, pp. 587–591, 2015.
114. Wang, X.W., Emotional state classification from EEG data using machine learning approach. *Neurocomputing*, *129*, 94–106, 2014.
115. Xu, H. and Plataniotis, K.N., Affect recognition using EEG signal, in: *2012 IEEE 14th International Workshop on Multimedia Signal Processing (MMSP)*, IEEE, pp. 299–304, 2012.
116. Yadava, M.K., Analysis of EEG signals and its application to neuromarketing. *Multimed. Tools Appl.*, *76*, 18, 19087–19111, 2017.
117. Yazdani, A.L., Implicit emotional tagging of multimedia using EEG signals and brain computer interface, in: *Proceedings of the first SIGMM workshop on Social media*, ACM, pp. 81–88, 2009.
118. Yoon, H.J., EEG-based emotion estimation using Bayesian weighted-log-posterior function and perceptron convergence algorithm. *Comput. Biol. Med.*, *43*, 12, 2230–2237, 2013.
119. Zander, T.O., Towards passive brain– computer interfaces: applying brain–computer interface technology to human–machine systems in general. *J. Neural Eng.*, *8*, 2, 025005, 2011.
120. Zhang, J.Y., Emotion recognition using multi-modal data and machine learning techniques: A tutorial and review. *Inform. Fusion*, *59*, 103–126, 2020.
121. Zhang, S.Z., Learning affective features with a hybrid deep model for audio-visual emotion recognition. *IEEE Trans. Circuits Syst. Video Technol.*, *28*, 10, 3030–3043, 2017.
122. Zhang, X.Y., *A survey on deep learning based brain computer interface: Recent advances and new frontiers. arXiv preprint arXiv:1905.04149*, 2019.
123. Zheng, W.L., EEG-based emotion classification using deep belief networks, in: *2014 IEEE International Conference on Multimedia and Expo (ICME)*, IEEE, pp. 1–6, 2014.

# 9

# An Extensive Survey of Applications of Advanced Deep Learning Algorithms on Detection of Neurodegenerative Diseases and the Tackling Procedure in Their Treatment Protocol

Vignesh Baalaji S., Vergin Raja Sarobin M.*, L. Jani Anbarasi, Graceline Jasmine S. and Rukmani P.

*School of Computer Science and Engineering, Vellore Institute of Technology, Chennai, India*

## Abstract

A degenerative disorder that results in deterioration of the structure or functions of the "nervous system", either by killing or rupturing the nerve cells, is known as a neurodegenerative disease. The most frequently occurring nerve disorder is "Alzheimer's Disease" (AD) and "Parkinson's Disease" (PD). The "National Institute of Environmental Health Sciences" has declared that, in the year 2016, around five million American citizens were living with AD. It focuses on application of deep learning models in the detecting the frequent occurrence of neurodegenerative diseases, the AD and PD. It also includes research works involving novel architecture for ensuring security in the deep brain stimulation (a treatment protocol for PD). This survey briefly reviews some significant literature on the application of advanced deep learning algorithms in the diagnosis of neurodegenerative diseases and in tackling the security threats in their treatment protocol. This chapter presented few techniques followed by various researchers; accuracy, sensitivity, and recall achieved by the methodologies have been presented for PD.

*Keywords:* Deep learning, Alzheimer's Disease, Parkinson's Disease, deep brain stimulation, machine learning

*Corresponding author*: verginraja.m@vit.ac.in

Archana Mire, Shaveta Malik and Amit Kumar Tyagi (eds.) Advanced Analytics and Deep Learning Models, (207–230) © 2022 Scrivener Publishing LLC

## 9.1   Introduction

The human nervous system is constructed with structures called the neurons. Our body does not replace these structures when they are ruptured or dead. This results in neurodegenerative disorders such as Alzheimer's disease (AD) or Parkinson's disease (PD). These diseases are not curable and slowly deteriorate the brain resulting in the death of the patient. The most commonly occurring neuro disorders are the dementias, and the frequent cause of dementias is the AD [14]. This chapter focuses on application of deep learning models [53, 54] in the detecting the frequent occurrence of neurodegenerative diseases, the AD and PD. It also includes research works involving novel architecture for ensuring security in the deep brain stimulation (DBS) (a treatment protocol for PD). This study is sorted as follows: Section 9.2 describes the story of AD, Section 9.3 describes the story of PD, Section 9.4 explains the deep learning algorithms using in detection of neurodegenerative diseases, Section 9.5 discusses about the methodology proposed by various researchers, Section 9.6 compares the results of the methodologies under various areas, and Section 9.7 gives the conclusion, followed by the references section.

## 9.2   Story of Alzheimer's Disease

Alzheimer's Disease: According to the textbook of "Clinical Psychiatry (1910)", there was a special set of cases involving death in the majority of the cerebral cortex with severe nutrition deficiency and nerve damage caused by the presence of huge numbers of plaques [1]. The author, named Kraepelin, was the person who defined the term AD [15]. The first case was introduced by Dr. Alois Alzheimer, who then gave the description of AD in 1907, followed by Proskin in 1909 [16]. Later in 1998, it was found that neurofibrillary cramps and amyloid plaques have affected certain parts of brain leading to AD [17]. It is one of the major causes of death for the elderly, in the USA [18].

Causes of Alzheimer's Disease: AD is caused when a special protein known as the A-Beta gets converted into plaques (insoluble deposits), which kills neuron synapses and disrupts communication between the brain cells. Though A-Beta contributes more to the cause of AD, another major reason is the tau tangles which, damages the stability of neural structure thereby killing them. The research so far suggests that the physical symptoms in the brain appear before the cognitive symptoms. We could infer that the sooner we detect the biomarkers, the sooner we could treat the patients to slow down or maybe even

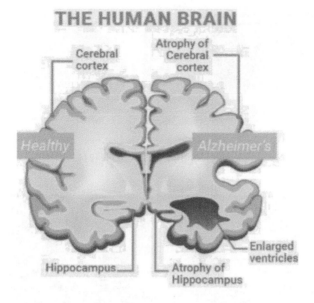

**Figure 9.1** Comparison of healthy brain and AD-affected brain.

prevent the disease. Figure 9.1 shows a comparison of healthy brain and AD-affected brain [19].

Stages of Alzheimer's Disease: AD can be classified into seven different phases based on the Global Deterioration Scale (GDS). In GDS phases 1 and 2, the patient will not face any impairment; in phase 4, there will be mild cognitive impairment (MCI); in phases 4 and 5, the patient will have mild to moderate dementia; and in phases 6 and 7, severe dementia will be experienced.

Diagnosis Methods: AD can be diagnosed using noninvasive methods such as MRIs, which can help us to comprehend the structure of patient's brain [45]. This can be divided into two groups, namely, as structural and functional imaging [46], where the first gives information on brain's structure and the latter reports about the activities [47–52].

Magnetic Resonance Image (MRI): The structure of the brain is captured as 3D or 2D format pictures, using magnetic fields and radio waves. A sample of sMRI is given in Figure 9.2a, and a sample of fMRI is given in Figure 9.2b. As mentioned above, fMRI captures activity related details of the brain.

Positron Emission Tomography (PET): "Positron Emission Tomography" is a neuroimaging technique that analyzes the activities of the brain as radioactive spheres, using radiotracers. Figure 9.3 shows and example image of PET scan during various activities such as looking listening, utilizing fluorodeoxyglucose and amyloid, which are the most commonly used tracers, for

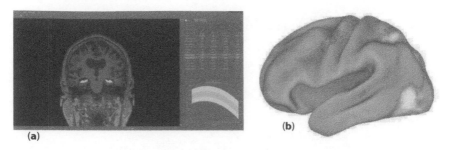

**Figure 9.2** (a) sMRI example and [20] (b) fMRI example [21].

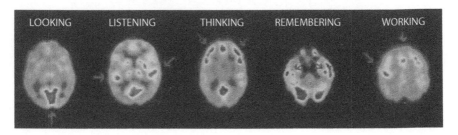

**Figure 9.3** Example of PET [22].

diagnosis of AD. A cost-efficient alterative for PET will be SPECT but is not well-suited for initial investigation.

## 9.3    Datasets

### 9.3.1    ADNI

The ADNI database consists of 509 cases out of which 137 belong to AD category and 67 belong to MCIc, 134 belong to MCInc, and 76 normal cases [23]. The idea is to see whether bio markers such as MRI ad PET can be used for advancement in early detection of AD. It holds sMRIs with a volume of 121 × 145 × 121 voxels [1].

### 9.3.2    OASIS

Developed by Dr. Randy Buckner and the Neuroinformatic Research Group at Harvard University [24], this database involves 100 cases of subjects aged older than 60 years old and 416 cases aged between 18- and 96 years-old subjects. Sample images from the OASIS dataset are given in Figure 9.4.

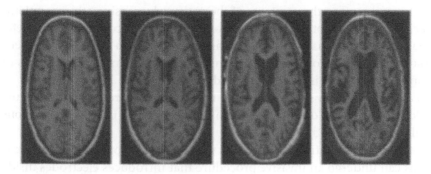

**Figure 9.4** OASIS example images [25].

## 9.4   Story of Parkinson's Disease

Parkinson's Disease: Parkinson's Disease or PD is a variant of neurode-generative ailment causing, involuntary trembling, kinetic difficulty, and loss in self-coordination. With its progress, the disease may challenge the patients with physical activities as well as in mentality, which may lead to a variety of problems such as depression, memory difficulties, behavioral changes, fatigue, and sleep problems. Elderly people are more likely to get affected by this ailment with the proportion of patients with "early-onset" is less than 10% [26, 27].

Causes of Parkinson's Disease: When nerves cell units become dead or rup-tured in the kinetic control area of the brain, it results in PD. The neurons in this part are responsible for the production of an essential brain chemical, dopamine. Consequently, as they become damaged or dead, they produce less dopamine, which results in the patient's movement issues. The death cause of these neurons is yet to be discovered. These patients also lose another chem-ical called norepinephrine, which acts as the messenger part of the "central-nervous-system", responsible for controlling involuntary body movements such as "blood pressure" and "pulse". This loss affects a person's non-physical health by causing irregular blood pressure, fatigue, etc. Though some cases of PD are genetic, some tend to be random as well. Thus, the scientific community believes its cause to be a combination of environmental and genetic factors.

Symptoms: Some common symptoms include the following:

- Resting tremor/tremble.
- Limbs and trunk stubbornness.
- Hindrance in kinetic activities.
- Loss of balance.

It can also affect the mentality of the patients by causing other symptoms like, depression, emotional and behavioral changes, difficulty in speaking, etc.
Diagnosis of Parkinson's Disease: Diagnosis of PD can be based on a neurological examination and medical history of a patient. The diagnosis of non-hereditary PD is challenging to diagnose.
Treatment of Parkinson's disease: At the time of this review, PD is incurable, but the effects of the disease can be alleviated by certain medications and invasive methods.
Deep Brain Stimulation: The patients who do not respond well for medications can undergo an invasive procedure that introduces electrodes inside the brain. These electrodes can combat by releasing minor electric charges that normalize kinetic disorders of the patient, thereby alleviating them from the symptoms.

**Datasets**

**PPMI**
"PPMI" or "Parkinson's Progression Markers Initiative" occurs at clinical sites in Australia, Europe, Israel, and the United States of America. Data and samples acquired from study participants will help develop a comprehensive database and biorepository for PD, available for research purposes to the scientific community. There are 72 data tables available in PPMI that comprises both lab and clinical data.

**PhysioNet—"DBS Dataset"**
This dataset contains rest tremor velocity (RTV) recordings of index finger for sixteen patients, who undertake "Electrical DBS" either it being unilateral or bilateral. DBS involves a surgical method that includes implantation of electrodes into the brain's subcortical structures for "long-term stimulation" at frequencies higher than "100 Hz".

## 9.5   A Review on Learning Algorithms

### 9.5.1   Convolutional Neural Network (CNN)

"Convolutional Neural Network" is a variant of deep neural network architecture that draws its inspiration from the brain's visual cortex. This architecture makes use of spatial data in two and three dimensional using continuous of convolution operation, which forms the basics of "CNN" and has been established as an efficient model for image processing [28, 29]. Apart from classification, they also act as excellent feature extractors for image-based data. Example architecture of the CNN is given in Figure 9.5.

## 9.5.2   Restricted Boltzmann Machine

"Restricted Boltzmann Machine" (RBM) is linked in-between hidden and visible layers but neurons within the same layer does not have any connections, which is similar to a bipartite graph. This model makes use of contrast divergence as its training technique, rather than traditional gradient-descent-based algorithms. It can generate input data from hidden representations, like an auto encoder as in [31, 32]. Deep Belief Networks or DBNs can be formed by used stacked RBMs, as in [33].

## 9.5.3   Siamese Neural Networks

"Siamese Neural Network" is a type of neural network architecture that contains two or more identical subnetworks, i.e., both the networks have

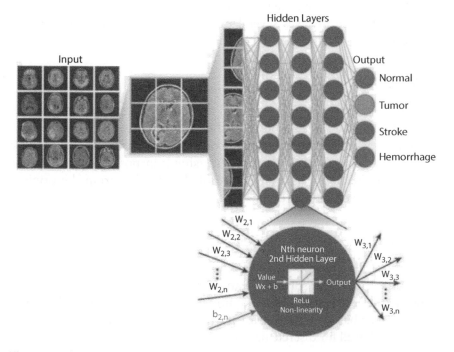

**Figure 9.5**  CNN—Example [30].

the same configuration with a similar weight and parameters. Upgradation of parameters is mirrored across both the sub-networks. It is used to find the inputs' similarity by comparing its feature vectors, which can be implemented in many use cases. As these SNNs learn a similarity function, they can be trained to see if the two images are similar. Thus, it can be used in classifying new classes of data without training the network again.

### 9.5.4    Residual Network (ResNet)

"Residual Network", also known as "ResNet", is a neural network architecture used as a backbone for many computer vision problems. ResNet's significant advantage is that it successfully enables the training of very deep neural networks, as it solves the vanishing gradient problem. The "ResNet50" consists of five stages, with each stage having an identity block and convolutional block. This architecture has its application in transfer learning, by acting as a feature extractor, where the extracted features can be passed on to a classifier for obtaining final results. It can also be fine-tuned, where, initially, it will be loaded with pre-trained ImageNet weights, and the new fully connected layer head replaces the original head to classify the data for our problem. To learn the skip weights, if an additional weight matrix is utilized, then it is known as the "HighwayNets", where if the architecture involves several parallel skips, then it is known as a "DenseNet".

### 9.5.5    U-Net

Olaf Ronneberger *et al.* [34] proposed a novel architecture for segmentation of biomedical images known as the "U-Net". It is a top-bottom convolution network and contains an encoder which uses conv and pooling layers to extract context and a decoder, using transposed convolution for accurate localization. The architecture of the "U-Net" from the original paper [34] is given in Figure 9.6.

### 9.5.6    LSTM

A variant of Recurrent Neural Networks (RNNs) with feedback connections is developed to solve the vanishing/exploding gradient problem, known as the "Long Short-Term Memory" (LSTM) [35]. This model is best suited for data based on time series. It can not only handle continuous data but can work well for discrete data as well.

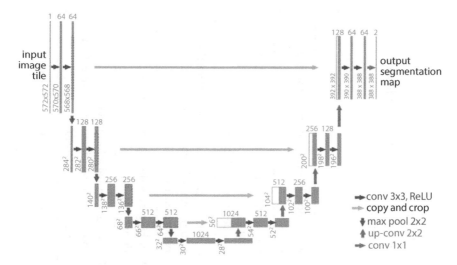

**Figure 9.6** Architecture—UUNet [34].

### 9.5.7   Support Vector Machine

Support Vector Machine, also known as SVM, can be defined as a linear classifier, an extension of the perceptron developed in 1958 by Rosenblatt. The perceptron guarantees to find a hyperplane if it exists, whereas SVM intends to find the hyperplane's maximum margin. A detailed comparison between various deep learning algorithms, applied in the discussed area, is summarized by Amir Ebrahimighahnavieh *et al.* [2] and is given in Table 9.1.

## 9.6   A Review on Methodologies

### 9.6.1   Prediction of Alzheimer's Disease

Santos Bringas *et al.* [3] proposed a method to identify AD patients' stages through accelerometer data and deep learning algorithms. The data is collected at the "AFAC Day Care Center", where the accelerometer data from the smartphones of 35 patients was collected, which was classified into three types namely, "early", "middle", and "late". This time series–based data is passed as input to the 1D-CNN to predict the stage of AD. An overview of the proposed [3] architecture is given in Figure 9.7.

This CNN-based method achieved an overall accuracy of 90.91% and F1-score of 0.897 [3], which is a significant improvement compared to the

**Table 9.1** Comparison on commonly utilized deep learning models [2].

| Models | | Strength | Limitations |
|---|---|---|---|
| Autoencoders | | Representation of highly nonlinear and complex patterns will be easier. Good initialization for CNNs. Well suited for dimensional reduction. Easy to implement. | Captures more information regardless of its relevance. |
| Restricted Boltzmann Machine (RBM) | | Can learn very good generative model. Able to create patterns if there are missing data. | Computationally expensive in the training process. |
| Deep Neural Network (DNN) | | Good for vector-based problems. Can handle datasets with a large number of samples. Detecting complex nonlinear relationships is efficient. | Slower training speed, not efficient for picture data. Has issues in generalization. |
| Deep Polynomial Network (DPN) | | Small sample feature representation efficient. | As it uses simple concatenation of hierarchical features learned across various layers, the performance is limited. |
| Recurrent Neural Network (RNN) | | Good for 2D images that are continuous. Suitable for longitudinal studies. | Vanishing/exploding gradients problem occurs during learning. |
| Convolutional Neural Network (CNN) | 2D CNN | Local feature extraction in images is optimal. Training is effortless. | Encoding of spatial information of the three-dimensional images across the third dimension is not possible. |
| | 3D CNN | Local feature extraction in images is optimal. Captures three-dimensional information from images. | Computationally expensive in the training process. |

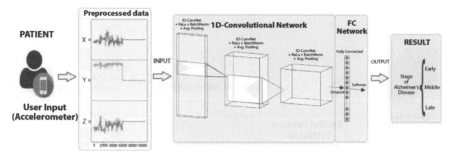

**Figure 9.7** Architecture of CNN presented by Santos *et al.* [3].

traditional feature-based classifiers' performance. This research has shown that the patient's mobility data can be a valuable resource for treating patients with AD and studying its progress. The use of the proposed CNN-based method improves the accuracy of identifying AD stages compared to standard supervised learning models.

Alejandro Puente-Castro *et al.* [4] proposed a methodology which makes use of deep learning techniques and sagittal MRI images, which are not generally used. The Transfer Learning [36] technique was implemented, using the ResNet [37] feature extractor with the SVM classifier [38]. The proposed methodology is evaluated based on some common performance metrics. The architecture of this [4] model is given in Figure 9.8.

The experimental results exhibit that the model delivers a satisfactory performance, especially in the detection of initial stages of the AD, in comparison with the previous works with horizontal plane MRI. The model is able to achieve an accuracy of 78.64% on ADNI dataset and 86.81% on OASIS dataset. This study also proves that deep learning models could be built in the where; obtaining samples for dataset can be very expensive, with transfer learning being a crucial tool for solving the problem with minimum examples.

A hybrid model (Figure 9.9) making use of VNet (an extension of UNet) is proposed by Manhua Liu *et al.* [5]. The initial image is passed to the "V-Net" which outputs segmentation map. This output is passed to the "3D DenseNet" for learning the features. Then, the output from "ResNet Block2" of the "V-Net" ad the "3D DenseNet" is concatenated ad then passed to a "Fully Connected Layer" for classification. This idea has achieved impressive results with the classification between AD patients and normal people being 88.9% accurate and the classification between MCI and normal

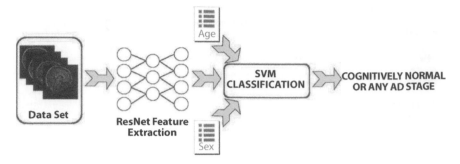

**Figure 9.8** Architecture of detection model presented by Alejandro *et al.* [4].

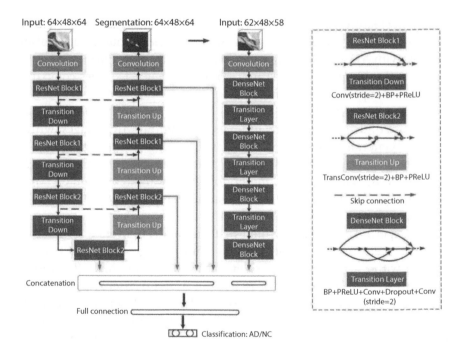

**Figure 9.9** Architecture of the hybrid model [5].

being 76.2%. The VNet is able to achieve a "dice similarity coefficient" of 87% for segmentation [5].

Bi Xiaojun and Wang Haibo proposed a method [6] using novel strategy which is based on the neural network architecture using hybrid feature maps, called the "Discriminative Contractive Slab and Spike Convolutional Deep Boltzmann Machine" or abbreviated as "DCssCDBM" [6]. This can be viewed as a discriminative extension of the "Contractive Slab and Spike

Convolutional Deep Boltzmann Machine" abbreviated as "CssCDBM" [39], where a label layer is induced to result in the discriminative version of "CssCDBM" known as the "DCssCDBM". For reduction of overfitting, a "Siamese Network" based is proposed where two "DCssCDBM" maintain shared parameters. The architecture of "DCssCDBM" is represented in Figure 9.10, whereas Figure 9.11 displays the "Siamese DCssCDBM architecture". This method is 95.04% accurate and is giving exceptional results in comparison with other models like "DBN-3", "GDBM-2", and "CDBN" [6].

Lin Liu *et al.* [7] have proposed an algorithm that utilizes spectrogram data to identify AD at an early stage. The speech data is collected from elderly people using a "Wearable IoT Device" designed for this purpose. The data is transmitted to cloud for encrypted storage, using secure transfer protocols. Then, after decryption, machine learning algorithms are applied on it. New speech data is collected for the experiment and then compared with "Dem@care" data. Logistic Regression CV exhibits optimal results.

This method by Chin-Fu Liu *et al.* [8] considers architecture, based on "Siamese Net" and the principle that the volume of two hemispheres of the

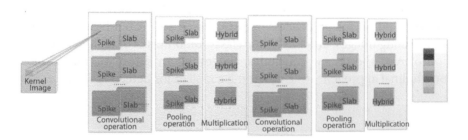

**Figure 9.10** Architecture of DCssCDBM [6].

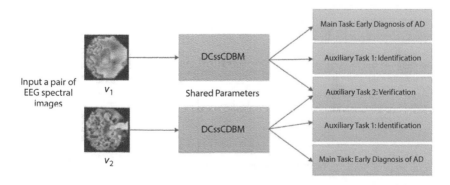

**Figure 9.11** "Siamese Net" Architecture [6].

brain must be "symmetric" or "same". The MRI is fed to the "MRICloud Pipeline" for extraction of volume features from it, for left and right hemispheres of the brain, separately. This is the passed to a "Siamese Network" model, where the left and right hemisphere volume details are passed to two different identical networks. Figure 9.12 shows the proposed algorithm that utilizes spectro-gram data to identify AD by Lin *et al.* Figure 9.13 displays the "MRICloud" representation, whereas Figure 9.14 shows the proposed [8] Siamese network architecture.

The outcome of these two networks is the features vectors, between which the absolute difference is calculated using a distance function. If the images are similar, the person is classified as "normal else as "symptomatic". This ideology is experimented on the ADNI and BIOCARD datasets, where it is able to achieve best results.

Suhad Al-Shoukry *et al.* [1] have presented an extensive survey that mainly focuses on neuro image analysis and biomarkers for AD. This study has also reviewed about the various datasets and various deep learning algorithms that can used in the detection of AD. Another review presented by Amir Ebrahimighahnavieh *et al.* [2] has presented a detailed survey on various deep learning algorithms, preprocessing techniques, and datasets related to AD. This study has suggested the use of intensity normalization and registration for preprocessing, ROI-based and patch-based methods for handling images, and CNNs for classification tasks of images in detection of AD. The review concludes, suggesting an automatic multimodal longitudinal approach while designing a system for detecting AD.

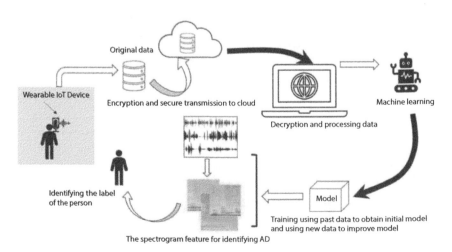

**Figure 9.12** Architecture of Lin Liu that utilizes spectrogram [7].

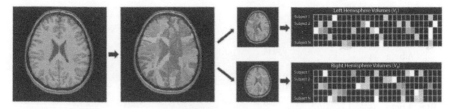

**Figure 9.13** "MRICloud" representation [8].

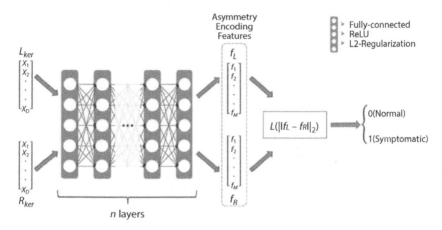

**Figure 9.14** "Siamese Net" architecture of [8].

### 9.6.2 Prediction of Parkinson's Disease

Wu Wang *et al.* [9] proposed an innovative deep learning technique which is based on "premotor features" to classify an individual as affected with PD or not. Three models, namely, the, "DEEP1", "DEEP2", and "DEEP3", along with an ensemble of the three models called the "DEEP-EN" are built with different hyper parameter configurations. These models consider several features such as the "rapid movement of eye" and "the level of spinal fluid" [9]. Figure 9.15 displays the architecture of the proposed [9] model. While comparing the proposed method with other algorithms on a dataset, which includes 183 healthy individuals and 401 early PD patients, the proposed deep learning model displays a superior detection performance, with a highest accuracy of 96.45% on an average.

Once again, a hybrid approach has been presented by K. H. Leung *et al.* [10], to predict the "MDS-UPDRS-III" score at "year 4" based on "year 0" and "year 1" data. The feature is extracted from the "DAT-SPECT" images, using the "Google InnceptionnV3" model [40] which is well-suited for

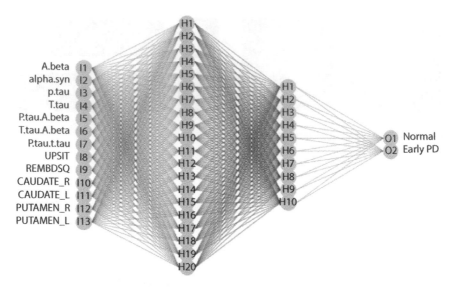

**Figure 9.15** Architecture of deep learning technique for Parkinson's [9].

medical data [41–43]. Then, an "LSTM"-based architecture is developed to extract the features from the "MDS-UPDRS-III" from "year 0" and "year 1". Then, these feature vectors are concatenated with patient details, such as "age" and "gender", and are forwarded to a "Fully Connected Layer" for the prediction of final outcome. The high-level architecture of the proposed [10] methodology is given in Figure 9.16.

This method is experimented as three studies and is evaluated with "10-fold cross validation". Study one using "InceptionV3" on image data achieved an "MAE" of 4.33 ± 3.36, where study two used "LSTM" on "MDS-UPDRS-III" data and achieved an "MAE" of 3.71 ± 2.91 and study three using both had an "MAE" of 3.22 ± 2.71 [10]. The image-based method of this model has been superseded by the non-image–based approach, but it can be clearly seen that the combined method, which utilizes image and non-image–based data performs better than either of the standalone methods.

Veronica Munoz Ramırez *et al.* [11] have proposed a deep learning method, using autoencoders and a technique called "anomaly scoring" to classify PD patients based on "quantitative Magnetic Resonance Imaging" data.

The data is imported from "Parkinson Progression Markers Initiative database". Two features were extracted from this data, namely, the "mean diffusivity" and the "fractional anisotropy". This method implements three auto-encoder-based models, namely, "Spatial Auto encoder" abbreviated as "sAE", "Spatial Variational Autoencoder" abbreviated as "sVAE", and

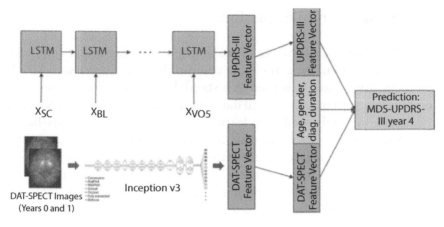

**Figure 9.16** Architecture of MDS-UPDRS [10].

"Dense Variational Autoencoder" abbreviated as "dVAE", which is evaluated by using ROC curve as the performance metric. This model obtained optimal results with "Area Under Curve" or "AUC" of 0.83, 0.80, and 0.74 for the "sAE", "sVAE", and "dVAE", respectively [11].

### 9.6.3    Detection of Attacks on Deep Brain Stimulation

Jonathan Pugh *et al.* [12] proposed a conceptual study on brain jacking in DBS and its autonomy. The authors have drawn three hypothetical case studies to explain the possibilities of brain jacking in a brain computing interface (BCI). This study also talks about the responsibilities and ethics that have to be followed with the development of advance BCI applications such as neurological implants, as in DBS.

Heena Rathore *et al.* [13] have presented an algorithm for the prediction of different attacks in DBSs by a third party. This method makes use of the LSTM (LSTM-RNN), to forecast and predict the RTV, which is a type of characteristic that helps evaluating of the intensity of neuro disorders. This model was developed with an idea of identifying duplicate simulation of electrode charges in DBS versus the real ones. When tested o detection of various types of attacks on PD patients, the model was able to do it and is able to notify about the patient probable occurrence of an attack. The proposed method includes two studies, where study 1 was evaluated using root mean squared error as its performance metric, achieving a RMSE score of 0.095, and study 2 analyzes the model performance for different attacks based on training loss, validation loss, and training duration, where, it achieves optimal results.

## 9.7   Results and Discussion

Majority of the research works in the area of AD makes use of computer vision–based approaches. The most commonly used dataset was ADNI, where, in some cases, it is used as a standalone and in some cases; it is combination with other standard datasets such as OASIS and BIOCARD. The most commonly used deep learning algorithms are the CNN-based ones. Some works, CNNs are used for classifications, whereas, in some of the hybrid approaches, feature extraction task is handled by the CNN architectures, which is passed to the classification algorithms such as the SVM or AdaBoost, for the handling of classification problem. Table 9.2 shows the comparison of proposed algorithms on detection of AD based on accuracy.

For detection of PD, a variety of approaches has been implemented; yet, again, we could see that transfer learning methodologies display good accuracy with minimal data. The work proposed in [10] makes use of a parallel hybrid methodology for detection of PD, using neuro image data and clinical data. Comparison of various algorithms on detection of PD is given in Table 9.3.

Table 9.4 tabulates the final results of a detection model that is trained to predict attacks on DBS. This area of research is still evolving with lots of areas to innovate. These types of models can not only be used in DBS but also can be used for ensuring security in BCI devices. This novel architecture is able to achieve minimum error value while detecting various simulated attacks on a DBS process.

## 9.8   Conclusion

Neuro disorders affect a large proportion of the world population every year [44]. As their early detection is crucial for treatment and is also a very challenging task, the use of intelligent systems together with medical experts plays a vital role in their detection. In this chapter, some of the advanced deep learning models have been reviewed in the areas of detection and enforcing security in their treatment protocol. In terms of detection of AD, majority of the works have made use of CNN-based approaches and have also reported better accuracies when compared to other deep learning models. Some advanced novel approaches (other than image-based) as in [6] and application of 1D CNN on mobile accelerometer data show promising results and open a pathway to new areas of research, which is yet to be explored. In classification of PD, the common dataset used for

**Table 9.2** Comparison of various algorithms on detection of AD.

| S. no. | Proposed algorithm | Dataset | Results |
|---|---|---|---|
| 1 | 1D – Convolutional Neural Network [3] | AFAC Daycare Dataset | ACCURACY - 91% |
| 2 | ResNet50 and Support Vector Machine [4] | ADNI | ACCURACY - 78.64% |
| | | OASIS | ACCURACY - 86.81% |
| 3 | V-Net and 3D DenseNet [5] | ADNI | ACCURACY 88.9% (AD vs. NC) and 76.2% (MCI vs. NC) |
| 4 | DCssCDBM [6] | Bejing Easy Monitor Technology Dataset | ACCURACY - 95.04% |
| 5 | Logistic Regression CV [7] | VBSD Dataset | ACCURACY - 83.33% |
| | | Dem@Care Dataset | ACCURACY - 84.44% |
| 6 | Siamese Neural Network [8] | ADNI | FI-SCORE 0.9512 (Latest) and 0.9372 (Scan Time) (displayed as mean) |
| | | BIOCARD | FI-SCORE 0.2275 (Scan Time) 0.5811 (Latest) (displayed as mean) |

detection of PD is the PPMI database. It is evident that the model based on a parallel approach [10] has shown to perform with exceptional results. We can also say that transfer learning approach helps to achieve maximum accuracy with minimum data. Though DBS provides hopes in treatment of PD, it has posed significant threats of its own. The security concerns raised by the use of such devices must be given importance, as it could directly influence the physical and mental orientation of the patients. Also, here,

**Table 9.3** Comparison of various algorithms on detection of Parkinson's disease.

| S. no. | Proposed algorithm | Dataset | Results |
|---|---|---|---|
| 1 | DEEP1 | PPMI | 96.45% (Average) |
| | DEEP2 | | |
| | DEEP3 | | |
| | DEEP_EN [9] | | |
| 2 | Google Inception V3 and LSTM [10] | PPMI | Method 1 - 4.33 ± 3.36 (MAE) |
| | | | Method 2 - 3.71 ± 2.91 (MAE) |
| | | | Method 3 - 3.22 ± 2.71 (MAE) |
| 3 | Autoencoders [11] | PPMI | sAE - 0.075 (Reconstruction Error) |
| | | | SVAE - 0.086 (Reconstruction Error) |
| | | | DVAE - 0.106 (Reconstruction Error) |

**Table 9.4** Results of the algorithm on detection of attacks on deep brain stimulation.

| Proposed algorithm | Dataset | Results |
|---|---|---|
| LSTM [13] | PhysioNet Dataset | RMSE: 0.095 |

we have reviewed a novel architecture [13] for the detecting the attacks on deep brain stimulators, which detected different attack patterns efficiently. These types of approaches would be essential to assure safe usage of BCIs. In conclusion, this study has reviewed some significant datasets related to AD and PD, applications of advanced deep learning algorithms in their detection, and to ensure security in the advanced neurodegenerative disorder treatments which make use of BCI.

# References

1. Al-Shoukry, S., Rassem, T.H., Makbol, N.M., Alzheimer's Diseases Detection by Using Deep Learning Algorithms: A Mini-Review. *IEEE Access*, 8, 77131–77141, 2020.
2. Ebrahimighahnavieh, M.A., Luo, S., Chiong, R., Deep learning to detect Alzheimer's disease from neuroimaging: A systematic literature review. *Comput. Methods Programs Biomed.*, 187, 105242, 2020.
3. Bringas, S., Salomón, S., Duque, R., Lage, C., Montaña, J.L., Alzheimer's Disease stage identification using deep learning models. *J. Biomed. Inform.*, 109, 103514, 2020.
4. Castro, A.P., Fernandez-Blanco, E., Pazos, A., Munteanu, C.R., Automatic assessment of Alzheimer's disease diagnosis based on deep learning techniques. *Comput. Biol. Med.*, 120, 103764, 2020.
5. Liu, M., Li, F., Yan, H., Wang, K., Ma, Y., Shen, L., Xu, M., Alzheimer's Disease Neuroimaging Initiative, A multi-model deep convolutional neural network for automatic hippocampus segmentation and classification in Alzheimer's disease. *NeuroImage*, 208, 116459, 2020.
6. Bi, X. and Wang, H., Early Alzheimer's disease diagnosis based on EEG spectral images using deep learning. *Neural Netw.*, 114, 119–135, 2019.
7. Liu, L., Zhao, S., Chen, H., Wang, A., A new machine learning method for identifying Alzheimer's disease. *Simul. Model. Pract. Theory*, 99, 102023, 2020.
8. Liu, C.F., Padhy, S., Ramachandran, S., Wang, V.X., Efimov, A., Bernal, A., Shi, L., Vaillant, M., Ratnanather, J.T., Faria, A.V., Caffo, B., Using deep Siamese neural networks for detection of brain asymmetries associated with Alzheimer's disease and mild cognitive impairment. *Magn. Reson. Imaging*, 64, 190–199, 2019.
9. Wang, W., Lee, J., Harrou, F., Sun, Y., Early detection of Parkinson's disease using deep learning and machine learning. *IEEE Access*, 8, 147635–147646, 2020.
10. Leung, K.H., Salmanpour, M.R., Saberi, A., Klyuzhin, I.S., Sossi, V., Jha, A.K., Pomper, M.G., Du, Y., Rahmim, A., Using deep-learning to predict outcome of patients with Parkinson's disease, in: *2018 IEEE Nuclear Science Symposium and Medical Imaging Conference Proceedings (NSS/MIC)*, IEEE, pp. 1–4, 2018, November.
11. Ramírez, V.M., Kmetzsch, V., Forbes, F., Dojat, M., Deep Learning Models to Study the Early Stages of Parkinson's Disease, in: *2020 IEEE 17th International Symposium on Biomedical Imaging (ISBI)*, IEEE, pp. 1534–1537, 2020, April.
12. Pugh, J., Pycroft, L., Sandberg, A., Aziz, T., Savulescu, J., Brainjacking in deep brain stimulation and autonomy. *Ethics Inf. Technol.*, 20, 3, 219–232, 2018.
13. Rathore, H., Al-Ali, A.K., Mohamed, A., Du, X., Guizani, M., A novel deep learning strategy for classifying different attack patterns for deep brain implants. *IEEE Access*, 7, 24154–24164, 2019.
14. https://www.neurodegenerationresearch.eu/

15. Vatanabe, I.P., Manzine, P.R., Cominetti, M.R., Historic concepts of dementia and Alzheimer's disease: From ancient times to the present. *Rev. Neurol.*, 176, 3, 140–147, 2020.

16. Sundberg, R.J., *The Chemical Century: Molecular Manipulation and Its Impact on the 20th Century*, CRC Press, USA, 2017.

17. Keuck, L., History as a biomedical matter: recent reassessments of the first cases of Alzheimer's disease. *Hist. Philos. Life Sci.*, 40, 1, 10, 2018.

18. Koh, H.K. and Parekh, A.K., Toward a United States of health: implications of understanding the US burden of disease. *JAMA*, 319, 14, 1438–1440, 2018.

19. Saraiva, C., Praça, C., Ferreira, R., Santos, T., Ferreira, L., Bernardino, L., Nanoparticle-mediated brain drug delivery: overcoming blood–brain barrier to treat neurodegenerative diseases. *J. Control. Release*, 235, 34–47, 2016.

20. Cuingnet, R., Gerardin, E., Tessieras, J., Auzias, G., Lehéricy, S., Habert, M.O., Chupin, M., Benali, H., Colliot, O., Alzheimer's Disease Neuroimaging Initiative, Automatic classification of patients with Alzheimer's disease from structural MRI: a comparison of ten methods using the ADNI database. *Neuroimage*, 56, 2, 766–781, 2011.

21. Lajoie, I., Nugent, S., Debacker, C., Dyson, K., Tancredi, F.B., Badhwar, A., Belleville, S., Deschaintre, Y., Bellec, P., Doyon, J., Bocti, C., Application of calibrated fMRI in Alzheimer's disease. *NeuroImage Clin.*, 15, 348–358, 2017.

22. Cohen, A.D. and Klunk, W.E., Early detection of Alzheimer's disease using PiB and FDG PET. *Neurobiol. Dis.*, 72, 117–122, 2014.

23. Vermunt, L., van Paasen, A.J., Teunissen, C.E., Scheltens, P., Visser, P.J., Tijms, B.M., Alzheimer's Disease Neuroimaging Initiative, Alzheimer disease biomarkers may aid in the prognosis of MCI cases initially reverted to normal. *Neurology*, 92, 23, e2699–e2705, 2019.

24. Marcus, D.S., Wang, T.H., Parker, J., Csernansky, J.G., Morris, J.C., Buckner, R.L., Open Access Series of Imaging Studies (OASIS): cross-sectional MRI data in young, middle aged, nondemented, and demented older adults. *J. Cogn. Neurosci.*, 19, 9, 1498–1507, 2007.

25. Matsuda, H., MRI morphometry in Alzheimer's disease. *Ageing Res. Rev.*, 30, 17–24, 2016.

26. https://www.nia.nih.gov/health/parkinsons-disease

27. https://physionet.org/content/tremordb/1.0.0/

28. Razzak, M.I., Naz, S., Zaib, A., Deep learning for medical image processing: Overview, challenges and the future, in: *Classification in BioApps*, pp. 323–350, Springer, Cham, 2018.

29. Litjens, G., Kooi, T., Bejnordi, B.E., Setio, A.A.A., Ciompi, F., Ghafoorian, M., Van Der Laak, J.A., Van Ginneken, B., Sánchez, C.I., A survey on deep learning in medical image analysis. *Med. Image Anal.*, 42, 60–88, 2017.

30. Vieira, S., Pinaya, W.H., Mechelli, A., Using deep learning to investigate the neuroimaging correlates of psychiatric and neurological disorders: Methods and applications. *Neurosci. Biobehav. Rev.*, 74, 58–75, 2017.

31. Li, F., Tran, L., Thung, K.H., Ji, S., Shen, D., Li, J., A robust deep model for improved classification of AD/MCI patients. *IEEE J. Biomed. Health Inform.*, 19, 5, 1610–1616, 2015.

32. Suk, H.I., Wee, C.Y., Lee, S.W., Shen, D., State-space model with deep learning for functional dynamics estimation in resting-state fMRI. *NeuroImage*, 129, 292–307, 2016.

33. Faturrahman, M., Wasito, I., Hanifah, N., Mufidah, R., Structural MRI classification for Alzheimer's disease detection using deep belief network, in: *2017 11th International Conference on Information & Communication Technology and System (ICTS)*, IEEE, pp. 37–42, 2017, October.

34. Ronneberger, O., Fischer, P., Brox, T., U-net: Convolutional networks for biomedical image segmentation, in: *International Conference on Medical image computing and computer-assisted intervention*, Springer, Cham, pp. 234–241, 2015, October.

35. Sak, H., Senior, A., Beaufays, F., *Long short-term memory based recurrent neural network architectures for large vocabulary speech recognition*, 2014, arXiv preprint arXiv:1402.1128.

36. Pan, S.J. and Yang, Q., A survey on transfer learning. *IEEE Trans. Knowl. Data Eng.*, 22, 10, 1345–1359, 2009.

37. He, K., Zhang, X., Ren, S., Sun, J., Deep residual learning for image recognition, in: *Proceedings of the IEEE conference on computer vision and pattern recognition*, pp. 770–778, 2016.

38. Cortes, C. and Vapnik, V., Support-vector networks. *Mach. Learn.*, 20, 273–297, 1995.

39. Xiaojun, B. and Haibo, W., Contractive slab and spike convolutional deep Boltzmann machine. *Neurocomputing*, 290, 208–228, 2018.

40. Deng, J., Dong, W., Socher, R., Li, L.J., Li, K., Fei-Fei, L., Imagenet: A large-scale hierarchical image database, in: *2009 IEEE conference on computer vision and pattern recognition*, IEEE, pp. 248–255, 2009, June.

41. Esteva, A., Kuprel, B., Novoa, R.A., Ko, J., Swetter, S.M., Blau, H.M., Thrun, S., Dermatologist-level classification of skin cancer with deep neural networks. *Nature*, 542, 7639, 115–118, 2017.

42. Gulshan, V., Peng, L., Coram, M., Stumpe, M.C., Wu, D., Narayanaswamy, A., Venugopalan, S., Widner, K., Madams, T., Cuadros, J., Kim, R., Development and validation of a deep learning algorithm for detection of diabetic retinopathy in retinal fundus photographs. *JAMA*, 316, 22, 2402–2410, 2016.

43. Rajpurkar, P., Hannun, A.Y., Haghpanahi, M., Bourn, C., Ng, A.Y., *Cardiologist-level arrhythmia detection with convolutional neural networks*, 2017, arXiv preprint arXiv:1707.01836.

44. https://www.niehs.nih.gov/research/supported/health/neurodegenerative/index.cfm

45. Hill, N.L. and Mogle, J., Alzheimer's disease risk factors as mediators of subjective memory impairment and objective memory decline: protocol for a construct-level replication analysis. *BMC Geriatr.*, 18, 1, 260, 2018.

46. Nolte, D.D., Turek, J.J., Jeong, K., Purdue Research Foundation, *Method and apparatus for motility contrast imaging*, 2014.
47. Makaretz, S.J., Quimby, M., Collins, J., Makris, N., McGinnis, S., Schultz, A., Vasdev, N., Johnson, K.A., Dickerson, B.C., Flortaucipir tau PET imaging in semantic variant primary progressive aphasia. *J. Neurol. Neurosurg. Psychiatr.*, 89, 10, 1024–1031, 2018.
48. SenthilKumar, A.L.P. *et al.*, "Breast cancer Analysis and Detection in Histopathological Images using CNN Approach.", 1272, 2021.
49. Anbarasi, L.J. and Anandha, M., "EPR hidden medical image secret sharing using DNA cryptography.". *Int. J. Eng. Technol.*, 6, 1346–1356, 2014.
50. Sharon, J.J., Anbarasi, L.J., Raj, B.E., "DPSO-FCM based segmentation and Classification of DCM and HCM Heart Diseases.". *2018 Fifth HCT Information Technology Trends (ITT)*, IEEE, 2018.
51. Jawahar, M. *et al.*, "Diabetic Foot Ulcer Segmentation using Color Space Models.". *2020 5th International Conference on Communication and Electronics Systems (ICCES)*, IEEE, 2020.
52. Sagnou, M., Mavroidi, B., Shegani, A., Paravatou-Petsotas, M., Raptopoulou, C., Psycharis, V., Pirmettis, I., Papadopoulos, M.S., Pelecanou, M., Remarkable Brain Penetration of Cyclopentadienyl M (CO) 3+(M= 99mTc, Re) Derivatives of Benzothiazole and Benzimidazole Paves the Way for Their Application as Diagnostic, with Single-Photon-Emission Computed Tomography (SPECT), and Therapeutic Agents for Alzheimer's Disease. *J. Med. Chem.*, 62, 5, 2638–2650, 2019.
53. Anbarasi, L., Prassanna, J., Sarobin, V., Rajarajeswari, S., Prabhakaran, R., Manikandan, R., Autistic Disorder Analysis Among Children and Adult. *Int. J. Curr. Res. Rev.*, 12, 21, 48–51, November, 2020. http://dx.doi.org/10.31782/IJCRR.2020.12217.
54. Sarobin, V.R.M. *et al.*, Swarm intelligence-based optimal device deployment in heterogeneous Internet of Things networks for wind farm application. *Int. J. Commun. Syst.*, 2021.

# 10

# Emerging Innovations in the Near Future Using Deep Learning Techniques

**Akshara Pramod[1], Harsh Sankar Naicker[1] and Amit Kumar Tyagi[1,2]\***

*[1]School of Computer Science and Engineering, Vellore Institute of Technology, Chennai, Tamil Nadu, India*
*[2]Centre for Advanced Data Science, Vellore Institute of Technology, Chennai, Tamil Nadu, India*

## Abstract

Due to recent development in technology, we can see many rapid changes in many sectors. Some popular rapid technologies of previous decade are deep learning, disruptive technology, blockchain technology (decentralized technology), cyber physical systems, Internet of Things, etc. Internet of Things is an interesting creation (development) of the previous decade and used today in many applications/sectors to make people's life easier to live and to increase productivity of businesses. Internet of Things provides device-to-device and machine-to-machine communication in this architecture. Also, it has data (communication) at rest and in motion mode. Generally, Internet of Things or internet-enabled thing devices generated a lot of data when these smart devices communicate together. For that, we require sufficient tools and efficient (also robust methods/algorithms) tools to analyze this large amount of data. Also, we require new measurements and standards to quantify this data and its respective results. Till now, machine learning was being used to analyze this data, but machine learning is unable to handle large amount of data, which is increasing every day. In near future, deep learning will take the place of machine learning for analyzing this massive data. Deep learning today is used in natural language processing, healthcare (mostly, i.e., to cure disease), etc., and will be used in many other applications like visual art processing, automatic speech recognition, facial recognition, and medical image recognition, etc. This chapter provides

*\*Corresponding author*: amitkrtyagi025@gmail.com
Amit Kumar Tyagi: ORCID: 0000-0003-2657-8700

Archana Mire, Shaveta Malik and Amit Kumar Tyagi (eds.) Advanced Analytics and Deep Learning Models, (231–254) © 2022 Scrivener Publishing LLC

complete details about every innovation possible in the filed of deep learning in the near future.

*Keywords*: Emerging innovations in near future, deep learning, computer vision, smart era

## 10.1    Introduction

Deep learning is one way of implementing machine learning (automated data analysis) via what are called artificial neural networks, i.e., algorithms that effectively mimic the human brain's structure and function [1]. With deep learning revolution, deep learning is useful to artificial neural networks, deep neural networks, automatic speech recognition, image recognition, visual art processing, natural language processing, drug discovery and toxicology, and many more. In near future, we see the tendency of deep learning in two ways. First, the huge advances in computational resources (CPU and GPU) allow the use of more complex and deeper models. The upper limit of this growth is difficult to predict. Second, as a researcher in machine learning, we feel a tendency toward the way the human learns. For example, currently, there is a lot of research focused on deep reinforcement learning, which integrates deep neural networks, such as convolutional neural networks (CNNs), with reinforcement learning theory. These models have proven to be very effective (in some cases, more than a human user) in several fields, for example, playing video games. With facial recognition, we use deep learning like the following:

a) unsupervised learning features with deep models and then using discriminative methods;
b) directly using class labels as supervision of deep models.

For implementation, deep learning is a complicated process in many applications, because of its black box problem [1]. Deep learning is one stream of exponential knowledge automation; the hidden layers of learning processes play a decisive role [2]. The progress with images will be faster than that with language; there are still a lot of heuristic enigmas to be solved. Generally, using deep learning is just complex architectures of neural networks. Note that we need to do precision during classification task, at the time training and testing of data.

Further, Figure 10.1 depicts evolution of computer science terms since 1950. Also, Figure 10.2 discusses working structure of deep neural network.

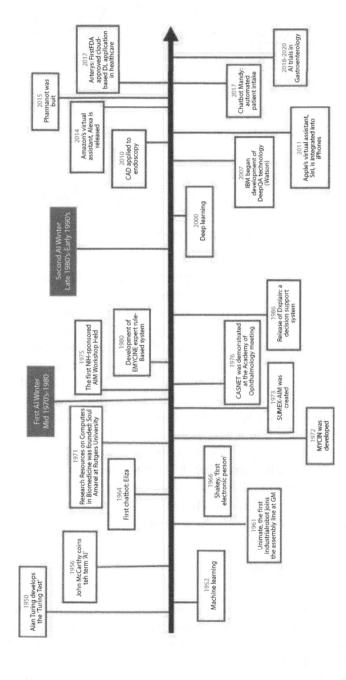

**Figure 10.1** Concepts and theories in deep learning.

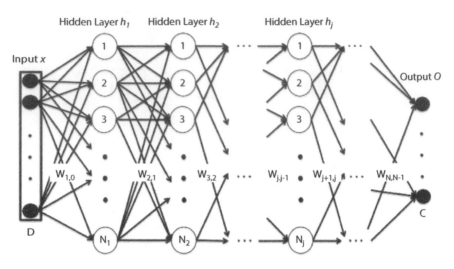

**Figure 10.2** Process of deep neural network (DNN).

In this, we can see that input layer, output layer, and hidden layers play an essential role in solving a problem or to do a task.

Hence, this chapter can be organized in further sections: Section 10.2 discusses related work behind this merging topic. Further, Section 10.3 discusses our motivation behind writing this chapter toward deep learning. Further, Section 10.4 discusses many emerging innovations in near future with deep learning. This section includes almost essential uses of nearly 20 applications, where deep learning is useful. Then, many open issues and opportunities or future research toward (excluding sectors) deep learning in near future have been discussed in Section 10.5. Then, opportunities and challenges have been discussed in Section 10.6. Further, an open discussion with augmenting the importance of deep learning over other learning techniques like data mining and machine learning is discussed in Section 10.7. In last, Section 10.8 concludes this work in brief with including several interesting future remarks.

## 10.2    Related Work

"Deep learning" refers to the immensely powerful form of machine learning which is being used in practice nowadays. It constructs complex mathematical structures called a neural network on large amount of data. Neural networks were first introduced in 1930. These are analogous to the functioning of the human brain. Our computers have become efficient enough to use these neural networks only in the past decade. Deep learning works on artificial neural networks (ANNs) and neural networks. People think that both are similar terms, but are not. ANNs work on neuron [1, 5], while neural networks work based on layers. ANN is a very old concept; it is nothing new to this world. Earlier, they were not even referred as neural networks and are rather quite different from what they were believed to be in their inception. Perceptron was what we had in the 1960s [3]. McCulloch-Pitts neurons basically laid the formation of these perceptrons. Earlier, there existed biased perceptrons, and ultimately, the world could witness the creation of multilayer perceptrons, which go with the definition of ANNs which exists in this present era.

Now, here a big question is that a neural network is active since the 1960s then why it was not popular in 20th century. Then, answer to such questions is like "we do not enough data to train and test our models". Also, we do not have computer processing power to do the same. But in today's scenario, what we observe is increase in rate of speed and power of our computers, and the collaboration of computers with internet, providing it all kinds of data sharing techniques. Many tools are popular in current for deep learning simulation. Five of the most popular open-source deep learning frameworks [1] (i.e., packages [17–25]) are listed below:

a) Caffe: https://github.com/BVLC/caffe;
b) TensorFlow: https://github.com/tensorflow/tensorflow;
c) Theano: https://github.com/Theano/Theano;
d) Torch7/PyTorch: https://github.com/torch/torch7 or
e) https://github.com/pytorch/pytorch; and
f) MXNet: https://github.com/apache/incubator-mxnet.

Few more comparisons on machine learning and deep learning tools have been made by Tyagi *et al.* [26–31]. Most of the popular frameworks provide multiple interfaces, such as C/C++, MATLAB, and Python. In addition, several packages provide a higher level library written on top of these frameworks, such as Keras. Hence, this section discusses work related to deep learning and status of deep learning in the previous decade. Now, next section will deal with motivation behind this work.

## 10.3    Motivation

In general, when a user starts buying some products over internet, then many websites starts recommending products during online shopping; in this process, machine learning took action on browsing history (previous). Note that even the "bought together" combination of products is another by-product of machine learning. Such techniques or methods used to increase the productivity of an item. This is how companies target their audience, and divide people into various categories to serve them better, make their shopping experience tailored to their browsing behavior. To provide, better service more things or scenarios are yet to be discovered. For example, in previous decade, digital marketing was not available, but today, it is on top position of marketing. So, in near future deep learning will have many innovative solution to solve people's daily problems in an efficient way.

Hence, to provide better service to customer/consumers or businesses is our main aim. For that, we want to write a write on this merging topic. This chapter shows us future capabilities of deep learning technology in detail, with example uses of deep learning in many possible applications. This section discusses motivation behind this work. Now, next section will discuss future with deep learning.

## 10.4    Future With Deep Learning/Emerging Innovations in Near Future With Deep Learning

Machine learning is used to do predictions, which is made based on experience [4, 7], i.e., collected previous data. In near future, vehicles/which will be driving themselves, fully autonomous vehicles which use Internet of Things/smart things to communicate each other. For example, there are various machines or devices which are programmed to create art. Generally, artificial intelligence (AI) technology is becoming the core/essential element of every application or of everything we do. Note that previous experience or backpropagation process is used by ANN [5]. Layers are just sets of neurons. We have an input layer which is the data we provide to the ANN. We have the hidden layers, which is where the magic happens. Lastly, we have the output layer, which is where the finished computations of the network are placed for us to use. Layers themselves are just sets of neurons. In the early days of multilayer perceptrons, we originally thought that having just one input layer, one hidden layer, and one output layer was sufficient.

Now, we introduce deep learning, which has more than one hidden layer. This is one of the reasons we have better ANNs now, because we need hundreds of nodes with tens if not more layers [5]. This leads to a massive amount of variables that we need to keep track of at a time. Advances in parallel programming also allow us to run even larger ANNs in batches. Our ANNs are now getting so large that we can no longer run a single epoch, which is iteration through the entire network, at once. We need to do everything in batches which are just subsets of the entire network, and once we complete an entire epoch, then we apply the backpropagation.

Today, we many layers (in deep learning); there is no limit and we got very efficient results. Due to this reason, deep learning provides a black box problem to outside world, i.e., no one knows "how this magic happens or outcome is generated". Note that ANNs are generally used all feed forward neural networks to do processing. For better results in specific/ different scenarios, we may use some other variants of deep learning like CNNs, sometimes, called LeNets [6], which works with images, long short-term memory (LSTM), recurrent neural networks (RNN), etc. Note that LSTM and RNN have been explained in [8]. In near future, we can apply reinforcement learning or genetic algorithm (GA) to build ANN architecture [9]. In near future, deep learning will be used many other sectors/ applications [1, 10–16] including language translation, animal recognition, picture captioning, and text summarization. In few applications like image classification and processing, medical image recognition, facial recognition, and clinical and health informatics, the usage of deep learning in discussed in next subsections.

## 10.4.1    Deep Learning for Image Classification and Processing

With highly evolved big data, it is almost impossible for human inspection on the accuracy of a machine which deals with huge pools of data. One such application is image, video processing (video is nothing, but images rolled at higher frame rates). It is speculated that more than 3.5 trillion photographs exist, with such mind baffling amount of data there is a desperate need for the machine to learn by itself more like humans without supervision. There is the vivid need for deep learning. Image processing and classification has been predicted to be one of the classic problems which are witnessed in the fields of computer vision and machine learning. This process came into existence in order to reduce the gap between computer and human vision. This mechanism involves differentiating images based on the context of vision so that it could achieve image classification.

## 10.4.2    Deep Learning for Medical Image Recognition

Whenever an epidemic occurs, there is a time delay in finding the antidote for the disease during which a very wide range of deaths and hospitalization effects occur in many parts of the world. Even during bio-wars, this effect occurs but in a wider range. In such cases, life stakes are very high, and solutions are required as early as possible to save lives of people. To analyze the complex chemistry of the medicines without crossing the investments, deep learning algorithms could be used.

It basically aims for improvisation of visual diagnosis in medicine with the support of deep learning algorithms based on image recognition. It is one of the rapidly growing fields of deep learning. Deep learning algorithms in medicine can be used to enable automation of medical image analysis. Rather than making this field completely computational, deep learning can add on to the transformation of pathology, radiology, etc.

### 10.4.3 Computational Intelligence for Facial Recognition

What if we met with an injury and our face is wounded? Our mobile most probably cannot recognise us because our face is in no shape. But if our mobile could learn to map other parts of our face and analyze them then a more intelligent face unlock system can be developed. It would be possible for unsupervised machine learning to differentiate between twins, provided it develops enough. Facial recognition is a mundane task because it happens in ease among humans, but it could be rather complex and often impossible for machines. For example, we can be recognized by our friends if we are in a clown's attire, but a recognition machine struggles to do so.

It comprises of improvisation in the fields of identification and public security. It involves the mechanism of calculating the distance between the nodal points present in the face. For accuracy, it must ensure calculating at least 80 of these nodal points. It is an emerging technology and can assure high amount of privacy and security as each individual has a different face print.

### 10.4.4 Deep Learning for Clinical and Health Informatics

A total of 12% to 14% of the total money in the world is used for health support. For a factor with such high weightage, informatics is an immediate result. In order to analyze the overall economic development of large boundaries like states, countries and continents we will need deep learning's assistance. Conventional processes will not be able to handle extreme amounts of data efficiently and therefore the need.

There is a huge onset of use of analytical data driven models. Deep learning can be very well applied into fields such as medical imaging, medical informatics, and translational bioinformatics.

## 10.4.5    Fuzzy Logic for Medical Applications

If we place the classical machine learning routines hierarchically, then fuzzy logic appears at the top of it. It uses the probabilistic approach than classical logic of vague True or False. It analyzes the pattern or input giving weightage between 0 and 1. It revolves around the basic idea of developing a knowledge-based medical system which aims on integration of Eastern and Western medicine and real-time monitoring of data of the patients. It is also used to interpret sets of medical functioning or differentiation of syndrome diagnosis of a disease.

## 10.4.6    Other Intelligent-Based Methods for Biomedical and Healthcare

It utilizes complex algorithms and software structures to emulate the human recognition. With the help of AI, the computer algorithms can select a decision boundary and predict the conclusions without direct human input.

## 10.4.7    Other Applications

If humans ever thought about making things which can think, implement, and analyze in real life situations, then there is a role played by deep learning. The concept of leaning using algorithms has gone far inside the roots of today's world machines. We kept on failing, albeit creating more and more advanced technologies. Deep learning can be drawn into a sophisticated version of machine learning. In today's era which is referred as weak AI era, since we are still in the infant stage of development, we are heavily dependent on the advancement of technology. The very need of improvement in approach exists rather than the implementation needs. It has become increasingly complex to perform supervised machine learning, in expert AI-based tasks. Deep learning is more complicated than supervised machine learning routine. Some of such tasks are briefly explained in this section. In near future, deep learning will impact affect our life with a major impact. The following examples depict the changes that deep learning will cause in our lives in near future:

   i.   Self-driven cars: Several companies have come forward with the idea of constructing driver assistance services in collaboration with full blown self-driving cars in order to take over the key features of driving with the help of digital sensors instead of human senses. Companies generally use a training algorithm on a large corpus of data. In near future, we should think "how a child learns through constant experiences and replication". New innovations could provide unexpected business models for industries and companies.

ii.   Healthcare: In order to diagnose a minute cold to a major problem like breast cancer, what would you prefer "Mobile and Monitoring" apps or the predicted or personalized medication based on the analysis done on the Biobank data? How does AI come into existence in this field? AI has provided a new direction to life sciences, medicines, and healthcare as an industry. Many new techniques; many new innovations all together are advancing the future of precision medicine and population health management in indefinite ways. Concepts of computer-aided detection, quantitative imaging, decision support tools, and computer-aided diagnoses will witness great recognition and good control over the healthcare in the coming few years.

iii.   Voice search and voice activation assistant: Deep learning has done a lot of enhancement in such fields. This field of deep learning in AI has priorly come across many developments and nowadays could be found on every smart phone. Significant increases by the tech giants in this area have made it the most popular usage of deep learning. Apple's Siri has rolled in the market since October 2011. Google Now, the voice-activated assistant for Android, just entered the market in less than a year after "Siri". The most recent voice-activated intelligent assistant is Microsoft "Cortana".

iv.   Automatic addition of sounds: This phenomenon is extensively used in silent movies. The system synthesis the sound and matches it with the silent videos. The system is provided with a training set of around 1,000 samples of videos containing sounds of a drumstick striking different surfaces producing different sounds. Further, a deep learning model is created where video frames act as the training data set which after the training and the learning process are associated and matched with the pre-recorded video datasets accordingly. A tuning test in performed later which is used to determine whether the video is synthesized with the fake or real sound. The process of determining is based on reward based learning (reinforcement learning) which is done by humans in this case. I basically involve the applications like CNN, LSTM, and RNN.

v. Automatic machine translation: It involves the translation of certain words, phrases, or sentences from one language into another. From quite a long time, automatic machine translation has been into existence. But as soon as deep learning entered this field, it gave success in majorly two arenas one Automatic text translation and Automatic Image translation being the other. The text translation does not require any pre-processing to be performed on the sequence; only the algorithm learns the dependencies between the words and maps them into a new language.

vi. Automatic text generation: The text generation model is created using a corpus of texts as its predictors. This large set of text is learnt and further generates texts either word by word or character by character. This model learns how to spell, punctuate, and capture the style of text in the set as well as sentence formation the learning process is done in order to find a relation between the items in the sequence of generated texts and input texts using large RNNs.

vii. Automatic handwriting generation: This is where a given set of handwriting samples which consists of words, phrases to generate a new handwriting. The sample is given as a sequence of coordinates where the pen moves while creating the sample. Further, the learning is done by finding the relationship between the letter and the pen movement, and hence, new samples are created.

viii. Image recognition: This is another popular department of deep learning. This majorly focuses on the recognition and identification of people, objects and images. It is also used to understand the text and content. It is already in existence in the fields of gaming, social media, retail, tourism, and many more. This work includes classification of objects within a photograph on the basis of the previously known objects. A complex variation added to this is the object detection part where recognition of one object is done within its frame and a box is drawn around them.

ix. Automatic image caption: In automatic image caption, a system is given as images as input, and the system generates a descriptive caption related to that image. In 2014, deep learning came into existence to solve such a problem statement and achieved tremendous results, leveraging the work from the top models for object classification and detection. Once the object is detected, next the major aim is to create labels for that object. After this step, we proceed by turning labels to coherent sentence descriptions. Large CNN is used for object detection by the system, whereas the system involves RNN and LSTM to turn the labels into coherent sentences.

x.  Automatic colorization: The main problem that arises is image colorization that is coloring the black and white images. Deep learning uses objects or their context in order to color the images. It works moreover like the human who would approach this problem. This phenomenon provided high quality as well as very large convolutional networks which were trained for ImageNet and opted for the problem of image colorization. This approach includes the usage of large CNNs and supervised layers which are used for the recreation of the colored image.

xi.  Advertising: This field has witnessed magnificent revolution with the entry of deep learning in this field. It is used by publishers as well as advertisers in order enhance the relevancy of advertisements and uplift returning policy on the investments of their advertising campaigns. In order to create scenarios of data driven predictions, real-time add bidding and precision in targeting display advertising, the idea of leveraging the content is chosen by the ad-networks and the publishers.

xii.  Predicting earthquakes: Harvard Scientists prepared a deep learning model. The model went through supervised learning process to perform viscoelastic computation. Viscoelastic computations are specifically used in the prediction of earthquakes. Earlier, the computations were preferred to be computer intensive but now with the evolution of deep learning the calculation time have been improved by 50,000%. In order to prevent any disaster and save all the lives the time prediction is stated to be as one of the factors for earthquake prediction.

xiii.  Neural networks for brain cancer detection: Many French researchers found out that they were numerous complications faced in spotting invasive brain cancer cells at the time of surgery. The major reason behind this complication was the effects of lighting in the operation theatres. In order to overcome such a problem neural networks in cooperation with the Raman spectroscopy made the detection of cancer cells easier and reduced the post operation cancer. Lately, this piece has matched advanced image recognition and classification with various forms of cancer and screening apparatus.

xiv.  Neural networks in finance: The future markets have encountered enormous success in the last four decades since their establishment across the world both in developed and developing countries. This success acts as an attribute to the resources the future would provide the market participants. It mainly focuses on analyzing the trading strategies and how can they be benefitted using Capital Asset Pricing Model (CAPM) and cost-of-carry relationship. A pre-existential set of technical trading ruler present in the spot market price is implemented on the future market price using CAPM based hedge ratio. Analysis of historical daily prices from 20 stocks from each of the ten markets is executed in parallel.

xv.  Energy market forecast: A very informative research is done by the Spain and Portugal researchers who have applied ANN on the energy grid. The main reason behind this application of deep learning is to predict the price and usage of fluctuations. Region wise daily and intraday markets are being conducted in daily sessions where the future sales and electricity purchase and transactions are analyzed. Further, in the six intraday sessions, the energy offer and demands which may arise along with the daily viability schedule fixed after the daily session grab the prime concern. The major predictions are mostly based on the patterns of consumption and availability of resources in order to reach maximum efficiency and cost saving.

Note that computer vision, AI, machine learning, and deep learning will help us achieve superintelligence in near future, which will change near future entirely, also solve real world's complex problems. Hence, as discussed above, deep learning has applications across a seemingly infinite number of fields, including speech recognition, supercomputing, social media, natural language processing, and cybersecurity. Hence, this section discusses several emerging innovations with deep learning in near future/ next decade. Now, next section will deal with various opportunities and challenges in deep learning today and tomorrow.

## 10.5   Open Issues and Future Research Directions

This section gives a marked outline for prospective research directions for deep recommender systems, which go beyond the groundwork laid down by existing works. Several open issues which are crucial to the current state of the domain have been addressed.

### 10.5.1   Joint Representation Learning From User and Item Content Information

A thorough understanding of item attributes and user's actual demands and preferences is necessary for making valuable, accurate recommendations. This can be realized by utilising the huge repository of supplementary data. For instance, contextual data regarding the user's environment can help in provision of tailored services and products as well as alleviation of cold start influence. Collecting explicit feedback is a resource-intensive process whereas implicit feedback is easily procurable. This feedback holds valuable information about the user's implicit intention. The deep learning model can mine user and item profiles, implicit feedback, contextual information, and review texts for recommendations. Its efficacy has been investigated yet they do not use this data in an effective way and do not reap the complete benefit of the same. A user's temporal interests and intentions can be deduced from thorough examination of users' footprints (e.g., Facebook posts or Tweets) from social media platforms and the physical world (e.g., Internet of Things). Deep learning method is a viable tool for integrating this supplementary data. It is highly capable in processing heterogeneous data sources which paves way for recommending diverse items with unstructured data such as textual, visual, audio, and video features.

The recommendation research community has not fully examined feature engineering. Nonetheless, it is extremely essential and widely employed in industrial applications. Even though it is time consuming and bothersome, manually crafted and selected features are used by the existing models. Manual intervention can be lowered considerably by automatic feature crafting using deep neural network. Representation learning through free images, texts, or the existing data in the "wild" without designing the intricate future engineering pipelines is one of the added benefits. Human efforts can be saved and recommendation quality can be improved by more by analyzing deep feature engineering specific for recommender systems more intensively. One of the more potential research problems is "how to design neural architectures that best exploits the availability of other modes of data". Joint representation learning framework is one recent work that has led the path toward models of such nature. Recommender system research might witness learning joint (possibly multi-modal representations) of users and items to be one of the emerging trends in future. From the perspective of deep learning, the research problem will be as follows: "how to design be.er inductive biases (hybrid neural architectures) in an end to end fashion?" For example, reasoning over different modalities (text, images, and interaction) data or recommendation performance.

## 10.5.2    Explainable Recommendation With Deep Learning

A common stereotype is that deep learning is highly non-interpretable. It is indeed a herculean task for making explainable recommendations. Subsequently, it is generally assumed that data is fitted in big and complex neural models with any proper understanding (for a clearer picture of the concept see the subsequent section on machine learning). There exists basically two domains where explainable machine learning holds great importance. First is enabling the comprehension of factor behind the network recommendation (i.e., reason for the recommendation of the item/service) through making explainable predictions to the user. Second is basically meant for probing weights and activation in order to learn about the model, this is considered to be its explain ability to the practitioner. Presently, attentional models have lessened the non-interpretability of neural models. The attention weights which give the idea about the internal execution of the model in addition to providing explainable results to the user have indeed increased the interpretability. Attentional models have been a part of research in "pre deep learning". They are capable of both, enhancing performance and providing greater explain-ability. As a result, it incites the usage of deep learning for recommendations. A model's explain-ability and interpretability depends on its application domain and content information use. A promising direction for future is to work toward designing better attentional mechanisms. Models can already depict what contributes to the decision. This can be elevated to the point where models are capable of providing conversational or generative explanations.

## 10.5.3    Going Deeper for Recommendation

It is already established that most neural CF models perform stably at three to four layers. Deeper networks perform far better than shallow network in various tasks. Despite this known fact there is ambiguity with respect to going deeper when it comes to deep neural network RS. If going deeper provides favourable results, then "how do we train such deep architectures?" If not, then why? There are two possibilities with respect to this. First is to explore the auxiliary losses at different layers hierarchically rather than sequentially. Second is to the layer-wise learning rates for each layer of the deep network or utilize some residual strategies.

### 10.5.4   Machine Reasoning for Recommendation

Myriad recent advancements have happened in the field of machine reasoning in deep learning. This machine reasoning can be over natural language or even visual inputs. Tasks like machine reading, reasoning, question answering and visual reasoning have a huge impact on recommender systems yet they are neglected as they seem completely arbitrary and irrelevant with regards to recommender systems. However, it is imperative that recommender systems often require reasoning over a single (or multiple) modalities (review, texts, images, and meta-data) which would eventually require borrowing (and adapting) techniques from these related fields. Recommendation and reasoning are related as they are both information retrieval problems. They key idea of attention is the most crucial architectural innovation in relation to neural architectures that have the capacity for machine reasoning. Several recommender problems have been effectively tackled using these key intuitions. Tay *et al.* Yi Tay, Luu Anh Tuan, and Siu Cheung Hui [32] proposed a co-attentive architecture that functions for reasoning over reviews. They highlighted that every recommendation domain has a different evidence aggregation pattern. In case of interaction-only recommendation, all similar reasoning architectures have used similar co-attentive mechanisms for reasoning over meta-paths. Adapting to situations that require multi-step inference and reasoning is the next level that recommender systems have to reach. For example, a user's social profile, purchases, etc., reasoning over multiple modalities to recommend a product. Reasoning architectures shall take the lead in recommender system research.

### 10.5.5   Cross Domain Recommendation With Deep Neural Networks

Several big companies provide varied products and services to customers. For example, Google provides us with web searches, mobile applications, and news services; we can buy books, electronics, and clothes from Amazon. Single domain recommender systems work on only one domain.

They neglect the user interests on other domains and this in turn worsens the sparsity and cold start problems. Since cross domain recommender system assists target domain recommendation with the knowledge learned from various source domains, it facilitates a pragmatic solution to these problems. In cross domain learning, transfer learning happens. This consequently improves learning in one domain by using knowledge acquired from other domains. Deep learning is suitable for this because it learns high level abstractions that disentangle the variations of different domains. The superior ability of deep learning in catching the generalizations and differences across different domains and gathering recommendations on cross domains is depicted in multiple works. Thus, this is a largely unexplored area which holds great promise for the future.

### 10.5.6    Deep Multi-Task Learning for Recommendation

Tasks like computer vision and natural language processing have been successfully tackled using multi-task learning. Several works have led to few improvements over single task learning by applying multi-task learning to recommender system in a deep neural framework. There are three main advantages of the aforementioned application of multi-task learning. Number 1: Overfitting is prevented as learning several tasks at a time generalizes the shared hidden representations. Number 2: The recommendation can be explained as the auxiliary task results in a comprehensible (interpretable) output. Number 3: Sparsity problem is allayed by implicit data augmentation. Multi-task can be used in traditional recommender systems. Deep learning facilitates a tighter integration of them. Multi-task learning can be used in such a manner that each specific task provides a recommendation for each domain, thus performing cross domain recommendation apart from introducing side tasks.

### 10.5.7    Scalability of Deep Neural Networks
          for Recommendation

The era we are living in is the era of big data which is flooded with enormous data which is proved to be a very big challenge for the real world applications. Scalability is a topic of major concern when we look forward to recommend some model whereas time complexity is also an area of prime consideration in order to choose the best fit models. Considerably, with the growth of GPU computation power deep learning has gained a very effective control on big data analysis. Majorly there are still areas under this which can be looked up to and there is still scope for implementation of new advancing techniques by exploring certain problems like (a) there exists a large corpus of non-stationery and streaming data, i.e., large volumes of incoming users and items which require incremental learning; (b) the extensive efficiency computation efficiency needed in multimedia data sources as well as high dimension tensors; (c) to maintain a balance between the model complexity and scalability when there is an exponential growth in the training parameters. There is an intense area of research which involves knowledge distillation which has come into existence for small and compact systems for recommendation. The basic idea behind this strategy is to train smaller student models which extract knowledge from the large teacher models and build a student-teacher relationship between them. Time being one of the major influencing factors in real-time applications becomes the area of vital concern and investigation. One another area which needs to be evolved is the compression techniques, i.e., the compression of high-dimensional input into compact embedding in order to reduce the computation time taken by the model to perform the given task.

## 10.5.8   Urge for a Better and Unified Evaluation

Every time a new model is propped, there is a necessary requirement of evaluation and judgement based on the pre-defined guidelines. Sever issues in the choices of datasets/baselines has been witnessed. Primarily, problems such as inconsistent scores are created because each author reports their own assortment of results. The general ranking of the systems is still vague which signifies that there exists a no free lunch theorem. The major problem which arises after this is the conflicting result scenario and each author comes up with different models and their results based on their own different norms. Also, the relative position change turns out to be a consequence in such a situation. Such a situation is when the NCF was ranked very low as compared to the original paper which had proposed the model. Thus, the relative benchmark of neural models has now become challenging. Now the major doubt that arises is how to solve this. Looking at the other fields this field seems to be a bit puzzled. We face problems due to the lack of **MNIST** and **ImageNet** for the recommender system. The visible idea as for now to overcome this is by proposing a suite of standardized datasets for evaluation of the model.

**MovieLens** dataset is a very common dataset which is in use by many of the practitioners to evaluate their models. The testing data is generally randomized. Secondly, the problem which is witnessed is uncontrolled evaluation procedure. To overcome this problem, the recommender system community needs to catch up with the CV/NLP communities as well as establish the hidden dataset so that the predictions can be only accessed (submitted) via web interface such as Kaggle. Finally, the third problem that arises is that there is no control over difficulty of test samples which are taken as input for the system. It is difficult to predict whether the test sample is too trivial or impossible to infer. The dependency on the dataset is also very doubtful. In order to overcome this problem, the system needs to learn from computer vision and NLP communities.

## 10.6    Deep Learning: Opportunities and Challenges

As we can see with development in technology, computers are learning more and learning faster, but we are learning more about how to improve their systems. Many issues like scalability and standardization, associated with modern deep neural networks, i.e., the number of connections in each Framework Class Library (FCL) grow quadratically with the number of nodes in the inputs and in the outputs. Convolutional layers provide a way around the quadratic FCL problem and lead to the breakthroughs in image processing models in the 2010's. Reduction of the dimension of the input data sufficiently for its piping in the FCLs before the production of the necessary input can be achieved through convolutions. The past knowledge of the structure is used by convolution to give effective results in problems of image processing, while on the other hand, it limits the computational cost required in the training of these models.

Figure 10.3 depicts a subclass of deep neural networks, known as CNN that is basically used in applications of analyzing visual imagery. Whereas, a class of ANNs, known as RNN which works on sequential data, where a

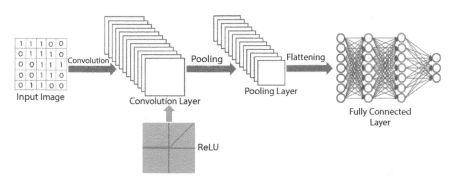

**Figure 10.3** Convolution layers feeding image data into a fully-connected layer [26, 27, 31].

directed graph is formed along a temporal sequence through connections between the nodes of the network. RNN basically works on the principle of using internal memory/state to process the sequence of inputs, which is not the case in FNN (feed forward neural networks). Deep learning carries with itself a great promise for the future and has a lot of hype built around it. Yet, it will undergo the same stages of development that all technological advances have gone through in the past. From a theoretical perspective, a lot of work is needed to comprehend and prove (analytically) the convergence of deep learning. While empirically it was already established since the introduction of CNNs (in parallel with the rise of connectionism in the 1980s with backpropagation) that at the cost of very large data and high computational power, representation learning, and wider hierarchical nets perform highly well. In scenarios where the data is highly non-stationary, we are yet to establish the usefulness of DL. The same goes for the more challenging tasks of unsupervised learning. A proposal by Hinton was made to surpass the backpropagation algorithm.

Future of deep learning depends on finding good data; in nature, deep learning can be useful for unsupervised learning. In near future, we should allow future projects to scale projects up to unprecedented scales. Also, quantum computer will be developed, which will also use deep learning. In next decade, many points have laid the ground for the quadratic increase in the deep neural networks model's learning capacity. With next learning models, we will be able to solve complex, real world's problems. Hence, this section discusses several challenges and opportunities in present and near future. Now, next section will discuss an open discussion, i.e., making a comparison of deep learning with other learning techniques, for proving that deep learning will rules next decade over other existed techniques.

## 10.7   Argument with Machine Learning and Other Available Techniques

Deep learning is a subset of machine learning, whereas machine learning is a subnet of AI [4, 33]. Many evolutions in deep learning has been mitigated and used in many sectors/applications. Hence, future of machine learning will be like

- Improved cognitive services
- The rise of quantum computing
- Rise of robots
- Other: courses, jobs, etc.

On another side, biggest impact on the future of deep learning will be

- Architecture search
- Compressing neural networks (compressing computer memory)
- Generative Adversarial Network (GAN)–based data augmentation [34]

In next decade, deep learning development tools, libraries, and languages will become standard components of every software development toolkit.

Note that one of the biggest challenges with building deep learning models is building the dataset. In other words, handling of unstructured data is too difficult for analysis purpose or for making a decision. Deep learning and CNNs are most common technique and structure in divers' fields expanding from predicting weather, cloud, etc., to diagnoses of serious diseases. But, we did not find an example which evaluates their computational complexity expenses and other disadvantages. Hence, this section discusses about importance or scope (with arguments) of deep learning over other existing learning techniques like data mining and machine learning and provides several facts with some real world's examples, that deep learning is the necessity of the future. Now, the next section will conclude this chapter in brief with identifying several research gaps for future research purpose (with respect to deep learning techniques).

## 10.8    Conclusion With Future Work

Deep learning is mostly used in many sectors nowadays like image recognition (healthcare) and natural image processing (translation). In near future, we will see many new innovations with deep learning and also will see the difference in living standards of people/businesses, whoever will use deep learning techniques. For example, CNN is (a feed forward neural network) used for Image recognition and object classification, whereas in RNN, the previous states is fed as input to the current state of the network. It (RNN) can be used in NLP, Time Series Prediction, Machine Translation, etc. Hence, other new medication of deep learning LSTM, ANN, etc., will cover the world and will be more helpful more in many applications, especially in healthcare like health informatics, clinical informatics, biomedical images, and radiography (i.e., CT scan and x-rays). Hence, this chapter discusses every possible innovation with deep learning in near future/decade, to solve complex problems. Also, in this chapter, we list out several opportunities and challenges toward deep learning. We believe that deep learning will change near future with doing major changes like architecture search, compressing neural networks, and using GANs to build deep learning datasets. In simple words, the goal of this work is to provide a systematic study/knowledge about deep learning for the computer science community and its possible innovations in other applications. Hence, all interested people locally/globally are looking or doing their research work toward deep learning and are kindly invited to continue their research work with above listed possibilities (opportunities).

## Acknowledgement

This research work is funded by the Anumit Academy's Research and Innovation Network (AARIN), India. The authors would like to thank AARIN, India, a research network for supporting the project through its financial assistance.

## References

1. Tyagi, A.K. and Rekha, G., Challenges of Applying Deep Learning in Real-World Applications, Book: *Challenges and Applications for Implementing Machine Learning in Computer Vision*, pp. 92–118, IGI Global, 2020.
2. Robins, M., *The Future of Deep Learning: Challenges & Solutions*, pp. ii–ii, 2017.
3. Alom, Md. Z., Taha, T., Yakopcic, C., Westberg, S., Sidike, P., Nasrin, Mst., Hasan, M., Essen, B., Awwal, A., Asari, V., A State-of-the-Art Survey on Deep Learning Theory and Architectures. *Electronics*, 8, 292, 2019.
4. Kumar, A.T. and Chahal, P., Artificial Intelligence and Machine Learning Algorithms, Book: *Challenges and Applications for Implementing Machine Learning in Computer Vision*, IGI Global, 2020
5. https://doi.org/10.1016/j.heliyon.2018.e00938
6. http://deeplearning.net/tutorial/lenet.html
7. Tyagi, A.K. and Rekha, G., Machine Learning with Big Data. *Proceedings of International Conference on Sustainable Computing in Science, Technology and Management (SUSCOM)*, February 26–28, 2019, Amity University Rajasthan, Jaipur - India, March 20, 2019, Available at SSRN: https://ssrn.com/abstract=3356269 or http://dx.doi.org/10.2139/ssrn.3356269.
8. https://colah.github.io/posts/2015-08-Understanding-LSTMs/

9. Idrissi, M.A.J., Hassan, R., Ghanou, Y., Ettaouil, M., *Genetic algorithm for neural network architecture optimization*, pp. 1–4, 2016.

10. Ranzato, M.A., Poultney, C., Chopra, S., LeCun, Y., Efficient learning of sparse representations with an energy-based model, in: *Proceedings of the 19th International Conference on Neural Information Processing Systems (NIPS' 06)*. MIT Press, Cambridge, MA, USA, 1137–1144, 2006.

11. Vincent, P., Larochelle, H., Bengio, Y., Manzagol, P.-A., "Extracting and composing robust features with denoising autoencoders," in: *Proc. ICML*, pp. 1096–1103, 2008.

12. Rifai, S., Vincent, P., Muller, X., Glorot, X., Bengio, Y., "Contractive auto-encoders: Explicit invariance during feature extraction," in: *Proc. ICML*, pp. 833–840, 2011.

13. Masci, J., Meier, U., Ciresan, D., Schmidhuber, J., Stacked Convolutional Auto-Encoders for Hierarchical Feature Extraction, pp. 52–59, ICANN, 2011.

14. Krizhevsky, A., Sutskever, I., Hinton, G.E., "Imagenet classification with deep convolutional neural networks," in: *NIPS*, pp. 1097–1105, 2012.

15. Zeiler, M.D. and Fergus, R., "Visualizing and understanding convolutional networks," in: *ECCV*, pp. 818–833, 2014.

16. Szegedy, C., Liu, W., Jia, Y., Sermanet, P., Reed, S., Anguelov, D., Erhan, D., Vanhoucke, V., Rabinovich, A., "Going deeper with convolutions," in: *Proc. CVPR*, pp. 1–9, 2015.

17. Center Berkeley, *"Caffe,"* [Online]. Available: http://caffe.berkeleyvision.org/.

18. Microsoft, *"Cntk,"* [Online]. Available: https://github.com/Microsoft/CNTK.

19. Skymind, *"Deeplearning4j,"*, [Online]. Available: http://deeplearning4j.org/.

20. Wolfram Research, *"Wolfram math,"* [Online]. Available: https://www.wolfram.com/mathematica/.

21. Google, *"Tensorflow,"* [Online]. Available: https://www.tensorflow.org/.

22. Universite de Montreal, *"Theano,"* [Online]. Available: http://deeplearning.net/software/theano/.

23. Collobert, R., Kavukcuoglu, K., Farabet, C., *"Torch,"* [Online]. Available: http://http://torch.ch/.

24. Chollet, F., *"Keras,"* [Online]. Available: https://keras.io/.

25. Nervana Systems, *"Neon,"* [Online]. Available: https://github.com/NervanaSystems/neon.

26. Tyagi, A.K. and Nair, M.M., Deep Learning for Clinical and Health Informatics, in the book, *Computational Analysis and Deep Learning for Medical Care: Principles, Methods, and Applications*, 28 July 2021.

27. Varsha, R., Nair, S.M., Tyagi, A.K., Aswathy, S.U., RadhaKrishnan, R., The Future with Advanced Analytics: A Sequential Analysis of the Disruptive Technology's Scope, in: *Hybrid Intelligent Systems. HIS 2020. Advances in Intelligent Systems and Computing*, Abraham A., Hanne T., Castillo O., Gandhi N., Nogueira Rios T., Hong TP. (eds), vol. 375, Springer, Cham, 2021.

28. Goyal, D., Goyal, R., Rekha, G., Malik S., Tyagi, A.K., Emerging Trends and Challenges in Data Science and Big Data Analytics, *2020 International Conference on Emerging Trends in Information Technology and Engineering (ic-ETITE)*, pp. 1–8, 2020.

29. Pramod, A., Naicker, H.S., Tyagi, A.K., Machine Learning and Deep Learning: Open Issues and Future Research Directions for Next Ten Years, in the book *Computational Analysis and Deep Learning for Medical Care: Principles, Methods, and Applications*, 28 July 2021.

30. Tyagi, A.K., Nair, M.M., Niladhuri, S., Abraham, A., Security, Privacy Research issues in Various Computing Platforms: A Survey and the Road Ahead. *J. Inf. Assur. Secur.*, 15, 1, pp. 1–16. 16p, 2020.

31. Nair M.M., Kumari S., Tyagi, A.K., Sravanthi, K., Deep Learning for Medical Image Recognition: Open Issues and a Way to Forward. In: *Proceedings of the Second International Conference on Information Management and Machine Intelligence. Lecture Notes in Networks and Systems*, Goyal D., Gupta A.K., Piuri V., Ganzha M., Paprzycki M. (eds), vol. 166, Springer, Singapore, 2021.

32. Tay, Y., Tuan, L.A., Hui, S.C., KDD '18, London, United Kingdom, August 19–23, 2018, https://arxiv.org/pdf/1801.09251.pdf

33. Mishra S., Tyagi A.K. (2022) The Role of Machine Learning Techniques in Internet of Things-Based Cloud Applications. In: Pal S., De D., Buyya R. (eds) Artificial Intelligence-based Internet of Things Systems. Internet of Things (Technology, Communications and Computing). Springer, Cham. https://doi.org/10.1007/978-3-030-87059-1_4

34. Malik S., Tyagi A.K., Mahajan S. (2022) Architecture, Generative Model, and Deep Reinforcement Learning for IoT Applications: Deep Learning Perspective. In: Pal S., De D., Buyya R. (eds) Artificial Intelligence-based Internet of Things Systems. Internet of Things (Technology, Communications and Computing). Springer, Cham. https://doi.org/10.1007/978-3-030-87059-1_9

# 11

# Optimization Techniques in Deep Learning Scenarios: An Empirical Comparison

**Ajeet K. Jain[1]\*, PVRD Prasad Rao[2] and K. Venkatesh Sharma[3]**

*[1]Department of Computer Science and Engineering, Koneru Lakshmaiah Education Foundation, Vaddeswaram, AP, India; (Association: CSE, KMIT, Hyderabad, India)*
*[2]CSE, KLEF, Vaddeswaram, AP, India*
*[3]CSE, CVR College of Engineering, Hyderabad, India*

*Abstract*

Machine learning has enormously contributed toward optimization techniques motivating new approaches for optimization algorithms and their usage that have played a pivotal role in data science. The optimization approaches in deep learning has wide applicability with resurgence of novelty starting from Stochastic Gradient Descent to convex and non-convex and derivative-free approaches. Selecting an optimizer is an important choice in deep learning scenarios, and the optimization algorithm chosen having convexity principles in their core determines the training speed and final performance predicted by the DL model. The complexity further increases with growing deepness due to hyperparameter tuning and as the datasets become larger and, in turn, they require a fitting optimizer.

In this chapter, we examine the most popular and widely optimizers algorithms in an empirical way. The augmenting behaviors of these are tested on MNIST, *SKLEARN* datasets. We empirically compare them pointing out their similarities, differences, and likelihood of their suitability for a given applications. Recent variants of optimizers are highlighted with their subtleties. The chapter focuses on the critical role and pinpoints which one would be a better option while making a trade-off.

*Keywords:* Deep learning, optimizers, Lipschitz constant, convexity, lottery ticket

---

*\*Corresponding author:* jainajeet123@gmail.com

---

Archana Mire, Shaveta Malik and Amit Kumar Tyagi (eds.) Advanced Analytics and Deep Learning Models, (255–282) © 2022 Scrivener Publishing LLC

## 11.1 Introduction

Deep learning (DL) algorithms are indispensable with statistical computations for higher efficiency when the datasets size increases. Interestingly, one on the pillar of DL is mathematical tactics of optimization process which makes decision based on previously unseen data. This is accomplished by parameters carefully chosen (near to optimal solution intuitively) for a given learning problem. *The hyperparameters are the parameters of a learning algorithm and not of a given model.* Evidently, the inspiration is to look forward to the optimizing algorithm which works well and predict accurately [1–4]. In ML, the study of text classification has been undertaken by many as it provides the fundamental problem of learning from examples. Similarly, speech and image recognition have been dealt with great success and accuracy yet offer the place for new improvements. In achieving higher goals, use of various optimizing techniques involving convexity principles are much more cited [5–7] nowadays and using logistic and other regression techniques. Moreover, the SGD has been very popular over last many years but also suffers from ill-conditioning and also taking more time to compute for larger datasets. At times, it also requires hyperparameter tuning and different learning rates adaptively.

With recent proliferation on convex theory intriguing with DL algorithms and first-order derivatives, these optimizers are giving high performance. The new entrants' variants are proving their superiors performance while adapted to a new datasets. We examine the most popularly used optimizers in DL networks on image dataset and on CNN and *sklearn*. We also emphasize about the criticalities of role played by optimizers and empirically compare them in response to their learning rate, suitability plus other selection criteria.

### 11.1.1 Background and Related Work

DL has made a strong pathway in all areas of engineering applications and has generated keen interest due to its closeness to human cognition. Machine learning (ML) has taken deep roots in addressing human life problems including healthcare, sociology, economic, logistics, and alike. So, now, we have intelligent products and services, e.g., speech recognition, computer vision, anomaly detection, game playing, and many such areas. The ever changing tools and techniques of ML have a widening impact to diagnose diseases, autonomous drive, animated movie making, smart recommended systems, and many more. To background work is owing to "optimizer and regularization methodologies"—ranging from

Gradient Descent (GD) to Stochastic GD to Momentum-based optimizers [8]. Meanwhile, the convex and non-convex theory of optimization is covered briefly and one can refer more on these topics in cited references [9, 10]. In fact, the whole convex optimization methods are relaxed now a day with conditioning and suitable niche algorithms are investigated to find the most probable accuracy results and thus less execution time and more result oriented.

In DL, the two sides of a coin are regularization and optimization and to achieve a perfect balance among the two is an artistic incredibleness. Firstly, in order to alleviate "*ovefitting*" in NN, regularization works well and thus improves the truthfulness toward the "*never-seen-before*" data. Effectively, doing so decreases the variance of the model with no increase in "bias" significantly. Varying regularization parameter "$\lambda$" decreases corresponding coefficients in tandem. So, regularization improves the generalization feature of DL (ML) and is by no means related to improvise the performance measure of the algorithm on the working dataset. Therefore, obtaining *generalization* is what exactly most desirable!

Secondly, to train the DL models, a number of different algorithmic approaches have been devised to update the model parameters to reduce the value of loss function while evaluating on the given training dataset. To accomplish this perfectly an in-depth understanding of optimizing techniques is needed to delve into. We require superior algorithms to train DL networks and it might take training time from a few minutes to aghast an hour or so alarmingly to get trained fully! With contemporary GPU technology on the fray, it is reduced much less than this though. As obviously expected, the optimum performance achievable from an algorithm greatly affects the training effectiveness and also intricate the role played for performance improvement. Moreover, since optimization problems are non-convex in nature, despite being so, many of them can be transformed and reshaped with suitable transformation as convex problems.

These two blending have been studied over the past many years "*separately*" with various paradigms and algorithms performing superiorly. However, when coming to DL scenario, many research papers in the literature seldom deal them in unison, and mostly, they are dealt as "*isolated*" island of wisdom. Foregoing with this forethought, the intriguingly motivating factor entails to delve deeper into the area of regularization and optimization to be explored collectively as a "*blend*" to get deeper insight of DL. Thus, the research study seeks a thoughtful process to answer most of the following questions and encompass the gamut of equilibrant to address the issues and challenges. The pertinent ones are enlisted as follows:

- How to measure the optimal performance? What are those attributes which empirically compares them using various techniques in deep learning?
- How non-convex methods could be transformed into convex methods?
- How derivative free algorithms are getting importance while reducing computational time?
- How hyperparameter tuning is done for optimization techniques?
- What is recent advancement-like Lottery Ticket Algorithm? How contemporary optimizers are useful to address distributed and deep learning scenarios?

## 11.2   Optimization and Role of Optimizer in DL

This section highlights about the role and criticality of optimizers and performance issues and challenges therein. It is naturally obvious that we need some way to evaluate whether our algorithm is performing accurately in order to narrow the bridge of gap between the current output and the targeted output. This measured difference works as a response indicator to regulate the difference obtained by the optimizer to make appropriate adjustments. The weights are fundamentally a bunch of numbers and are stored as pattern carrying information what a layer does with its input data. Thus, the learning is primarily to discover new updated weight values for all the layers such that it accurately maps them to their connected targets. This is easier to say than happening in practice! Here lies the problem—a deep network may contain hundreds (or even more!) of parameters, so discovering them out with precise value for each and every one is a formidable task, particularly knowing that amending value of one parameter influences the rest.

To control the output from layers, we assess them against expected. The closeness between them is what is desired as expectation. This is the work of the *loss function* of the network- aka, objective function [1, 3, 4]. It takes the predicted value and compares against the true target, i.e., what we wanted as actual output and calculates the difference, suggestive of our performance on this specific input dataset, as depicted in Figure 11.1.

The basic principle utilizes this scored difference as a pointer to regulate the value of the weights accordingly leading toward lesser loss score. This adjustment is the function performed by "*optimizer*", which augments

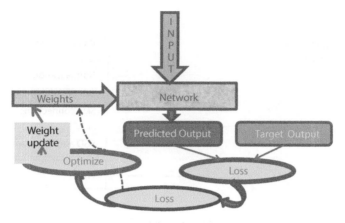

**Figure 11.1** An optimizer framework.

what is conventionally known as back propagation algorithm. *In factual terms, this is the fundamental part of machine learning algorithms* [11–14].

Initially, the weights are given random values (smaller values in the beginning) and the network performs a sequence of arbitrary transformations. As expected the discrepancy should be lowered against the larger values. Nevertheless, the network update weights in correct direction for every input and thereby propitiating toward decrease of loss. This process continues as iteration and the training loop is repeated (known as epoch)—and each epoch yields a correct weight update values augmenting to reduce the loss further less. Ideally, the idea is to reduce it toward near zero. A cost function usually just calculates the mean squared error (loss) between an actual output and the desired output when performing supervised learning tasks. So, a loss function can be considered synonymously with a cost function [15].

How to train a NN successfully? To accomplish this we need (i) power engine (latest multi-core CPU/GPU), (ii) a suitable network, and (iii) a suitable algorithm with accurate training artifices (tricks).

## 11.2.1   Deep Network Architecture

The architectural and activation functions are most important and one can think of a deep network with at least four to five layers and sufficient connections. Achieving good performance, one can go to even a deep level of 20 or more and add skip connections. Primarily, **ReLU (Re**ctified **L**inear **U**nit) activation function begins a good choice, but depending upon the characteristics of dataset, using **tanh** or **swish** activation functions might

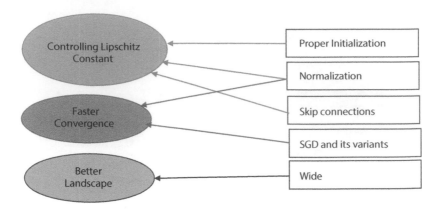

**Figure 11.2** Proposed choices for training of a NN.

prove a superior choice while training the algorithm [16]. Additionally, another criticality is to use SGD with well-tuned constant step-size, however, momentum and adaptive step size offers additional profit. A prototypical is depicted in Figure 11.2 interposing three aspects with their effects.

These propositions have three characteristics of algorithmic convergence: make convergence possible, faster convergence, and better global solutions. All three aspects are interrelated.

The Lipschitz constant is the maximum ratio between variations in the output space and variations in the input space of $f$. This measures the sensitivity of the function with respect to input perturbations.

A function $f: \mathbb{R}^n \rightarrow \mathbb{R}^m$ is called Lipschitz continuous if there exists a constant $L$ such that

$$\forall x, y \in \mathbb{R}^n, \; \|f(x) - f(y)\|_2 \leq L\|x - y\|_2 \qquad (11.1)$$

For locally Lipschitz functions, it may be computed using the differential operator. For more details, one can refer to [17, 18].

### 11.2.2   Proper Initialization

This is extremely significant to start in order to train a network having many layers and two extra artifices can improvise: adding normalization layers and adding skip connections. Imperatively, which one is a design or a critical choice? Typical these include: initialization strategies, normalization methods, the skip connections, and over-parameterization as depicted in Figure 11.3.

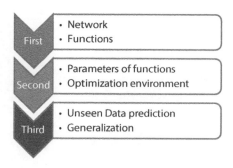

**Figure 11.3** Three steps toward generalization.

## 11.2.3    Representation, Optimization, and Generalization

Firstly, for a supervised learning scenario, we need to find a function that approximates observed samples. Secondly, we need to identify those parameters for minimizing loss. Thirdly, we need to use a function from the previous step to make predictions on test data and calculate the resultant test error, which can be further divided into *representation, optimization*, and *generalization* errors, respectively.

Note worthily in DL, these three errors are often studied disparately—while noting the representation supremacy of a certain class of functions, we often do not try to look into optimization problem closely. Similarly, while noting the generalization error, we often take for granted that the global optima have been found and in the same way tend to ignore the generalization error while noting optimization properties, assuming the representation error is *zero* [19–21].

## 11.2.4    Optimization Issues

The criticalities of optimization issues in DL are fairly intricate and a pictorial representation is in Figure 11.4 with enumeration as follows:

(i)   Making the algorithm starts run and converging to a realistic solution.

(ii)  Making the algorithm to converge fast and speed up convergence rate.

(iii) Ensuring convergence with a stumpy value–like global minimum.

Roughly speaking, all issues and challenges are chiefly inspired by optimization techniques. Moreover, this vertical divide is never precise due

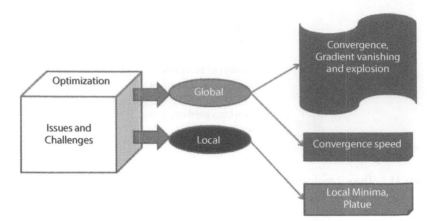

**Figure 11.4** Optimization: Issues and challenges.

to blur boundaries. For example, some algorithms provide better convergence rate—citing it as a global issue (mostly). Others view these three as sub-areas of DL optimization techniques as an important art.

### 11.2.5   Stochastic GD Optimization

Ironically, SGD closely follow the gradient of a mini-batch selected at random. While training a network, we estimate the gradient using a suitable loss function. At an iteration "**k**", the gradient will be updated accordingly. Hence, the calculation for "**m**" examples input from the training set having y(i) as target is as follows:

$$
\left.
\begin{aligned}
\hat{g} &\leftarrow \frac{1}{m}\nabla_\theta \sum_i L(f(x^{(i)};\theta), y^{(i)}) \\
\theta &\leftarrow \theta - \eta\hat{g}
\end{aligned}
\right\}
\tag{11.2}
$$

here "η" (eta) is learning rate. Further, the learning rate is of paramount importance as the magnitude of an update at "$k^{th}$" iteration is dictated by this. For instance, if η = 0.01 (very small to small), then evidently more number of iteration updates will be required for convergence. On the contrary, if η = 0.5 or more, then, in this case, the recent updates shall be highly dependent on the recent instance. Eventually, an obvious wise decision is to select (choose) it arbitrary by trial—this is one very important hyperparameter tuning in DL systems. On the parallel side of it, yet another way could be "*choose one among several learning rates*" which provide smallest loss value. This intrigue technique is known as **"line search"**—a very popular scheme for DL fraternity to tuning. Yet another intuitive way is to monitor for first few beginning epochs and make a prudent choice of "$\eta$" offering best or near-to-best performance. In subsequent Section 11.4.3 on **MAS** (**M**ixing **A**dam and **S**GD), more details about the seemingly interesting technique is discussed.

## 11.2.6    Stochastic Gradient Descent with Momentum

From the preceding section and paragraphs, it is obvious that SGD has a trouble to get toward global optima and has a tendency to get stuck into local minima, as depicted in Figure 11.5.

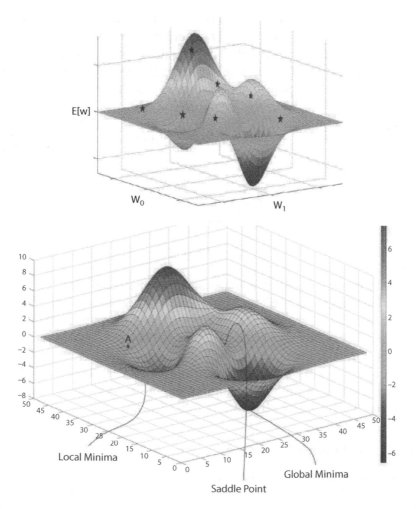

**Figure 11.5** A 3-D representation with local and global minima (maxima).

Moreover, smaller values of gradient or noisy ones can create another problem of vanishing gradient issue! To overcome this problem, the method involving momentum (a principle borrowed from physics) is adopted to accelerate the process of learning. The momentum method aims to resolve two very important issues:

(i)    variance in SGD.
(ii)   variance when solving Hessian Matrix for poor conditioning.

The method takes the brevity of running moving average by incorporating previous update in the recent change as if there is a momentum due to preceding updates.

The momentum-based SGD will converge faster with reducing oscillations. To achieve this, we use another hyperparameter "$v$" known as velocity. This hyperparameter tells the speed and, of course, the direction by which its moves in the given parameter space. Usually, "$v$" is set as negative of gradient value of exponential decaying average. Moving further on, we would require yet one more hyperparameter $\alpha$ (alpha): $\alpha \in [0, 1]$, known as momentum parameter and its contribution is to find how fast the previous gradient exponentially decays. The new (updated) values are computes as follows:

$$
\left.
\begin{aligned}
v \leftarrow \alpha v - \epsilon \frac{1}{m} \nabla_\theta \left( \sum_{i=1}^{m} L(f(x^{(i)};\theta), y^{(i)}) \right) \\
\theta \leftarrow \theta + v
\end{aligned}
\right\}
\qquad (11.3)
$$

From Equation (11.3), it is obvious that the velocity vector "$v$" keeps on adding the gradient values. Moreover, for a bigger value of $\alpha$ (alpha) relative to $\epsilon$, the gradient affects the current direction more from previous iteration. This in fact lays the foundation on which ADAM (see Section 11.3.3) principally works.

The commonly used values of $\alpha$: from 0.5 to 0.99. Despite being so intuitive and nice technique, the limitation of this algorithm is additional parameter inclusion and extra calculations involved.

## 11.2.7   SGD With Nesterov Momentum

This is another variant of standard momentum feature motivated by using Nesterov acceleration [22]. Basically, it calculates gradient of functional loss ahead in the momentum direction rather than at the local point position in-place [23, 24]. In short, the technique estimates gradient while applying recent velocity as in Equation (10.4):

$$\tilde{\theta} \leftarrow \theta + \alpha v \qquad (11.4)$$

Subsequently, the provisional estimation of gradient is accomplished and parameters get updated, as per Equation (10.5):

$$g \leftarrow \frac{1}{m} \nabla_{\tilde{\theta}} \sum_{i=1}^{m} L(f(x^{(i)}; \tilde{\theta}), \gamma^{(i)})$$

$$v \leftarrow \alpha v - \epsilon g \qquad (11.5)$$

$$\theta \leftarrow \theta + v$$

This modified technique is also getting lot of attention in DL scenarios.

## 11.3 Various Optimizers in DL Practitioner Scenario

The DL practice is more of the optimization and regularization process. The currently available optimizers with their process framework are briefly described with their relative merits and limitations. Each one has some peculiarities or the other and an insight of those will an exemplary thought progression [25, 26].

### 11.3.1 AdaGrad Optimizer

The simplest of optimizing algorithms to begin with is **AdaGrad**, where the algorithm's names itself suggest, the algorithm adapts, i.e., dynamically changes the learning rate with model's parameters Here, for parameters whose partial derivative are higher (larger) for them decrease their corresponding learning rate substantially. Contrary to this intuition, the algorithm takes inversely to where derivatives are lower. A natural question to ask is *"why one needs different learning rates?"* The choice of answer suggests that we need this adaptive feature of learning rate for following reasons [25]:

(i) *Learning Rate for Sparse Features*—where quite a large number of zero value features are present-like in a bag of words (Deepak likes to watch movies on Amazon Streaming). This necessitates that we should have a mechanism to perform larger updates on those features.

(ii)   *Learning Rate for Dense Features*—where quite a large number of non-zero values are present (House price/Number of stocks/population, etc.). This kind of dense features when present in the dataset necessitates for the mechanism to perform smaller updates on those ones.

So to accomplish these characteristics, **AdaGrad** employs square value of the gradient vector using a variable "**r**" for gradient accumulation, as stated in following Equation (11.6).

$$g \leftarrow \frac{1}{m}\nabla_\theta \sum_i L(f(x^{(i)};\theta),(y^{(i)}) \tag{11.6}$$

Using this Equation (10.6), the square of gradient is collected, and subsequently, the update of parameters is computed by a scaling factor "**δ** + √**r**", where **δ** is a very low value constant for numeric stability. The update applied as per the following Equation (11.7) now:

$$r \leftarrow r + g \odot g$$

$$\Delta\theta \leftarrow -\frac{\epsilon}{\delta + \sqrt{r}} \odot g \tag{11.7}$$

$$\theta \leftarrow \theta + \Delta\theta$$

Here, ⊙ operator implies element-wise multiplication of vectors. As can be inferred from above equations, when "**r**" is close to a "near-zero" value, the term in the denominator should not be evaluated as "NaN = Not A Number", and thus, the term δ helps to avoid this to happen. Also, the term "**ε**" stands for global learning rate.

**Advantages of AdaGrad**

- Well suited for simple learning task problems and easier to use.
- Manual tuning of learning rate is eliminated—set to a value of 0.01 as default.

**Disadvantages of AdaGrad**

- Only suitable for simple problems having quadratic space.
- Stops early while training even medium complexity networks, as scaling factor affects convergence and also stops before trying to get toward better solutions.

## 11.3.2   RMSProp

The modified version of **AdaGrad** is **RMSProp** (Root Mean Square **Prop**ortional) [27]. In order to alleviate the problems of **AdaGrad**, here we recursively define a decaying average of all past gradients. By doing so, the running exponential moving average at each time step depends only on the average of previous and current gradients. It performs better in the non-convex setting as well with same characteristics features. Comparison wise, **AdaGrad** contracts the learning rate according to the entire history of the squared gradient whereas **RMSProp** exploits an exponentially decaying average to discard history from the extreme past such that it can converge quickly after finding a convex bowl. The pertinent equation to implement is as follows:

$$r \leftarrow \rho r + (1 - \rho)\, g \odot g \tag{11.8}$$

here, $\rho$ is the decay rate. Then, parameter update is computed and applied as follows:

$$\Delta \theta = -\frac{\epsilon}{\sqrt{\delta + r}} \odot g \tag{11.9}$$
$$\theta \leftarrow \theta + \Delta \theta$$

**Advantages of RMSProp**

- Can adapt increase or decrease of learning rate with each epoch—meaning it chooses different learning rate for each parameter.
- New input data does not dramatically changes the gradient and hence convergence to local minima in shorter path smoothly.

## 11.3.3   Adam

**Adam** (**Ada**ptive Momentum) one majorly used optimization algorithms in DL and joins the heuristic of both the momentum and **RMSProp** and interestingly been designed for deep neural nets [28]. This algorithmic technique has the squared gradient feature of **AdaGrad** (Section 11.3.1) and to scale the learning rate analogous to RMSProp (Section 11.3.2) and feature of momentum using moving average. The fine algorithm calculates individual learning rate for each parameter using a term called "*first moment*" (similar to velocity vector) and "*second moment*" (similar to acceleration vector). The algorism coalesce the characteristics of AdaGrad having sparse gradient and RMSProp having the mechanism for on-line and non-stationary datasets.

Let us closely look at some salient features, which has made this much more popular among DL fraternity. These emanate from the followings:

- Momentum term is in-built as an estimate of first-order moment.
- In-built bias correction while estimating for first and second order moments, sometimes called as initialization at origin (start point).
- Update moving exponential averages of gradient "$m_t$" and square gradient "$u_t$" with hyperparameters ρ1 and ρ2 (in original paper by the authors, they are denoted by β1 and β2, respectively) as these control the cited decaying rates.

These moving averages are estimation of mean (first moment) and uncentered variance (second moment) of gradient. Moving ahead in the pipeline process, at time step "t", the various estimates are as follows:

$$m_t \leftarrow \rho_1 m_{t-1} + (1-\rho_1)\, g_t$$

$$u_t \leftarrow \rho_2 u_{t-1} + (1-\rho_2)\, g \odot g$$

$$(11.10)$$

Then, bias is corrected in first and second moments. By using the corrected moment estimates, parameter updates are calculated and applied:

$$\hat{m}_t \leftarrow \frac{m_t}{1-\rho_1^t}$$

$$\hat{u}_t \leftarrow \frac{u_t}{1-\rho_2^t}$$

$$\Delta\theta = -\epsilon \frac{\hat{m}_t}{\sqrt{\hat{u}_t}+\delta}$$

$$\theta_t \leftarrow \theta_{t-1} + \Delta\theta$$

$$(11.11)$$

From [28], the default values are ρ1 (β1) = **0.9** and ρ2 (β2) = **0.999** and δ = **$10^{-8}$**. Adam works quite well in DL scenarios and is one of the most favored adaptive learning method algorithms.

**Advantages of Adam**

(i)   No manual tuning required for learning rate and is straight forward as no modifications (alternations) needed to rescale gradients.

(ii)  Due to less "on-board" memory requirements, algorithm is proficient.

(iii) Suitable for gradients having noisy and meagreness (sparsity) characteristics.

## 11.3.4   AdaMax

Extending Adam algorithm with infinity norm yields another variant, known as AdaMax [28]. The idea borrowed here is that, as Adam algorithm updates individual weights with respect to inversely proportional to $L_2$ norm, this technique is more generalized with Lp norm taken for updating.

Here, at time step "**t**", we calculate gradient with respect to stochastic way for biased first moment via training infinity norm. Subsequently, the parameters are updated according to Equation (10.12):

$$g_t \leftarrow \nabla_\theta f_t(\theta_{t-1})$$
$$m_t \leftarrow \rho_1 m_t + (1 - \rho_1) g_t$$
$$\gamma_t \leftarrow max(\rho_2 \gamma_{t-1}, |g_t|) \tag{11.12}$$
$$\theta_t \leftarrow \theta_{t-1} - (\epsilon / (1 - \rho_1^t)) m_t / \gamma_t$$

The basic advantage of using AdaMax is that we need not to make correcting the values of initialization bias and parameter updates a much easier bound in comparison to Adam [28, 29].

## 11.3.5   AMSGrad

In the progression pipeline, can we a technique where the exponential moving averages promises convergence as one of the features? The expected answer is: *yes* and this is exactly what AMSGrad technique stands for [30]. It combines the features of Adam and RMS Prop together and in the present time getting quite a bit of attention in DL scenarios. As noticed from the previous discussions, the first and second order moments variables are modified as per Equation (10.13):

$$m_t \leftarrow \rho_1^t m_{t-1} + (1 - \rho_1^t) g_t$$
$$u_t \leftarrow \rho_2 u_{t-1} + (1 - \rho_2) g_t^2 \qquad (11.13)$$
$$\hat{u}_t \leftarrow max(\hat{u}_{t-1}, u_t)$$

The fundamental differentiation from Adam algorithm is as per Equation (10.14):

$$\theta_{t+1} \leftarrow \prod_{F, \sqrt{\hat{u}_t}} (\theta_t - \epsilon_t m_t / \sqrt{\hat{u}_t} \qquad (11.14)$$

Noting that, it keeps the maximum of all $u_t$ until present time step and takes this value for normalizing averages successively instead of $u_t$ as their counterpart in Adam. By accomplishing this way, **AMSGrad** achieves a non-increasing step size and the parameters are revised as per (14). The most noticeable feature is that **AMSGrad** neither way decreases nor increases the learning rate. In addition to this, it reduces $u_t$, which guides to non-decreasing rate in the event when gradient is huge in future expected iterations.

## 11.4    Recent Optimizers in the Pipeline

In the recent past, many things in the optimization research have been undertaken by many practitioners and academicians. The research community in ML and DL are striving for more with better parameter tuning and exponential decay rates and using state-of-the-art technology to improve the performance on CNN, GAN, RNN, and other datasets. Here, we enlist a few recent optimizers with different blends which they exhibit close relationships with the optimizers presented so far. It is worth to be aware on this emerging field of research where lots of floruit ideas are taking new heights with statistical techniques [31].

### 11.4.1    EVE

There are two learning rates of paramount interest as depicted in Figure 11.4 (Section 11.4), and these influence the convergence and other virtues of optimizer. Recapturing the thinking toward this, we can have the adaptive gradient feature of SGD where the intended these is well suited too.

So, this one is cited as modification of Adam optimizer with coefficient confining two themes—firstly adapting the learning rate locally for each parameter and secondly combining all parameters together and performing an update globally. This sounds great! And in fact, it has shown to be outperforming Adam and others while training deep neural network (DNN)–like CNN for classification of pictures (photographs) and RNN for language translation task [32]. It seems as though a companion of **Adam**— as name suggests.

## 11.4.2    RAdam

The problem of adaptive learning rate and its big variance is usually noticed in the early stage of training the network and the idea of "*warmup*" works as a supplement in order to reduce the variance. The term "*warmup*" step is just a parameter used to lower the learning rate to reduce impact of model deviation from learning on new data suddenly. This implies that we can use a very low learning rate for a set number of training steps, i.e., "*warmup steps*". Afterward, we use our "*regular*" learning rate or better known as "*learning rate scheduler*". We can also gradually increase your learning rate over the number of warmup steps.

The proposed **Rectified Adam (RAdam)** is a modification by introducing a term to rectify the variance of the adaptive learning rate. The experimental results on image classification, language modeling, and neural machine translation verify our intuition and demonstrate the efficacy of this new variant [33, 34].

## 11.4.3    MAS[1] (Mixing ADAM and SGD)

Another variant that join together Adam and SGD by weighing the contributions collectively with the task of regular (constant) weights and exploit them at the same time by taking the best of them. This intuitive blending idea is illustrated in Figure 11.6 with a side caption therein. Recently, various demonstrations are cited with CNN DNN incorporating different images and the conventional classification of text data with MAS optimizer and cited that it produced better results than their single SGD or ADAM counterpart optimizers individually [35].

---

[1] https://gitlab.com/nicolalandro/multi optimizer

### 11.4.4    Lottery Ticket Hypothesis

From the passion of gambling world, the inspiration is to select (get) a ticket whose chance of winning is highest! In the same way, the training of DL models is often compared with lottery to buy every possible ticket. However, if we know the winning process, then it seems that we can make a prudence choice about selection process. By the same token, in DL models, the training processes produce large structures of inter-connections of NN equivalent to a large container of lottery tickets. In this hypothesis, the model undergoes optimization techniques-like pruning that remove unnecessary weights from NN in order reduce model size without compromising the performance. Thus, this is, in turn, equivalent to searching of winning tickets from the container leaving the rest. Such pruning process produces structures which are almost 90% smaller than the original NN structure [34]. This idea leads to the hypothesis that a large NN contains a smaller sub-network that, if trained properly, will attain a similar accuracy in counterpart.

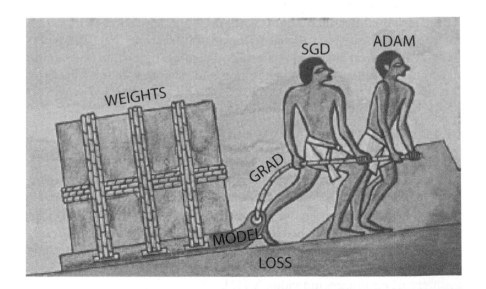

Intuitive idea representing MAS: weights are modified jointly by both paradigm techniques. It combines automatically to move fast in the direction toward the loss function plane when duo agrees.

**Figure 11.6** A MAS mixing logo.

> *LT premise:* An arbitrarily initialized DNN includes a sub-network so initialized with the intention of while separately being trained — it matches test accurateness of the original network after training for at most the same number of iterations.

Thus, looking at the brevity of this hypothesis, it opens more fronts for understanding and research to become one of the most important DL fields as it challenges the conventional wisdom in DL network training. For more insightfulness, one can refer to [33–36].

## 11.5   Experiment and Results

### 11.5.1   Web Resource

*https://scikit-learn.org/stable/modules/generated/sklearn.datasets.make_blobs.html*

The various optimizers were tested using classification from the **sklearn** datasets by generating random classification. Initially, this creates a cluster of points normally distributed with standard deviation as 1 about the vertices of an **n_informative** hyper cube with sides of length **2\*class_sep** and assigns an equal number of clusters to each class. Further, it also introduces interdependence between these features and adds various types of noise to the data. The numbers of samples were taken as 100 (default) and number of features as 20. The testing dataset generates isotropic Gaussian blobs for clustering. The purpose of using this data set is to create random samples artificially of a given controlled size and complexity, thus providing a way to test various optimisers algorithm with varying 'learning rate' with number of epochs. The generated dataset produce a matrix of features with their corresponding target values. The plot of generated clusters for 3 categories is shown in Figure 11.7

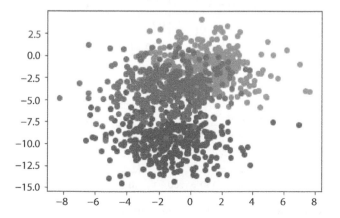

**Figure 11.7** Sample output showing three different classes.

```
pyplot.savefig('sgd.png')
pyplot.show()
```

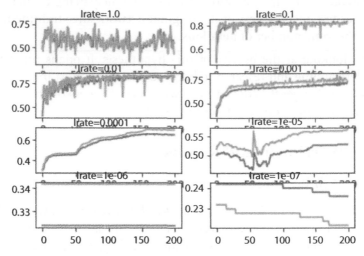

**Figure 11.8** (a)  SGD with "lrate" and accuracy with number of epochs.        (*Continued*)

```
pyplot.savefig('adam.png')
pyplot.show()
```

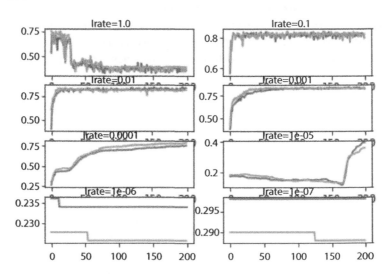

**Figure 11.8 (Continued)** (b)  ADAM with "lrate" and accuracy with number of epochs.
(*Continued*)

```
pyplot.savefig('adagrad.png')
pyplot.show()
```

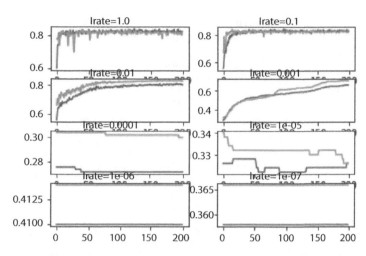

**Figure 11.8 (Continued)** (c)  AdaGrad with "lrate" and accuracy with number of epochs.
(*Continued*)

```
pyplot.savefig('rmsprop.png')
pyplot.show()
```

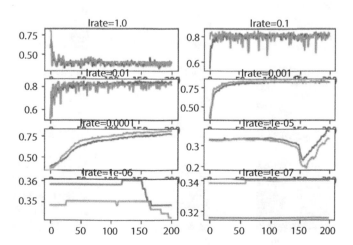

**Figure 11.8 (Continued)** (d)  RMSProp with "lrate" and accuracy with number of epochs.
(*Continued*)

```
pyplot.savefig('amsgrad.png')
pyplot.show()
```

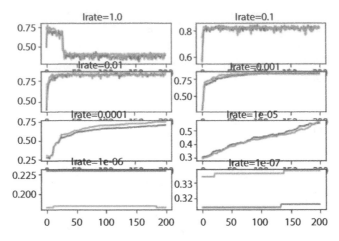

**Figure 11.8 (Continued)** (e)  AMSGrad with "lrate" and accuracy with number of epochs.

*(Continued)*

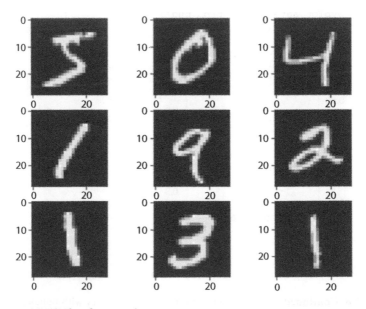

**Figure 11.9**  MNIST handwriting data.

with orange, green and blue colors. Different optimizers were tested keeping 'lr' and 'epoch' as parameters and their behavior and intricacies are depicted in Figure 11.8(a)-(e).

## 11.5.2   Resource

Simple MNIST ConvNet (CONVolutional neural NETwork) Handwritten Digit Classification (keras.io) is shown in Figure 11.9.

The MNIST dataset contains 60,000 small square 28 × 28 pixel grayscale images of handwritten single digits between 0 and 9 and to classify them into 1 of 10 classes representing integer values from 0 to 9. Figure 11.10(a,b)

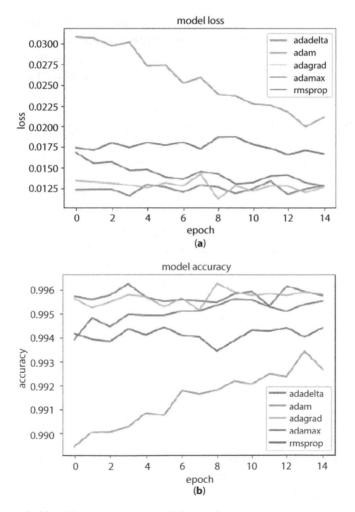

**Figure 11.10** (a, b)  Different optimizers with loss and accuracy.

clearly depicts the accuracy v/s epochs for different optimizers. As one can visible guess intuitively, different optimizing algorithms and therefore their named optimizer empirically have varied virtues and need to be considerer carefully - depending upon the data set and other optimizing parameters, in order to produce better results!

## 11.6   Discussion and Conclusion

As can be visually analyzed from various graphs from the experimental analysis, some salient points emerge:

- – A good start is to have technique that usually works well with ReLU and tuning of a few hyperparameters.
- – Error function should reflect the learning goals so that it could provide intuitive learning idea and guessing with approximations.
- – DL is more about straightening-out the factors, and an appropriate data representation can provide meaningful data transformations.
- – Start with a simple dataset having fewer (easier) samples with a simple network, and after obtaining promising results gradually increase the complexity of both data and network while tuning hyperparameters and trying regularization methods.
- – Training with random initialization is first choice and later one can go with pre-trained model to speed up.
- – Begin with well-known optimizer to get results and trying out with each will provide a reconnaissance and might lead to improvement. The correctly chosen optimizer with learning rate and other parameters makes a good deal. However, there no way a *single one optimizers will fit for all types of date set* (*NO FIT ALL RULE!*).
- – *Selecting a Particular Optimizer*: Choose a well-understood optimizer with default learning rates and other parameters settings. Try to change these parameters with iterations (epochs) and see the loss (accuracy) results. Subsequently, shift toward other similar-featured optimizer and observe the changes. *This is indeed an exhaustive process!* Nevertheless, keep experimenting by increasing toward momentum based and other current blends of optimizers (like Adam, AMSGrad or RADam, etc.).

> Caveat: Selecting proper learning rate is "hit-and-try again" scenario. Tuning hyperparameters require intuition and experience. Nonetheless, to achieve distinction in performance, the deep learning rule is simple—try differently with patience, shall definitely lead to improved results.

We have provided with an understanding of reasons for a particular optimizer for a given dataset and it gives foundation for the pros and cons of their suitability. The most popular in DL research community are Adam and RMSProp, and the results were shown as promising ones. However, this imperativeness provides an insightful for making a visionary choice of optimizers. Also, getting an overview of their criticalities and understanding the reasons for choice makes a footing platform in DL [37–39].

Furthermore, there are several promising results one can obtain from different set(s) of optimizer(s) and this might require more investigations and deeper delving into. The upcoming and already announced optimizers, like YOGI, have to be integrated into the DL framework, so that it can be empirical tested against others. The Lottery Ticket technique is already gaining momentum in this area, and sooner, hopefully, more insight shall we be able to explore with. The blue sky is the limit to gaze!

# References

1. Goodfellow, I., Bengio, Y., Courville, A., *Deep Learning*, MIT Press, USA, 2016.
2. Bishop, C.M., *Neural Network for Pattern Recognition*, Clarendon Press, USA, 1995.
3. Chollet, F., *Deep Learning with Python*, 1st Ed, Manning Pub., NY, USA, 2018.
4. Jain, A.K., Prasad Rao, Dr. PVRD., Sharma, Dr. K. V., "A Perspective Analysis of Regularization and Optimization Techniques in Machine Learning", in: *Computational Analysis and Understanding of Deep Learning or Medical Care: Principles,Methods and Applications*". *CUDLMC 2020*, Wiley-Scrivener, USA, April/May 2021.
5. Mueller, J.P. and Massaron, L., *Deep Learning for Dummies*, John Wiley, USA, 2019.
6. Patterson, J. and Gibson, A., *Deep Learning: A Practitioner's Approach*, O'Reilly Pub. Indian Edition, New Delhi, India, 2017.
7. Jain, A.K., Prasad Rao, Dr.PVRD., Sharma, Dr. K. V., Deep Learning with Recursive Neural Network for Temporal Logic Implementation. *Int. J.*

Adv. Trends Comput. Sci. Eng., 9, 4, 6829–6833, July – August 2020. online (https://doi.org/10.30534/ijatcse/2020/383942020

8. Srivasatava, N. et al. Journal of Machine Learning Research, JMLR, Inc. and Microtome Publishing (USA), Vol.15, 2014 , pp 1929-1958. http://jmlr.org/papers/volume15/srivastava14a.old/srivastava14a.pdf.

9. Bertsekas, D.P., Convex Optimization Theory, Athena Scientific Pub., MIT Press, USA, 2009.

10. Boyd, S. and Vandenberghe, L., Convex Optimization, Cambridge University Press, USA, 2004.

11. LeCun, Y., Boser, B., Denker, J.S., Henderson, D., Howard, R.E., Hubbard, W., Jackel, L.D., Backpropagation applied to handwritten zip code recognition. Neural Comput., 1, 4, 541–551, 1989.

12. Hinton, G., Srivastava, N., Krizhevsky, A., Sutskever, I., Salakhutdinov, R., Improving neural networks by preventing co-adaptation of feature detectors, 3 Jul 2012, arXiv:1207.0580v1 [cs.NE]

13. Glorot, X. and Bengio, Y., Understanding the difficulty of training deep feed-forward neural networks, in: Proceedings of the International Conference on Artificial Intelligence and Statistics (AISTATS), pp. 249–256, 2010.

14. Glorot, X., Bordes, A., Bengio, Y., Deep sparse rectifier neural networks, in: Proceedings of the International Conference on Artificial Intelligence and Statistics (AISTATS), pp. 315–323, 2011.

15. Zeiler, M. and Fergus, R., Stochastic pooling for regularization of deep convolutional neural networks, in: Proceedings of the International Conference on Learning Representations, ICLR, 2013.

16. Ramachandran, P., Zoph, B., Le, Q.V., Semantic Scholar, SWISH: A Self-Gated Activation Function, 16 Oct 2017, arXiv:1710.05941v1 [cs.NE]. (https://www.semanticscholar.org/paper/4f57f486adea0bf95c252620a4e8af-39232ef8bc )

17. Latorre, F., Rolland, P., Cevher, V., Lipschitz Constant Estimation Of Neural Networks Via Sparse Polynomial Optimization. ICLR, 2020.

18. Asadi, K., Misra, D., Littman, M.L., Lipschitz Continuity in Model-based Reinforcement Learning. Proceedings of the 35th International Conference on Machine Learning, PMLR, Stockholm, Sweden, p. 80, 2018.

19. Hinton, G., Srivastava, N., Krizhevsky, A., Sutskever, I., Salakhutdinov, R., Improving neural networks by preventing co-adaptation of feature detectors, arXiv:1207.0580v1 [cs.NE] Jul 2012.

20. Duchi, J., Hazan, E., Singer, Y., Adaptive subgradient methods for online learning and stochastic optimization. J. Mach. Learn. Res., 12, 2121–2159, 2011.

21. Prabhu, C.S.R., Gandhi, R., Jain, A.K., Lalka, V.S., Thottempudi, S.G., Prasada Rao, P.V.R.D., "A Novel Approach to Extend KM Models with Object Knowledge Model (OKM) and Kafka for Big Data and Semantic Web with Greater Semantics", in: Advances in Intelligent Systems and Computing, vol. 993, p. 544, 2020.

22. Bottou, L., Online algorithms and stochastic approximations, in: *Online Learning and Neural Networks*, D. Saad, (Ed.), Cambridge University Press, Cambridge, 1998.

23. Sutskever, I., Martens, J., Dahl, G., Hinton, G., On importance of initialization and momentum in deep learning. *International Conference on Machine Learning*, Atlanta, USA, pp. 1139–1147, 2013.

24. Nesterov, Y., A method of solving a convex programming problem with convergence rate O(1/k2). *Sov. Math. Dokl.*, 27, 372–376, 1983.

25. Duchi, J., Hazan, E., Singer, Y., Adaptive subgradient methods for online learning and stochastic optimization. *J. Mach. Learn. Res.*, 12, 2121–2159, 2011. https://dl.acm.org/doi/10.5555/1953048.2021068

26. Jain, A.K., Prasad Rao, Dr.PVRD., Sharma, Dr.K V., "Extending Description Logics for Semantic Web Ontology Implementation Domains". *Test Eng. Manage.*, 83, 7385, 2020.

27. Hinton, G., *Neural networks for machine learning, Coursera, Video Lectures*, 2018. https://www.youtube.com/watch?v=cbeTc-Urqak

28. Kingma, D. and Ba, J., *Adam: A method for stochastic optimization*, 2014, arXiv:1412.6980. arXiv:1412.6980v9 [cs.LG] 30 Jan 2017 - https://arxiv.org/pdf/1412.6980.pdf

29. Reddi, S.J., Kale, S., Kumar, S., On the convergence of Adam and beyond. *International Conference on Learning Representations, Vancouver, Canada*, 2018.

30. Zaheer, M., Reddi, S., Sachan, D., Kale, S., Kumar, S., Adaptive methods for nonconvex optimization, in: *Advances in Neural Information Processing Systems*, pp. 9793–9803, 2018.

31. Londhe, A. and Prasada Rao, P.V.R.D., "*Platforms for big data analytics: Trend towards hybrid era*". *International Conference on Energy, Communication, Data Analytics and Soft Computing, ICECDS*, 2017.

32. Hayashi, H., Koushik, J., Neubig, G., *Eve: A Gradient Based Optimization Method with Locally and Globally Adaptive Learning Rates*, 11 Jun 2018, arXiv:1611.01505v3 [cs.LG]. https://sciencedocbox.com/Physics/72482944-Optimization-for-training-i-first-order-methods-training-algorithm.html

33. Liu, L. *et al.*, *On The Variance Of The Adaptive Learning Rate And Beyond*, International Conference on Learning Representations (ICLR), 17 Apr 2020, arXiv:1908.03265v3 [ cs.LG]. https://arxiv.org/abs/1908.03265

34. []https://d2l.ai/chapter_optimization/lr-scheduler.html

35. Landro, N., Gallo, I., La Grassa, R., *Mixing ADAM and SGD:a Combined Optimization Method*, 16 Nov 2020, arXiv:2011.08042v1 [cs.LG]. https://www.researchgate.net/publication/345970892_Mixing_ADAM_and_SGD_a_Combined_Optimization_Method

36. Frankle, J. and Carbin, M., *The Lottery Ticket Hypothesis: Finding Sparse, Trainable Neural Networks*, 4 Mar 2019, arXiv:1803.03635v5 [cs.LG]. https://arxiv.org/abs/1803.03635

37. Yadla, H.K. and Prasad Rao, P.V.R.D., "Machine learning based text classifier centered on TF-IDF vectoriser. *Int. J. Sci. Technol. Res.*, 9, 03, 583–586, 2020.

38. Varakumari, S., Prasad Rao, P.V.R.D., Sirisha, M., Mohan Rao, K.R.R., MANOVA- A multivariate statistical variance analysis for WSN using PCA. *Int. J. Eng. Technology(UAE)*, 7, 8, 4, pp 70-74, 2018. https://www.sciencepubco.com/index.php/ijet/article/view/10976/4101%20pp.779–782, https://www.sciencepubco.com/index.php/ijet/article/view/10976/4101 pp.779-782

39. Phani Madhuri, N., Meghana, A., Prasada Rao, P.V.R.D., Prem Kumar, P., "Ailment prognosis and propose antidote for skin using deep learning". *IJITEE*, 8, 4, 70–74, 2019.

# Part 3

# INTRODUCTION TO ADVANCED ANALYTICS

# 12

# Big Data Platforms

## Sharmila Gaikwad[1]* and Jignesh Patil[2]†

*¹University of Mumbai, Computer Engineering, Mct's Rajiv Gandhi Institute of Technology, Andheri Mumbai, India*
*²University of Mumbai, Mct's Rajiv Gandhi Institute of Technology, Andheri Mumbai, India*

## Abstract

Big data refers to huge datasets which gives the advanced analysis about the system. Information is increasing nowadays due to more advanced technology, tools, and techniques. When there is a huge increase in information, it has some merits and demerits like maintaining the data, data visualization, and securing the data. Big data offers various tools and techniques to maintain and secure data. This chapter focuses on two important parts of big data, namely, visualization and security. It is really challenging task to visualize data in simple way but big data makes easy to understand and interpret. This study explains different techniques such as 1D, 2D, and multidimensional with current pandemic case study on COVID-19 with a diagrammatic representation for easy understanding of the techniques. Data visualization makes communication insights from data through visual representation. Its main aim is to still the datasets into visual graphics to allow easy understanding with complex relationships within the data. Data visualization promotes that creative data exploration [3]. Data visualization is applied in every field of knowledge. Researchers use computer techniques to model complex events and visualize phenomena that cannot be observed directly such as weather patterns and medical conditions. Today, the world is facing pandemic situations like COVID-19, and big data has played vital role in analysis and predictions [1]. Visualization made great help to society to visualize the patients in different areas or in the world. By using plotly data visualization analysis, different datasets of COVID-19 are covered in this study. Today, almost every institute is thinking big data as they are seeing growth of big data using Hadoop, Spark, Pig, etc. HDFS (HADOOP Distributed File System) is distributed file system. All types of files can be stored in the HDFS. Biggest challenge for big data

*Corresponding author*: sharmilagaikwad170@gmail.com
†*Corresponding author*: jigpatil1999@gmail.com

Archana Mire, Shaveta Malik and Amit Kumar Tyagi (eds.) Advanced Analytics and Deep Learning Models, (285–310) © 2022 Scrivener Publishing LLC

from a data security point of view is the protection's user details. As per studies, it is demonstrated the flow of big data is in three layers: incoming, stored, and outgoing data. The organizations may face the problem of encryption while storing huge data. There are some major issues while handling big data about security such as data breach, data access, and privacy violations. Due to larger data sets, there may serious data branches problem which can result more devastating consequences than normally seen in any system. This chapter covers part of data breaches in the year 2018 to 2019 and conclusion of 2020. This study also demonstrates an investigation about virtual reality which radically changes the world of big data.

*Keywords*: Plotly, data visualization, HDFS, privacy, COVID-19, security, data breaches

## 12.1    Visualization in Big Data

### 12.1.1    Introduction to Big Data

The term Big Data is collection of huge datasets which gives high performance while performing operations; there are three many characteristics of big data such as volume, value, and veracity. This macro data is increasing tremendous day by day. Technology has increase in all over world, so collection of data is also increase [1].

Big data is the field which focuses on collection of huge datasets to solve complex problem of the system in few seconds; we know that the operations performed by user require high performance of resources for quick results. It is related with following features:

1) Volume: Volume refers to the memory of the data array that must be studied and achieved in seconds bigger than TB. Example: Transactions is data set which will be stored in big storage and also wants the quick update in system.
2) Variety: Variety creates huge quantity data in a system. Records are originated from an extreme method of foundations and normally are of three types: structured, semi-structured, and unstructured data.
3) Velocity: Velocity refers rapid with which information is generated. Example: Posting and searching on the multimedia.
4) Veracity: Quality of the record that is being analyzed is refer to Veracity. So, correctness of scrutiny depends on the veracity of the source record. For example: Prediction on some topic.
5) Value: Value decides market cost of data in earlier and what will be value of such data in future. Each value of data gets

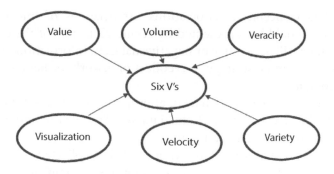

**Figure 12.1** Characteristics of Big Data [2].

pool of record progress in the system; it helps the big data to gather the data as per feature of data.

6) Visualization: Conception makes the computerized data more innovative which helps the data to present on real-time using different methods.

7) Variability: Variability means constantly changing it, making big data incredibly special because these are different solutions, different techniques, etc. Example: Seasonal effect on health on human's analysis (today, world corona analysis is done by big data and this special property) [4].

The above Figure 12.1 elaborates big data characteristics in which visualization we have added and our chapter focus on the data visualization.

## 12.1.2    Techniques of Visualization

Big data comprises the arrangement of information of nearly any form in a graphical format that makes it easy to recognize and interpret. Visualizing difficult huge information in a few second is not a simple task for anybody; imaging data in an easy way using graph bars, histogram, and dendrogram make computerized data without difficult to read to humans. Big data visualization trusts on dominant IT system to get fresh segmented data and methods is to produce graphical representation that agree users to take in and know massive of statistics in seconds.

Visualization techniques [2] offer a fast and effective way to the following:

1) Proper Documents Represent: You want to realize your viewers what correctly they require and define data in such way that viewers will attract on product. Visualization of product should be that it makes interest and change the mindset of the people.

2) Data Conception Associations: Associations of information should be represented by seeing all factors of the data which will be positive or negative datasets. Information used before can be strategy to recollect or rework for benefits of company

3) Adhesive Data: To fix data in appropriate position is difficult but big data made easy to fix data in early and is an opportunity that can be acted upon.

4) Data Complication: Vast amount of data collected in database big data provide various operations to complete capacity as soon as possible. As we know, seven V's characteristics of big data make effortless work. There are numerous big data visualization techniques [3], which are as follows:

a) **Linear (One Dimensional):** The one-dimensional data visualization is a set of information in array which is systematized by individual condition for instance in alphabetic series (Figure 12.2) [5].

b) **Two-Dimensional:** Two-dimensional data visualization is a flat graph using the horizontal and vertical (X and Y) dimensions data items are represented, according to the data provided by user.

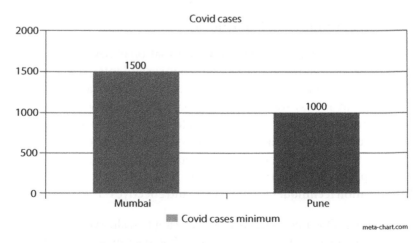

**Figure 12.2** One dimensional illustration (COVID-19 cases maximum in Mumbai and Pune at the end of March) [15].

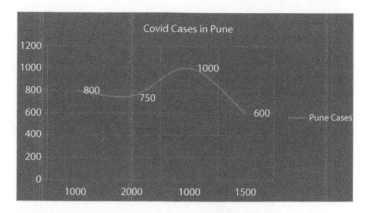

**Figure 12.3** Two-dimensional representation of Covid Cases in Pune [15].

As shown in Figure 12.3, we see that zigzag line represent data of Pune cases which is increasing and decreasing. X-axis represents predicated cases on 4 days.

There are few types of two-dimensional data visualization listed below:

1) **Cartogram:** The cartogram is a map in which the structure of areas is slanted in direction to take the data of substitute variable. The section zones is magnified and flattened according to numerical values. Cartogram is represented in three types such as Contiguous, Non-Contiguous, and Dorling Contiguous (Figure 12.4).

Algorithm:

- Read the value of polygon.
- Calculate region and center (using current margins of polygon).
- Find angle of centroid of each polygon determine the error.
- Verify points again and plot data.
- Output is ready.

2) **Dot Distribution Maps:** A distribution maps is chosen to refer the concentration of elements. Individual spot on the map signifies one or more singularities being charted.

As shown in Figure 12.5, each dot seen in map represents different population. Big dots represent high number of populations.

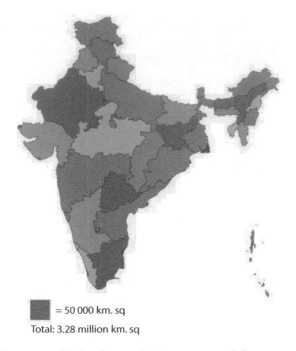

= 50 000 km. sq

Total: 3.28 million km. sq

**Figure 12.4** Cartogram of India where each color represents different states of India [2]. For following cartogram we have use the tool to represent the India map [18].

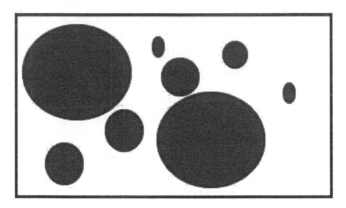

**Figure 12.5** Distribution of population.

Algorithm:

- Regulate the assignment zone.
- Compute probable dot places.
- Make a separate but repeatable dot shape.

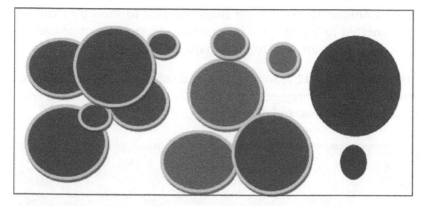

**Figure 12.6** Proportional map for Highest cases in different zones [11]. Left area is red zone. Right area represents orange zone which consists of normal to critical patients. Middle area represent the green zone which is the safest.

- Estimate the dot rate and verify the mistakes.
- Final report of the dot illustration.

**3) Proportional Symbol Maps:** A proportional symbol map is a category of map that integrates signs that transform in size based on the data they are plotted. Proportional symbol maps are classically used to display totals and can be envisage classed or unclassed data. There are two types of proportional symbol maps (Figure 12.6):

1) Single Variable Proportional Symbol Map
2) Multi Variable Proportional Symbol Map

Biggest circle represents high number of cases in specific area, which is categorize into zones (Red, Orange and Green).
Algorithm:

1. Search and store square root make a dataset.
2. Select a greater symbol size—example, a circle with 2 cm diameter.
3. Now, you read the full array of values, from the square root array. For each value, we get a symbol size.
4. Draw the mark using different shapes; we can see diameter of circle side triangle and picture of leaves etc. They will be all in the proper proportion.

4) **Contour Maps:** Contour maps are used to show data connected to topographic information. Most of the time contour maps are used to show maps linked to geology.

As seen in Figure 12.7, Sub 1, Sub 2, and Sub 3 are assumed regions, for
example. In these subregions, total patients are counted (serious, ventilator, normal symptoms, and death).

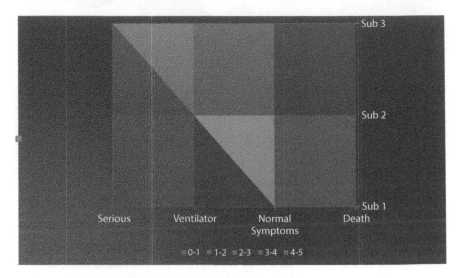

**Figure 12.7** Contour map for COVID-19 patients [16].

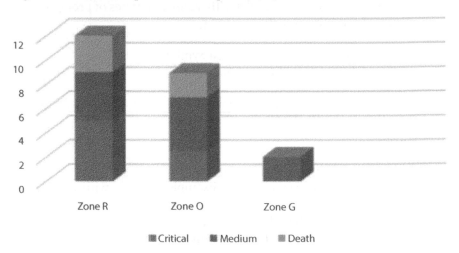

**Figure 12.8** Three-Dimensional Visualization of Zones and the count of Patients in
particular zone. Zones are divided according to patients' cases and health. Zone Green is
safest place where numbers of patients are less [15].

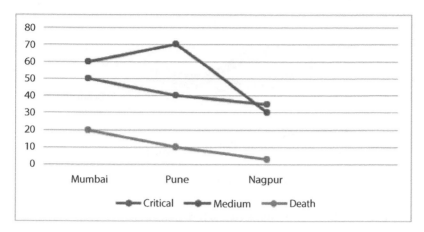

**Figure 12.9** COVID-19 cases in three major cities of Maharashtra from March to June [15].

Algorithm:

- Collect information make a dataset.
- Assume the shape rectangle divide it in four parts.
- Check possibility intersection points with all parts.
- Plot points in map via various algorithms according to requirement of user (Figure 12.8 and Figure 12.9).

We of scientific displaying achieved on system which is calculated to forecast the performance of or the consequence of physical life. In big data, 3D prototypes are important since its existing data and fix data in real world smoothly.

**I. Temporal Visualization:** Temporal visualizations are like 1D linear visualizations. Because schedule is universally used and dynamic plenty for medical records, project organization, and early appearances. It is a pigeon-holed by items that have an initiate and end period and items may intersect each.

Examples: timeline, time service charts, and scatter plot.

**a. Timeline:** A timeline is a graph way of showing an array of procedures in linear direction. Few timelines work on a rule while others simply show incident. Timeline permits you to see when things occur by permitting the observer to watch some forms survey; some nominated time stages or how actions is circulated that time period (Figure 12.10).

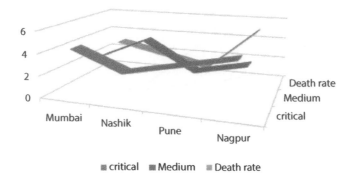

**Figure 12.10** COVID-19 cases from March to June in timeline chart [17].

Example: The latest algorithm of timeline is concentrating in Facebook to gather more friend and relatives not on brand promotion. Nowadays, Facebook is integrated new algorithm such as creating room and contact to friends and sharing post memes to friends and pages to global world.

**b. Time Series:** A time series diagram similarly called a time series graph, respectively, point on the diagram matches to mutually a time and quantity that is being calculated. Time series is also for predicating future of any situations such as weather conditions (heavy rainfall in particular area and water increase in dam is predicated by watching weather condition).

Different algorithms are used for forecasting data using machine learning python language for programming [14].

1. Auto regression: This type of algorithm learns previous information to find predication of future movements [10].
2. Moving average: Basically, it focuses on a fault which is occurring in past and in current situations.
3. Autoregressive moving average: It is the sandwich of Auto regression and Moving average.
4. Vector auto regression: It use for predicating multiple times using single model.
5. Simple exponential smoothing: As seen overhead algorithms, we can see past data, current data, and fault data, which are used for predicating. This algorithm concentrates on data cleaning eliminate noise such as in digital signal.
   Example: predictions of stock market and GDP of countries.

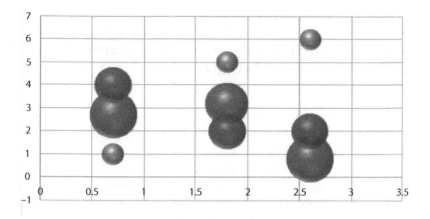

Figure 12.11  COVID-19 cases in different areas [16].

**c. Scatter Plots:** A scatter plot is an information imagining that shows the cost of two dissimilar variables as ideas. The information for individually vision is characterized by horizontal (X) and a vertical (Y) spot of visualization. Scatter plots is also called Scatter gram.

Different circle represents zone of cases in specific area if big circle is spotted that is called red zone, medium circle is orange zone, small circle represents green zone. There are few conditions of scatter plot (line of best fit, interpolation, correlation) (Figure 12.11).

**d. Multi-Dimensional:** Multi-dimensional represents one dimension as a point two dimensions as an object or graph and three Dimensions as 3D object or graph. Some examples are listed below:

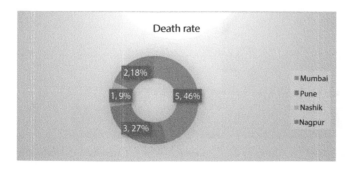

Figure 12.12  Death rate of Maharashtra in metro cities [16].

**1) Pie Charts:** Pie charts help show sizes and portions between classes by isolating a circle into comparative sectors. Each curve length denotes a proportion of each group while the whole circle characterizes the overall amount of the data equal to 100% (Figure 12.12).

Algorithm:

1. Search the middle angle for all modules.
2. Draw a circle of any range.
3. Draw a horizontal range.
4. Starting with horizontal range, draw radii making middle angle corresponding values to respective module.
5. Repeat all process for all components.
6. These radii isolate the whole circle into various sectors.

**2) Histograms:** A histogram is graph that signifies the possibility delivery of a dataset. A histogram has categories of vertical bars where each bar characterizes a solo value or a limit values for a variable. The heights of the bars designate the occurrences or chances for the dissimilar values or range of values.

Categories are follows: category 1 (normal symptoms), category 2 (medium symptoms), category 3 (serious cases), and category 4 (ventilator).

Algorithm:

Step 1: Calculate the cumulative frequency distribution Figure (12.13).

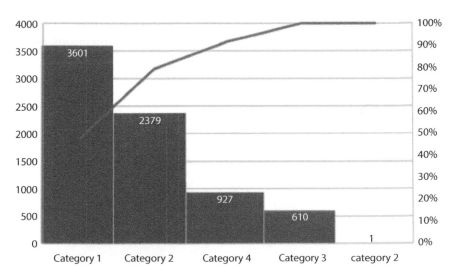

**Figure 12.13** Most case in March-April (Mumbai) [16].

Step 2: Compare with the CuF of an equalized histogram.

Step 3: Design mapping.

Step 4: The new histogram will be displayed [9].

**3) Heat map:** Heat map is a way to imagine guest performance data in the procedure of warm and icy region engaging a hot to cold system. The dark colors represent divisions with the maximum visitor interaction, red color covers regions of maximum interaction, and the cool colors specify divisions with the minimum interaction.

Example: weather prediction on the further locations (Figure 12.14).

Algorithm:

There are two procedures elaborated in calculating the range (lower bound and upper bound) of values of each container.

Implement the below steps to calculate range:

1. Compute the container size by isolating the total number of process cases with total number of containers. The total number of containers is always nine.
2. Analyze the range (lower bound and upper bound) of values of each container.

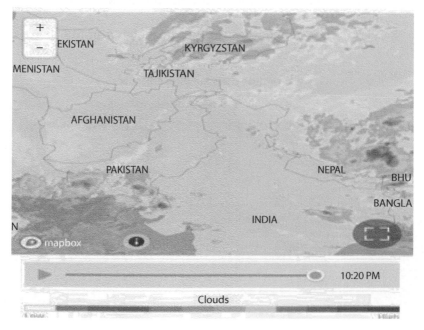

**Figure 12.14** Weather prediction [16].

The range of the first bin (bin with index of zero) would be larger than zero and less than 2. The range of the second bin (bin with index of one) would be over and above 2 and less than 4 (Figure 12.15).

**4) Tree maps:** Tree maps are visualizations for classified data. They are made of sequence of embedded rectangles of sizes comparative to the equivalent data value. A branch of tree is the large rectangle, and it is segmented into smaller rectangles that signify the dimensions of each node within that branch [7, 8].

Algorithm:

1. Take Rectangle R, select pivot P and order list having specific region.
2. Divide R into four rectangles.
3. Divide the list in to three segments to be placed out in r1, r2, and r3.
4. If the number of items is smaller than equal to 4 lay them out in either pivot.
5. Choose appropriate pivot
   a. Pivot by size.
   b. Pivot by middle
   c. Pivot by split size
6. L1 contain of items whose index is < than P and L2 have items having index < than those in L3 and the feature fraction of RP is near to 1 as possible.
7. Pick the best design whose feature fraction is near to 1.

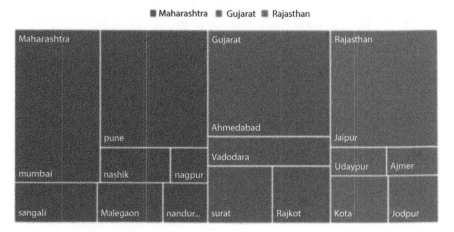

Covid cases in three states and there major cities

■ Maharashtra  ■ Gujarat  ■ Rajasthan

**Figure 12.15** Major cases in three states of India [16].

**5) Spider Charts:** A spider chart is a graphical method of demonstrating one or more variable data in the procedure of a 2D chart of three or more measureable variables symbolized on axes opening from the similar point. It is also recognizing as web charts and radar charts Figure (12.16).

Algorithm:

1) Plot a point along each axis and then connect them using different shape of forms.
2) Search which category axis represents.
3) Check how categories are related to one another as you read around the circle.
4) Zero is the center of the circle of each axis.

a. **Tree/Network Chart:** Tree Chart is a different way of envisioning the hierarchical structure of tree diagram while also showing measures for each group via area size. Tree chart summarizes each data such that it makes the user connect the thinks rapidly.

b. **Dendrogram:** A dendrogram is a diagram that displays the hierarchical connection between objects. The purpose of dendrogram is to work out the top way to allocate items

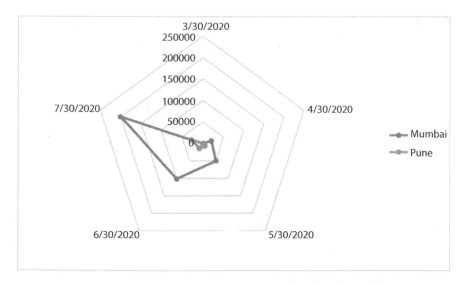

**Figure 12.16** Covid cases in Mumbai and Pune (March-July) [9]. We can say that two region of Maharashtra Mumbai and Pune patients count from April to June 2020. We can also see that how rapidly patients is increased [16].

to bunches. Dendrogram contains of set branches that break down into smaller branches.

Algorithm:

1. We allocate all the points to specific group (cluster). For example, different size points will show different groups (cluster).
2. We search for smallest distance in the contiguity matrix and will join points with smallest distance then change contiguity matrix.
3. We will repeat the procedure till one single cluster is left behind.

   **d.** **Hyperbolic Tree Charts:** A hyperbolic tree is an emphasis framework visualization technique: It offers an exhaustive view on a small area, while still only if an overview of the whole structure. This is obtained by first laying out in a uniform way the hierarchy as an tree on a non-Euclidean hyperbolic plan.

Considering root node as first public transmitted country and last node represents the last infected patient in world. In Figure 12.17, we can see that blue shape triangle as root node and other nodes as last leaf node.

Algorithm:

Step-1: Assign S has root node of the tree which include dataset.

Step-2: Search for best feature in the dataset using Attribute Selection Measure (ASM).

Step-3: Distribute the S into subgroups that comprises likely values for the best features.

Step-4: Generate the decision tree node, which contains the best feature.

Step-5: Periodic take new decision trees using the subgroups of the information formed in Step-3. Stay with this procedure till a phase is touched where you cannot extra establish the nodes called as a leaf node.

We have seen different techniques of big data visualization. Today, there are different data visualization tools which the companies use for making presentation of data.

1) Fusion Charts Suite XT
2) QlikView
3) Tiblo Specific

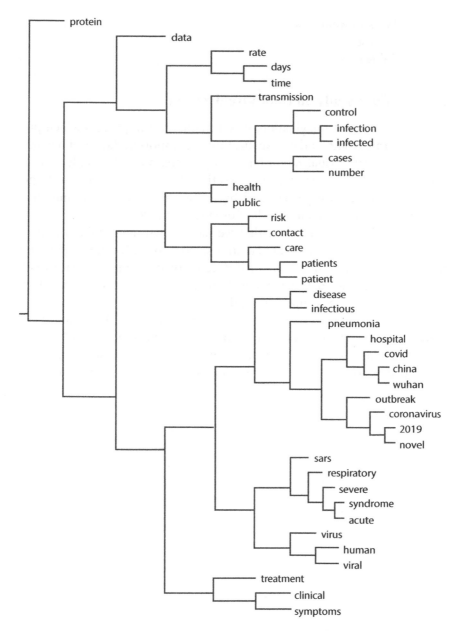

**Figure 12.17** Dendrogram data analysis of COVID-19 [12].

4) Watson Analytics
5) Sisense
6) Tableau

## 12.1.3   Case Study on Data Visualization

Visualization is not imagination; it is a mathematical process which provides accurate result. Today, visualization has important factor of big data; from 1990s, data visualization has changed this mode to Golden Era of visualization. We have seen in above sections how various charts and algorithms are representing small and big information with neat and clean quality which is understand to all of us (Figure 12.18).

The world faces a huge war that we have to win and make the world free of virus. In these pandemic situations, most countries started planning with long-term war situation; governments of different countries firstly choose the approach of visualization. Our chapter focuses on visualization, so we will focus on visualization module.

As seen in Figure 12.19, we can see that awareness by visualization (explaining corona to world and how it is impact on health), media (narrating daily situation to world), and social media such Facebook has added module safety and precautions in Facebook application with

**Figure 12.18** Spreading of Corona virus from root node to last node [16].

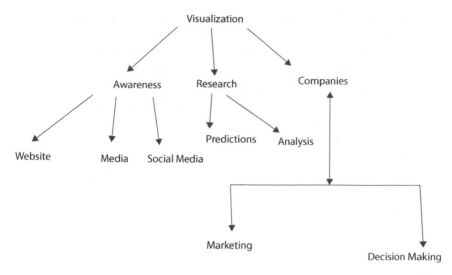

**Figure 12.19** Hierarchy of data visualization according to department [12].

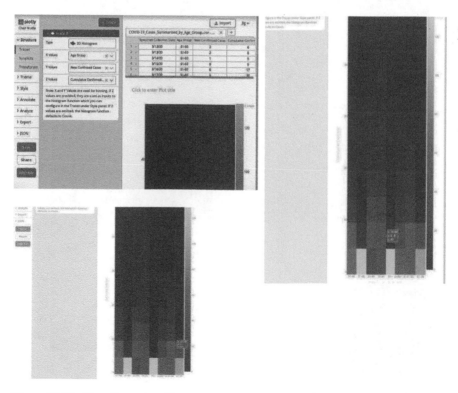

**Figure 12.20** Two-dimensional histogram (different colour) shows age group and total of age group patients [9].

helpline numbers. Tracking records of patients to stop transmission with other community. Analysis of patient's health after covid and before virus impacted on their health, evaluating mental and physical health of the patient. Companies have taken challenge of working from home as new system or architecture with dealing customers. Managers and employees plan for better output result and get quality decision making from various visualization tools. Visualization makes more innovative presentation and explanation of product in market.

As shown in Figure 12.20 plotly chart studio is used for visualization and dataset for visualization age group (Figure 12.21 and Figure 12.22) and new confirmed cases of COVID-19 [9].

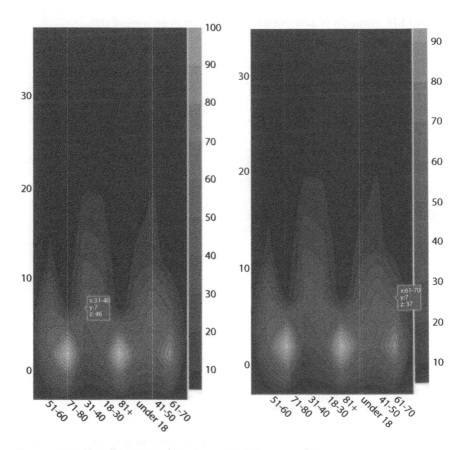

**Figure 12.21** Two-Dimensional Contour with different age [9].

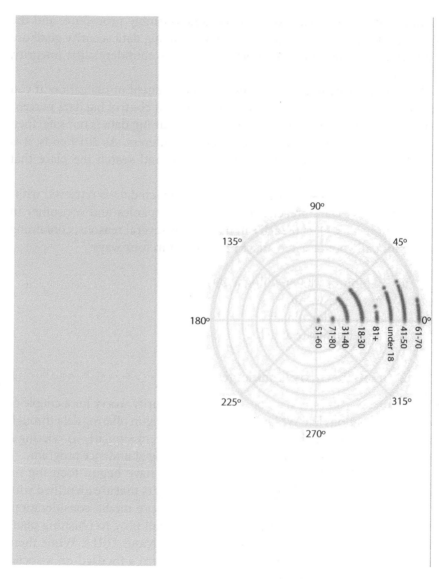

**Figure 12.22** Polar scatter in which age and new confirmed cases is shown in 0° to 45° [16].

## 12.2   Security in Big Data

### 12.2.1   Introduction of Data Breach

Bearing in mind in big data there is a group of errors that want to be measured. These contain the data lifecycle (provenance, rights, and sorting of information), the data construction and assembly procedure, and the shortage of security techniques. Eventually, the big data security goals are no altered from any further information forms confidentiality, integrity, and availability [1].

Big data security huge information can be a benefit or obligation. If you examine your data and keep it safe, then you can control big data perceptions and recover your business. However, if your big data is not safe, then you may look financial and brand authority sufferers. As 2019 ends, it is vital to evaluate our previous security efforts, and search the place that need extra enhancement.

Big data breach is a security happening in which data is retrieved without permission. Data breaches can wound companies and consumer in form of traditions. Data breach can happen for several reasons, containing unintentionally but targeted attacks passed out in four ways:

a. Exploiting system vulnerabilities
b. Weak passwords
c. Drive by downloads
d. Target malware attacks

## 12.2.2   Data Security Challenges

Open-source weaknesses have been a notable security worry for a couple of years. Organizations like White Source [13] have begun offering data through free weakness information bases. The EU even went similarly as offering a prize pool of USD\$1 million for its open source bug abundance program.

Advanced Persistent Threats (APT) assaults have begun focusing on end-clients through phishing plans. Insider dangers that are identified with traded off certifications have been increasing more media consideration. Studies uncover that not just non-nerd clients fall prey to phishing plans and social designing—even CSOs fall prey to noxious URLs. While there are insider dangers that purposefully look to harm a focused-on association, most of insider dangers are casualties [12].

The term data information security alludes to practices and apparatuses utilized to ensure information and examination measures. The large information edge is normally partitioned into three classes:

1. Approaching information—helpless while on the way.
2. Capacity information—powerless while very still.
3. Yield information—prepared for examination, helpless being used.

**Table 12.1** Comparison of 2018 vs. 2019 data security [1].

|  | 2018 | 2019 |
|---|---|---|
| Total amount of records exposed during the year | Over records 4.5 billion | Over records 5.3 billion |
| Total amount of records exposed during the biggest data breach | Over records 500 million | Over records 885 million |
| Average cost of a data breach | $3.86 million USD | $3.92 million USD |
| Top cause of the breach | 99% of breaches were caused were caused by external attackers | 90% of breaches were caused by phishing attacks |

### 12.2.3   Data Breaches

If we compare this year's data breach statistics to 2018, then we determine a frightening growth in data breaches. According to IT Governance, in October 2019, 412 million data breach cases were recorded. That is a big rise from October 2018; 44 million histories were breached [6] (see Table 12.1).

### 12.2.4   Data Security Achieved

Standard enormous information security best practices include the following: Encryption is the way toward encoding data such that renders it futile for aggressors. After the information is encoded, the framework creates keys. Just the correct key can unscramble the information, and the framework pivots keys. This security strategy depends on the notion that assailants would not have the option to re-make the right decoding key.

Tokenization is the information is shipped off an outsider arbiter, which sends a token to the site. The tokenization framework spares the data in a vault, and the site is not putting away any money related data. This security strategy depends on the speculation that aggressors would not access the tokenization framework.

Cutting edge Firewall (NGFW) as indicated by Garner, this is a "profound bundle review firewall". NGFW moves past stateful port/convention investigation and hindering. NGFW is dynamic, and offers highlights, for example, application investigation, interruption counteraction, and cloud danger knowledge.

For endpoint assurance, associations can utilize the following:

Endpoint Protection Platforms (EPPs) is a latent layer of guard against known dangers. Basic EPP arrangements utilize antivirus and Next-Generation Antivirus (NGAV), encryption, DLP, and NGFW. EPPs normally utilize protection procedures, for example, signature coordinating, sandboxing, boycotting, and whitelisting. End-point Detection and Response (EDR) is a functioning layer of protection against endpoint dangers. EDR arrangements for the most part apply information assortment, identification, and investigation methods. The critical objectives of EDR are giving ongoing danger knowledge, cautions, and criminology. Some EDR arrangements give mechanized reactions and trace back instruments.

On the off chance that an EPP arrangement incorporates EDR devices, it increases dynamic protection capacities. The objective is to guarantee that all focuses on the organization are secured, to dispose of unapproved admittance to your information. The greater perceivability you gain, the less vulnerable sides you will have.

**Table 12.2** Data breach from February to June 2020 [1].

| Data breaches size | Name of company | Date of data breaches caused |
|---|---|---|
| Over 1 Million | One class | June 2020 |
| Over 2 Billion | Blue Kai | June 2020 |
| Across 8 Million | Postbank | June 2020 |
| 5vBillion | Keepnet | June 2020 |
| 47.5 Million | True caller | May 2020 |
| 26 Million | Live Journal | May 2020 |
| 91 Million | Tokopedia | May 2020 |
| 25 Million | Math way | May 2020 |
| 1,60 Lakh | Nintendo | April 2020 |
| 5.2 Million | Marriot | March 2020 |
| 6.9 Million | Dutch Government | March 2020 |
| 81 Million | Antheus technology | March 2020 |
| 9 lakh | Virgin Media | March 2020 |
| 3,50 lakh | Slickwraps | February 2020 |

### 12.2.5 Findings: Case Study of Data Breach

2019 was one more "Year of the Data Breach" year. Most of security assaults concentrated on information. Indeed, by taking a gander at security information and examples, a sheltered derivation would be that the target of assaults is quite often information. In the advanced circle, information is a significant item that can open monetary data and accreditations. Aggressors can deliver information, offer it to the most noteworthy bidder, use it to dispatch another assault, erase it to harm the association, and control it to spread disinformation. Big data examination storehouses are particularly powerless and merit a balanced security approach that covers a wide range of organization focuses and clients. Companies during the pandemic situation and highest data breaches from February to June 2020 are shown in Table 12.2.

## 12.3 Conclusion

The term big data is collection of huge datasets which gives high performance while performing operations. This book chapter focuses on the three main characteristics of big data, namely, volume, value, and veracity. This macro data is increasing tremendous day by day.

Collections of huge data like documents, images, and videos, as potential sources of discovery and explicit knowledge, require tactical analysis techniques. Technology has increase in all over world, so collection of data is also increase. Data visualization is the graphical illustration of information and data. This chapter explains with the use concept of data visualization with the help of graphical representation for COVID-19 case study.

## References

1. Ping Wang, Hubert D'Cruze, David Wood "Economic Costs and Impacts of Business Data Breaches" Issues in Information Systems Volume 20, Issue 2, pp. 162–171, 2019.
2. Friendly, M., Hardle, W.K.K., Chen, C.H., Unwin, A., *A Brief History of Data Visualization*, pp. 3–25, Springer, Verlag, 2006.
3. Nseok Ko Hyejung Chang, Interactive Visualization of Healthcare Data Using Tableau, (2017) DOI: 10.4258/hir.2017.23.4.349, pp. 349–354).
4. Gennady Ardrienko, Steven Drucker (2019), Big Data Visualization and Analytics: Future Research Challenges and Emerging Applications, 3rd Intl. Workshop on Big Data Visual Exploration & Analytics pg (1-8)1 https://bigvis.imsi.athenarc.gr/bigvis2020 Published in the Workshop Proceedings of the EDBT/ICDT 2020 Joint Conference (March 30-April 2, 2020, Copenhagen, Denmark) on CEUR-WS.org. Use permitted under Creative Commons License Attribution 4.0 International (CC BY 4.0).

5. Sharmila Gaikwad, Rajesh Thasal, Subhada Yelkar, "Information Retrieval and Deduplication for Tourism Recommender System, International Research Journal of Engineering and Technology (IRJET), pp. 6–9, 2018.

6. Supriya More, Sharmila Gaikwad, "Secure Cloud using Secure Data De-Duplication Scheme", International Research Journal of Engineering and Technology (IRJET) Volume No: 05 Issue No: 5, Page 793-799, May 2018.

7. Gharat, M. *et al.*, Enhancing Speed of Map Reduce Classification Algorithms using Pre-Processing Technique. *Int. J. Adv. Res. Comput. Eng. Technol.*, 5, 10, 2482–2487, October 2016.

8. Maya Gharat, *et al.*, "Review on Enhancing the Speed of Map Reduce Classification Algorithms using preprocessing Technique", *International Journal of Computer Science Trends and Technology (IJCST)*, 4, 2, 32–37, Mar–Apr 2016.

9. Sharmila Gaikwad, Jignesh Patil, "Analysis of Data Visualization in Pandemic Situation" IJEAST, Vol. 5, Issue 7, Pages 251–254, November 2020.

10. Rathod, N. and Wankhade, S., An Enhanced Extreme Learning Machine Model for Improving Accuracy, in: *Proceedings of Integrated Intelligence Enable Networks and Computing*, pp. 613–621, Springer, Singapore, 2021.

11. Gaikwad, S., Study on Artificial Intelligence in Healthcare. *2021 7th International Conference on Advanced Computing and Communication Systems (ICACCS)*, pp. 1165–1169, 2021.

12. Esmaeili, L. *et al.*, A novel tourism recommender system in the context of social commerce. *Expert Syst. Appl.*, 149, 113301, 2020.

13. White source computer Software Agile Open Source License Management, container security, open source security, application security. *DevSecOps, and AppSec.*, 2011.

14. Rathod, N. and Wankhade, S.B., Improving Extreme Learning Machine Algorithm Through Optimization. *Advanced Computing Technologies and Applications: Proceedings of 2nd International Conference on Advanced Computing Technologies and Applications—ICACTA 2020*, Springer Nature, SVKM's Dwarkadas J. Sanghvi College of Engineering, Mumbai, India, from 28 to 29 February 2020.

15. Nazeer, F. and Akbar, I., Data Visualization Techniques – A Survey. *Int. J. Res. Emerg. Sci. Tech.*, 4, 3, 2017.

16. Teyseyre, A.R. and Campo, M.R., IEEE Trancations on visualizations and computers graphics, 15, 1, January-February 2009.

17. Sadiku, M.N.O., Shadare, A.E., Musa, S.M., Akujuobi, C.M., International Journal of Engineering Research And Advanced Technology (IJERAT), 02, 12, December– 2016]

18. The State of the Art in Cartograms Sabrina Nusrat and Stephen Kobourov, vol. 35, 3, STAR – State of The Art Report, 2016.

# 13

# Smart City Governance Using Big Data Technologies

K. Raghava Rao* and D. Sateesh Kumar

*Koneru Lakshmaiah Education Foundation, Guntur, India*

## Abstract

The population of urban (UN, 1993) was claimed to be 2.96 billion in 2000 and 3.77 in 2010. There are 50 million people that are added to urban population and almost 35 million people that are added to the rural population each year in the world. Almost 37% of the urban population was staying in million plus cities. There are 12 cities containing million plus population as per India 2001 census; they are Agra, Allahabad, Amritsar, Asansol, Dhanbad, Faridabad, Jabalpur, Jamshedpur, Meerut, Mumbai, Nashik, Rajkot, and Vijayawada. In the future, ICT (Information and Communications Technologies) will play progressively dominant role in the governance of these cities. Using the ICT to revamp the working efficiency, sharing information with the public, and ameliorating the quirk of government services to the citizen's welfare is called "smart cities". The work pressure in the governments is rising to hike their productivity in the world and, especially, to do more with less. In the late global downturn, governments are struggling to provide a top drawer of public services in a low budget. They are trying to reduce high budget deficits and built up the debt levels through spending public money heavily to stimulate growth. The reason could be lack of transparency and coordination between government departments that work together to realize better services to citizens. Governments are trying to take advantage through information to improve performance and transparency in the governance. Fortunately, in India, mazer details in the civic sector managerial functions are in digital form; still, there are uncertain data formats and obstacles that are associated with legacy systems. So, it is very critical to resolve but it needs to be overcome. This chapter highlights the need of smart governance to integrate planning, policy, and information across all the government departments and services provided by the city and all its stakeholders. So, government needs a better information engineering

---

*Corresponding author*: krraocse@gmail.com

---

Archana Mire, Shaveta Malik and Amit Kumar Tyagi (eds.) Advanced Analytics and Deep Learning Models, (311–324) © 2022 Scrivener Publishing LLC

pipeline and a better governance process. The adoption of big data technologies is being deployed in support of processes within government. This can show a remarkable economic role to the assistance of the national economies and citizens.

*Keywords*: Big data, smart city, e-governance, city governance, smart governance, city administration, Hadoop, MapReduce

## 13.1    Objective

The process of globalization is a gift of information technology and, due to the technology and its benefits, the concept of e-governance is introduced in India. The concept of the e-governance is illustrated in Figure 13.1. This chapter objective is to show the integration across the government departmental data that are available to citizen services (paperless) and assessment of confidential information by authorities based on Aadhar card number (or) any other unique ID. The citizens from anywhere (or) from any address can access information of any department with analysis, which is being done by data analytics algorithms.

## 13.2    Introduction

This chapter is focused on implementation and application of big data technology and analysis to improve and to provide city a smart governance for the essential services, such as revenue, road and transport, land and buildings, and medical and police departments, and further, it can be extendable

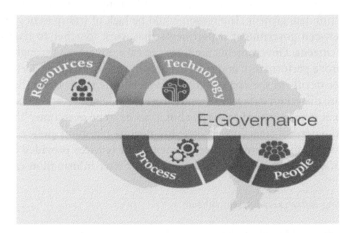

**Figure 13.1** Addressing e-governance.

to other departments. This problem, being the most important at this time for a country like India, were central government and state government emphasizing to develop more cities to be smart cities, essentially, first and foremost, needs smart governance. The problem of implementing smart city governance has much relevance to the big data technology; addressing problems of unlimited data, generated from different formats and dimensions such as structured, unstructured, audio, video, and images, is considered to gather, to analyze, and to draw conclusions; and decision-making is possible with more accuracy and close to real-time conditions with larger data sets instead of sample data. In India, big data initiative has started in recent years and government also identified its importance as it is evident that DST started a separated division BDI to develop big data science technologies. This chapter proposes to adopt open-source technologies to smart governance that is economical and not any commercial or vendor specific, so that public and government can utilize and access software and analytical tools freely, and also uniformity can be achieved in the process and implementation. Bureaucratic effort is the basement of heaps of public precinct functions, and this is common across many departments. Using data, the government employees and their related agencies can achieve fast work progress. This can reduce wastage of time and search times among the departments that can dream up a momentous section of the time of jurisdiction employees. The big data use in city administration benefits in operational efficiency, reduction of cost, and elimination of fraud and errors. All citizen services are based on key input of Aadhar card or unique ID. In departmental information sharing, government provides smart services to citizens and employees within departments, and further, each department's performance can be evaluated. Lack of transparency is eliminated in government departments, and also budget allocation, spending, and recorded results are taken into account and can be displayed in public as much as needed. RTI act is available online to any citizen. Every service and progress of the work of any individual in the department can be tracked by government officials, identifying where the problem/process got stuck to complete a particular file case. Every citizen is well identified in the city with Aadhar card as input to know the entire history of any citizen across any department with authenticated login of government official. This work brings closer the invisible bridge of processes between government departments and citizens up to the extent of acceptable policy, rules, and guidelines of the government. Government departments where this project was initially implemented in a city want to have smart governance; later, five key departments, such as Revenue, Transport, Police, Medical, and Road and Buildings, are considered. Citizens can avail smart services by Aadhar card input key. Government department officials process it in the department's automated file systems and transparency process moves from official to official, leading to fast service performance and efficiency of the government operation; hence, smart governance can be achieved.

## 13.3   Literature Survey

During World War II, the United States' scientific inquest and advancement director, Dr. V. Bush, who struggled for years in reconciling science with battle, puts forward on an enigma, which is an immense boost in information and productively access to recuperate society [1]. According to Bush, in the aspect of palisade battle science, American industrial cities revet the issue of infrastructure fashion to support 19th and 20th century recession and those community which had blast to uphold them his decades of invention. He [2] said that cities fit a strange vision on a fiscal conversion carries out all from redevelopment projects to robust reuse [3]. Admix problems for cities are well-cataloged [4–6] flights to moderate areas and the arising concept of astute prosperity [7]. The recipients from US cities have been observed ("Emerging Trends in Information Technology", May 28, 2012, by Jason Repko and Steve DeBroux). Anciently, city populace has raised and flowed with the pulse of tradition industrial frameworks [8]. Eighty percent of the population lives in urban places of Europe. India and China [9] planned to add over 600 million humans with a momentous trend toward population in urban centers over the coming 30 years. This will upsurge pressure on city services—"environmental, economy conditions, and community cultures". Smart city is a concept; it is unfolded to reiterate strategies affecting sustainability, civilian well-being, and economic advancement. The information and communication technologies (ICTs) lie within the fabric of a smart city. Anuj Tiwari and Kamal Jain [10] explained in their paper titled "G.I.S steering smart destiny for smart Indian cities" the effect of three pillars of smart progress model with brunt of their verdict and the prospect state of assets. The development of smart urban infrastructure in India is a vision of Yogesh Meena et al. [11].

## 13.4   Smart Governance Status

### 13.4.1   International

Today, half of a mankind appears in urban environments and that number will lead to 81% by the midst of this century. North America is earlier with 80% of population in cities and will increased to 90% by 2050. The cities are the resource of consumption, economy, and innovation places. These are all roots of our imminent sustainability problems; however, those problems must be solved. Cities must be efficient, resilient, and sustainable. It must address quality life of its citizens. The city must be as great as it can be in the global race for talent and capital.

As pointed by John Chicago, Chief Technology Officer, "We experience cities mediated by the digital technology. We need to learn discipline that does not really exist yet, to merge urban planning and design with urban informatics along networked public space". European government sector reduces the cost potentially of bureaucratic action by 16% to 21%, creating the reciprocal of 150 billion to 300 billion euros or even higher. The big data provides gigantic statistical samples, which enhance results analytically (write-up by Philip Russom). According to IDC (2011), the amount of information replicated and created this year will surpass 1.8 zettabytes; it is growing nine times just in 5 years. According to the study by a website (http://ubdc.ac.uk/our-research/our-research/urban-research/neighbourhoods-housing), it is noted that the amount of knowledge created by entity photos, music, record, document files, blog posts, etc., is lower than the amount of knowledge being themselves in the digital universe. The UK data web portal (http://www.Data.gov.uk) and the Spain web portal (https://datos.gob.es/) are the examples of usage and disclosing big data service to citizens. The databases made available in http://where-doesmymoneygo.org/ through the government's open data. U.K. makes the citizens to view and figure out public spending of United Kingdom through visualization and analyzation of the data shown in Figure 13.2.

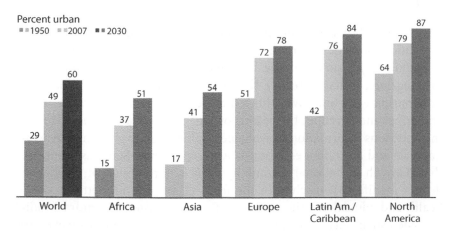

**Figure 13.2** Urban population fraction in various geographical regions.

The citizens struggle for their intercommunication with government agencies, but they will better gain services for their needs. The information translucence creates and improves accountability in public sector bureau and enhances trust of the public. In the United States, FTC (Federal Trade Commission) uses the biggest data application, for instance, to practice its clean information basis as a guidance for dealing with privacy and security issues. Germany monitors industries for data protection compliance using a federal commission. Through two government agencies, South Korea's protects the data. In 2003, United Kingdom's NS (National Statistics) reacts with the Atkinson review and established a CMGA (Centre for the Measurement of Government Activity). It began to produce a productiveness index. Management systems are the hints of "smart systems". Environment uses of ICT-based technologies convey more efficient and effective public services that improve the living and working conditions. It creates high sustainable urban environment. Smart city is an interconnected instrumented intelligent. The President of United States in 2009 has released Order M10-06, the "Open Government Directive". This decree needs to take accurate decisions to achieve the following goals through departments and executive agencies: 1. publishing the information of government in online; 2. bettering the quality in the government information; and 3. building and regulating a culture of open government and making administrative framework for open government. The government of UK has grasp a very akin effort through their open government data initiative and the government digital service unit like Norway, Canada, Finland, Brazil, and France.

### 13.4.2    National

This is a belief that the complication of the city could be solved over the scientific approaches of urban design in modernism master plan. In 2007, Benjamin *et al.* surveyed the land record digital preservation project in Bangalore, India. In reality, this project promoted as a pro-poor and pro-transparency initiative. This led to decrease the heighten corruption and bribes and to reduce the vesting of time in land transactions. Through this, previous information is available to all related to the lands. A Nobel Laureate and an Indian economist, Amartya Kumar Sen, has mentioned that "Growth in national income by itself is not enough, if the benefits do not manifest themselves in the form of more food, better access to health and education". The respected Prime Minister, Narendra Modigi, launched smart city project for major urban development. However, this concept is very new to India. The country is admitting a lot of minds in the last few years. The smart cities' mission and housing project are illustrated in Figure 13.3.

India has witnessed the massive urban transformation; it is observed that, every minute, there are 30 people leaving agronomic India with this rate, by 2050, India needs 500 new cities to bear 700 million more. This leads to wanton the modernization of the urban cities in India. Government urban planning bureaus anticipate ingenious technologies and solutions to manage the burgeoning demands on city infrastructures. It is expected that, by 2030, it is grown to be five times. At this time, the labor force of the country is expected to grow by 270 million. In this rate, the urban jobs account to 75% of that improvement. India's first planned hill city is roughly 10,000 rolling acres. It is located on the backwaters of Warangalone dam between Pune and Mumbai. To develop considerable style of living, private infrastructure sector in India created unified township at a cost around Rs 1,400 billion. India will have 82 cities with population more than 6 million and six megacities with population of 10 million or more. The main purpose of GIFT, i.e., Gujarat International Finance Tec-City, is to provide high-quality physical infrastructure (that contains water, electricity, gas, cooling roads, telecoms, and broadband). It started their operations from Mumbai, Bangalore, Gurgaon, etc. In this scenario, now, Indian state and central governments realized to develop smart cities with smart services such as

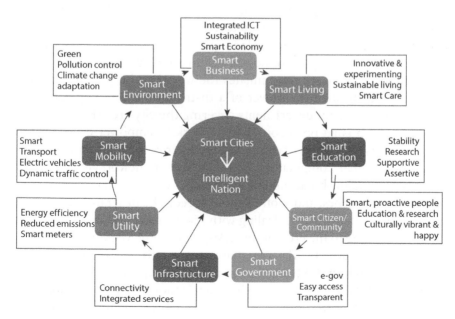

**Figure 13.3** Smart cities' mission and housing in India.

smart city governance, which is the need of hour to move to bring cities under data protection and safeguarding government wealth by recorded spending, proper utilization, and fraud elimination. The government inter-departmental information sharing will help faster governance and transparency and smart citizen service.

## 13.5   Methodology and Implementation Approach

Government collects the huge amount of data regularly from all the sectors and individuals through agencies. This big data helps to know the uncovered attainment within different parts of a government and private departments that are operating broadly identical functions. In the proposed design, the basic step is digitalizing and structuring the data. It contains the steps that assure that the data is created, structured, and organized in such a way that they can be used directly for further analysis. Later, these techniques are used to identify and remove the errors from the data and assure data quality. This helps to placing data into usual forms and adding metadata that characterize the data being collected. It is very important to protect critical IT (Information Technology) as cyber-attacks become increasingly sophisticated. Framework is important to assure that institutions can access and use data securely and safely. Nowadays, big data are used in automated design for sophisticated applications to inspect large data sets to take superior decisions. In this work, it is proposed to adopt Apache Hadoop framework which is considered as the best novel approach for design and implementation of this project. The Hadoop framework reformulates the way that the data are handled and analyzed through the power of a distributed computing resources across all government departments covering the city area (Figure 13.4).

The Hadoop is an open-source framework to empower processing of huge data sets on clusters of computers configuration management, workflow, and parallel computation. The Hadoop framework is more cost effective to handling broad complicated or disorganized data sets than conventional approaches, and it offers more speed. The programming framework MapReduce simplifies dealing with big data sets and then provides a common method to the programmer. Applications of MapReduce are connected with social networks, entertainment, electronic commerce, fraud detection, search and advertisement mechanisms, data warehouse, etc. HDFS provides real-time access to big data. Hadoop framework adopts big data platforms to government departments to integrate information sharing across government departments. The framework is divided into four

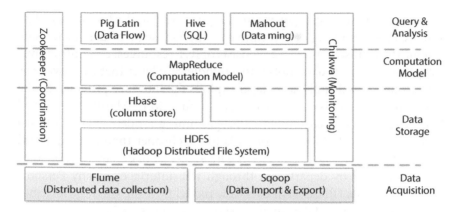

**Figure 13.4** Apache Hadoop framework architecture adopted for smart city governance.

components: 1) data generation, 2) data acquisition, 3) storage of data, and 4) data analysis. This employs a variety of mining process to investigate big data sets.

### 13.5.1 Data Generation

It is bothered on how data are generated. The term "big data" is nominated too disparate, complex, and huge data sets that are spawn from various longitudinal distributed data sources, from all government departments.

### 13.5.2 Data Acquisition

It indicates the process of reap information and is partitioned into data pre-processing, data collection, and data transmission. Data storage perturbs persistently storing and executing large-scale data sets. It can be divided into two parts: hardware infrastructure and data management.

### 13.5.3 Data Analytics

It is the science of analyzing raw data in order to make conclusions about that information. Analytics research can be classified into six technical areas: structured data analytics, text analytics, multimedia analytics, web analytics, network analytics, and mobile analytics.

Further, to implement smart city governance by the adoption of Hadoop architecture, we propose a layered design (Figure 13.6), which affords a visionary pecking order to underscore the intricacy of a big data system application for smart city governance. Figures 13.5 and 13.6 show the layered architecture of big data technology and key steps of data processing system. The infrastructure layer consists of ICT resources; computing layer encapsulates various data tools into a middleware layer that runs over raw ICT resources; and application layer exploits the interface provided by the programming models to the data analysis functions. MapReduce Dryad Pregel and Dremel are exemplified programming models. HDFS is based on the principle of "Moving Computation is cheaper than Moving Data". Lost, the user access layer consists of data access from department or communicating user by department through web interfaces or any Personal Digital Assistants (PDAs). An overview model flow for smart governance for citizen services and data analysis shown in Figure 13.7.

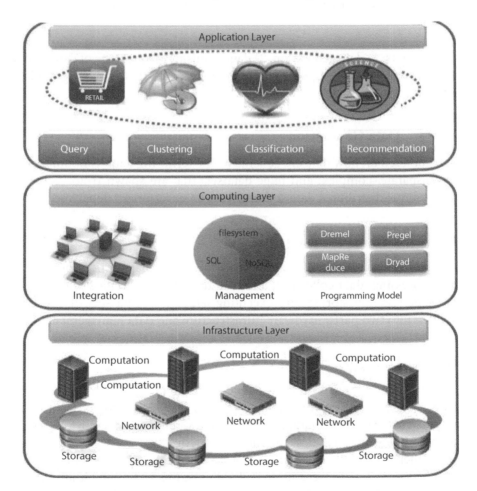

**Figure 13.5** Layered architecture of big data system (from bottom to up).

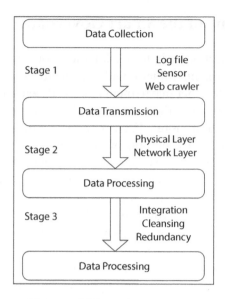

**Figure 13.6** Three stages of data acquisition system.

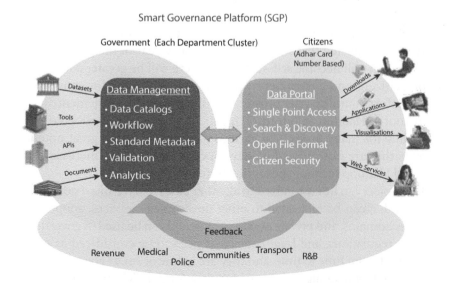

**Figure 13.7** An overview model flow for smart governance for citizen services and data analysis.

## 13.6   Outcome of the Smart Governance

The proposed project is ready to use for the public and with limited five government departments initially with full features and services, which can be extendable to other departments easily. Based on the feedback and corrections and omission, the project will be extended to other government departments, and more citizen services of smart city can be called smart city governance. The outputs of this project work bring a change of city society into a knowledge society where information flows across government departments. Every city citizen has recorded his full information, to be identified in the city, so that tracking and obtaining information is faster. Citizen services and government departments' transparency bring faster growth in economic development. All government welfare schemes, budge spending, and timely completion of work are open to public, and interdepartmental work becomes faster without delay. Another key output of this project is that anyone has to utilize Aadhar card number to access any government service and government department; all employees filing data process is faster and they can access data of any department as possible. The impact will be, initially, people feel difficult to get into this system on the side of city; citizens and government departments disinterest with fear of the whole process in recording and storing in short period. Impact will be so great after 1 year of implementation where smart service and smart governance with a culture and discipline across the city society and suburban people will also be aware of working of government and public, which is time saving, prompt service, without corruption, and everything online. It is expected that without fail after once year of the project implementation, it will become self-sustained. There will be greater cooperation among citizens and government departments' employees for convenience and comfort found in this project. As this project is implemented with open-source Hadoop architecture, it gets popular and it is adopted internationally for many projects in various domains and with great potential benefits that are experienced by developed countries. The increase of big data and Hadoop technologies is illustrated in Figure 13.8.

The project can be customized to all other cities to have smart governance across India; can be replicated to other government services, adoptable to business domains, and private organizations; and can be used in government policies, regulations, and legal issues that need to be considered as part of this project from time to time, and they are in line of smart governance. The research outcome as algorithms for big data for parallel processing and for high speed computation is big scope for replicability into other domains.

Big Data and Hadoop Market Size Forecasy Worldwide 2017-2022
Size of Hadoop and Big Data Market Worldwide From 2017 To 2022
(in billion U.S. dollars)

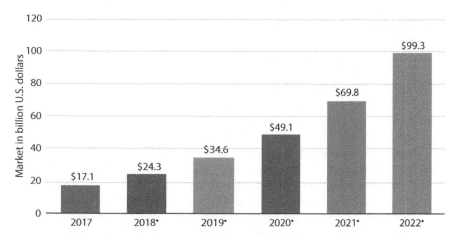

**Figure 13.8** Worldwide big data and Hadoop market size.

## 13.7   Conclusion

Introducing smart governance in existing manual procedure, how over-comes difficulties earlier, with a timeline, how smart governance gives benefits public, and how does it takes its path in to future are mentioned in this chapter. This study reveals that big data technologies have actually big potential for smart governance, where it can easily improve its day-to-day operations, enhance the cooperation of citizens, access to decid-ing information, and improve democracy, financial and social admittance, sustainable feature, involvement of private sector, public service delivery, policy-making decision, and other services. The extension and limitations are also specified.

## References

1. Bush, V., *As we may think*, ACM SIGPC Notes, 312, New York, NY, United States, April 1979, https://doi.org/10.1145/1113634.1113638.
2. Widner, R.R., Physical Renewal of the Industrial City. *Ann. Am. Acad. Pol. Soc Sci.*, 488, 47–57, Nov. 1986.

3. Wikipedia contributors, "Adaptive reuse," Wikipedia, the free encyclopedia. Wikimedia Foundation, Inc, 21-May-2012.

4. Frey, W.H., Black In-Migration, White Flight, and the Changing Economic Base of the Central City. *Am. J. Sociol.*, 85, 6, 1396–1417, May 1980.

5. Brueckner, J.K., *Urban Sprawl: Lessons from Urban Economics*, pp. 65–97, Brookings-Wharton Papers on Urban Affairs, Chicago, 2001.

6. Downs, Smart Growth: Why We Discuss It More than We Do It. *J. Am. Plann. Assoc.*, 71, 4, 367–378, 2005.

7. Mitra and B. Mehta, Cities as the Engine of Growth: Evidence from India. *J. Urban Plann. Dev.*, 137, 2, 171–183, Jun. 2011.

8. Repko, J. and DeBroux, S., Smart Cities Literature Review and Analysis. *IMT 598 Spring 2012: J. Emerg. Trends Comput. Inf. Sci.* IMT 598, 1–18, 2012, https://www.researchgate.net/publication/236685572.

9. UN Department of Economics and Social Affairs, Population Division, Population Estimates and Projections Section, "UN: World Urbanization Prospects, 2011 Revision," United Nations Department of Economics and Social Affairs, 25-Apr-2012. [Online]. Available: http://esa.un.org/unpd/wup/Country-Profiles/country-profiles_1.htm. [Accessed: 27-May-2012].

10. Tiwari, A. and Jain, Dr. K., 3D City Model Enabled E-Governance For Sustainable Urbanization. *14th ESRI India User Conference id:UCP0024*, pp. 11–12, Dec. 2013.

11. Meena, Y. *et al.*, Smart City Development. *Int. J. Educ. Res.*, 3, 3, 38–41, 2017. http://ierj.in/journal/index.php/ierj/article/view/740.

# 14

# Big Data Analytics With Cloud, Fog, and Edge Computing

**Deepti Goyal[1], Amit Kumar Tyagi[2,3]\* and Aswathy S. U.[4]**

[1]*Department of Computer Science and Engineering, Lingaya's Vidyapeeth,*
*Faridabad, Haryana, India*
[2]*Centre for Advanced Data Science, Vellore Institute of Technology, Chennai,*
*Tamil Nadu, India*
[3]*School of Computer Science and Engineering, Vellore Institute of Technology,*
*Chennai, Tamil Nadu, India*
[4]*Department of Computer Science and Engineering, Jyothi Engineering College,*
*Thrissur, Kerala, India*

## Abstract

The uses of Internet of Things (IoT)–based devices are increasing in the world by people, and life without such smart devices becomes impossible these days. The essential of human being has been increasing day by day and, along with the improvements in IoT, has led to demand on evolving platforms like edge computing and fog cloud.

Here, we can define cloud computing terms as follows: "Cloud computing service was initially proposed due to small works in industries (to reduce the number of computer system in an organization), but later, it was implemented on a large scale". Today, major companies like IBM and Amazon are providing such efficient services of the cloud to consumers (or millions of customers world-wide). When comes to company side of cloud computing, they actually prefer resources that are in the form of utility such as Virtual Machine (VM) and other applications, and some services involve cloud storage, hybrid cloud intelligence, and applications. Mainly, these services are classified into three main groups such as IaaS (Infrastructure as a Service), PaaS (Platform as a Service), and SaaS (Software as a Service). These services are explained in this chapter in detail.

*\*Corresponding author:* amitkrtyagi025@gmail.com
Amit Kumar Tyagi: ORCID: 0000-0003-2657-8700

Archana Mire, Shaveta Malik and Amit Kumar Tyagi (eds.) Advanced Analytics and Deep Learning
Models, (325–350) © 2022 Scrivener Publishing LLC

*Keywords*:  Cloud computing, fog computing, edge computing, big data analytics, Internet of Things

## 14.1    Introduction to Cloud, Fog, and Edge Computing

Cloud computing gives us the authorization of several applications over the Internet and helps in creating and customizing the applications online. We can define the cloud as it refers to a network or internet. It provides services on network which is of two types: public or private networks, which is further categorized into WAN, LAN, or VPN. It also offers storing data online, infrastructure for building, and application for the user to use that, and also it overcomes the platform dependency issue [1].

It can be remotely accessed through any web browser, and these files are stored in centralized format rather than in some hard drives [2]. Analytics part comes where we apply principle of analytics on available cloud drives rather than with individual servers. There are several models that are being used for end users and two of them are deployment models and service models.

As each provider has its own functions, we need to pick a cloud provider by comparing it with available providers, and if the respective technology on its working has a change, then we can purchase even more space from the cloud provider. Cloud providers are being categorized into three: Software as a Service (SaaS), Platform as a Service (PaaS), and Infrastructure as a Service (IaaS).

    a.   SaaS: It gives access to both resources and applications and also gives clients a membership or month free subs (e.g., Salesforce CRM, Google Apps, and Desk Away).

    b.   PaaS: It gives authorization to components that each provider wants to develop and operate the application they are building.

    c.   IaaS: It deals with computational infrastructure where they can completely outsource resources.

Field of IT brings evolving change with day-to-day life, and edge computing is a new paradigm when comes adding this with new technologies like Internet of Things (IoT), Machine Learning (ML), and Big Data Analytics.

a. **Edge computing** brings computing as new distinct level of cloud environments and that is one reason in smart application where data are not sent to cloud to avoid latency. This computing combination with IoT brings a great development in sensor in future, and it needs to be used so vastly that it is not only brings some good in sensor itself. Edge computing always brings data processing and locally processing of real-time data and several edge-related components are data processing, rule engine, and local database. Mahadev Satyanarayanan, who is considered to be the "father" of Edge Computing, explains the birth of edge computing in his article [4].

b. **Cloud computing** offers great resources in the terms of memory, storage, and processing for the computation needs that can be used in mobile applications. But there comes a problem when bringing entire computational needs and that is latency issues and availability of bandwidth. Since these packets have to travel through several routers which also signifies in increasing RTT (Round-Trip Times) that is been provided and controlled by Internet Service Providers (ISPs), operating at different levels. Due to ISPs and some network conditions, the end-end path may also change (Medianova R&D Center proposed a research paper on this issue to IEEE ISNCC 2019). It will be way hard to face issues like face bandwidth and bottlenecks as evolving of IoT increases. Therefore, distant cloud environments are not an option [10]. In Figures 14.1a and b, cloud computing to edge computing transition is shown, where edge computing gives a latency issue.

In the view point of transition of cloud to edge computing, the evolving of cloudlets, fog, and mobile edge computing came to release [5, 8]. When this mobile edge computing brings every network to its base station, the devices within the range of Radio Access Network (RAN) can easily do computation and storage jobs to certain mobile edged nodes.

a. **Cloudlet computing** performs its computation on the latency sensitive applications and also in computer-based application that can potentially run on servers located in LAN. They can be called as the data center in a box [3].

### The Best Uses of Data Analytics

a. Social Media: With the help of cloud data analytics, we can have the records of all the activities happened over social media. Earlier, being without a cloud drives could drive us in a hard way of keeping records of social websites of different servers.

b. Tracking Products: It was a long thought, but these days, Amazon is using data analytics to have the track on the records anytime when it is required. The use of cloud drives for remote analysis by Amazon along with the help of Redshift initiative provides analysis tools and storage capabilities as Amazon to the small organizations and acts as an information warehouse.

c. Tracking Preference: "Netflix" is the best example to describe this because it keeps on tracing the records of user choice movies likes and watch, and based on that, it recommends

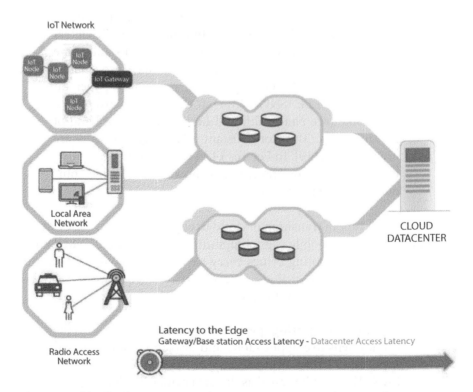

**Figure 14.1 (a)** Cloud computing to edge computing transition. (*Continued*)

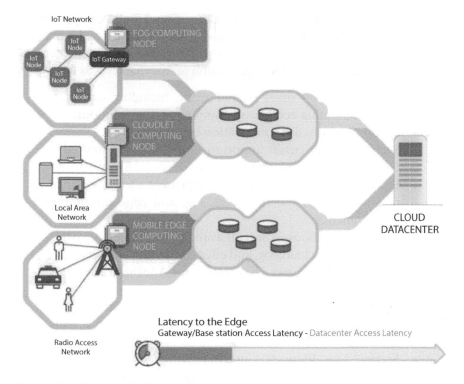

**Figure 14.1 (Continued)** **(b)** Cloud computing to edge computing transition.

some other choices to the user. Users would not prefer changing of storage from one system to another as every user's information is stored remotely in cloud drives.

d. Records Keeping: Regardless to local servers, cloud activity keeps on simultaneous record keeping process. In most of companies, this feature helps them keep track on several sales related and stock related information. If there is no proper selling of product happens, then they do not need to wait for inventories to get into, instead everything is updated in cloud drives. These constant updating brings more efficient version of business and the behavior of the customers.

**Internet of Things:** According to study by Gartner, there will be around 26 billion IoT-based devices by 2020 and the amount of data that is being created from each device and those needs to store in cloud drives brings so much add on features such as [11] flexibility, multiple processing systems, and disparate datasets along with cloud computing.

Hence, the section of this chapter discusses several useful components as related to different computing that we discussed earlier. Related work and evolution of this useful technology with useful review and timeline (decade-wise) will be briefed. Finally, the organization of this chapter is as follows:

- Section 14.2 discusses related work, including evolution cloud computing and its issues and respective solutions.
- Section 14.3 discusses motivation behind this work.
- Section 14.4 discusses importance of cloud, fog, and edge computing in various applications.
- Section 14.5 discusses several requirement and importance of analytics (general) in cloud, fog, and edge computing environment.
- Section 14.6 discusses several available tools to do analytics of big data/for cloud, fog, and edge computing environment.
- Section 14.7 discusses several tools for Advanced Analytics in this smart era.
- Section 14.8 includes information regarding importance of Big Data Analytics for Cyber-Security and Privacy for Cloud-IoT Systems in detail.
- Section 14.9 discusses a use case with real world's application (with respect to big data analytics) related to cloud computing, fog computing, and edge computing.
- Section 14.10 discusses issues and challenges in big data and problems/application related to three computing.
- Section 14.11 discusses several opportunities toward cloud computing, fog computing, and edge computing.
- Section 14.12 summarizes this work in brief.

## 14.2   Evolution of Computing Terms and Its Related Works

Through message passing interface, several tasks have been divided among several networks and they communicate with each other for performing in a decentralized format, which brings us the distributed computing. Since the task is given and each process communicates through message passing method to perform that task, and this process has been bring out in early 1960s [27]. LAN was the first distributed computing, and it shows the communication between multiple computers and brings out respective solutions. Thereby, distributed computing started evolving slowly starting from utility computing then to emerging of cloud computing and lately mainframe for fog computing. Figure 14.2 shows the timeline of distributed computing.

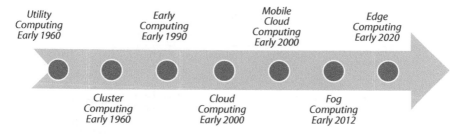

**Figure 14.2** The timeline of DC.

The name utility computing came as per requirement of the end user as users have their own needs to satisfy on their end product. In early days, users need to pay for the services, and this concept was first presented by John McCarthy in 1961 [32]. Though it was not that much popular and it again being introduced in 1990s where there is a huge drop in cost due to the hardware and practical case. In previous sections, there was no exact access to resources and further unavailability of support for completion within deadline situation over these systems, thereby giving user a proper valuation of their services. Marketplace has huge impact of utility computing where there is huge competition among services and services providers. Single-time sharing system is one of plus point of this computing and also it supports high throughput in case of multiple servers [33–36].

When comes to cluster computing [31–37], computers interconnect to perform several tasks and even though they are connected, they act like single system and all will do same tasks assigned and are controlled by schedulers. The different components of cluster computing are on Figure 14.4. With the help of switches and high-speed network property the interfaces of networks and communication software's of each personal computer. Reliability and the availability are some merits of this computing. As we have redundancy in clusters, it thereby reduces the system failure rate [38–42].

Cloud computing was started in early 2000. It had been seen for the first time when a large number of systems have a single problem which is scientific in nature and needs high level of parallel computation. In the 1990s, the concept of virtualization was came into existence which expands beyond virtual servers to higher levels of abstraction, i.e., first the virtual platform, including storage, and network resources. In the case of overlay networks, the usage of applications which have two properties such as scalable and decentralized came to play from 2001. When we overlay networks, it brings efficiency in fault-tolerant routing, object location, and load balancing, thereby changes in the overall load in network and improved latency. Fog computing brings to solve the issues mentioned [3]. Also, Figure 14.3 depicts the taxonomy of fog framework in detail.

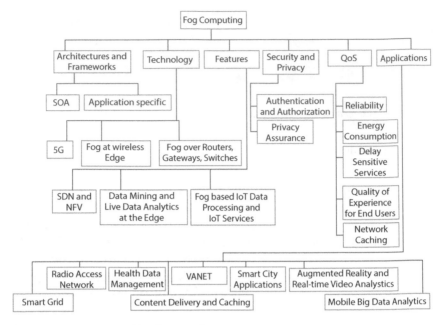

**Figure 14.3** Taxonomy of fog framework.

Cisco introduces fog computing in 2012, and its main aim was to promote scalability [6]. Data are sent to the nearby localities like gateway and phones for analysis purposes rather than sending to the cloud. Edge computing concept pushes that intelligence into several technologies to bring some useful and efficient product that can be useful for valid purposes and also analyzing. It also processes many real-time applications like streaming. The major plus point is minimized latency, lower costs, reduce load, and improved security [7].

Edge computing when combined modern applications like drones and autonomous cars brings huge data consumption (a self-driving car, for instance, could create up to 4,000 GB of data a day). Hence, this section deals with history of cloud and its several applications. The coming session will be of motivation toward cloud computing.

## 14.3   Motivation

Today, IoT is being used almost in every possible computing environment. These smart devices are helping citizens a lot to do everyday task, i.e., have made people life convenient and easier to live. These internet devices generate a huge number of data at end nodes which is complex to handle and require efficient tools to handle and to make some predictive and useful decisions for improving business or organization's growth. But, together IoT many other new concepts like cloud computing, fog computing, and edge computing are also attracting researchers' attention around the world. Cloud clouding is oldest version of edge computing. Edge computing produces services at edges of the nodes, i.e., reduce latency. Hence, providing convenient, reliable, and secured services is our main/primacy goal for users. For that, we need to secure cyber infrastructure with efficient algorithms. Hence, such concepts are needed to be defined in a clear and concise manner. This chapter tries to fulfill such goals and provides complete information about cloud computing and its extended environments with big data analytics in detail.

Now, next section will discuss importance of cloud, fog, and edge computing in many applications in detail.

## 14.4 Importance of Cloud, Fog, and Edge Computing in Various Applications

Cloud computing is one the flamboyant innovation in 21st century, and this all happens just because of the easily adapted into the mainstream. It can be used in various applications:

  a. Disaster recovery: with the help of this faster recovery at lower cost from the devices at different physical locations can be possible.
  b. Testing and development: With respect to assets, power, and time, we need to build that much budget to test and develop and lastly the installation and configuration.
  c. Hybrid cloud: Ability to expand during peak usage, for large infrastructure.

The potential of fog computing brings new innovative services and applications with other emerging technologies [9, 43] which are discussed here as:

  • Smart Switchers: Sometimes, some devices need to switch their networks automatically as the current service provider is unavailable at the time. If congestion gets felt, then it will automatically jump to another network.
  • Smart Cities: To keep an area well organized, we must use the self-regulating technological systems (e.g., traffic light sensor)

- Smart Home Appliances: The sensors embedded devices which help in monitoring their components at home. If the devices detect/found any problem, then they will send an alert to the owner with the problem.

Now, some real-life application examples of edge technology and distributed computing [9, 23–26, 28, and 30] included here as:

- Autonomous Vehicles: GE Digital partner, Intel, has estimated that autonomous cars, with hundreds of on-vehicle sensors, thereby generating up to 40 TB data for every 8 hours of driving condition, and thereby, edge computing comes into play. Sending all the data to cloud is unsafe and impractical. The car immediately response to the events which has valuable data when coupled into digital twin and performance of other cars of its class.
- Fleet Management: For example, considering a trucking company, the main goal is to combine and send data from multiple operational data points like wheels and battery, to the cloud. Health key operational components are analyzed by the cloud. Thus, essentially, a fleet management solution encourages the vehicle to lower the cost.

Hence, this section discusses about scope and importance of cloud and its advanced technology in various (existing) applications. Now, next section will discuss about existing (available) tools for implementing scenarios in a cloud (with explaining a use case).

## 14.5    Requirement and Importance of Analytics (General) in Cloud, Fog, and Edge Computing

Cloud computing and data science go hand in hand together. A data scientist will analyze the data that are stored on a cloud. Cloud analytics provides many benefits such as follows:

- **Improved decision-making**: A study of HBR giving around 82% of them is likely to analytics tool because of the improved quality, and thereby, those organizations gain new customers and good revenue.

- **Improved planning and forecasting**: It mainly allows business partners in finance section to incorporate data from different sources available to build a data models [18].
- **Single source of data**: The tool cloud analytics gives easier use for validating and integrates their data into a single source.
- **Agility**: Using the above tool, they can quickly respond and change to the market condition.
- **User satisfaction**: Preferring cloud tools than traditional tool for more and improved employee morale.

In summary, we can say that cloud analytics gives the benefits of cloud computing as well as big data analytics. Benefits of big data in cloud computing are better analysis, infrastructure that is been simplified, low cost, security, and virtualization. In this section, we have discussed about the benefits of cloud analytics. Now, next section will discuss several available tools for analyzing big data (collected by IoT devices) for different applications (which use cloud applications).

## 14.6    Existing Tools for Making a Reliable Communication and Discussion of a Use Case (with Respect to Cloud, Fog, and Edge Computing)

The term "Cloud" is vastly used in today's environment. It is a concept that exists from the early years of 1970s. Its primary used is for data transfer (point to point) which is also known as Virtual Private Network (VPN). Cloud computing uses central remote services and the internet to maintain, process, and manipulate software applications and databases. The list of existing tools is as follows.

### 14.6.1    CloudSim

Clouds Laboratory put forwarded this "CloudSim" at University of Melbourne, Australia [12]. It acts as toolkit for simulation and helps for evaluating policies done by user. It is not easy to arrive at the solution, instead it needs to write java coding and thereby collects the required data and comes into desired result in cloud that needs to be stored. Layered architecture of CloudSim is given in Figure 14.4; all the components communicate through message passing.

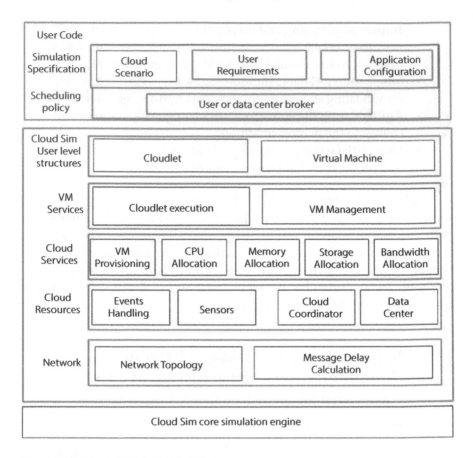

**Figure 14.4** Layered CloudSim architecture.

## 14.6.2   SPECI

SPECI stands for Simulation Program for Elastic Cloud Infrastructures used for scaling. As input, we give size and middleware design; we get result as performance and behavior of data [13]. SPECI is given in Figure 14.5.

## 14.6.3   Green Cloud

Kliazovich put forward this idea, and it is nothing but a simulator for energy aware data centers that mainly concentrate on cloud communication. It gives detailed consumption of equipment's, such as servers, switches, and communication links [14] and also used as solutions for monitoring, allocation, and workload scheduling.

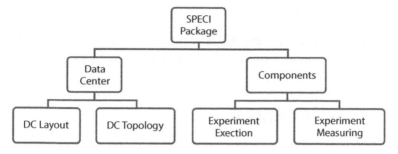

**Figure 14.5** SPECI package.

## 14.6.4 OCT (Open Cloud Testbed)

Grossman *et al.* put forward this OCT and mainly used for investigating interoperability [5]. It is also used now in small-scaled version and also used to develop [15] cloud computing software and infrastructure. The architecture of OCT is shown in Figure 14.6.

## 14.6.5 Open Cirrus

Hewlett-Packard (HP) along with other collab put forwarded this open cloud computing testbed. It helps in achieving goals as follows:

- Foster systems-level research in cloud computing.
- Collection of experimental datasets.
- Develop open-source stacks and APIs for the cloud.

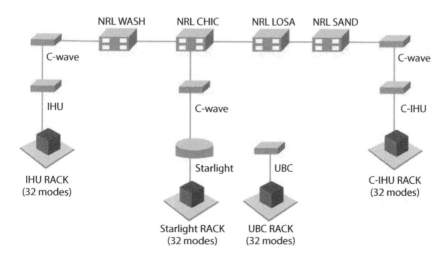

**Figure 14.6** Architecture of the OCT cloud simulator.

### 14.6.6    GroudSim

Ostermann proposed this event-based simulator for grid and cloud environments. It can be parameterized and extend easily by probability packages for failures cases [16].

### 14.6.7    Network CloudSim

S.K. Garg and Rajkumar Buyya put forwarded this, and [17] this is an extension of Cloud Sim that allows more accurate evaluation of scheduling and resource provisioning policies [17].

Hence, this section discusses many existing tools available for implementing or solving problems in cloud. Now, next section will discuss about requirement and importance of data and data analytics in cloud, fog, and edge computing environments.

## 14.7    Tools Available for Advanced Analytics (for Big Data Stored in Cloud, Fog, and Edge Computing Environment)

Big data is a wider term, and to perform analytics on this, some tools are required. With the help of tools, analytics becomes easier and faster to perform. Several data mining, ML, and big data analytics tools have been discussed in [20] for predicting/making effective decisions from big data. Some of the tools have been discussed in the following.

### 14.7.1    Microsoft HDInsight

It provides two categories: Standard and Premium, and it also gives enterprise scale to run big data workloads. Some features are listed as follows:

- Industry with reliable scaling-leading SLA
- Enterprise security and monitoring
- Protect data assets
- High productivity
- Integration
- Deploy Hadoop in the cloud without purchasing new hardware

### 14.7.2    Skytree

Big data tools empower data scientists to build accurate models [19]. Some features are as follows:

- Algorithms which are highly scalable
- Artificial Intelligence
- Interpretability
- Solve robust predictive problems
- Programmatic and GUI Access

### 14.7.3    Splice Machine

Big data tools are portable for public clouds such as AWS and Google. Some features are follows:

- Dynamically scale from a few to thousands
- Reduce risk
- Consume fast streaming data

### 14.7.4    Spark

Open-source big data analytics tools are for building parallel apps [19]. Some features are here listed as follows:

- Runs applications faster
- Ability to integrate with Hadoop and existing Hadoop data
- Provides built-in APIs in Java, Scala, or Python

### 14.7.5    Apache SAMOA

Big data tools enable new ML algorithms. It also helps in data mining and ML tasks.

### 14.7.6    Elastic Search

JSON-based search and analytics engine is for solving number of use cases and also offers scalability, maximum reliability, and easy management.

### 14.7.7    R-Programming

Statistical computing and graphical language for big data analysis: it provides a wide variety of statistical tests. Some features are as follows:

- Data handling and storage facility
- Suitable operation for calculation

Hence, this section discusses several available tools in current for analyzing data (big data), for generating useful decision based on tracking/analyzing actions of events. Now, the next section will explain a popular use case related to real world's application and with respect to integration of big data analytics and cloud, fog, and edge computing.

## 14.8    Importance of Big Data Analytics for Cyber-Security and Privacy for Cloud-IoT Systems

Big data is like a coin having two phases; it can be threat or can be savior. As we all know, big data is used to examine, observe, and detect irregularities within a network which makes a huge merit to cybercrimes. According to CSO report, 84% business users use this technology to block several attacks like Malware, Worm, Spyware, Botnet [46], etc.

### 14.8.1    Risk Management

Handling these threats by timely manner gives us that much power to withstand other organizations and tools are need to be backed by risk management insights.

### 14.8.2    Predictive Models

A predictive model can be used to set as an alert when these attacks reach the entry point, and here, technologies like ML and AI come into play.

### 14.8.3    Secure With Penetration Testing

For exploiting vulnerabilities, we use this testing against our computers and network. Penetration testing has become a crucial step in IT and business sector.
Penetration testing involves five stages:

- Planning
- Scanning
- Gaining access
- Maintaining access
- Analysis and web application firewall (WAF) configuration

Once done with configuration and process strengthening, thereby a new test is done.

### 14.8.4    Bottom Line

Bringing ML and AI give a huge hope to it as well as business sector and thereby give greater efficiency to the models. Monitoring and improving and also periodic penetrations help to save from cyber threats.

### 14.8.5    Others: Internet of Things-Based Intelligent Applications

Several IoT-based applications (depend on Cloud) for this smart era can be discussed here as:

- IoT for smart agriculture
- Smart home
- Smart grid
- Smart manufacturing
- Smart logistics systems
- Smart Transportation
  - Autonomous vehicles
  - Intelligent vehicles
  - Hybrid vehicle
  - Autonomous intelligent vehicles
- Other smart applications

## 14.9    A Use Case with Real World Applications (with Respect to Big Data Analytics) Related to Cloud, Fog, and Edge Computing

Today, every sector is moving to cloud for the betterment of the society. Let us take an example of healthcare. In healthcare, there are several uses of cloud such as disaster recovery to ensure the availability of critical systems in case of an outage. These services help to meet HIPAA Requirements for an organization. It is a very cost-effective alternate as compared to data centers. Addition to all this, companies like Microsoft and VMWare introduced some security aspects to cloud which can be used to assist users in protecting their data. Some other information for this use case is included as follows:

- Healthcare deals with a tremendous amount of data which is generated by their internal clinical systems. This unwieldy mountain of information has encouraged many organizations to consider cloud options for mining the information for meaningful insights and for providing them with an elastic and scalable environment where storage is more affordable and protected. Cloud providers can tailor different packages according to a hospital's data needs.
- Cloud providers can store their clients' data and they can offer powerful engines that can mine the data for insights using advanced algorithms and ML capabilities. In addition, business intelligence capabilities, such as interactive dashboards, encourage many businesses to look to these vendors as a quick and effective way to analyze their information without the need for significant upfront hardware and software investments.
- The cloud may be easy to adopt, but it can also be very difficult to leave. That should be taken in consideration when evaluating the different services for cloud in healthcare.

Hence, this section gives about cloud computing and IoT devices in healthcare appositions. Also, it discusses "how these devices can change future of healthcare sector". For example, infection rates of any diseases through getting pre-alert message by smart devices can be reduced to a certain level. Now, next section will be of challenges and issues faced by big data analytics in current era.

## 14.10   Issues and Challenges Faced by Big Data Analytics (in Cloud, Fog, and Edge Computing Environments)

Big data comes to play when complex problem occurs rather than traditional problems. In this section, we discuss the challenges and issues that can be faced during the process.

**Cloud Analytics Challenges:** As cloud analytics offers a numerous benefit, enterprises will also have to face some challenges such as follows:

- Security: One of the major concerns when comes to public computing service. In order to secure data of customer, we must caution on both transactional and customer service data and making sure strong data protective measure taken.

- Lack of skills: Many organizations do not have expertise for selecting several cloud-related solutions along with that they need to invest for ensuring success.
- Data migration: The process of moving the data from one place to another is always a challenging task and, when we have huge data (petabytes) in house data centers and needs to move on cloud, it will be a difficult task because the volume of data will be always growing.
- Lack of customization: Organizations always try to customize itself to meet their requirements. This happens when vendor takes to meet the needs.
- Vendor lock-in: As there is no of cloud analytics, vendors and each vendor use different technologies and tools for the support they are offering. For selecting a vendor, organizations must take proper time for the selection process because changing a vendor will effect on the cost of the loss.

Apart from this, several challenges of IoT-based cyber-physical attacks also have been included in [21]. Some of the major challenges that big data analytics program is facing today include the following:

a. Uncertainty of data management: As the big data is continuously growing every day, it is very difficult to choose that which technology is best for the future of the company with the less of risks and problems.
b. The talent gap: As the big data is building and to find an expert who can understands the complexity in this field are very few thereby evolving of talent gap exists.
c. Getting data into the big data platform: As the source of data is increasing (mobile phones), then the data is also increasing and to tackle this huge data every time is a difficult task, thereby we need to make that data simple and convenient.
d. Synchronization: As data gets bigger, there is a need to create some sort of synch; else, it may lead to wrong insights.

## 14.10.1   Cloud Issues

When it comes to security of cloud, there is doubt still, and we stand on is authenticity. Based on a survey in 2008 [4], the major challenges that prevent cloud computing are described below:

    a.   Security: The most crucial challenge that needs to ensure day by day from being attacked by third party and, for that, organizations use the cloud as (SaaS, PaaS, and IaaS) and deployment models (private, public, hybrid, and community) [4].

    b.   Costing Model: When comes to choosing, a model is another important thing. Problems occur when community having hybrid where data is evenly distributed in public/private community.

    c.   Service-Level Agreements (SLA): Agreement forms between the providers and consumers. Agreement is kept in such a way that appropriate trade-off happen and should cover consumer expectation to be verified.

    d.   Cloud Interoperability: Each cloud has its own operating way to connect and it is also important that both cloud should be satisfied as well as clouds from local body.

Hence, this section discusses several open issues and challenges existing during big data analytics, i.e., analysis for cloud and edge computing environments. Now, next section will discuss several future opportunities related to cloud, fog, and edge computing environments for future researchers.

## 14.11   Opportunities for the Future in Cloud, Fog, and Edge Computing Environments (or Research Gaps)

Both the technologies go with aim of enhancing the revenue of the company by reducing cost. The usage of these evolving technologies brings reliable and improved security, giving rise to store data remotely rather in physical location. Moreover, cyber-physical systems are the interconnection of several IoT devices. IoT is the major function of cyber-physical infrastructure or internet-enabled/cyber infrastructure. In continuation to this, several future research opportunities have been discussed in [21]. As discussed above, IoT and big data produce many new challenges like data storage, integration, and analytics. All these emerging technologies that are part of our life nowadays required attention from research communities. Cloud/fog/edge computing and IoT merged together to solve popular real-time problems (related to many applications). Many serious issues which are required efficient solution have been discussed in [22]. In near future, researchers and scientists are invited to focus/work on the issues mentioned in [22].

Fog computing is very important step because we can easily check that how much and what different type of operational data moves in the past and helps in decision-making for future. In this way, fog computing helps in tamp down on bandwidth usage and even slow down your need to engage in costly upgrades. It also helps in keeping your infrastructure to run smoothly.

- Artificial for cloud computing
- Artificial intelligence for edge computing
- Artificial intelligence and blockchain for IoT-based cloud applications
- ML to automated analytics

In [43–45, 47] readers can find the possible use of cloud and edge computing in detail (including raised issues ad challenges).

Hence, this section discusses several opportunities (or provide some future research directions) for future researchers toward cloud, fog, and edge computing. Now, next section will conclude this work in brief (with identifying some research gaps for readers).

## 14.12   Conclusion

Cloud computing got the attention from research communities in the previous decade. Many good articles for this technology have been written by renewed scientists and researchers. But today, cloud become out of trend because of change in demand of user/customers. So, this place is now taken by its extended technology, like fog and edge computing. As we can see today, two important technologies, i.e., big data and cloud computing, can change the face/center of IT/concerns of real world and can provide efficient services to citizens of a nation. The combination of both technologies is much useful and beneficial for the industries/organizations. In near future, using big data analytics and IoT, we can send alert message to doctor regarding a patient's health. Also, patient can access information accordingly form anywhere or based on his/her availability. Hence, this chapter discusses several useful terms, concepts, importance, open issues and challenges, and, lastly, future research directions for future readers/ researchers. In future, we can focus more big data analytics with integration of IoT devices and cloud computing. Also, blockchain technology plays a crucial role in protecting data from unwanted user on internet/an open (public) network.

# References

1. Hashizume, K., Rosado, D.G., Fernández-Medina, E., Fernandez, E.B., An analysis of security issues for cloud computing. *J. Internet Serv. Appl.*, 4, 5, December 2013.
2. Neves, P.C., Schmerl, B., Bernardino, J., Big Data in Cloud Computing: features and issues. *Proceedings of the International Conference on Internet of Things and Big Data - IoTBD*, Rome, Italy, pp. 307–314, 2016.
3. Peter, N., FOG Computing and Its Real Time Applications. *IJE TAE*, 5, 6, June 2015.
4. Satyanarayanan, M., How we created edge computing. *Nat. Electron.*, 2, 1, 42–42, 2019.
5. Hassan, N., Gillani, S., Ahmed, E., Yaqoob, I., Imran, M., The Role of Edge Computing in Internet of Things. *IEEE Commun. Mag.*, 56, 11, 110–115, 2018.
6. Yu, W., Liang, F., He, X., Hatcher, W.G., Lu, C., Lin, J., Yang, X., A Survey on the Edge Computing for the Internet of Things. in *IEEE Access*, vol. 6, pp. 6900–6919, 2018.
7. Nebbiolo Technologies - pioneers of fog Computing - difference between Fog and Edge Computing.
8. Dolui, K. and Datta, S.K., Comparison of edge computing implementations: Fog computing, cloudlet and mobile edge computing. *2017 Global Internet of Things Summit (GIoTS)*, 2017, pp. 1–6, 2017.
9. Spice, B., Carnegie Mellon University, Microsoft join forces to advance Edge Computing Research. News. Retrieved, 2018. November 22, 2018, from https://www.cmu.edu/news/stories/archives/2018/november/edge-computing-partnership.html.
10. Bastug, E., Bennis, M., Debbah, M., Living on the edge: The role of proactive caching in 5G wireless networks. *IEEE Commun. Mag.*, 52, 8, 82–89, 2014.
11. Gartner Identifies Top 10 Strategic IoT Technologies and Trends. *Analysts Explore Internet of Things Opportunities and Pitfalls at Gartner Symposium/ITxpo 2018, November 4-8 in Barcelona*, Spain BARCELONA, Spain, November 7, 2018.
12. Calheiros, R.N., Ranjan, R., Beloglazov, A., De Rose, C.A.F., CloudSim: A Toolkit for Modeling and Simulation of Cloud Computing Environments and Evaluation of Resource Provisioning Algorithms. *Software Pract. Exp.*, 41, 1, 23–50, January 2011.

13. Sriram, I., SPECI, a Simulation Tool Exploring Cloud-Scale Data Centres. *IEEE International Conference on Cloud Computing, CloudCom*, Cloud Computing, pp. 381–392, 2009.
14. Radu (Genete), L.D., Green Cloud Computing: A Literature Survey. *Article (PDF Available) Symmetry*, 9, 12, 295, November 2017.
15. Sinha, U. and Shekhar, M., Comparison of Various Cloud Simulation tools available in Cloud Computing, IJARCCE4(3) : 171–176, March 2015.
16. Ostermann, S., Plankensteiner, K., Prodan, R., Fahringer, T., GroudSim: An Event-Based Simulation Framework for Computational Grids and Clouds. *European Conference on Parallel Processing, Euro-Par 2010: Euro-Par*, Parallel Processing Workshops, pp. 305–313, 2010.
17. Garg, S.K. and Buyya, R., Cloud Computing and Distributed Systems (CLOUDS), in: *Laboratory Department of Computer Science and Software Engineering*, The University of Melbourne, Australia, 2006.
18. Muntean, M., Driving Business Agility With The Use Of Cloud ANALYTICS. *International Conference on Informatics in economy, At Bucharest, Volume: Proceedings of the 14the International Conference on Informatics in economy (IE 2015)*.
19. Karthiga, S., Janahan, S.K., Anbazhagu, U.V., Research on Various Tools in Big Data. *Int. J. Innov. Technol. Explor. Eng. (IJITEE)*, 8, 6S4, April 2019.
20. Tyagi, A.K. and Rekha, G., Machine Learning with Big Data (March 20, 2019). *Proceedings of International Conference on Sustainable Computing in Science, Technology and Management (SUSCOM)*, Amity University Rajasthan, Jaipur - India, February 26-28, 2019, Available at SSRN: https://ssrn.com/abstract=3356269 or http://dx.doi.org/10.2139/ssrn.3356269.
21. Amit, K., Cyber Physical Systems (CPSs) – Opportunities and Challenges for Improving Cyber Security. *Int. J. Comput. Appl.*, 137, 19–27, 2016. 10.5120/ijca2016908877.
22. Tyagi, A.K., Rekha, G., Sreenath, N., Beyond the Hype: Internet of Things Concepts, Security and Privacy Concerns, in: *Advances in Decision Sciences, Image Processing, Security and Computer Vision. Learning and Analytics in Intelligent Systems, ICETE*, vol. 3, S. Satapathy, K. Raju, K. Shyamala, D. Krishna, M. Favorskaya (Eds.), Springer, Cham, 20202019.
23. Leopold, C., *Parallel and Distributed Computing: A survey of Models, Paradigms and approaches*, John Wiley & Sons, Inc, 2001.
24. Bermond, J.-C., Comellas, F., Hsu, D.F., Distributed loop computer-networks: a survey," Elsevier. *J. Parallel Distrib. Comput.*, 24, 1, 2–10, 1995.
25. Huebscher, M.C. and McCann, J.A., A survey of autonomic computing-degrees, models, and applications. *ACM Comput. Surv. (CSUR)*, 40, 3, 7, 2008.
26. Bal, H.E., Steiner, J.G., Tanenbaum, A.S., Programming languages for distributed computing systems. *ACM Comput. Surv. (CSUR)*, 21, 3, 261–322, 1989.

27. Gropp, W., Lusk, E., Doss, N., Skjellum, A., A high-performance, portable implementation of the MPI message passing interface standard," Elsevier. *Parallel Comput.*, 22, 6, 789–828, 1996.
28. Clark, D.D., Pogran, K.T., Reed, D.P., An introduction to local area networks. *Proceedings of the IEEE*, vol. 66, pp. 1497– 1517, 1978.
29. Limb, J. and Flamm, L., A distributed local area network packet protocol for combined voice and data transmission. *IEEE J. Sel. Areas Commun.*, 1, 5, 926–934, 1983.
30. Tsao, C., A local area network architecture overview. *IEEE Commun. Mag.*, 22, 8, 7–11, 1984.
31. Buyya, R., High performance cluster computing: Architecture and systems, volume i, in: *Prentice Hall, Upper SaddleRiver*, vol. 1, p. 999, NJ, USA, 1999.
32. Garfinkel, S. and Abelson, H., Architects of the information society, in: *35 years of the Laboratory for Computer Science at MIT*, MIT Press, Cambridge, MA, United States, 1999.
33. Padala, P., Shin, K.G., Zhu, X., Uysal, M., Wang, Z., Singhal, S., Merchant, A., Salem, K., Adaptive control of virtualized resources in utility computing environments, in: *Proceedings of the 2007 ACM SIGOPS Operating Systems Review*, vol. 41, ACM, pp. 289–302, 2007.
34. Nurmi, D., Wolski, R., Grzegorczyk, C., Obertelli, G., Soman, S., Youseff, L., Zagorodnov, D., Eucalyptus: A technical report on an elastic utility computing architecture linking your program stouseful systems, in: *UCSB Technical Report*, Citeseer, Cambridge, MA, United States, 2008.
35. Ross, J.W. and Westerman, G., Preparing for utility computing: The role of it architecture and relationship management. *IBM Syst. J.*, Cambridge, MA, United States, 43, 1, 5–19, 2004.
36. Buco, M.J., Chang, R.N., Luan, L.Z., Ward, C., Wolf, J.L., Yu, P.S., Utility computing sla management based upon business objectives. *IBM Syst. J.*, 43, 1, 159–178, 2004.
37. Valentini, G.L., Lassonde, W., Khan, S.U., Min-Allah, N., Madani, S.A., Li, J., Zhang, L., Wang, L., Ghani, N., Kolodziej, J. *et al.*, An overview of energy efficiency techniques in cluster computing systems," Springer. *Clust. Comput.*, 16, 1, 3–15, 2013.
38. Werstein, P., Situ, H., Huang, Z., Load balancing in a cluster computer, in: *Proceedings of 2006 IEEE Seventh International Conference on Parallel and Distributed Computing*, Applications and Technologies, IEEE, pp. 569–577, 2006.
39. Bohn, C.A. and Lamont, G.B., Load balancing for heterogeneous clusters of PCs," Elsevier. *Future Gener. Comput. Syst.*, 18, 3, 389–400, 2002.
40. Maguluri, S.T., Srikant, R., Ying, L., Stochastic models of load balancing and scheduling in cloud computing clusters, in: *Proceedings of the 2012 IEEE International Conference on Computer Communications (INFOCOM)*, IEEE, 2012702–710.

41. Agbaria, A.M. and Friedman, R., Starfish: Fault-tolerant dynamic MPI programs on clusters of workstations, in: *Proceedings of the 1999 IEEE Eighth International Symposium on High Performance Distributed Computing*, IEEE, pp. 167–176, 1999.

42. Fu, S., Failure-aware resource management for high-availability computing clusters with distributed virtual machines," Elsevier. *J. Parallel Distrib. Comput.*, 70, 4, 384–393, 2010.

43. Tyagi, A.K., Fernandez, T.F., Mishra, S., Kumari, S., Intelligent Automation Systems at the Core of Industry 4.0. in: *Intelligent Systems Design and Applications. ISDA 2020. Advances in Intelligent Systems and Computing*, A. Abraham, V. Piuri, N. Gandhi, P. Siarry, A. Kaklauskas, A. Madureira (Eds), vol 1351, Springer, Cham, 2021.

44. Tyagi, A.K., Nair, M.M., Niladhuri, S., Abraham, A., Security, privacy research issues in various computing platforms: A survey and the road ahead. *J. Inf. Assur. Secur.*, 15, 1, 1–16, 16p, 2020.

45. Nair, M.M., Tyagi, A.K., Sreenath, N., "The Future with Industry 4.0 at the Core of Society 5.0: Open Issues, Future Opportunities and Challenges," *2021 International Conference on Computer Communication and Informatics (ICCCI)*, pp. 1–7, 2021.

46. Tyagi, A.K. and Aghila, G., "A Wide Scale Survey on Botnet". *Int. J. Comput. Appl.*, 34, 9, 9–22, 2011.

47. Kumari, S., Tyagi, A.K., Aswathy, S.U., The Future of Edge Computing with Blockchain Technology: Possibility of Threats, Opportunities and Challenges, in: *Recent Trends in Blockchain for Information Systems Security and Privacy*, CRC Press, 2021.

# 15

# Big Data in Healthcare: Applications and Challenges

V. Shyamala Susan[1]*, K. Juliana Gnana Selvi[2],
and Ir. Bambang Sugiyono Agus Purwono[3]

*1Department of Computer Science, A.P.C. Mahalaxmi College for Women,
Thoothukudi, Tamil Nadu, India*
*2Department of Computer Science, Rathinam College of Arts and Science,
Coimbatore, Tamil Nadu, India*
*3Department of Mechanical Engineering, State Polytechnic of Malang,
Malang City, Indonesia*

## Abstract

The demand for the healthcare sector has increased rapidly which, in turn, has drastically increased the need to manage healthcare and innovative medicines. This demand has been the main reason for the need for new technologies being initiated in the healthcare industry. The use of big data analysis in the healthcare industry will be one of the major challenges that may take place in the coming years according to International Data Corporation (IDC). The IDC reports that big data will show immense growth in the healthcare industry when compared to other industries. There are many tools that come along with big data. These tools will collect, manage, analyze, and assimilate huge loads of data which are the output of the present healthcare system. This makes it evident that, by 2025, the data from the healthcare industry will show a Compound Annual Growth Rate (CAGR) of 36%. This chapter highlights the huge impact of the big data in the healthcare industry and the various factors that makes it very challenging to manage and process big data in the healthcare sector before the healthcare implements big data.

*Keywords*: Big data analysis, healthcare system, international data corporation, challenges, factors

*Corresponding author*: shyamalasusan@gmail.com

Archana Mire, Shaveta Malik and Amit Kumar Tyagi (eds.) Advanced Analytics and Deep Learning
Models, (351–364) © 2022 Scrivener Publishing LLC

## 15.1   Introduction

The start of the 21st century has observed incredible jumps in computerized innovation and healthcare services across the world. The transition between paper document records to digital documents is taking place slowly and methodically in the healthcare sector, causing unrest [1]. These improvements give high effectiveness and adaptability to healthcare facilities by giving a display place that productively shares medical care information between various partners. Electronic Medical Records (EMR), Electronic Health Records (EHR), Electronic Health Data (EHD), and Personal Health Records (PHR) are examples of document records that have been replaced by digital documents as a result of this revolution (EHD). These records are involved a wide assortment of medical care information. Dissimilar to paper documents, EHR incus less labor, time, and actual stockpiling [2]. The preferred position of HER incorporate simpler and quick clinical information access, capacity to keep up compelling clinical work processes, relief of clinical blunders, upgrading understanding wellbeing, decreased clinical expenses, and better and more grounded uphold for clinical dynamic. The selection of EHRs was delayed toward the beginning of the 21st century; it was becoming considerably high after 2009 [3, 4]. The capacity of EHDs to give better administration of healthcare services has been learned and affirmed by different clients. These qualities uphold the verification that healthcare data meet the high-speed measure. This healthcare information has not been utilized for decision-making to its fullest degree. Investigation of immense volumes of expanded healthcare data is a difficult assignment.

### 15.1.1   Big Data in Healthcare

Big data in healthcare services introduces the incredibly huge healthcare data from a wide assortment of sources. The information can emerge out of a group of sources including HER, PHR, drug research, genomic sequencing clinical gadgets, RPM wearables, insurance agencies, doctors, and medical clinics and that is just the beginning. According to the IDC Data Age 2025 study, the rise of the Internet of Things (IoT), computerized and cloud progress, and tech-savvy clinicians will result in a 36% increase in revenue from 2018 to 2025. These huge data sets are so enormous, complicated, and with conventional management approaches; it is almost impossible to handle them. Presented with a problem, in order to produce actionable insights, healthcare systems need to implement technologies capable of capturing, storing, and analyzing this knowledge.

## 15.1.2    The 5V's Healthcare Big Data Characteristics

The five important qualities that have been initiated in most works [5, 6] to characterize healthcare big data are as follows.

### 15.1.2.1    Volume

Contrasted with different industries, the healthcare sector produces huge measures of information as EHRs biometric information, clinical information, radiology images, and genomic information. Any of this information in healthcare sector generates big data [7–9].

### 15.1.2.2    Velocity

The pace at which data are generated, as well as data obtained from various healthcare frameworks [10], is referred to as velocity.

### 15.1.2.3    Variety

The term "variety" refers to the variety and diversity of knowledge. This same healthcare industry generates and collects data at an incredible pace from a diversity of ways, including social media platforms, sensor devices, sensors, and mobile phones. In any case, the healthcare information may be ordered, unstructured, or semi-structured.

### 15.1.2.4    Veracity

It applies to the data dependability, although in this context equates to data quality confirmation. It indicates the degree of validity of healthcare details.

### 15.1.2.5    Value

The most important factor is value and unmistakable qualities of the five V's of healthcare big data, since it has the potential to alter healthcare details into worth of data. Its idea is actually in accordance with that of healthcare data.

## 15.1.3    Various Varieties of Big Data Analytical (BDA) in Healthcare

BDA specializes in three types of analytics: descriptive analytics, prescriptive analytics, and discovery analytics.

This same descriptive analysis allows for the discussion of ideas and the consideration of what is really going on in a specific circumstance by healthcare professionals [11, 12]. It analyzes the collected data to view, comprehend, interpret, and illustrate relevant details related to health. Predictive research, on the other hand, allows doctors to be able to make choices [13]. Prescriptive analytics forecast the future and have the opportunity to do something. Although in order to evaluate interrelationships, patterns, and outliers, discovery analytics uses machine learning to analyze raw data. It tries to analyze what we really need to explore more but original data can restrict its effectiveness by being inaccurate or incomplete.

### 15.1.4   Application of Big Data Analytics in Healthcare

Big data is a talking point in the digital environment and is in short supply in each and every field, particularly in the healthcare sector. It has built a cornerstone in the healthcare sector for various applications. By finding the correlations from large amounts of health data, public healthcare BDA has the potential to improve healthcare efficiency and reduce patient medical costs by offering a wider perspective of clinical knowledge regarding medical evidence and various tests [14]. Public healthcare BDA further enables doctors and policymakers to enhance government policy and patient care by using data from accessible healthcare data, disease occurrence data, and socioeconomic distress data [15]. The key areas for BDA implementations in healthcare are described follows, according to the researchers in [16–19].

**Tracking for Healthcare:** Healthcare data management can be used to continuously monitor the health status of customers (patients) in order to change their actions [20].

**Healthcare Risk Prediction:** A profound examination of healthcare data helps medical care partners and clinical specialists to create answers for hazard forecast. It additionally empowers clinicians to be fit for settling on patient-related choices based on framework expectations [21]. In medical care, data analytics can also be used to identify and manage patients who are at high risk and cost a lot of money [22].

**Behavioral Checking:** Another pending usage of BDA in healthcare services is observing of patients who are acting strangely [23]. Nambe *et al.* initiated home health services in 2005 to catch the behavior information of patients for the purpose of determining their illnesses [24].

**Fraud Recognition and Counteraction:** Misrepresentation detection and correction is one of the most important applications of data investigation in the healthcare sector. Data mining and AI procedures are often used for misrepresentation position in healthcare facilities, according to the developers in [25].

**Clinical Decision Supportive Networks:** Clinical support networks are used in the medical industry to encourage healthcare experts in creating clinical choices to analyze sicknesses depending on patient's ailment [26, 27].

**Personalized Healthcare Proposal Framework:** Big data in healthcare sector intends to create a customized framework to give exact and pertinent clinical suggestion (counsel) to an individual in light of their present wellbeing status and clinical history [28].

**Drug Disclosure and Clinical Preliminaries:** Healthcare BDA is generally utilized by the drug business for drug revelations so it can help doctors, drug designers, and other healthcare experts in order to get the right drug to the right patient at the right time [29–31].

**Telediagnosis and Image Informatics:** Imaging informatics is the examination of techniques for developing, handling, and interacting with imaging data in a variety of biological applications. It is involved only with sharing and analysis of imaging data around various healthcare systems [32, 33]. The investigation's creators [34] propose a revolutionary tele-mammography system for early breast cancer detection through the assistance of picture preparing and AI procedures.

**Healthcare Data Framework:** As per [35], Healthcare Data framework is created to help clinical decision-making.

Based on the studies of various scholars, it is demonstrated that the BDA in health has a significant potential to improve healthcare efficiency, minimize patient outcomes, and lower patient hospital expenses by examining the relationships and understanding the nature of healthcare data. Image processing, signal processing, and genomics are currently the three primary areas for the implementation of data analytics in the healthcare sector.

### 15.1.5    Benefits of Big Data in the Health Industry

Through digitizing, integrating, and effectively utilizing healthcare analytical tools and techniques for big data, healthcare markets that extend from a particular doctor's office to a wide range of platforms of suppliers of healthcare services may find significant advantages. The below are some of the key advantages, based on the newly published studies [36–38].

**Clinical operations:** The health data aids in the creation of more clinically relevant and expense diagnosis and treatment strategies. Health knowledge can help clinicians make the best decision and boost clinicians' health, thereby lowering healthcare costs.

**Providers of healthcare:** Data gathered from health organizations aid stakeholders in developing creative patient healthcare programs that eliminate unnecessary hospital admissions.

**Research and product development:** Health data assists doctors and scientists in developing increasingly accurate and efficient approaches to improve healthcare outcomes.

**Public health:** Health data also helps to determine health risks and analyze disease patterns to improve and monitoring of public health.

**Innovative work:** Healthcare information uphold analysts and researchers to improve Healthcare services administrations through more exact and proper therapies.

**Public health:** Health data is useful for identifying health hazards and analyzing disease trends in order to enhance public health surveillance.

## 15.2  Analytical Techniques for Big Data in Healthcare

To store, process, and manage data, data analysts have historically relied on traditional technology and data repositories. Conventional database systems, techniques, and methods, on the other hand, would not be able to deal with the revolution of massive data collections in healthcare. The data analyst has traditionally used conventional technology and data warehouses to store, process, and handle data. However, it is not possible to tackle the revolution of large data volumes in healthcare using traditional database systems, instruments, and techniques.

To counter the reduced productivity and complexity of conventional systems, many advanced systems with high storage capacity and large storage have been installed in recent years. As a result, big data technology [39] can be described as innovative materials that have a high level of resource utilization and processing capability to absorb great quantities of data extracted from multiple sources in order to extract information. Big data techniques, according to the authors in [40], cover a broad range of areas, including machine learning, statistical analysis, and image analysis. Big data is relevant in all sectors, including government agencies, trade unions, healthcare, education, and technology development. In the healthcare industry, BDA also encourages the main use of patient images [41]. Big data awareness has grown significantly, from 17 in 2015 to 53 in 2017, according to Forbes [42].

### 15.2.1 Platforms and Tools for Healthcare Data

Currently, there are many methods for conducting BDA. Hadoop, Apache HDFS, Hadoop Map Reduce, Apache Hive, Pig, HBase, and Mahout are some of the instruments and techniques that support the distributed platform.

## 15.3 Challenges

Big data provides tremendous opportunities to optimize patient outcomes, provide reliable medicine, minimize costs, reduce hospital readmissions, increase revenue, ensure patient safety, and comply with regulations. Yet there are an equal number of barriers to compliance. Big data research in healthcare, as today's big data is distributed in multiple ways through different outlets.

The real problem is how such nuanced knowledge can be obtained, evaluated, and managed to forecast the effects and make possible decisions. The healthcare data problems fall into many groups, like challenges in data, challenges in the process, and management challenges.

### 15.3.1 Storage Challenges

Encrypting is one of the ways to store big data safely. Even then, scaling and managing a fully equipped server network can be expensive and challenging. With declining costs and rising reliability, it seems that cloud-based storage using its technology is a safer choice that most healthcare organizations have selected. Cloud partners must be selected by organizations that understand the significance of particular enforcement and protection concerns surrounding healthcare. Cloud technology, in particular, has a lower initial investment, a faster recovery plans, and faster growth. Institutions may now use a customized approach to digital management software, which is the most adaptable and realistic solution for businesses with varying data access and processing times.

## 15.3.2    Cleaning

In order to ensure precision and correctness, the data must be cleaned or scrubbed. Consistency is after acquisition, significance, and purring. Using logical guidelines, this cleaning method can be performed manually or automated to ensure a high degree of consistency and integrity. Data cleaning is indeed an equally essential feature in most healthcare businesses. Machine learning methods are used by more advanced and reliable tools to minimize costs and effort and to avoid foul data from big data ventures derail.

## 15.3.3    Data Quality

The majority of healthcare knowledge is unstructured and is accessible in text, images, numerical, paper, audio, and visual formats. Such unstructured and untapped information typically includes the patients, workers, and performers' most relevant and genre bending information. The task is making such knowledge more valuable and interoperable. Developers need to create the correct data metadata and convert it into a standardized format.

## 15.3.4    Data Security

As cyberattacks in this sector are growing exponentially, protecting patient data is a priority for all health organizations. About 18 PHI elements that must be covered are listed by HIPAA. The job is to eliminate certain key PHI components and still make knowledge usable for study. This legislation also addresses some safeguards that must be adopted by organizations in order to ensure privacy and protection. In order to resolve data privacy and use patient data for invention or research, balance is needed.

## 15.3.5    Missing or Incomplete Data

Patients often appear to conceal some of their personal facts. When work is done with such empty or incorrect fields, it may or may not be processed and incorrect research will be made. If we leave any documents because they are null, then our study is not based on cumulative data. Unless we assume incorrect value fields, therefore the analysis is again incorrect and inaccurate and it is important to answer such a problem.

## 15.3.6    Information Sharing

Clinical information needs to be exchanged through several organizations such as hospitals, research centers, hospitals, and more to establish a good health initiative and clinical outcomes; however, data sharing raises data privacy concerns. Thus, in order to exchange information in a secure way, it is vital to keep the HIPAA regulations in consideration. The other big sharing problem is that there is no standardized data storage solution, making it hard to attain interoperability with the other systems of medical data processing. The health sector provided by today's suppliers actually makes it impossible to copy exactly or share data to other misaligned fonts, various data fields, and proprietary formals from electronic medical record software or other healthcare technology, ensuring that data must be manipulated and sanitized until it can be incorporated into other systems. To ensure that the data from sources is valid information and is of good quality, we need a method. In the case of social media data, assessing data validation and accuracy is another major challenge. The development and use of specifications for health data forms the basis for allowing interoperability between organizations and electronic health record systems. Yet no single norm exists. This lack of general practice for patient data collection, delivery, receipt, storage, and management causes delays and inconsistencies that are a major obstacle.

### 15.3.7    Overcoming the Big Data Talent and Cost Limitations

In order to handle and analyze huge amounts of real-time data, each organization needs trained professionals. Large businesses use trained data scents and big data analytics to optimally use and optimize big data. At present, however, data scientists and big data researchers are in short supply but in high demand. Big data is mostly used by small companies and start-ups because of a shortage of capital and expertise. Large organizations often find it challenging to effectively handle large data through the deployment of additional data scientists.

### 15.3.8    Financial Obstructions

These relate to the expense of designing and improving health information systems to meet constantly evolving requirements and health services, including the shortage of information-sharing opportunities and the need for secondary data-use business models.

### 15.3.9    Volume

The huge amount of data and the vast scale present a significant challenge. Heterogeneity, iniquity, and the diverse nature of multiple tools and devices for data generation, as well as the enormous scale of data alone, would make recovering, processing, and interfering with real world data a difficult task. Healthcare data is not really static and, in order to stay current and important, most components need reasonably frequent updates. It can be a challenge for an enterprise that does not regularly track its data search to update the volatizing and big data or, now often, and to what degree is change. Yet companies frequently neglect the fact that the volume and workload of big data is increasing quickly. Enterprises must build an infrastructure that enables the inclusion of new datasets to be processed periodically. They will need to ensure that ample resources are available to meet the steady growth in the size and complexity of big data.

### 15.3.10   Technology Adoption

Health organizations generate vast quantities of data on a regular basis, but once they have the right infrastructure, technology, and instruments, they will not be used. Sometimes, healthcare centers lack the right technologies that can help their attempts to analyze data. Although large healthcare organizations are increasingly embracing emerging technology such as smart devices, mobile computing and cloud services, it is time to embrace the same for small- and medium-sized healthcare professionals. In addition, innovation can take place not only in healthcare innovations but also in those that concentrate on the corporate structure.

## 15.4   What is the Eventual Fate of Big Data in Healthcare Services?

Big data will be embraced in larger numbers by healthcare organizations in the future as it becomes more important for success. Big data analytics will also strive to support make touch points smarter and much more integrated for marketing. In addition, with mobile technology and the IoT gaining popularity, the amount of available data will expand. Continual healthcare monitoring will become normal through wearable devices like IoT and will add enormous amounts of data to big data stores. Healthcare advertisers will combine a vast amount of healthcare data with this knowledge to identify and attract patients with the greatest propensity for services.

Big data analytics is gaining traction as a promising way to extract information from massive volumes of data and improve results while lowering costs. Its ability is exceptional.

## 15.5   Conclusion

Data analytics has the power to change the way doctors utilize cutting-edge technology to produce knowledge and make intelligent choices based on clinical and other data. For the meantime, we might see a rapid and extensive implementation and use of data analytics in the healthcare system and the healthcare industry. To this same end, it is critical to address the numerous issues listed above. As big data analytics becomes more popular, issues like maintaining security, maintaining security, establishing standards and administration, and continuously developing instruments and innovations become more popular. Big data analysis and healthcare technologies are in a preliminary phase of development, but rapid progress in phases and tools will speed up their development cycle.

## References

1. Dong, N., Jonker, H., Pang, J., Challenges in ehealth: From enabling to enforcing privacy. *Proc. Int. Symp. Found. Health Inform. Eng. Syst*, pp. 195–206, 2011.
2. Kruse, C.S., Mileski, M., Vijaykumar, A.G., Viswanathan, S.V., Suskandla, U., Chidambaram, Y., Impact of electronic health records on long-term care facilities: Systematic review. *JMIR Med. Inform.*, 5, e35, 2017.
3. Reisman, M., EHRs: the challenge of making electronic data usable and interoperable. *Pharm. Ther.*, 42, 9, 572–5, 2017.
4. Murphy, G., Hanken, M.A., Waters, K., *Electronic health records: changing the vision*, p. 627, WB Saunders Company, Philadelphia, 1999.
5. Nazir, S., Nawaz, M., Adnan, A., Shahzad, S., Asadi, S., Big data features, applications, and analytics in cardiology-a systematic literature review. *IEEE Access*, 7, 143742–143771, 2019.
6. Sarkar, B.K., Big data for secure healthcare system: A conceptual design. *Complex Intell. Syst.*, 3, 2, 133–151, 2017.
7. Widmer, A., Schaer, R., Markonis, D., Müller, H., Gesture interaction for content–based medical image retrieval, in: *Proceedings of International Conference on Multimedia Retrieval*, Glasgow, Scotland, pp. 503–506, April 2014.
8. Seibert, J.A., Modalities and data acquisition, in: *Practical Imaging Informatics*, pp. 49–66, Springer, New York, NY, USA, 2009.
9. Panayides, A.S., Pattichis, M.S., Leandrou, S., Pitris, C., Constantinidou, A., Pattichis, C.S., Radiogenomics for precision medicine with a big data analytics perspective. *IEEE J. Biomed. Health Inform.*, 23, 5, 2063–2079, 2018.

10. Cyganek, B., Graña, M., Krawczyk, B. *et al.*, A survey of big data issues in electronic health record analysis. *Appl. Artif. Intell.*, 30, 6, 497–520, 2016.

11. Phillips-Wren, G., Iyer, L.S., Kulkarni, U., Ariyachandra, T., Business analytics in the context of big data: a roadmap for research. *Commun. Assoc. Inf. Syst.*, 37, 1, 23, 2015.

12. Watson, H.J., Tutorial: big data analytics: concepts, technologies, and applications. *Commun. Assoc. Inf. Syst.*, 34, 1, 65, 2014.

13. Gandomi, A. and Haider, M., The hype: Big data concepts, methods, and analytics. *Int. J. Inf. Manage.*, 35, 2, 137–144, 2015.

14. Sukumar, S.R., Natarajan, R., Ferrell, R.K., Quality of big data in healthcare. *Int. J. Healthcare Qual. Assur.*, 28, 6, 621–634, 2015.

15. Cleland, B., Wallace, J., Bond, R. *et al.*, Insights into antidepressant prescribing using open health data. *Big Data Res.*, 12, 41–48, 2018.

16. Oussous, A., Benjelloun, F.-Z., Ait Lahcen, A., Belfkih, S., Big data technologies: a survey. *J. King Saud Univ.- Comput. Inf. Sci.*, 30, 4, 431–448, 2018. (100-104).

17. Bahri, S., Zoghlami, N., Abed, M., Tavares, J.M.R.S., Big data for healthcare: a survey. *IEEE Access*, 7, 7397–7408, 2019.

18. Sukumar, S.R., Natarajan, R., Ferrell, R.K., Quality of big data in healthcare. *Int. J. Healthcare Qual. Assur.*, 28, 6, 621–634, 2015.

19. Cleland, B., Wallace, J., Bond, R. *et al.*, Insights into antidepressant prescribing using open health data. *Big Data Res.*, 12, 41–48, 2018.

20. Agnihotri, N. and Sharma, A.K., Proposed algorithms for effective real time stream analysis in big data, in: *Proceedings of the 2015 Third International Conference on Image Information Processing (ICIIP)*, IEEE, Waknaghat, India, pp. 348–352, December 2015.

21. Rumsfeld, J.S., Joynt, K.E., Maddox, T.M., Big data analytics to improve cardiovascular care: promise and challenges. *Nat. Rev. Cardiol.*, 13, 6, 350–359, 2016.

22. Bates, D.W., Saria, S., Ohno-Machado, L., Shah, A., Escobar, G., Big data in healthcare: using analytics to identify and manage high-risk and high-cost patients. *Health Aff.*, 33, 7, 1123–1131, 2014.

23. Mehta, N. and Pandit, A., Concurrence of big data analytics and healthcare: a systematic review. *Int. J. Med. Inform.*, 114, 57–65, 2018.

24. Nambu, M., Nakajima, K., Noshiro, M., Tamura, T., An algorithm for the automatic detection of health conditions. *IEEE Eng. Med. Biol. Mag.*, 24, 4, 38–42, 2005.

25. Platt, R., Carnahan, R., Brown, J.S. *et al.*, The U.S. Food and drug administration's mini-sentinel program. *Pharmacoepidemiol. Drug Saf.*, 21, 1–303, 2012.

26. Berner, E.S., *Clinical Decision Support Systems*, vol. 233, Springer Science+ Business Media, LLC, New York, NY, USA, 2007.

27. Mayo, C.S., Moran, J.M., Bosch, W. *et al.*, American association of physicists in medicine task group 263: standardizing nomenclatures in radiation oncology. *Int. J. Radiat. Oncol. Biol. Phys.*, 100, 4, 1057–1066, 2018.

28. Kos, A. and Umek, A., Wearable sensor devices for prevention and rehabilitation in healthcare: swimming exercise with real-time therapist feedback. *IEEE Internet Things J.*, 6, 2, 1331–1341, 2018.

29. Hamburg, M.A. and Collins, F.S., The path to personalized medicine. *N. Engl. J. Med.*, 363, 4, 301–304, 2010.

30. Wang, G., Jung, K., Winnenburg, R., Shah, N.H., A method for systematic discovery of adverse drug events from clinical notes. *J. Am. Med. Inform. Assoc.*, 22, 6, 1196–1204, 2015.

31. Luo, J., Wu, M., Gopukumar, D., Zhao, Y., Big data application in biomedical research and healthcare: A literature review. *Biomed. Inf. Insights*, 8, 1–10, 2016.

32. Doi, K., Computer-aided diagnosis in medical imaging: historical review, current status and future potential. *Comput. Med. Imaging Graph.*, 31, 4-5, 198–211, 2007.

33. Manogaran, G., (ota, C., Lopez, D., Vijayakumar, V., Abbas, K.M., Sundarsekar, R., Big data knowledge system in healthcare, in: *Internet of 7ings and Big Data Technologies for Next Generation Healthcare*, pp. 133–157, Springer, Cham, Switzerland, 2017.

34. Saheb, T. and Izadi, L., Paradigm of IoT big data analytics in healthcare industry: a review of scientific literature and mapping of research trends. *Telemat. Inform.*, 41, 70–85, 2019.

35. Wang, Y., Kung, L., Byrd, T.A., Big data analytics: understanding its capabilities and potential benefits for healthcare organizations. *Technol. Forecast. Soc Change*, 126, 3–13, 2018.

36. Mehta, N. and Pandit, A., Concurrence of big data analytics and healthcare: a systematic review. *Int. J. Med. Inform.*, 114, 57–65, 2018.

37. Bahri, S., Zoghlami, N., Abed, M., Tavares, J.M.R.S., Big data for healthcare: a survey. *IEEE Access*, 7, 7397–7408, 2019.

38. Gantz, J. and Reinsel, D., Extracting value from chaos. *IDC Iview*, 1142, 1–12, 2011.

39. Ngufor, C. and Wojtusiak, J., Learning from large-scale distributed health data: an approximate logistic regression approach, in: *Proceedings of the ICML 13: Role of Machine Learning in Transforming Healthcare*, Atlanta, GA, USA, 2013.

40. Zhang, R., Simon, G., Yu, F., Advancing Alzheimer's research: a review of big data promises. *Int. J. Med. Inform.*, 106, 48–56, 2017.

41. Cano, I., Tenyi, A., Vela, E., Miralles, F., Roca, J., Perspectives on big data applications of health information. *Curr. Opin. Syst. Biol.*, 3, 36–42, 2017.

42. https://www.forbes.com/sites/louiscolumbus/2017/12/24/53-of-companies-are-adoptingbig-data-analytics/#50bf384239a1.

# 16

# The Fog/Edge Computing: Challenges, Serious Concerns, and the Road Ahead

**Varsha. R.[1], Siddharth M. Nair[1] and Amit Kumar Tyagi[1,2]\***

*[1]School of Computer Science and Engineering, Vellore Institute of Technology, Chennai Campus, Chennai, Tamil Nadu, India,*
*[2]Centre for Advanced Data Science, Vellore Institute of Technology, Chennai, Tamil Nadu, India*

## Abstract

Cloud computing is the innovative solutions of the past decade, developed to shared data anytime, anywhere (from any remote location) and to reduce complexity and enhanced accessibility of resources. This technology has seen several enhancements in the form of fog and edge computing. Moreover, this in the recent years, we are facing several other issues also with this emerging technology. Privacy, security, and scalability are the major (common) problems faced in the fog/edge networking-based solutions. But today, in the 21st century, we can use several emerging concepts to resolve above listed issues, i.e., artificial intelligence can help in service provider to store data at nearest node in edge computing. Similarly, user can access the required data from nearest node (without any hassle). Also, blockchain technology can help in securing this data in perfect way and can provide trusted services to users or consumers, i.e., it can help in building a highly trusted relationship among service providers and consumers. Today, cloud/ fog or edge computing is using by many industries to reduce e-waste and save cost of installation of infrastructure, etc. These industries also used cloud/edge computing in providing reliable services to its users and increase profits of their businesses. Hence, this work discusses such interested topics, areas, threats mitigated in cloud/fog/edge computing, opportunities and problems faced during implementation of cloud/edge computing in many sectors, etc. This work also discusses various challenges faced during implementation of these emerging technologies

*Corresponding author*: amitkrtyagi025@gmail.com
Amit Kumar Tyagi: ORCID: 0000-0003-2657-8700

Archana Mire, Shaveta Malik and Amit Kumar Tyagi (eds.) Advanced Analytics and Deep Learning Models, (365–390) © 2022 Scrivener Publishing LLC

like AI and blockchain with cloud computing and suggest countermeasure for the same for researchers/scientific community.

*Keywords*: Artificial intelligence-based edge computing, IoT-based edge computing environment, blockchain technology, threats, security, privacy

## 16.1    Introduction

The cloud permits clients to perform work and access data with a protected Internet association whenever and from anyplace (to further develop productivity and asset reuse). Cloud-based administrations may likewise incorporate applications for clinical picture documenting and security administrations, permitting medical care suppliers to trade clinical information across a safe organization. Note that an approximate of 1.3 million individuals are killed through street mishaps (consistently around the world). Concerning this, IoT gadgets or brilliant gadgets innovation can gather, examine, and computerize fitting reactions and activities to ongoing information from sensors and different gadgets in homes or different properties in a safe way. For instance, contamination paces of any infection, through pre-ready messages by brilliant gadgets can be diminished to a specific level. Likewise, about any cardiovascular failure or mental or jumble ready message about a patient can be shipped off particular specialist. At the point when these keen gadgets associate together, it makes a huge size of framework (digital and physical) to do ordinary undertaking. [1] This sort of foundation called Cyber-Physical Systems (CPS), whose tasks are checked, composed, controlled, and incorporated by a registering and correspondence center. The present web changed "how people connect with each other", though digital actual frameworks will change "how we associate with the actual world around us". We are (moving) to another time, i.e., in fourth mechanical unrest, and that this new modern transformation is a CPS upheaval. We can see that IoT is a critical capacity of this transformation (advancement). Together, large information investigation comes into picture for Internet of Things (IoT), to create compelling choices and to check conduct financial aspects (by means of social examination).

Consequently, the present big information and cloud registering is an ideal mix for changing the associations mindsets. Both the innovations mean to upgrade the income of the organization while decreasing the venture cost. While cloud deals with the nearby programming, big data helps in business choices. There are different advantages of big data investigation in cloud, as further developed examination, simplified infrastructure, lowering the expense, security, and protection, and virtualization.

Fog computing is an infrastructure which is distributed in nature and several processes, services, and applications are supervised at the network edge by smart devices, while others are supervised in the cloud framework. In essence, it is a layer which lies in between the cloud framework and the hardware resources to enhance processing of data, analysis, storage and visualization. This occurs because the data required to be transported to the cloud has been substantially reduced. In this computing scenario, information is prepared by a smart gadget subsequently lessening the measure of information shipped off the cloud workers. Fogging does not completely supplant distributed computing; it serves to supplement and make the information preparing, investigation, and capacity more proficient. The favorable position that fog computing adds is that it carries the insight to the nearby organization [2].

Rather than anticipating that gadgets should encounter the association spine structure, haze registering licenses contraptions to interface clearly no perspiration and grants them to manage their affiliations and endeavors any way they respect fit [3]. As needs be, haze registering works on the idea of organization, diminishes latency, and gives a decent customer experience. Mist registering effectively supports the emerging trap of things, frameworks that are embedded with sensors to engage them to send/get data. Mist registering can be executed using a crucial correspondence system as opposed to being realized using a significant spine association. Appropriately, it has a denser consideration. This ideal position simplifies it to run a constant, enormous data movement with the ability to help billions of center points in outstandingly novel, different conditions. Edge handling conveys the limits of the cloud close to the end-customer or end-device. There are talks around edge computing versus fog enrolling. In fact, the two have tantamount objections. A little difference is that fog enlisting can recall running knowledge for the end-contraption and is more IoT focused. Telcom directors habitually treat edge as indistinguishable from convenient edge preparing or multi-access edge figuring— register reliant upon the edge of the association. Regardless, telco edge figure joins remarkable jobs that need to be done running on customer premise gear and various motivations behind quality at the customer site. Like the cloud, edge registering structures are adaptable and versatile. In contrast to static, on-premise workers, it has the ability to deal with unexpected spikes in jobs from spontaneous expansions in end-client movement. It likewise helps scale when testing and sending new applications so an incredible answer for big business. Once more, the effectiveness and versatility are money saving advantages here.

We state telco edge is the best thought of a scattered figure, administered by the overseer, which might connect past the association edge and onto the customer edge. Telco edge cloud joins the upsides of cloud and close by enlisting, and "neighborhood" can be on-contraption or on-premises. Customers can run low inactivity applications, similarly as hold or cycle data close to the data source. This can similarly diminish backhaul traffic volumes and costs.

### 16.1.1   Organization of the Work

Section 16.2 discusses our inspiration for composing this article on cloud/edge computing. Further, Section 16.3 talks about foundation or advancement of the history of haze processing/edge registering exhaustively. Section 16.4 discusses fog and edge computing–based applications. Machine Learning and Internet of Things–based cloud, fog, and edge computing applications are discussed in section 16.5. Difficulties and serious threats toward fog/edge computing and its applications have been examined in Section 16.6. Section 16.7 discusses critical challenges and serious concerns of fog/edge computing and its applications. Then, Section 16.8 recommends potential countermeasures for the raised/alleviated assaults. Further, Section 16.9 talks about a few opportunities for the 21st century toward fog and edge computing, an absolute necessity for 5G and IoT achievement, artificial intelligence (AI) for cloud computing and edge registering, and so on. In closing, Section 16.10 reviews different and fascinating comments for future scientists.

## 16.2   Motivation

Cloud computing is an environment, i.e., public, private, and hybrid which provide services to users anytime, from anywhere. Fog/edge computing has evolved over the years and has risen to be one of the most promising and assuring technologies in the present and in the future and has triggered a massive number of novel applications and methods. Moreover, this methodology does possess some striking features and characteristics which enhance the safety, security, privacy [20], and scalability of data being stored. Further, with the incorporation of blockchain, data storage, and maintenance advances to a higher level from numerous aspects. Cloud along with fog/edge computing is the necessity of future. On other side, IoT is being used almost in every possible computing environment. These smart devices are helping citizens a lot to do everyday task, i.e., have made people life convenient and easier to live. In another words, IoTs are storing huge amount of data at cloud/edge networking after communicating together. These internet (smart) devices generate a huge amount of data at end nodes which is complex to handle and require efficient tools to handle, to make some predictive and useful decisions for improving business or organization's growth. But, together with IoTs, many other new concepts like cloud computing, fog computing, and edge computing are also attracting researcher's attention around the world. Cloud clouding is oldest version of edge computing. Edge computing produce services at edges of the nodes, i.e., reduce latency. This article includes all possibilities where fog or edge computing can be used, with threat mitigated in many applications, and suggesting countermeasure for the same applications in detail.

Hence, this part examines about our inspiration driving composing this article identified with cloud, mist, and edge processing. Presently, next area will examine foundation of these terms exhaustively.

## 16.3  Background

To accomplish constant mechanization, information catch and examination must be done continuously without managing the high dormancy and low transmission capacity gives that happen during the handling of organization information. Regardless of the way that the cloud gave a flexible and versatile climate for data examination, correspondence, and security challenges between close by resources and the cloud lead to personal time and other danger factors. To moderate these dangers, fog computing and edge registering were created. These ideas carried registering assets closer to information sources and permitted these resources for access significant insight utilizing the information they delivered without speaking with far off figuring framework [4].

The term fog computing is related with Cisco, who enlisted the name "Cisco Fog Computing", which played on distributed computing (refer Figure 16.1). In 2015, an Open-Fog Consortium was made with establishing individuals ARM, Cisco, Dell, Intel, Microsoft, and Princeton University, and extra contributing individuals including GE, Hitachi, and Foxconn. IBM presented the firmly associated and generally interchangeable (in spite of the fact that in certain circumstances not actually) term "edge processing".

The origin of edge computing can be followed back to the 1990s, when Akamai dispatched its substance transport association (CDN). The idea in those days was to introduce centers at regions geographically nearer to the end customer for the movement of put away substance, for instance,

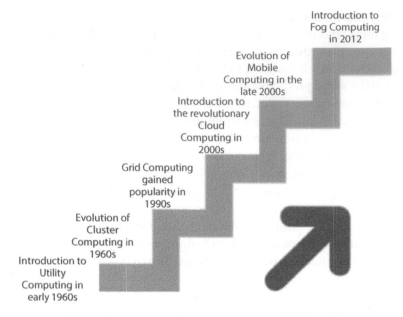

**Figure 16.1** Evolution of computational methods.

pictures and accounts. In 1997, in their work "Quick application-careful change for transportability", Nobel *et al.* shown how different sorts of uses (web programs, video, and talk affirmation) running on resource obliged mobile phones can offload certain tasks to stunning laborers (proxies) [5].

The goal was to facilitate the pile on the handling resources. Additionally, as proposed in a later work, to further develop the battery life of cells. Today, for example, talk affirmation organizations from Google, Apple, and Amazon work thusly. In 2001, versatile and decentralized appropriated applications utilized, as proposed, diverse shared (alleged disseminated hash tables) overlay organizations. These self-putting together overlay networks empower proficient and shortcoming open minded directing, object area, and burden adjusting. Additionally, these frameworks likewise make it conceivable to abuse the organization closeness of fundamental actual associations in the web, subsequently evading significant distance joins between peers. These abatements the general organization load as well as improves the inertness of utilizations. In the previous few years, there has been a moving improvement in big data which has prompted the development of cloud. Enormous information utilizing cloud has been the most doable decision for some organizations to get to the huge measure of information. As modernized social data have gotten continuously widespread, many have coordinated their focus toward harnessing these tremendous instructive lists to make purportedly progressively exact and complete understandings of social methodology and have given it a term of "enormous information". Data volumes will continue to addition and move to the cloud.

Billions of related contraptions and introduced systems that make, assemble, and offer a bounty of IoT data assessment reliably, wherever all through the world. As adventures acquire the opportunity to store and take apart huge volumes of data, they will find the opportunity to make and manage 60% of huge data as soon as possible. Experts acknowledge that the limit of PCs utilizing their cloud and different approaches to acquire data will improve widely as a result of additional created independent computations, more significant personalization, and abstract organizations. We consider significant to be in huge data as they have a multi-layered nature of social and spatial methodology. In the current world enormous data infers working with huge datasets that are consistently unstructured. The datasets being worked with will be a mix of prohibitive in-house data and openly available data. Working with these datasets will require gadgets that license the unstructured data to be worked with and can, moreover, manage the enormous volumes. Data security and assurance have reliably been pressing issues, exhibiting a tremendous compounding potential. Steadily creating data volumes make additional challenges in safeguarding it from interferences and cyberattacks, as the levels of data protection cannot remain mindful of the data improvement rates. Several months prior to NASA has revealed the image of the dim opening, anyway there is a huge play of data science behind the revelation of Blackhole. Information sciences and data getting ready are the critical factors in the production of smoothed out self-administering vehicles that is self-driving vehicles. To enhance this development further, dim information will progress and engraving the possible destiny of gigantic data in the coming years or even months. Security hole which was achieved by a shortfall of guidance and planning openings and the headway of cyberattacks where the perils are used by developers are progressing and end up being continuously improving too [6].

## 16.4    Fog and Edge Computing–Based Applications

With edge registering, the IoT information is gathered and broke down straight by regulators, sensors, and other associated gadgets, or the data is communicated to a nearby data handling framework for investigation.

While mist registering is similar to edge figuring and that they are frequently confused with each other, there is a little distinction between them. In mist registering, there is just 1 brought together PC liable for preparing information from various endpoints inside the organizations. On the contrary hand, in edge registering, each organization partakes in preparing information. Edge registering pushes correspondence capacities, handling force, and insight information straightforwardly into gadgets like programmable mechanization regulators. The most innovative applications are smart cities, in the manufacturing departments and healthcare department where even blockchain plays a major rule. Augmented reality devices such as glasses and headsets are major applications of fog and edge computing and the most important application is the AI Virtual Assistant.

a) Healthcare applications: this is a territory where constant preparing assumes a significant job. Henceforth, information should be prepared quick, and the reaction time should be as less as conceivable.

b) Augmented reality: for augmented reality (AR), overlaying valuable data onto the actual world continuously is significant. Utilizing haze registering will help accomplish this part of enlarged reality.

c) Smart utility administrations: utility administrations like power, water, and phone can be overseen by fog computing [7].

d) Traffic administration framework: mist registering can expand the proficiency of the traffic light framework by decreasing the idleness. The communications between vehicles, traffic lights, and passageways can be upgraded by the fog framework.

e) Caching and preparing: mist processing can likewise be utilized for improving the presentation of sites. Certain sites have a ton of information bases and information to be handled, for instance, person-to-person communication locales and library or internet shopping centers. These sites can utilize the mist layer for reserving and preprocessing its information and henceforth decreasing reality unpredictability.

f) Gaming: in the previous, not many, years, there has been a tremendous advancement in the gaming business. Aside from games being computationally mind boggling, they are generally multiplayer nowadays and rely enormously upon constant handling.

g) Decentralized brilliant structure control: like keen utility administrations, even on account of savvy building, control mist processing will assume an enormous part in making it more effective and secure [8].

h) Retail advertising: targeted advertisements and data for retail associations depend on key boundaries, for example, segment data and set on field gadgets. In this utilization case, edge figuring can help secure client protection. It can scramble the information and keep the source as opposed to sending unprotected data to the cloud.

i) Smart speakers: Smart speakers can get the ability to translate voice rules locally to run fundamental orders. Turning lights on or off, or changing indoor controller settings, whether or not web network bombs would be possible.

j) Video conferencing: Poor video quality, voice delays, and set screens—a moderate associate with the cloud can cause various video conferencing disappointments. By setting the specialist side of video conferencing programming closer to individuals, quality issues can be lessened.

k) Portable edge registering is a provisioning answer for AR applications on cell phones. AR portable applications have natural shared properties as far as information assortment in the uplink, figuring at the edge, and information conveyance in the downlink. In this letter, these highlights are utilized to propose a novel asset assignment approach over both correspondence and calculation assets. The methodology, actualized by means of progressive raised estimate, apparently yields significant increases in versatile energy utilization when contrasted with traditional autonomous offloading across clients.

l) A clever sewer vent covers the board framework (IMCS) is one of the main fundamental stages in a keen city to forestall successive sewer vent cover mishaps. Sewer vent cover dislodging, misfortune, and harm present dangers to individual security, which is in opposition to the point of shrewd urban areas. This paper proposes an edge processing–based IMCS for keen urban areas. An interesting radio recurrence distinguishing proof tag with tilt and vibration sensors is utilized for every sewer vent cover, and a narrowband IoT is embraced for correspondence. Then, edge registering workers communicate with relating the executive's faculty through cell phones dependent on the gathered data.

## 16.5   Machine Learning and Internet of Things–Based Cloud, Fog, and Edge Computing Applications

With the ascent of the IoT, applications have become more astute and associated gadgets offer ascent to their abuse in all parts of an advanced city. As the volume of the gathered information expands, Machine Learning (ML) procedures are applied to additionally upgrade the insight and the capacities of an application [9]. ML and the IoT-based cloud, fog, and edge computing with each other are commonly prevalent today. The speed, flexibility, and transparency which can be achieved with the combination with each other cannot be achieved with anything else, the safety of the data and the quality of deliverables are attributed top priority. They widely include facial recognition tools, to filter the spam mails from general mails, chatbots for services, and the self-driving cars; in fact, the Google search engine technology is using a combination of the two.

Smart location tracking, navigation becomes easier, the control of the cabin conditions, the combination of them helps in automating the environment, helps with the connectivity of the mobile devices, not just with each other but with other points which can improve the connectivity, and helps in building signals. The control of the drive modes, like the self-driving cars, makes it much more efficient and time saving, the safety of the car and the surroundings is being monitored with the help of fog computing and ML, the assistance of parking cars or vehicles in general is yet another application which makes use of these concepts. Intelligent mobile and mobile apps are in process. The monitoring of the driver with the car in general and self-driving cars is being kept on track with the IoT-based cloud and fog computing. Sports applications/wearables powered by ML are yet another application which is of extreme importance and the success rates can be achieved by using ML and IoT. Predictive maintenance for battery monitoring and solar tracking systems in Industry 4.0 is the final and the most important forthcoming application which will make a huge difference in the society. There are many possible use cases for fog and edge computing and ML including the following:

a)   Remote monitoring for corporations: This can be the distinction between day-by-day activities and a cataclysm. Regular concentrated examination of information can educate you what caused individual time or can expect dissatisfaction subject to oversaw learning applied to different sorts of exercises or disillusionments reliant upon a pre-arranged dataset. However, setting up of choices that can move toward second examination at the site as the data is being made can see the signs of a disaster and take measures to prevent a catastrophe before it even starts.

b) Behavioral analysis of customers: Retail analytics to diminish relinquishment of trucks and further develop customer responsibility using close second edge examination where bargains data, pictures, coupons used, traffic models, and accounts are made gives marvelous encounters into purchaser direct. This understanding can help retailers with bettering target item, arrangements, and headways and assist with overhauling store configurations and thing game plan to further develop the customer experience. For example, use signs to accumulate information, for instance, trade history from a customer's wireless, by then objective headways and arrangement things as customers walk around the store.

c) Driverless cars: With state-of-the-art frameworks to help drivers, vehicles will end up being much safer and more successful as they become dynamically aware of and react to the enveloping driving environment and conditions. Veritable accomplishment will mean the democratization of ΛDAS where the development is open in entry level to premium vehicles, for first-time drivers to seniors, in voyager and business vehicles, and any place in the center. Vehicles should cycle to match the development and sending of state-of-the-art progresses—and self-driving vehicles in the not-so-distant future—it is basic to look at how the total plan of systems inside the vehicle can pass on a better experience as gone against than pushing toward the vehicle as a little pack of free innovations [10].

d) Grape development has social and monetary significance in India. In India, Maharashtra positions first in quite a while creation. In the course of the most recent couple of years, the nature of grapes has corrupted in light of numerous reasons. One of the significant causes is illnesses on grapes. To forestall illnesses ranchers, shower gigantic measure of pesticides, which bring about expanding the expense of creation? Additionally, ranchers cannot recognize the infections physically.

Note that IoT devices will be a part of smart environment in near future, and when all applications will be connected internet, then this environment can be considered as Internet of Everything [21]. In near future, we will see fully automation process in industries, manufacturing, education, healthcare, etc. [22–24].

## 16.6   Threats Mitigated in Fog and Edge Computing–Based Applications

Important information gets leaked which puts the data into danger. A fake/false identity leaks the original data to the network of the attackers. This interferes with the radio frequencies which when reaches the wrong set of people can change the entire network and redirect to their group of attackers. If a malicious node is added, then it affects the entire network. The DDOS attack cuts down the system service. The fog system has comparatively less memory resources and it contains insufficient storage in comparison to the cloud; however, these resources can be increased. They gather huge amounts of data from various sources of data. The system is both scarcely distributed and dense based on its location geographically. They reinforce communication between machines and connection wirelessly. Fog computing systems can be installed on devices which have low specifications including switches and IP cameras. It is essentially deployed in mobile phones and other devices which are portable in nature. Fake data is often replaced with the original data and this affects the whole network. Certain messages are turned to a false message which gives false information and eventually, the link is blocked [11].

   a) Decoy system: Decoy documents which is used to detect unusual information that can be generated on demand and to "poison" the exfiltrated information. At the point when the unapproved admittance to cloud is seen, distraction data is returned by the cloud and conveyed in such manner it seems, by all accounts, to be ordinary. This is innovation might be joined with client conduct profiling innovation to make sure about user's data in cloud.

b) Client behavior profiling: It is depended upon that induction to a client's information in cloud will show nice strategies for access. Client profiling is recognizable innovation that can be applied to demonstrate how, how much, when client access a data in cloud. Such "normal user" can be consistently checked to decide if irregular admittance to a user's data is emerging. This strategy is generally utilized in extortion identification applications. Encryption, fixing and the utilization of man-made brainpower to screen to recognize and react to potential dangers are largely fundamental, and the obligation regarding actualizing these safety efforts falls decisively on organizations, not end client. Various proposition for cloud-based administrations depict strategies to store records, documents, and media in a distant assistance that might be gotten to any place a client may interface with the Internet. An especially vexing issue before such administrations are extensively acknowledged concerns ensures for making sure about a client's information in a way where that ensures just the client and nobody else can access that information. The issue of giving security of private data stays a center security issue that, until this point in time, has not given the degrees of affirmation a great many people want.

Various suggestions have been made to ensure about far off data in the cloud using encryption and standard access controls. Most would concur the whole of the standard techniques have been displayed to fall at times for a collection of reasons, including insider attacks, misplanned organizations, broken executions, code with bugs, and the innovative improvement of fruitful and progressed attacks not envisioned by the implementers of safety frameworks. Building a solid circulated processing framework is not adequate, considering the way that disasters continue to happen, and when they do, and information gets lost, it is incredibly far-fetched to get it back. One need is to anticipate such setbacks [12].

Edge Clouds empower a lot further and more extensive security arrangements by putting them closer to the gadgets enduring an onslaught. The register, stockpiling, and systems administration assets offered by Edge Clouds can be used to make extremely refined intrusion detection and prevention that can divert DoS assaults, securing basic edge applications and lessening further upstream presentation. By adding extra security administrations at the edge, for example, Deep Packet Inspection, Edge Clouds can forestall the noxious contamination of information that could be utilized to create neighborhood or upstream assaults. Also, since Edge Clouds give a "division" model by separating huge populaces of edge computing and IoT gadgets over different mists, the effect of enormous scope assaults can be overseen and segregated on a more granular level. Edge computing has been exceptionally useful for lightweight gadgets to accomplish convoluted assignments adequately in any case, its surged improvement prompts the negligence of security perils to a huge degree in edge processing stages and their engaged applications; certain issues such as latency issues. Edge computing can dispose of the slack time between smart devices and can send responses to customers' requests quickly. This can make a more dependable interface between the buyer and the gadget. This issues incredibly to a portion of the brief instant choices that sway new IoT devices from your Alexa to self-governing vehicles. Security can portion with edge computing. Edge designs permit the limitation of information blackouts to the neighborhood preparing focus and the applications administered by that gadget. Constant information is passed by the IoT devices (and its sensors) and this information is stored at cloud in a decentralized structure. Edge computing is a siloed substance zeroed in totally on explicit additions of information, with less preparing slack time. The expense can diminish on the edge, lessening capital and working costs. The administration of edge figuring networks is kept up by IT business initiative. Controlling information at the source takes out cloud goes between and builds IT possession.

## 16.7   Critical Challenges and Serious Concerns Toward Fog/Edge Computing and Its Applications

Organizations dependent on the IoT are needed to offer strong and secure sorts of help to the EUs. This requires all devices that are significant for the haze organization to have a particular level of trust on one another. Check accepts a huge part in setting up the beginning game plan of relations between IoT contraptions and mist center points in the organization. Be that as it may, this is not sufficient as contraptions can by and large glitch or are also defenseless against malicious attacks. In such a circumstance, trust expects a critical part in developing relations subject to past associations. Trust ought to expect a two-way part in a haze organization. That is, the processing networks that offer organizations to IoT contraptions should have the choice to support whether the devices referencing organizations are confirmed. Of course, the IoT contraptions that send data and other regarded dealing with requesting should have the choice to affirm whether the normal mist networks are to be certain protected.

Fog computing expands disseminated figuring and circles back to IoT. The cycle of mist figuring has additional accumulating resources at the edges to manage the requirements. Hereafter, the fog laborer needs to change its organizations provoking the leaders and upkeep cost. Additionally, the manager needs to encounter the going with issues:

a)  Security fog enlisting being overpowered by far off basically, there is a significant concern for network assurance. Association chairman produces plans truly, haze hubs being passed on at the edge of Internet, immense upkeep cost is incorporated. The spillage of private data is getting thought while using organizations. The end customers are more accessible to the fog centers. Thusly, more delicate information is assembled by fog center points than far away cloud. Encryption strategies like HAN (Home-Area Network) can be used to counter these issues.

b)  Security: The guideline security issue is the affirmation of the devices related with fog enlisting at different entryways. Each device has its own IP address. A malicious customer might use a fake IP address to move to information set aside on the particular fog center. To overcome this passage control, an interference area structure should be applied at all layers of the stage.

c)  Organization management: Being related with heterogeneous devices, managing the mist hubs and the association, relationship between each center will be raise a ruckus aside from if SDN and NFV techniques are applied.

d)  Position of fog servers: Putting a social affair of murkiness laborers with the goal that they pass on most outrageous help of the close by necessities is an issue. Inspecting the work done in each center point in the laborer preceding putting them diminishes the upkeep cost.

e) Deferment in computing delays in light of data aggregation: Resource over-usage diminishes the effectives of organizations gave by the haze center points, creating setback for preparing data. Data aggregation ought to happen before data taking care of; resource-limited mist hubs ought to be arranged booking by using need and flexibility model.

**Edge Computing:**

i. Before moving altogether to edge processing, cloud suppliers will start the change by actualizing half breed cloud/edge frameworks, as per Dave McCarthy, an exploration chief for IDC.

ii. Due to the COVID-19 pandemic, edge registering development will be deferred because of breaks in sending 5G organizations.

iii. While 5G will reinforce edge processing, it may not end up being the main thrust many have anticipated that it should be. "5G broadens the stage that applications are based on. Now and again, this will permit production of new applications, yet as a rule, it will essentially permit existing applications to work better."

iv. Many organizations that put resources into IoT are as of now managing an excess of information they did not foresee. Not exclusively will edge figuring give them a spot to store that information, it will likewise bring down the expense of capacity while scaling back the requirement for correspondence. With assistance from man-made brainpower and AI, it will likewise give these organizations knowledge into how information patterns influence their tasks.

v. When it comes to actualizing arising advances, the conventional ethos is to begin little; however, that is probably not going to apply to edge processing. Edge processing plans and designs must be created in view of operationalizing the whole venture. Verification of idea models seldom work.

vi. As the COVID-19 pandemic inclines up the requirement for organizations to put resources into new advances to remain serious, they are probably going to see edge figuring as a feasible arrangement. "As organizations further digitize their activities and investigate new information streams that help illuminate business choices, they will be more inspired by edge figuring as an expansion of their cloud model".

## 16.8    Possible Countermeasures

Assailants could abuse privacy of clients by getting genuine personality, area, or even his propensities. For example, assailants can get to delicate data through shrewd TV far off controls if information is shipped off the fog nodes without encryption. Nonetheless, encoding all communicated information is expensive and causes dormancy. By the manner in which clients' presses and solicitation channels on far off gadgets, assailants can recognize what their identity is, their propensities, and their area. It has been recommended that insignificant information for usefulness should be shipped off the fog nodes to limit security dangers, by the accompanying framework:

- The fog nodes get just the most critical removed highlights through the distant TV.
- Adding distortions to the communicated information can be eliminated by the fog nodes by basic calculations.
- Data can be sent as broken and rearranged bundles without encryption, while the request is sent encoded, utilizing the public key of the fog nodes to reorder it.

Of course, the proposed structure could achieve the goal of grouping and reliability, and be a respectable protection against man-in-the-middle and savage force attacks. In this system, as opposed to the over the top option of cover encryption of all data, the imparted data is darkened, apportioned, and revamped to diminish the customer's exercises and addition the capability of consistent organizations. Such protects are moreover satisfactory to thwart man-in-the-middle assailants, snoops, and savage force aggressors from achieving their goals. Regardless, while this proposed structure gets customer assurance, it requires a huge load of simultaneous errands (clouding, filtering, encryption, unscrambling, and mentioning and reordering), which increase the overhead weight for both the customer and the mist hubs, especially as the TV far off sends data continually. This assessment region needs greater evaluation of time usage to show its effect on continuous organizations, and to lessen overheads for the components.

The "System for Efficient Privacy Preservation Aggregation" (EPPA) revolves around sharp meters used in wise cross section structures and suggests to work on the security of exchanges, approval costs, and assurance concerns.

There is a gadget known as the keen meter which is utilized to screen and keep up with the utilization of the energy on the client side. Over the long haul, the energy saved is shipped off the activity community and a reaction is sent back from that point. It is utilized to keep the mist hubs from unscrambling the client information.

- The splendid meter data is imparted by the Paillier cryptosystem, which intrinsically guarantees data against the picked plain substance attack; furthermore, it does not leave a chance for meddlers.
- Each conveyed record has a timestamp imprint to ensure its authenticity, and confirm the sharp meter. We figure it will also avoid a replay attack.
- The comparing fog nodes confirms the mark and the time stamp; whenever confirmed, it signs the scrambled record with its signature and sends it to the activity place, without unscrambling the information.
- The functioning spot checks the sign of the sending haze hubs and subsequently unscrambles the customer's record by the expert key. The framework did not accomplish the goal of accessibility as the correspondence between the gadgets of fog nodes-clients and the fog nodes-control focus is the expensive Wi-Fi, which is as yet compromised by over-burdening bandwidth

In the case of edge computing, the greater part of the dangers is exacerbated because of configuration blemishes, usage bugs, and gadget misconfigurations in the edge gadgets and workers. Likewise, the absence of undeniable UIs in many edge gadgets regularly makes it difficult to recognize a continuous/unfolded assault. Considering the above mentioned, understanding the security dangers (and safeguards) in edge figuring accepts most extreme importance. Countering zero-day assaults anxious processing equipment is more troublesome because of the inaccessibility of unique source codes for the projects running on the machine, and furthermore because of the way that as a rule the product comes installed in a firmware and is not manageable for inspection. The most well-known information irritation calculation is k-secrecy which adjusts the identifier data in the information before distributing its delicate properties. In conclusion, it is critical to take note of that unexpectedly most safeguard instruments are themselves powerless against side-channel assaults. Safeguard systems against infusion assaults by and large depend on static examination for noxious code discovery and fine-grained admittance control. Examination on concocting intends to moderate firmware change is additionally being done for avoidance of such assaults.

## 16.9   Opportunities for 21st Century Toward Fog and Edge Computing

Cloud advances give a main issue of information stockpiling, with gadgets sending information to and fro to this middle. Along these lines, information the executives in mists brings about postponements, which is the reason edge registering is viewed as more effective in shrewd city frameworks. Edge figuring implies performing information investigation continuously in an area close to the end-client. It additionally gives more stockpiling assets closer to the activity, as it were. Brilliant city applications and IoT gadgets require moment examination administrations, and these functionalities require edge registering (source). With the registering power drew nearer to the source, edge figuring and 5G will empower IoT sensors to investigate information quicker and cause robotized and moment reactions without having to depend on an online cloud community. Few of possibilities with edge computing are as follows:

- Edge computing—A must for 5G and IoT success
- 5G and edge computing as vehicles for transformation of mobility in smart cities
- AI for cloud and edge computing

### 16.9.1   5G and Edge Computing as Vehicles for Transformation of Mobility in Smart Cities

Video reconnaissance to a great extent relies upon data transmission. Top quality recordings require extraordinary assets and extra room, making HD observation unreasonable in current conditions. Notwithstanding, 5G and edge registering will definitely change this image. Today cloud computing/edge computing have been moved to many applications/sectors like transportation [14–19], retail, education, and healthcare. As per numerous industry investigators, 5G will be critical in interfacing public and city-wide organizations of cameras and sensors. As a result of the higher transmission capacity, HD recordings will be quickly accessible, and the utilization of edge processing will empower situational mindfulness and examination and dynamic on the spot.

5G and edge registering will empower parking spots mechanization over the city (something Barcelona previously attempted to execute). Street sensors and HD cameras can be utilized to screen gridlock continuously, telling drivers and putting together traffic in a flash. These and numerous other traffic applications will give street clients a vastly improved encounter, moreover sparing time and diminishing contamination in urban communities. Also, IoT sensors, robots, and robots can be adequately utilized as track trash specialists and screens, conveyance frameworks, and registration focuses. With nearby information the board and high data transmission, these keen gadgets can perform complex AI calculations continuously. With the development of 5G and edge registering, we are drawing nearer to a definitive dream of a profoundly working brilliant city. In 21st century, IoT is accepting a huge capacity in making smart metropolitan regions. With the advancement of IoT, data is creating with accelerating. As the data is fostering the need to store data is also extending. More the data, the dormancy will be high to store and recuperate data from the cloud. Mist figuring was started to diminish the inaction for getting to the data to and from the cloud. Haze figuring gives the limit, preparing similarly as frameworks organization organizations close to the end motivation behind the association. Haze center points moreover have limited computational limits. On account of specific inadequacies, haze handling and conveyed figuring cannot help alone, so both these advances are joined to manufacture splendid IoT establishment for Smart city. Haze figuring have a huge work and exceptional commitment being created of a Smart city. This work examines about various employments of mist enrolling and their utilization in a Smart metropolitan networks. It also proposes a model for Waste organization system in a city. Mist preparing can help with regulating the waste variety of the city in a canny manner. In light of our overview, a couple of open concerns and hardships of mist preparing are inspected, and the orientation for future experts has also been discussed.

## 16.9.2    Artificial Intelligence for Cloud Computing and Edge Computing

The current generation of the smart environment; technologies including AI and cloud computing are completely turning people's lives for the better. To explain it better, AI and cloud computing along with edge computing when they come together. We can also see that edge computing is a nascent technologically advanced version of cloud computing [8]. The present numerous digital (keen) gadgets blending AI and distributed computing in our lives each day, like Siri, Google Home, and Amazon's Alexa. For a bigger scope, AI abilities are attempting to make organizations more successful, key, and understanding driven in the business distributed computing world. As a rule, through facilitating information and programming in the cloud, distributed computing gives associations more noteworthy flexibility, spryness, and cost reserve funds. A cloud in business (industry) can be public, private, and mixture, furnishing end-clients with administrations like SaaS, PaaS, and IaaS. A vital distributed computing administrations is foundation that incorporates the arrangement of registering and capacity gadgets. Cloud suppliers additionally give server farm benefits that cover the different information bases accessible. This advancement chain is moving innovation toward the development of AI and cloud computing.

To deliver better outcomes from enormous measure of information put away by IoT (through their correspondence), cloud appears with AI. Man-made reasoning advancements consolidate with cloud/edge registering and assist organizations with dealing with their information, look for information patterns and bits of knowledge, give better client support, and improve work processes [9]. AI has colossal business qualities, the requirement for innovative assets and huge framework has made it less attainable for some organizations. Advantage from AI innovation can resemble on the off chance that we need top specialized ability, and admittance to enormous informational collections, AI can assist us with its monstrous figuring power for refining this information (in clever way), cost-effectiveness, increased productivity, reliability, and availability of advanced infrastructure. For instance, such an AI-fueled valuing module guarantees that evaluating for a business is constantly upgraded. It is not just about utilizing information; without the requirement for human inclusion, it is playing out the exploration and afterward placing it into impact. That is, the cloud is democratizing admittance to AI by permitting organizations the opportunity to utilize it now. Some other helpful advantages will be the following:

- Critical and promising AI and distributed computing applications: Powering an AI self-managing cloud is incorporated into the IT framework to assist with smoothing out jobs and robotize rehash undertakings.
- Further developing AI information the executives: Artificial insight arrangements at the cloud level are additionally further developing information the board.

- Having things accomplished with AI-SaaS integration: Artificial knowledge innovations are currently being applied to offer more benefit as a component of more extensive Software-as-a-Service (SaaS) frameworks.
- Utilizing dynamic cloud services: As a help, AI is likewise changing the manner in which organizations depend on instruments.

The present cloud and edge registering go about as a motor to expand a region's span and AI impacts. At all levels, AI and cloud (additionally, edge) figuring are changing business, particularly with a huge effect for huge scope business. A smooth AI stream and cloud-based instruments are making many administrations a reality [11]. For instance, it is feasible to appreciate administrations (without making a remarkable ML mode) which equal frameworks, i.e., text preparing, voice, vision, and code interpretation, are accessible to end-clients. In any case, beforehand, we need to give more significant information, more human labor forces for breaking down huge measure of information, then, at that point expectation improves and the precision is improved.

With these AI-based stages, the quantity of associations further developing discussions benefits the hankering to place cash into psychological innovation capacities. Taking everything into account, the utilization of AI in distributed computing is unquestionably not a radical or progressive move. It is a progressive one, from numerous points of view. We need AI and the cloud's "test and learn" abilities. We are hopeful that the consolidation of distributed computing administrations and AI innovation would carry significant improvement to the innovation area. In not so distant future, AI will turn into a factor of creation with having ability of enormous stockpiling. With presenting numerous models/conceivable use (in next subsections) for future analysts, researchers, and so forth, toward AI for cloud and edge figuring, we guarantee that with the development of distributed computing, AI field needs to arise, interest in AI would propel the cloud area and have the option to hit another level as far as pay and efficiency. Accordingly, in the following not many years, we should trust that the market will start to detonate, with AI pushing distributed computing higher than at any other time, as the cloud market will send AI's advantages to the mainstream [13].

An arising innovation has additionally crested in 2017–2018. As appeared in the cloud computing engineering, the center or second layers of the cloud arrangement are spoken to by the Fog processing. For certain applications, delay in correspondence between the figuring gadgets in the field and information in a cloud (frequently actually separated by a huge number of miles) is unfavorable of the time necessities, as it might cause significant postponement in time touchy applications. For instance, preparing and capacity for early notice of fiascos (charges, tsunami, and so on) must be progressively. For these sorts of utilizations, figuring and putting away assets should be set nearer to where processing is required (application territories like computerized road). In these sorts of situations, fog processing is viewed as appropriate.

## 16.10    Conclusion

Cloud computing provides several services like Infrastructure as a Service, Software as a Service, Network as a Service, Internet as a Service, and Data as a Services, in the form of public, private, and hybrid cloud. In this smart era, we have seen a rapid growth for cloud computing, and today, extension of or variants of cloud computing in form of edge computing is being used everywhere, i.e., in important applications. Also, with this, we have faced several critical attacks, issues, and challenges on this advancement. This article includes such topics and have discussed in detail and leaves readers to new horizons of edge computing, i.e., possible use of edge computing with big data analytics, computing, AI, and blockchain uses in edge computing. Also, edge computing can be a major resource for the popularity of quantum computing and dew computing. Readers and inventors are suggested to look through the possible advancement of edge computing with emerging technologies and work toward for the same for better of society (in an efficient manner).

## References

1. Patil, S.S. and Thorat, S.A., Early detection of grapes diseases using machine learning and IoT. *2016 Second International Conference on Cognitive Computing and Information Processing (CCIP)*, Mysore, pp. 1–5, 2016.
2. Jia, G., Han, G., Rao, H., Shu, L., Edge Computing-Based Intelligent Manhole Cover Management System for Smart Cities. *IEEE Internet Things J.*, 5, 3, 1648–1656, June 2018.
3. Ni, J., Zhang, K., Lin, X., Shen, X., Securing Fog Computing for Internet of Things Applications: Challenges and Solutions. *IEEE Commun. Surv. Tutor.*, 20, 1, 601–628, Firstquarter 2018.
4. Peralta, G., Iglesias-Urkia, M., Barcelo, M., Gomez, R., Moran, A., Bilbao, J., Fog computing based efficient IoT scheme for the Industry 4.0. *2017 IEEE International Workshop of Electronics, Control, Measurement, Signals*

and their Application to Mechatronics (ECMSM), Donostia-San Sebastian, pp. 1–6, 2017.

5. Fan, Q. and Ansari, N., Application Aware Workload Allocation for Edge Computing-Based IoT. *IEEE Internet Things J.*, 5, 3, 2146–2153, 2018.

6. Tedeschi, P. and Sciancalepore, S., *Edge and Fog Computing in Critical Infrastructures: Analysis, Security Threats, and Research Challenges.*

7. Shi, W. and Dustdar, S., The Promise of Edge Computing. *Computer*, 49, 5, 78–81, May 2016.

8. Xiao, Y., Jia, Y., Liu, C., Cheng, X., Yu, J., Lv, W., Edge Computing Security: State of the Art and Challenges, in: *Proceedings of the IEEE*, vol. 107, pp. 1608–1631, Aug. 2019.

9. Svorobej, S., Takako Endo, P., Bendechache, M., Filelis-Papadopoulos, C., Giannoutakis, K.M., Gravvanis, G.A., Tzovaras, D., Byrne, J., Lynn, T., Simulating Fog and Edge Computing Scenarios: An Overview and Research Challenges. *Future Internet*, 11, 55, 2019.

10. Fernandes, E., Jung, J., Prakash, A., "Security analysis of emerging smart home applications". *Proc. IEEE Symp. Secur. Privacy (SP)*, pp. 636–654, May 2016.

11. Na, W., Jang, S., Lee, Y., Park, L., Dao, N., Cho, S., Frequency Resource Allocation and Interference Management in Mobile Edge Computing for an Internet of Things System. *IEEE Internet Things J.*, 6, 3, 4910–4920, 2019.

12. Stojmenovic, I. and Wen, S., The Fog computing paradigm: Scenarios and security issues. *2014 Federated Conference on Computer Science and Information Systems*, Warsaw, pp. 1–8, 2014.

13. Nair, M.M., Tyagi, A.K., Sreenath, N., The Future with Industry 4.0 at the Core of Society 5.0: Open Issues, Future Opportunities and Challenges. *2021 International Conference on Computer Communication and Informatics (ICCCI)*, pp. 1–7, 2021.

14. Rekha, G., Tyagi, A.K., Anuradha, N., Integration of Fog Computing and Internet of Things: An Useful Overview. *Proceedings of ICRIC 2019. Lecture Notes in Electrical Engineering*, vol. 597 Springer, Cham, 2020, https://doi.org/10.1007/978-3-030-29407-6_8.

15. Tyagi, A.K. and Sreenath, N., Providing trust enabled services in vehicular cloud computing. *2016 International Conference on Research Advances in Integrated Navigation Systems (RAINS)*, Bangalore, pp. 1–7, 2016.

16. Tyagi, A.K. and Niladhuri, S., Providing Trust Enabled Services in Vehicular Cloud Computing, in: *Proceedings of the International Conference on Informatics and Analytics (ICIA-16)*, vol. Article 3, Association for Computing Machinery, New York, NY, USA, pp. 1–10, 2016.

17. Tyagi, A.K., Kumari, S., Fernandez, T.F., Aravindan, C., P3 Block: Privacy Preserved, Trusted Smart Parking Allotment for Future Vehicles of Tomorrow, in: *Computational Science and Its Applications – ICCSA 2020. ICCSA 2020. Lecture Notes in Computer Science*, vol. 12254 Springer, Cham, 2020.

18. Sravanthi, K., Burugari, V.K., Tyagi, A., Preserving Privacy Techniques for Autonomous Vehicles. 8, 5180–5190, 2020.
19. Varsha, R. *et al.*, Deep Learning Based Blockchain Solution for Preserving Privacy in Future Vehicles. 1, 223 – 236, Jan. 2020.
20. Tyagi, A.K., Nair, M.M., Niladhuri, S., Abraham, A., Security, Privacy Research issues in Various Computing Platforms: A Survey and the Road Ahead. *J. Inf. Assur. Secur.*, 15, 1, 1–16, 16, 2020.
21. Tyagi, Amit Kumar; Nair, Meghna Manoj "Internet of Everything (IoE) and Internet of Things (IoTs): Threat Analyses, Possible Opportunities for Future, *JJ. Inf. Assur. Secur.*, 15, 4, 2020.
22. Tyagi, A.K., Fernandez, T.F., Mishra, S., Kumari, S., Intelligent Automation Systems at the Core of Industry 4.0, in: *Intelligent Systems Design and Applications. ISDA. Advances in Intelligent Systems and Computing*, vol. 1351, A. Abraham, V. Piuri, N. Gandhi, P. Siarry, A. Kaklauskas, A. Madureira (Eds.), Springer, Cham, 2020.
23. Varsha, R., Nair, S.M., Tyagi, A.K., Aswathy, S.U., RadhaKrishnan, R., The Future with Advanced Analytics: A Sequential Analysis of the Disruptive Technology's Scope, in: *Hybrid Intelligent Systems. HIS 2020. Advances in Intelligent Systems and Computing*, vol. 1375 Springer, Cham, 2021.
24. Kumari, S., Tyagi, A.K., Aswathy, S.U., The Future of Edge Computing with Blockchain Technology: Possibility of Threats, Opportunities and Challenges, in: *Recent Trends in Blockchain for Information Systems Security and Privacy*, CRC Press, 2021.

# Index

# Also of Interest

## Check out these published and forthcoming titles in the "Next-Generation Computing and Communication Engineering" series from Scrivener Publishing

**Advanced Analytics and Deep Learning Models**
Edited by Archana Mire, Shaveta Malik and Amit Kumar Tyagi
Forthcoming 2022. ISBN 978-1-119-79175-1

**Medical Imaging and Health Informatics**
Edited by Tushar H Jaware, K Sarat Kumar, Svetlin Antonov, and
Ravindra D Badgujar
Forthcoming 2022. ISBN 978-1-119-81913-4

**Data Science Handbook**
**A Practical Approach**
By Kolla Bhanu Prakash
Forthcoming 2022. ISBN 978-1-119-85732-7

**Integration of Renewable Energy Sources with Smart Grids**
Edited by A. Mahaboob Subahani, M. Kathiresh and
G. R. Kanagachidambaresan
Published 2021. ISBN 978-1-119-75042-0

**Cognitive Engineering for Next Generation Computing**
**A Practical Analytical Approach**
Edited by Kolla Bhanu Prakash, G.R. Kanagachidambaresan,
V. Srikanth and E. Vamsidhar
Published 2021. ISBN 978-1-119-71108-7

**Role of Edge Analytics on Sustainable Smart City Development**
Edited by G.R. Kanagachidambaresan
Published 2020. ISBN 9781119681281

www.scrivenerpublishing.com

Printed and bound by CPI Group (UK) Ltd, Croydon, CR0 4YY

27/10/2024

14580174-0003